SAT PREP PROGRAM
First Choice College

SAT PREP PROGRAM: First Choice College

First Choice College
75 New Haven Avenue
Milford, CT 06460
Email: info@firstchoicecollege.com

Test Prep Genius
PO Box 25321
Arlington, VA 22202
Email: support@tpgenius.com

This product was developed by Test Prep Genius, a premiere education support services company that delivers a comprehensive package for education institutions and services, in partnership with First Choice College Prep, an educational service provider.

Website: http://www.tpgenius.com/

TABLE OF CONTENTS

Evidence-Based Reading

Introduction
Explicit and Implicit Information
Understanding Relationships
Author's Intent
Analyzing Arguments
Structure
Citing Textual Evidence
Words in Context
Word Choice
Analogical Reasoning
Quantitative Information
Analyzing Multiple Texts
Practice Passages

What is the Evidence Based Reading Section?

The Evidence Based Reading Section is part of your Evidence Based Reading and Writing score. Each section is scored on a scale from 10-40, and the combined scores are then calculated on a scale from 200-800.

You will have 65 minutes to complete the Evidence Based Reading Section, which consists multiple passages. Look at the "Reading By the Numbers" list on the right to see what kinds of passages and how many questions you should expect to see. Part of preparing for the Evidence Based Reading Section is to familiarize yourself with the kinds of passages that you can expect to encounter. Below is a chart detailing the specific topics covered by the passages:

Reading By the Numbers:

- 65 minutes
- 4 passages with 500-750 words per passage
- 1 paired passage with 1000-1500 total words
- 52 total questions
- 3 sections with 10 questions
- 2 sections with 11 questions
- 2 Words-in-Context questions per passage
- 2 Evidence questions per passage

Passage Type	Topics	Number of Passages
Literature	Classic and contemporary pieces representing works from authors both the United States and the rest of the world.	1
History and Social Studies	Topics covered within the social sciences include anthropology, geography, political science, psychology, economics, linguistics, sociology, and the relevant subfields.	1
Founding Documents or Great Global Conversation	Culturally and historically important texts about the founding documents of the United States and other issues at the heart of civic and political life.	1
Science	Science texts cover foundational concepts and recent developments in the sciences, including earth science, biology, chemistry, physics, and the relevant subfields.	2

Here are some of the strategies students use on the reading section:

- **Skim the Passage.** Read the whole first paragraph, the first and last sentences of the middle paragraphs, and then the whole last paragraph. Then you go to the questions and go back and read in more detail when they give you line numbers.

- **Read the questions first.** Read the questions first, then read the passage, and then go back and answer the questions.

- **Just answer the questions, never read the passage.** Don't read the passage at all. You just go directly to the questions, and answer all the questions that give you line numbers. After you have answered all of the questions with line numbers, the thinking is that you will know enough about the passage to go back and answer the rest of the questions.

- **Actively Read and Take Margin Notes.** Carefully read the passage and look for the main idea of each paragraph. Then write a summary of each paragraph in the margins.

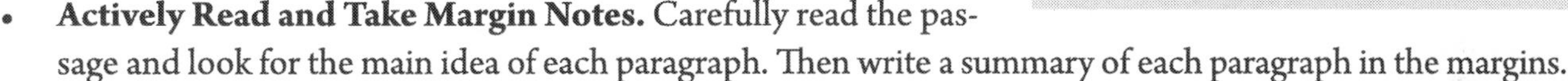

Helpful Tip:

Sometimes these passages are boring (no really!), so it might help to break the passages into either 2 or 3 pieces and focus in bursts. Draw 1 or 2 lines through the passage. Read up to the first line and then answer all the questions before that line. Then, read the next piece, and answer all questions covered in that piece of the passage.

Given that there are many ways to approach the passages, what should you do? Overall, we find that students who use "active reading" have the greatest amount of success.

So what does it mean to "actively read" the passage? What does active reading look like? It looks like marked up passages, with underlines and notes in the margins. Use your pencil! This will keep your mind engaged.

- Don't expect these passages to be entertaining. They are usually dry and awkwardly written - one of the most common complaints that students have is that they lose focus during the reading sections. **You can avoid this by reading with your pencil.**
- Underline and mark up the passage as you go.
- Passages/questions are not arranged in order of difficulty
- The questions are broken up by passage and will usually be arranged in an order that follows the passage. You never know if the last question in the section is one of the easiest.
- Time management skills will be crucial for this part of the test.
- There is only one right answer
- Use process of elimination
- Try to think about the author's point, her intention, how the information is organized and the tone of the passage (persuasive, angry, amused, informative, etc.) while you are reading the passage and don't be afraid to write it down.
- Underline transition words like *but, however, nevertheless, despite*
- Try to avoid being distracted by difficult words, names or places. If a certain question does ask you about a specific section you had trouble with, you can always go back and read that section of the passage.
- Since the passages don't go in the order of difficulty, read the first line or two of each passage and decide which one you like best. Do that one first.
- Do all of the questions for a passage before going on to the next passage.

As you read and mark up the passage, keep these questions in mind:

- Why did the author write this?
- What is s/he trying to explain or convince me of?
- How does the author feel about this subject?
- What is the tone/ attitude?
- What is the main idea of the passage overall?
- What is the main point of each paragraph?

Explicit Information

Explicit information questions are all about your ability to identify the information that is stated in the passage. Part of answering these questions is knowing where different topics appear in the passage. Overall, explicit information questions tend to be straightforward because what they require is that you recall information that you have read. The more you must hunt through the text to find the answers, the longer these questions will take.

HOW TO ANSWER EXPLICIT INFORMATION QUESTIONS

- Explicit information questions are looking for information that is stated in the passage.
- Try to match an answer choice with specific information in the passage.
- Process of elimination is critical – get rid of any answers that are incorrect based on the information given. Eliminate answer choices with common errors:
  - Lack of evidence or being off topic.
  - Too specific or too general.
  - Answer choice from the wrong part of the passage.
  - Answer choices that are just plain wrong.

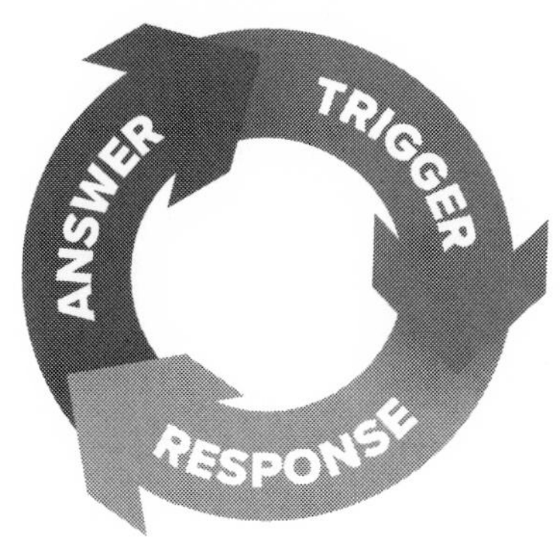

Trigger: The question sends you to specific line numbers or uses words like "according to the passage," or "based on the information given in the passage," and some tricky questions will ask you, "which of the following is NOT true"

Response: If the question gives you specific line numbers, then go back to the area referenced and go a little above and a little below where they send you. See if you can clearly support just one answer choice. If you still have answer choices left, start eliminating wrong answer choices using the strategies above.

KEY CONCEPTS

Implicit Information

Implicit information questions are often some of the more difficult ones to grasp. Getting to the answer is going to require using logic to make inferences based on information in the passage.

HOW TO ANSWER IMPLICIT INFORMATION QUESTIONS

- **Draw the smallest conclusion possible.** One mistake that people often make in life is to draw broad conclusions from just a little bit of information. The SAT is looking to see if you'll make this mistake – so make sure that you make logical steps, rather than leaps!

- **Avoid the hunt and peck method.** In order to do this, you need to utilize active reading, which allows you to gain a better understanding of the author's intent in writing, his attitude toward his subject, and his overall tone. This information provides valuable clues to help answer implicit information questions, since you won't be able to find the answer explicitly stated.

- **Inverse Conclusions are a common type of inference question found on the SAT.** If I tell you that Kelly is taller than Jaime, then you can conclude that Jaime is shorter than Kelly. That's an inference! You can't infer that Kelly is tall, however.

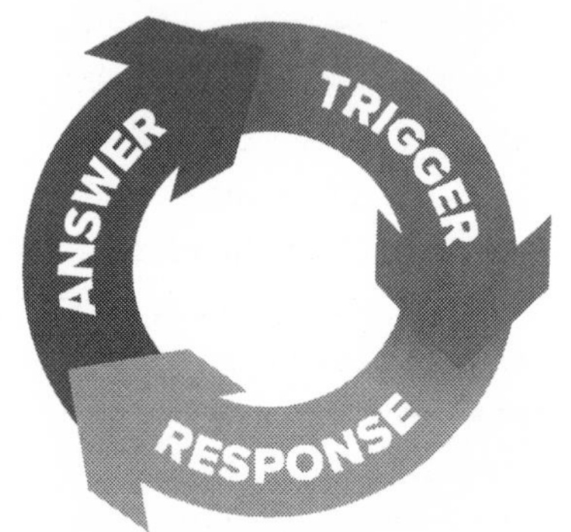

Trigger: The question uses phrases such as suggest, implies, infer, or conclude.

Response: Use your notes from active reading to see if you can support one of the answer choices. Eliminate answer choices that do not match the author's tone. Test inverse conclusion questions by imagining a scenario where the facts from the passage are true, but the answer choices is still false. If you can imagine such a scenario, then the answer choice cannot be inferred from the passage and you can eliminate it.

KEY CONCEPTS

Explicit and Implicit Question Practice Passage

This passage, written by a biologist, is an excerpt from an article about how common misunderstandings in biology result from the way key concepts are defined and presented in textbooks

Textbook and popular writers have a difficult task. Their job is to present science to students and other members of the public who, increasingly, come from disparate cultural and economic backgrounds, live in states that have conflicting guidelines for what should be presented in science texts, and are being subjected to deteriorating state support and increasing political factionalism. With less money to spend on instructional materials, competition is tougher than ever.

Teachers who compare closely the treatments of subjects in competing textbooks will notice that they promise the moon, advertising the individual and unique effectiveness of their pedagogical approach. Be that as it may, the science content is peculiarly uniform among publishing houses, although specific examples and details of concepts "may vary" (to quote traditional textbook jargon). And sometimes that content is wrong, and it has been for many years. Textbook writers are reluctant to change their presentations, even when they are long outdated, because they worry about being "too different" from other textbook programs, and confusing some teachers who expect certain content and cannot always keep up with new developments in the field. An example is how long it is taking textbooks to get rid of the Linnaean classification system and teach phylogenetic systematics (cladistics).

Because the treatment of scientific subjects is so uniform among textbooks, specific errors and misrepresentations are common to most publishing houses. These have been picked up by other media, and many of them are longstanding. In the following suggestions, I try to point out why certain conventions in science texts and popular publications are either incorrect or technically correct but could be presented better, and to suggest alternative treatments.

About half the American populace has trouble of some kind with understanding evolution. The word "evolution" itself has several meanings. Evolution is a fact: science understands that life has evolved through time, and there is no reasonable doubt about this anywhere in the scientific community. It is a theory: it comprises a great many patterns, processes, observations, and hypotheses—all testable. Evolution has patterns, such as the patterns of diversity through time. It has processes, such as natural selection, sexual selection, species selection, drift, and more. Evolution is a big subject with a lot of dimensions. As long as you are clear about which dimension of evolution you mean, there's no conflict for readers.

Following the paragraph above, how does one choose a definition of evolution to use? Because science has no catechisms, there is not a single, standard definition of evolution. But some are more and less useful. A popular one, especially among scientists who work on population biology, is 'a change in gene frequency in a population'. This means, for example, that an allele with a frequency of 0.75 in one generation can change to 0.73 in the next, and this is evolution. Well, sort of. In the next generation, the frequency can change back to 0.75. So what has evolved? It is like defining a football game as the process of hiking the ball. This simple (or simplistic) definition gets to one level of the processes of evolution (yet it misses many processes from speciation to what causes changes in gene frequencies in populations).

Other definitions, such as 'the history of life', get to the patterns of evolution, but do not describe their causes. So both kinds of definitions are inadequate on their own.

Darwin's definition, which he used in *On the Origin of Species,* was "descent with modification." Although it may seem at first glance simplistic or vague, it embodies both the patterns of evolution (descent) and its processes (modification). It is as useful on a short timescale as on a long one; it suggests minor evolutionary modifications as well as major ones. In the last paragraph of Chapter 6 of *On the Origin,* Darwin used this simple definition to settle a century of debate about what controls the morphology of form in the first place. Geoffroy St. Hilaire and others had stressed "unity of type," the features that characterize major groups of animals (mollusks, arthropods, vertebrates) and separate them from others. Baron Georges Cuvier had emphasized "conditions of existence," circumstances that made it advantageous for herbivorous animals to have cropping teeth, complex guts, and hooves for fleet escape. Darwin brushed away this conflict in a single paragraph by showing that common descent could explain the common body plans of related organisms, and that natural selection could explain their adaptive differences as they were modified to fit the conditions of existence.

1. It can be inferred from the first paragraph of the passage that the author believes that

   A) some scientific theories may be inherently difficult to understand for people raised in cultures that do not embrace those theories.
   B) some people have politically-motivated reasons for wanting to influence the context of science curricula.
   C) the quality of textbooks would improve if their writers received more financial support from government.
   D) some politicians seek to remove accurate explanations of evolution from biology textbooks.

2. It can be inferred from the second paragraph (lines 12-31) that

   A) science teachers rely on a level of familiarity with the material in the textbooks they use.
   B) the "Linnaean classification system" (lines 30-31) is no longer taught in any biology classes or textbooks.
   C) science teachers are widely ignorant of new developments in their own fields.
   D) science textbooks may use jargon to obscure gaps in the information they cover.

3. The distinction between the position of Geoffroy St. Hilaire (lines 93-94) and that espoused by Georges Cuvier (lines 97-98) is most nearly that they respectively emphasized

   A) groups of related traits versus specific traits.
   B) form versus function.
   C) historical lineages versus present-day selection pressures.
   D) differences between animals versus similarities between animals.

4. Darwin's conception of evolution as "descent with modification" (lines 82-83) resolved a long-standing dispute in biology by

   A) providing a simultaneous explanation for two competing sets of observations.
   B) accounting for both short and long time scales.
   C) offering a simpler definition of a term than those that had already been in use.
   D) offering the first explanation as to why groupings of animals with similar characteristics exist.

5. Which choice provides the best evidence for the answer to the previous question?

   A) Lines 77-80 ("Other… on their own.")
   B) Lines 86-88 ("It is… major ones.")
   C) Lines 89-92 ("In the last… first place.")
   D) Lines 101-106 ("Darwin brushed… existence.")

Understanding Relationships

Several questions will ask how one part of the passage relates to another. This could be an idea that the author states (and how it relates to the evidence the author gives), relationships between events mentioned in the passage, or relationships between individuals mentioned or quoted in the text. If the reading is a paired passage, these questions may ask about the relationship between ideas or topics mentioned in both.

TYPES OF RELATIONSHIPS

- **Cause-and-Effect/Sequence.** What happens first? What happened next? These relationships are generally chronological in nature.

- **Comparison-Contrast.** While trying to argue a point, an author may bring in another idea to either provide contrast or show similarity. Are these two things alike in any way? Or are they completely different? Do they support or refute the other?

- **Adding Support.** Especially after the author makes some sort of claim, the passage will often offer evidence to support the claim. This may include citing a study or quoting an expert whose opinions agree with the author.

- **Personal Relationships.** These relationships are between people mentioned in the passage. Are these people related, or are they coworkers? Do they have similar views, or is the author showing us the difference between their viewpoints?

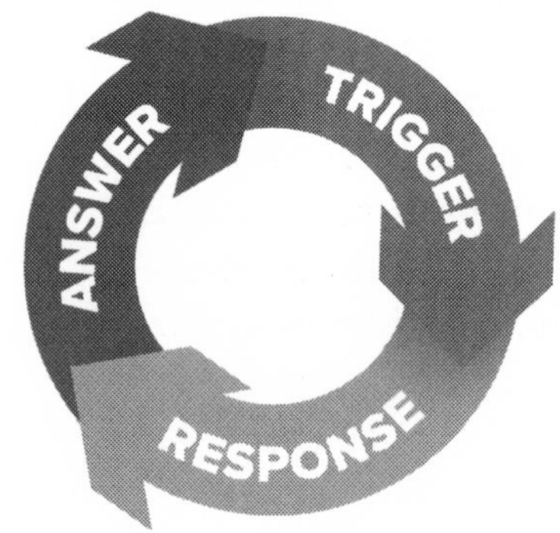

Trigger: The question uses words or phrases such as "what is the relationship...", "connects with," "related to", or "caused by."

Response: Find the two parts of the passage that are mentioned before you do anything else. Determine the relationship in your own words, using the relationships described above. Find the choice that most closely resembles that relationship. Eliminate any choices that don't properly describe the relationship.

KEY CONCEPTS

Understanding Relationships Practice Passage

This passage is and excerpt from Emma *by Jane Austen.*

Emma Woodhouse, handsome, clever, and rich, with a comfortable home and happy disposition, seemed to unite some of the best blessings of existence; and had lived nearly twenty-one years in the world with very little to distress or vex her.

She was the youngest of the two daughters of a most affectionate, indulgent father; and had, in consequence of her sister's marriage, been mistress of his house from a very early period. Her mother had died too long ago for her to have more than an indistinct remembrance of her caresses; and her place had been supplied by an excellent woman as governess, who had fallen little short of a mother in affection.

Sixteen years had Miss Taylor been in Mr. Woodhouse's family, less as a governess than a friend, very fond of both daughters, but particularly of Emma. Between *them* it was more the intimacy of sisters. Even before Miss Taylor had ceased to hold the nominal office of governess, the mildness of her temper had hardly allowed her to impose any restraint; and the shadow of authority being now long passed away, they had been living together as friend and friend very mutually attached, and Emma doing just what she liked; highly esteeming Miss Taylor's judgment, but directed chiefly by her own.

The real evils, indeed, of Emma's situation were the power of having rather too much her own way, and a disposition to think a little too well of herself; these were the disadvantages which threatened alloy to her many enjoyments. The danger, however, was at present so unperceived, that they did not by any means rank as misfortunes with her.

Sorrow came—a gentle sorrow—but not at all in the shape of any disagreeable consciousness.—Miss Taylor married. It was Miss Taylor's loss which first brought grief. It was on the wedding-day of this beloved friend that Emma first sat in mournful thought of any continuance. The wedding over, and the bride-people gone, her father and herself were left to dine together, with no prospect of a third to cheer a long evening. Her father composed himself to sleep after dinner, as usual, and she had then only to sit and think of what she had lost.

The event had every promise of happiness for her friend. Mr. Weston was a man of unexceptionable character, easy fortune, suitable age, and pleasant manners; and there was some satisfaction in considering with what self-denying, generous friendship she had always wished and promoted the match; but it was a black morning's work for her. The want of Miss Taylor would be felt every hour of every day. She recalled her past kindness—the kindness, the affection of sixteen years—how she had taught and how she had played with her from five years old—how she had devoted all her powers to attach and amuse her in health—and how nursed her through the various illnesses of childhood. A large debt of gratitude was owing here; but the intercourse of the last seven years, the equal footing and perfect unreserve which had soon followed Isabella's marriage, on their being left to each other, was yet a dearer, tenderer recollection. She had been a friend and companion such as few possessed: intelligent, well-informed, useful, gentle, knowing all the ways of the family, interested in all its concerns, and peculiarly interested in herself, in every pleasure, every scheme of hers—one to whom she could speak every thought as it arose, and who had such an affection for her as could never find fault.

How was she to bear the change?—It was true that her friend was going only half a mile from them; but Emma was aware that great must be the difference between a Mrs. Weston, only half a mile from them, and a Miss Taylor in the house; and with all her advantages, natural and domestic, she was now in great danger of suffering from intellectual solitude. She dearly loved her father, but he was no companion for her. He could not meet her in conversation, rational or playful.

1. Which of the following characters most strongly influences Emma's decisions?

   A) Emma's sister
   B) Miss Taylor
   C) Emma's father
   D) Emma's mother

2. Which choice provides the best evidence for the answer to the previous question?

   A) Lines 11-15 ("Her mother… affection")
   B) Lines 20-28 ("Even… own")
   C) Lines 29-34 ("The real evils… enjoyments")
   D) Lines 37-39 ("Sorrow… married")

3. The marriage of Emma's sister Isabella had which effect on Emma's life?

   A) Emma made many acquaintances but few close friends
   B) Emma saw marriage as a wonderful achievement
   C) Emma turned to her father for friend-ship
   D) Emma developed a strong friendship with Miss Taylor

4. Emma's relationship with Miss Taylor is most like which of the following?

   A) an employer and an employee
   B) a strict teacher and a disobedient student
   C) a fine lady and a maid
   D) two close friends who grew up together

Author's Intent

Everything you read was written for a reason. The author may have a point to argue, information to share, or a story to tell. Many questions on the SAT will ask you to determine and describe what the author's intent was when writing the passage. These include questions that focus on central ideas and themes, the author's purpose, and the author's point of view.

CENTRAL IDEAS AND THEMES

When reading a passage, it's important to keep an eye on the big picture. Consider how you would summarize the primary ideas of the passage. If you were asked what the question is about, how would you respond? One way to determine this is to make small notes to the side of the passage that summarize each paragraph while you read. By the time you've finished reading, you should be able to look at your notes to summarize the passage in your own words – this will help you with main idea questions.

ANALYZING PURPOSE

Knowing what the passage is about is just one aspect of these questions. You'll also need to know why the author wrote this passage. In addition, you want to determine the author's intended audience – is it a friend? A specific scientific community? The world? Is the language very simple and clear, or is it highly technical? Speakers or writers will write differently and phrase their ideas differently depending on the audience to whom they're speaking.

POINT OF VIEW

Not every passage is written by an EPA official or American President. Often a big part of determining the author's intent is to figure out where he or she is coming from. Is the writer writing from a position of authority? How formal or informal is the language used? What is the writer's tone? Does the writer himself/herself have a vested interest in what he or she is writing about?

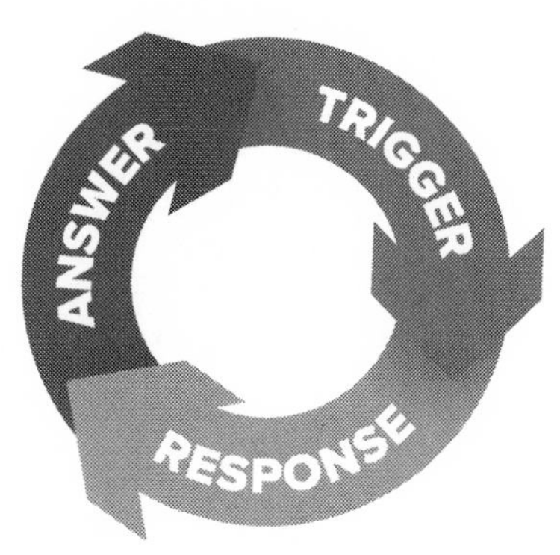

Trigger: The question asks about central ideas and themes usually use the phrases "main idea", "primary point", or "central theme," or the question asks about analyzing purpose and uses the phrases "what is the author's purpose?" or "why did the author write this?"

Response: Active reading is the key. You want to be able to anticipate answers by knowing what each paragraph is about and the main idea of the passage overall. Also, anticipate the purpose of the passage. Use what you have in your head to match to a correct answer. If you cannot support an answer choice, then work backwards and cross out wrong answer choices.

KEY CONCEPTS

Analyzing Arguments

When you try to make an argument, you can't simply state your opinion and be done with it. You've got to back yourself up with proof. The same goes for the writers of the passages you read on the SAT. Many of the passages you read will be making a central claim and you must not only identify the main idea but determine how the author argues it.

CLAIMS AND COUNTERCLAIMS

Claims and counterclaims questions ask you to identify the claims or counterclaims that the author makes in the passage. A claim is an argument that is made by the author. A counterclaim is something that the author says in response to defend the author's argument. Note: what the author is responding to may not be an actual person, but rather "Some people worry that..."

ANALYZING REASONING

Analyzing reasoning questions are a bit trickier because they can come in several forms. These questions require you to understand the reasoning behind the author's argument and whether that reasoning is valid. Examples of faulty reasoning include:

Faulty causation: ______________________________

Circular reasoning: ______________________________

Over-generalization: ______________________________

Over-simplification: ______________________________

ANALYZING EVIDENCE

Analyzing evidence requires you to determine whether the evidence the author uses is relevant or pertinent to the argument the author is making. If the author is citing an expert, is that expert a good source? Are the statistics the author cites clearly supporting the author's argument, or are they misleading?

Evidence can generally be divided into four basic categories:

Examples: ______________________________

Analogies: ______________________________

Statistics: ______________________________

Testimony: ______________________________

Trigger: The question might ask what assumptions the author or the author's sources make. It may ask you to identify the author's reason for including a word or phrase in the context of making an argument.

Response: If it gives you an area of the passage, make sure you return to the passage and put the argument in your own words. Understanding the argument is critical. Eliminate wrong answer choices. If it is taking you too long, guess and move on, as these types of questions are very difficult.

KEY CONCEPTS

Author's Intent and Analyzing Arguments Practice Passage

This passage talks about the recovery and improvement of Haiti since the 2010 earthquake that caused massive destruction.

Haiti, often cited as one of the least developed countries in the Western Hemisphere, has reached – or nearly reached – several of the Millennium Development Goals ahead of the 2015 deadline, according to a report launched by the United Nations Development Program (UNDP) a month ago.

Among other achievements, the country has seen a steady boost in enrollment rates in primary education from 47 percent in 1993 to nearly 90 percent, achieving equal participation of boys and girls in education. Haiti has also halved the number of underweight children under the age of five some three years ahead of the 2015 deadline.

As Secretary-General Ban Ki-moon wrapped up a visit to the Caribbean nation earlier this week, poverty reduction was a central theme in his discussions with UN officials and Haitian authorities. It is also a priority for the government. Haitian Prime Minister Laurent Lamothe recently remarked, "Our initiatives will be increasingly strengthened and we invite civil society to join us in the fight against poverty and to improve Haitians' living conditions."

Since the quake, which killed at least 200,000 people, UNDP reports that 97 percent of the debris has been removed from the streets; 11,000 displaced families have been relocated and 50 camps housing the displaced have been closed; and more than 4,000 meters of river bank protection structures have been constructed to guard against flooding.

Haitian and international efforts have succeeded in significantly reducing the toll from the cholera epidemic, reflected in a 74 percent decrease in the number of new cases so far this year, while Haitian communities are rebuilding, recovering and becoming more resilient to future catastrophes four years after the devastating 2010 earthquake.

The country's Gross Domestic Product (GDP) rose from $1,548 per capita in 2009 to $1,602 per capita in 2012, with extreme poverty stabilizing at 24 percent in 2012, according to the new Haiti MDG report.

Haiti has made notable progress in health indicators, with infant mortality decreasing 44 percent since 1990, faster than the global average, and HIV/AIDS has stabilized with a prevalence of 0.9 percent among the population aged 15 to 24.

Moreover, nearly 65 percent of households now have improved access to water, compared to 36.5 percent in 1995, according to the report. Despite the progress made, however, weak water, sanitation and health systems – demonstrated by the lack of access to safe water by more than a third of the Haitian population – are still enabling cholera, acute diarrhea or other waterborne diseases to persist.

So when Secretary Ban travelled to the village of Los Palmas this week, he and Haitian Prime Minister Laurent Lamothe together launched the country's "Total Sanitation Campaign" which aims to scale up sanitation and hygiene interventions in rural areas.

The Secretary-General called the campaign "a development milestone" for the country, where half the population lacks access to adequate sanitation systems.

He said the UN stands ready to help expand the initiative to the most remote areas and to places where cholera persists.

Together with the World Bank, the UN plans to assist the Haitian Government to provide schools and health centers in an initial 20 targeted communities affected by the disease, covering 3 million people within the next five years because cholera is still an emergency in Haiti and efforts need to be pursued to sustainably eliminate the disease.

From October 2010 to the end of June 2014, the Government of Haiti has reported over 700,000 suspected cholera cases and 8,500 cholera-related deaths. Even with the decline in rates over the first five months of 2014 compared to the same period last year, and a fatality rate below the 1 per cent target rate set by the World Health Organization, cholera is still an emergency.

1. The author's stance in the passage is best described as a

   A) Haitian bragging about the country's successes.
   B) developer attempting to get more investors interested in Haiti.
   C) opponent of foreign involvement in Haiti's internal struggles.
   D) journalist outlining the recent problems and successes in Haiti.

2. Which of the following statements is a counterclaim used by the author?

   A) Lines 12-15 ("Haiti has… deadline.")
   B) Lines 22-25 ("Our initiatives… conditions.")
   C) Lines 34-36 ("Haitian and… epidemic")
   D) Lines 56-61 ("Despite the… persist.")

3. What is the author's tone in the second to last paragraph (Lines 75-82)?

   A) Neutral
   B) Dismissive
   C) Hopeful
   D) Despondent

4. Which of the following counterclaims, if made by the author, would increase the amount of foreign assistance that Haiti is receiving?

   A) The Haitian government is weak and cannot handle its own infrastructure without UN assistance.
   B) The Haitian people are refusing UN assistance due to cultural and religious differences.
   C) The UN is hindering the growth of Haiti by helping them too much.
   D) Thanks to the donations from other countries, Haiti is recovering and will soon become an independent country.

Structure

When you read a passage, the ideas aren't simply arranged in the order the author thought of them. Each speech, excerpt, or report has been carefully laid out to best communicate its ideas. Answering questions about the passage's structure can be difficult, as this skill requires a thorough understanding of everything the passage is trying to say.

OVERALL TEXT STRUCTURE QUESTIONS

The best method to approach text structure questions is to analyze the structure of the passage as you read. Here are some examples of different kinds of organization:

- chronologically and/or cause-effect
- thesis statement followed by support (evidence or quotes from experts)
- from general statements to specific statements
- contrasting ideas – pro/cons of a situation, problems and solutions, examples and counter-examples

PART-TO-WHOLE STRUCTURE QUESTIONS

These questions ask what role certain paragraphs, sentences, and phrases play in the structure of the overall passage. Is that third paragraph providing additional evidence, or is it refuting a previously stated point? As with any question on the SAT, put it in your own words first.

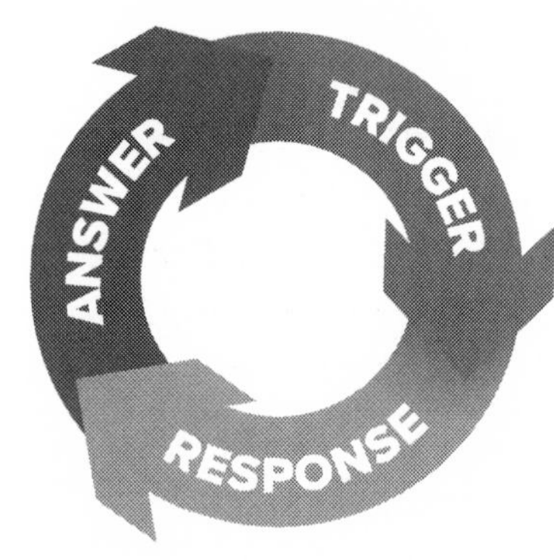

Trigger: Look for phrases such as "the author included the information in lines 42-53 in order to..." or "what purpose does the third paragraph (lines 22-29) play in the passage as a whole?"

Response: Start by putting the question in your own words. Determine if the question is about overall structure or how a part fits in. While you were reading, you should have noted any changes in tone, subject, or purpose. If it is about overall structure, does it match one of the structure types above? If it is a part to whole, ask yourself, " In light of the overall purpose, why did the author include this piece?" Finally, reread the italicized introduction to see if these provides a clue.

KEY CONCEPTS

Citing Textual Evidence

Citing textual evidence questions will appear on every reading passage on the SAT. These questions ask you to identify which part of the passage supports your answer to an earlier question. Many students despair upon seeing them because they seem difficult at first glance. Don't worry! We're going to give you some strategies that will help.

APPEAR IN PAIRS

Citing textual evidence questions will appear within a pair of questions. The first question of the pair focuses on analysis, asking you to draw a conclusion or make an inference about something in the passage. The second question in the pair is the citing textual evidence question, which provides four sets of lines from the passage and asks which one provides the best evidence in support of the answer to the analysis question.

HOW TO ANSWER CITING TEXTUAL EVIDENCE QUESTIONS

There are two ways to approach Citing Textual Evidence Questions.

1. **When you already know the answer to the analysis question.** If this happens, circle your answer to the first question. Then, look for where in the text you found that answer. See which of the answers to the second question points you to the right lines. Note that the two should line up clearly! If they do, great! Be confident in your answer and move on. If they don't, then you may want to rethink your answer to the analysis question, and move on to scenario two.

2. **When you don't know the answer to the analysis question.** Here, you can use the citing textual evidence question to locate the answer. First, decide what kind of information you need to answer the question. Then, look through the line numbers and see which ones are on topic – eliminate any that aren't. Focus on the remaining lines, and summarize what they say. Eliminate any answer choices from the analysis question which are off topic from the lines that you have remaining. Of any remaining choices, pick the ones that best answer the question and provide evidence for that answer.

Trigger: The second question refers to the first question and cites 4 different sets of line numbers as support for the answer.

Response: Look for answer choices from the first question to pair up with supporting choices from the second question. Get rid of any questions that aren't paired up. Of the pairs of lines and answers that you have left, choose the one that best answers the question. Sometimes the supporting lines will be adjacent to each other. Then you are going to have to be careful and make certain to select the area which provides the best evidence.

KEY CONCEPTS

Words in Context

Every reading passage on the SAT will test your knowledge of vocabulary through words in context questions. Read the sentence with the word in it before you choose your answer – you'll be surprised what context can do to a word!

ADDRESSING WORDS IN CONTEXT QUESTIONS

Words in context questions are easy to spot because they always appear in the same format:

As it is used in line ##, "*word*" most nearly means...

The answer choices will always be either a single word or, much more rarely, two- or three-word phrases. Remember what the goal of these questions is. It's not about fixing the word that the author used – the assumption is that the author chose the right word or phrase! Instead, imagine that this is the scenario. Your friend is reading the text, and they don't understand what the sentence means because they are unfamiliar with the word. What words of phrases could you replace it with so that they could understand it?

Trigger: The question uses phrases like "best captures the meaning of" and "most nearly means."

Response:

- Refer back to the text before choosing your answer
- Choose your own words to fill in the blank before looking at the answer choices
- Don't be afraid to pick a word whose meaning you're unsure of
- Move quickly through these questions – there comes a point where you will just have to guess, and there are other questions where your time will be better spent
- If you are running short on time, answer these questions first as they are short and you will know right away if you know the right answer or not
- Positive/Negative/Neutral – this helps with process of elimination

KEY CONCEPTS

Structure, Citing Textual Evidence, and Words in Context Practice Passage

This passage, written by a biologist, is an excerpt from an article about how common misunderstandings in biology result from the way key concepts are defined and presented in textbooks

Textbook and popular writers have a difficult task. Their job is to present science to students and other members of the public who, increasingly, come from disparate cultural and economic backgrounds, live in states that have conflicting guidelines for what should be presented in science texts, and are being subjected to deteriorating state support and increasing political factionalism. With less money to spend on instructional materials, competition is tougher than ever.

Teachers who compare closely the treatments of subjects in competing textbooks will notice that they promise the moon, advertising the individual and unique effectiveness of their pedagogical approach. Be that as it may, the science content is peculiarly uniform among publishing houses, although specific examples and details of concepts "may vary" (to quote traditional textbook jargon). And sometimes that content is wrong, and it has been for many years. Textbook writers are reluctant to change their presentations, even when they are long outdated, because they worry about being "too different" from other textbook programs, and confusing some teachers who expect certain content and cannot always keep up with new developments in the field. An example is how long it is taking textbooks to get rid of the Linnaean classification system and teach phylogenetic systematics (cladistics).

Because the treatment of scientific subjects is so uniform among textbooks, specific errors and misrepresentations are common to most publishing houses. These have been picked up by other media, and many of them are longstanding. In the following suggestions, I try to point out why certain conventions in science texts and popular publications are either incorrect or technically correct but could be presented better, and to suggest alternative treatments.

About half the American populace has trouble of some kind with understanding evolution. The word "evolution" itself has several meanings. Evolution is a fact: science understands that life has evolved through time, and there is no reasonable doubt about this anywhere in the scientific community. It is a theory: it comprises a great many patterns, processes, observations, and hypotheses—all testable. Evolution has patterns, such as the patterns of diversity through time. It has processes, such as natural selection, sexual selection, species selection, drift, and more. Evolution is a big subject with a lot of dimensions. As long as you are clear about which dimension of evolution you mean, there's no conflict for readers.

Following the paragraph above, how does one choose a definition of evolution to use? Because science has no catechisms, there is not a single, standard definition of evolution. But some are more and less useful. A popular one, especially among scientists who work on population biology, is 'a change in gene frequency in a population'. This means, for example, that an allele with a frequency of 0.75 in one generation can change to 0.73 in the next, and this is evolution. Well, sort of. In the next generation, the frequency can change back to 0.75. So what has evolved? It is like defining a football game as the process of hiking the ball. This simple (or simplistic) definition gets to one level of the processes of evolution (yet it misses many processes from speciation to what causes changes in gene frequencies in populations).

Other definitions, such as 'the history of life', get to the patterns of evolution, but do not describe their causes. So both kinds of definitions are inadequate on their own.

Darwin's definition, which he used in On the Origin of Species, was "descent with modification." Although it may seem at first glance simplistic or vague, it embodies both the patterns of evolution (descent) and its processes (modification). It is as useful on a short timescale as on a long one; it suggests minor evolutionary modifications as well as major ones. In the last paragraph of Chapter 6 of *On the Origin,* Darwin used this simple definition to settle a century of debate about what controls the morphology of form in the first place. Geoffroy St. Hilaire and others had stressed "unity of type," the features that characterize major groups of animals (mollusks, arthropods, vertebrates) and separate them from others. Baron Georges Cuvier had emphasized "conditions of existence," circumstances that made it advantageous for herbivorous animals to have cropping teeth, complex guts, and hooves for fleet escape. Darwin brushed away this conflict in a single paragraph by showing that common descent could explain the common body plans of related organisms, and that natural selection could explain their adaptive differences as they were modified to fit the conditions of existence.

1. The author's observation that "science content is peculiarly uniform" (line 17) is most nearly

   A) misleading, because in fact the details of such content vary in important ways from one book to the next.
   B) unsurprising, because lack of resources means that publishers cannot always update their textbooks to incorporate the latest scientific knowledge.
   C) reassuring, because it means that most textbooks contain basically accurate information despite occasional factual discrepancies.
   D) ironic, because textbook marketing often involves the promise of uniqueness.

2. Which choice provides the best evidence for the answer to the previous question?

   A) Lines 2-9 ("Their job… factionalism.")
   B) Lines 12-16 ("Teachers who… pedagogical approach.")
   C) Lines 18-22 ("although specific… many years.")
   D) Lines 22-24 ("Textbook writers… outdated")

3. As used in line 32, "treatment" most nearly means

   A) conduct.
   B) manipulation.
   C) presentation.
   D) regimen.

4. The purpose of the fourth paragraph (lines 43-58) in context of the passage as a whole is to

   A) provide a transition from a general discussion to a specific example.
   B) lay out the key ways in which a common scientific term can be misunderstood.
   C) illustrate the amount of controversy that surrounds a central concept of biology.
   D) carefully define a term that will be used in subsequent paragraphs.

5. As used in line 102, "common" most nearly means

   A) characteristic.
   B) conventional.
   C) prevailing.
   D) shared.

6. The distinction between the position of Geoffroy St. Hilaire (line 94) and that espoused by Georges Cuvier (line 98) is most nearly that they respectively emphasized

   A) groups of related traits versus specific traits.
   B) form versus function.
   C) historical lineages versus present-day selection pressures.
   D) differences between animals versus similarities between animals.

7. Darwin's conception of evolution as "descent with modification" (lines 83-84) resolved a long-standing dispute in biology by

   A) providing a simultaneous explanation for two competing sets of observations.
   B) accounting for both short and long time scales.
   C) offering a simpler definition of a term than those that had already been in use.
   D) offering the first explanation as to why groupings of animals with similar characteristics exist.

8. Which choice provides the best evidence for the answer to the previous question?

   A) Lines 78-81 ("Other… on their own.")
   B) Lines 86-88 ("It is… major ones.")
   C) Lines 88-92 ("In the last… first place.")
   D) Lines 101-106 ("Darwin brushed… existence.")

Word Choice

The SAT will test your ability to analyze an author's choice of words within a given passage. Remember that an author almost always chooses his words carefully, so an author's choice of words is typically done with some purpose in mind.

ADDRESSING WORD CHOICE QUESTIONS

Answering word choice questions will often require that you understand the author's intent in writing the passage; after all, the author's choice of words will generally be determined by the author's purpose in writing.

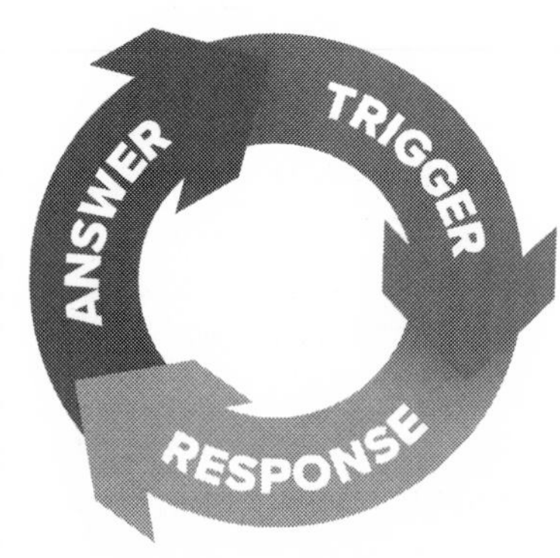

Trigger: Word choice questions will usually either ask why an author has chosen a particular phrasing or how the author's choice affects the passage.

Response:

- Return to the text and read more of the text than you think you need to, as these questions are all about context clues .

- One strategy for handling these types of questions is to imagine that the author had said something differently. How would using "walked" instead of "sauntered" change the image that you have of the scene?

KEY CONCEPTS

Word Choice Practice Passage

The following is an excerpt from The Time Machine, *an 1895 novel by English writer H. G. Wells.*

I think that at that time none of us quite believed in the Time Machine. The fact is, the Time Traveller was one of those men who are too clever to be believed: you never felt that you saw all round him; you always suspected some subtle reserve, some ingenuity in ambush, behind his lucid frankness. Had Filby shown the model and explained the matter in the Time Traveller's words, we should have shown him far less scepticism. For we should have perceived his motives; a pork butcher could understand Filby. But the Time Traveller had more than a touch of whim among his elements, and we distrusted him. Things that would have made the frame of a less clever man seemed tricks in his hands. It is a mistake to do things too easily. The serious people who took him seriously never felt quite sure of his deportment; they were somehow aware that trusting their reputations for judgment with him was like furnishing a nursery with egg-shell china. So I don't think any of us said very much about time travelling in the interval between that Thursday and the next, though its odd potentialities ran, no doubt, in most of our minds: its plausibility, that is, its practical incredibleness, the curious possibilities of anachronism and of utter confusion it suggested. For my own part, I was particularly preoccupied with the trick of the model. That I remember discussing with the Medical Man, whom I met on Friday at the Linnaean.

The next Thursday I went again to Richmond—I suppose I was one of the Time Traveller's most constant guests—and, arriving late, found four or five men already assembled in his drawing-room. The Medical Man was standing before the fire with a sheet of paper in one hand and his watch in the other. I looked round for the Time Traveller, and—'It's half-past seven now,' said the Medical Man. 'I suppose we'd better have dinner?'

'Where's——?' said I, naming our host.

'You've just come? It's rather odd. He's unavoidably detained. He asks me in this note to lead off with dinner at seven if he's not back. Says he'll explain when he comes.'

'It seems a pity to let the dinner spoil,' said the Editor of a well-known daily paper; and thereupon the Doctor rang the bell.

The Psychologist was the only person besides the Doctor and myself who had attended the previous dinner. The other men were Blank, the Editor aforementioned, a certain journalist, and another—a quiet, shy man with a beard—whom I didn't know, and who, as far as my observation went, never opened his mouth all the evening. There was some speculation at the dinner-table about the Time Traveller's absence, and I suggested time travelling, in a half-jocular spirit. The Editor wanted that explained to him, and the Psychologist volunteered a wooden account of the 'ingenious paradox and trick' we had witnessed that day week. He was in the midst of his exposition when the door from the corridor opened slowly and without noise. I was facing the door, and saw it first. 'Hallo!' I said. 'At last!' And the door opened wider, and the Time Traveller stood before us. I gave a cry of surprise. 'Good heavens! man, what's the matter?' cried the Medical Man, who saw him next. And the whole tableful turned towards the door.

He was in an amazing plight. His coat was dusty and dirty, and smeared with green down the sleeves; his hair disordered, and as it seemed to me greyer—either with dust and dirt or because its colour had actually faded. His face was ghastly pale; his chin had a brown cut on it—a cut half healed; his expression was haggard and drawn, as by intense suffering. For a moment he hesitated in the doorway, as if he had been dazzled by the light. Then he came into the room. He walked with just such a limp as I have seen in footsore tramps. We stared at him in silence, expecting him to speak.

1. The main rhetorical effect of the phrase "like furnishing a nursery with egg-shell china," in line 21, is to

   A) emphasize the vulnerability of children in an age of technological experimentation.
   B) express the impracticality of such far-fetched schemes as the invention of a time machine.
   C) suggest the reluctance to invest in scientific research without proven commercial applications.
   D) convey the dangerousness of entrusting reputations to someone likely to damage them.

2. The references to other guests by their occupations in lines 51-53 and elsewhere serves the purpose of

   A) conveying the unreliability of the narrator by suggesting that he has difficulty with remembering the other guests' names.
   B) contributing to the plausibility of the account by identifying guests' scientific occupations instead of using their specific names.
   C) undermining the plausibility of the account by indicating that the guests want to remain anonymous so they cannot be asked for testimonies.
   D) creating a sense of the universality of the time traveling experience by using the guests' occupational categories instead of their specific names.

Analogical Reasoning

The SAT will ask you to identify similar situations through analogical reasoning questions. These questions ask you to analyze something in the passage and to apply the characteristics of that something to another, unrelated situation. There is usually at most one of this type of question on the test.

ADDRESSING ANALOGICAL REASONING QUESTIONS

Analogical reasoning questions will usually ask which of a given set of situations most closely mirrors a situation given in the passage. These questions require that you go beyond the superficial details of the passage. For example, the situation in the passage might involve a politician hoping to address the achievement gap in education by attacking the root issue of poverty. The superficial details here are the actor (the politician) and the problem (the achievement gap). The underlying detail is how the politician hopes to address the problem - by solving the root of the problem.

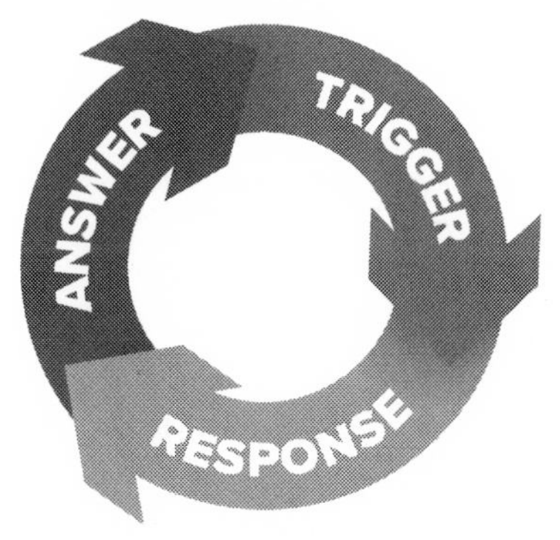

Trigger: The question uses phrases such "situation most nearly resembles" or "is analogous to".

Response: Return to the area of the passage, if a specific area is mentioned, and get the gist of what is happening. Examine the answer choices, and look out for traps that try to make a superficial connection. Try to create a logical equation to help you see what the deeper connection is, and look for an answer choice that uses that same logical equation.

KEY CONCEPTS

Quantitative Information

Quantitative information questions involve the use of graphs, tables, charts, and other graphics. Using the evidence available in the passage and the graphic, you must draw conclusions in order to answer quantitative information questions.

ADDRESSING QUANTITATIVE INFORMATION QUESTIONS

Quantitative information questions require synthesis, meaning that you must combine information from two sources. This means that no matter what the answer to the question is, it must agree with both the passage and the graphic. Having two sources of information to draw from can help you to eliminate answer choices more easily.

Trigger: The question contains a phrase like, "according to the graphic" or "according to the passage and the graphic."

Response:

- Refer back to the passage and the graphic. Check your axes! Always read any titles and labels that are on the graph or chart.

- Think about what kind of information you're looking for before you start to look for it. Eliminate any answer choices that don't agree with the chart, and then eliminate any answers choices that don't agree with the passage. Of the answer choices that remain, choose the one that best answers the question.

KEY CONCEPTS

Analogical Reasoning and Quantitative Information Practice Passage

The following excerpt is from the Report of the Presidential Commission of the Space Shuttle Challenger Accident.

With the 1982 completion of the orbital flight test series, NASA began a planned acceleration of the Space Shuttle launch schedule. One early plan contemplated an eventual rate of a mission a week, but realism forced several downward revisions. In 1985, NASA published a projection calling for an annual rate of 24 flights by 1990. Long before the *Challenger* accident, however, it was becoming obvious that even the modified goal of two flights a month was overambitious.

In establishing the schedule, NASA had not provided adequate resources for its attainment. As a result, the capabilities of the system were strained by the modest nine-mission rate of 1985, and the evidence suggests that NASA would not have been able to accomplish the 15 flights scheduled for 1986. These are the major conclusions of a commission examination of the pressures and problems attendant upon the accelerated launch schedule.

On the same day that the initial orbital tests concluded - July 4, 1982 - President Reagan announced a national policy to set the direction of the U.S. space program during the following decade. As part of that policy, the President stated that:

"The United States Space Transportation System (STS) is the primary space launch system for both national security and civil government missions."

Additionally, he said:

"The first priority of the STS program is to make the system fully operational and cost-effective in providing routine access to space." From the inception of the Shuttle, NASA had been advertising a vehicle that would make space operations "routine and economical." The greater the annual number of flights, the greater the degree of routinization and economy, so heavy emphasis was placed on the schedule. However, the attempt to build up to 24 missions a year brought a number of difficulties, among them the compression of training schedules, the lack of spare parts, and the focusing of resources on near-term problems.

One effect of NASA's accelerated flight rate and the agency's determination to meet it was the dilution of the human and material resources that could be applied to any particular flight.

The part of the system responsible for turning the mission requirements and objectives into flight software, flight trajectory information and crew training materials was struggling to keep up with the flight rate in late 1985, and forecasts showed it would be unable to meet its milestones for 1986. It was falling behind because its resources were strained to the limit, strained by the flight rate itself and by the constant changes it was forced to respond to within that accelerating schedule. Compounding the problem was the fact that NASA had difficulty evolving from its single-flight focus to a system that could efficiently support the projected flight rate. It was slow in developing a hardware maintenance plan for its reusable fleet and slow in developing the capabilities that would allow it to handle the higher volume of work and training associated with the increased flight frequency.

Pressures developed because of the need to meet customer commitments, which translated into a requirement to launch a certain number of flights per year and to launch them on time. Such considerations may occasionally have obscured engineering concerns. Managers may have forgotten - partly because of past success, partly because of their own well-nurtured image of the program - that the Shuttle was still in a research and development phase.

1. Which of the following scenarios is most analogous to the situation at NASA leading up to the *Challenger* accident?

    A) A manufacturer takes a contract to supply the U.S. Open with tennis balls but is unable to meet the increased demands on its manufacturing lines.
    B) A doctor overloads his schedule with patients, and eventually ends up fatally botching a surgery due to exhaustion.
    C) An oil company takes on too many supply contracts, and is unable to fulfill any of them completely when one of its wells runs dry.
    D) An automobile company attempts to cut corners to save money and produces a car with a fatal defect.

The following graph represents the number of space shuttles that were launched in the years before and after the Challenger *disaster. The year of the disaster, 1986, is indicated by a vertical line.*

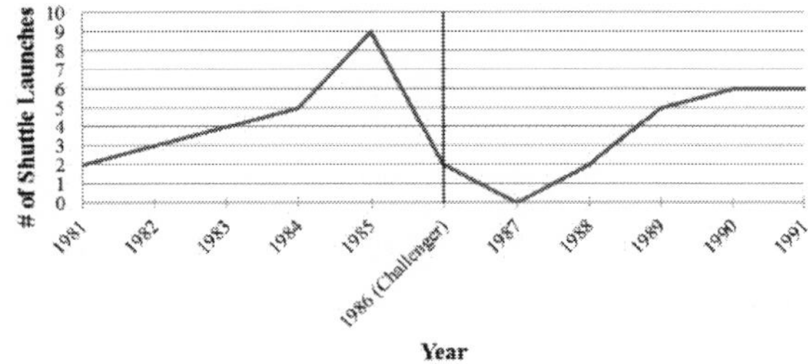

2. The evidence in this graph best supports which of the following claims from the passage?

    A) Despite overwhelming pressure to launch more shuttles in less time, NASA employees were unable to keep up with their new and demanding launch schedule.
    B) Immediately after President Reagan's statements, NASA instituted a much tighter shuttle launch schedule than it had ever used before.
    C) Operation, economy, and routine were the first priorities of the STS program until after the *Challenger* disaster, when safety became the most important issue.
    D) NASA was already showing steady increase in launch frequency in the early 1980s, but it suddenly faced enormous pressure for more dramatic improvement.

3. Which of the following most directly relates to the information presented in this graph?

    A) Lines 1-3 ("With the... launch schedule.")
    B) Lines 14-18 ("the capabilities... for 1986.")
    C) Lines 33-35 ("'The first... to space.'")
    D) Lines 62-66 ("Compounding the... flight rate.")

Analyzing Multiple Texts

Two of the passages on the SAT will be shorter, and will be part of a pair that require you to analyze multiple texts. These questions will require that you be able to identify the points of view of two different authors in order to compare or contrast the passages.

ADDRESSING ANALYZING MULTIPLE TEXTS QUESTIONS

Some multiple text questions will ask how the author of one passage would respond to information or claims made in the other passage. Other questions may ask about the differences or similarities between the points of view of the two authors. Regardless of the form the question takes, all multiple choice questions are made easier through active reading. To answer these questions, it is important to be able to identify the main ideas/claims, author's intent, and style/tone of each passage.

HOW TO APPROACH MULTIPLE TEXT QUESTIONS:

- First, treat the passages separately.
- Read the first passage as usual, and answer any questions that talk about only that passage. Answer detail questions first, then move on to the main idea questions.
- Read the second passage. Take note of similarities and differences between the two passages as you work through the second passage. Answer all the questions that pertain to only the second passage.
- Finally, answer the questions that talk about both passages. There will usually be around three of these.
- When answering those questions, break them into parts! Eliminate any answer choices that only apply to one passage or the other. Sometimes, it helps to give the authors of the two passages names. That lets you keep them separate in your head in a simple way.

Careful reading will save you time

Don't take on too much at once – treat each passage separately at first

Give names to the authors if you are having trouble separating the points of view

KEY CONCEPTS

Analyzing Multiple Texts Practice Passage

The first passage is from the U.S. Department of Energy website. The second was adapted from environmental research.

Pellet Fuel Appliances

Pellet fuel appliances burn compacted pellets usually made of wood, but they can also be derived from other organic materials. Some models can burn nutshells, corn kernels, and small wood chips.

Pellet fuel appliances are more convenient to operate than ordinary wood stoves or fireplaces, and some have much higher combustion and heating efficiencies. As a consequence of this, they produce very little air pollution. In fact, pellet stoves are the cleanest solid fuel residential heating appliance. Pellet stoves that are certified by the EPA are likely to be in the 70 to 83 percent efficiency range. Pellet stoves have heating capacities that range between 8,000 and 90,000 British thermal units (Btu) per hour. They are suitable for homes as well as apartments or condominiums.

Most pellet stoves cost between $1,700 and $3,000. However, a pellet stove is often cheaper to install than a conventional wood-burning heater. Many can be direct-vented to the room and do not need an expensive chimney or flue. As a result, the installed cost of the entire system may be less than that of a conventional wood stove. . . .

All pellet fuel appliances have a fuel hopper to store the pellets until they are needed for burning. Most hoppers hold between 35 and 130 pounds (16 and 60 kilograms) of fuel, which will last a day or more under normal operating conditions. A feeder device, like a large screw, drops a few pellets at a time into the combustion chamber for burning. . . .

Pellet appliances usually require refueling only once a day. However, because the fuel is compressed, the bagged pellets can be difficult to lift. Some models use bulk-filled storage systems and are fully automatic.

Most pellet appliance exteriors (except glass doors) stay relatively cool while operating, reducing the risk of accidental burns. Pellet stoves burn fuel so completely that very little creosote builds up in the flue, posing less of a fire hazard.

Unfortunately, pellet appliances are also more complex and have expensive components that can break down. Moreover, they need to be cleaned by the homeowner on a weekly basis and by a professional on an annual basis. They also require electricity to run fans, controls, and pellet feeders. Under normal usage, they consume about 100 kilowatt-hours (kWh) or about $9 worth of electricity per month. Unless the stove has a back-up power supply, the loss of electric power results in no heat and possibly some smoke in the house.

A Local Choice

Schools districts in the colder states of the U.S. should replace their heating systems that burn oil and natural gas with ones that burn wood pellets. This is not only a matter of cost and environmental awareness; it is also a matter of supporting local economies.

Since 1995, the Pilgrim Unified School District has budgeted and spent over $400,000 annually for oil, gasoline, and natural gas. A recent analysis by an accredited energy auditor concludes that the district could save as much as $4 million over the next twenty years by reducing those costs by 35 to 40 percent. It is impossible to consider using less fuel if student populations remain fairly constant. However, the district could change the type and amount of fuel that it uses with one simple change. The school board should approve the purchase of wood pellet furnaces for all school buildings.

Wood pellet technology is the wave of the future. Between 2006 and 2010, pellet production more than doubled in the U.S. A 2012 report from the Biomass Energy Resource Center projects that it will double again in the next five years. These high-efficiency boilers offer combustion efficiencies between 75 and 90 percent. In addition, they add much lower levels of toxic emissions into the air than those produced by our current systems.

Most importantly, rather than burning fuels that are imported from thousands of miles away, pellet boilers use a local product. Since wood pellets are made from sawdust or wood shavings, they do not even require the harvesting of more trees. Pellets are an extremely efficient fuel that produces a consistent heat and very little ash.

What an excellent example the school board would set for students if the district embraced a local product, downshifted costs, upgraded efficiency, and invested in a future more liberated from dependence on foreign oil. The board should take action immediately and support wood pellet furnaces for all of its schools.

1. Based on both passages, which of the following best describes the purposes of the two authors?

   A) Entertainment vs. argument
   B) Informative vs. persuasive
   C) Descriptive vs. directive
   D) Advisory vs. narrative

2. Which of the following is the most likely response of the author of "A Local Choice" to the claims made in the last paragraph of "Pellet Fuel Appliances"?

   A) Students and their families can learn to clean and maintain their home heating units on a regular basis.
   B) The additional costs of cleaning and maintaining may prevent schools from purchasing wood pellet furnaces.
   C) Custodial staff will clean and maintain the furnaces, and all schools have back-up generators in case of power failures.
   D) Residential heating issues help inform about potential heating issues in large institutions such as schools.

3. Which of the following is used by both authors to support their arguments and opinions?

   A) Efficiency ratings
   B) Ventilation issues
   C) Appliance costs
   D) Safety concerns

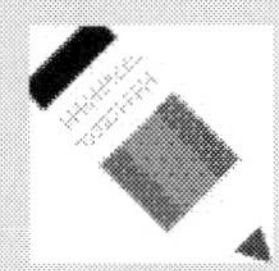

Practice Passage 1

This passages details one way in which scientists are trying to meet the challenges caused by global climate change.

People around the world depend on food crops adapted to an array of temperature and precipitation regimes, but those conditions are in flux because of global climate change.

Among the climate changes we can expect in the future are rising temperatures and increases in greenhouse gases such as methane and carbon dioxide (CO_2). So scientists want to identify plant traits that could be used to develop food-crop cultivars that thrive despite—or perhaps because of—shifts in CO_2 levels, water availability, and air temperature.

As part of this effort, plant physiologist Lewis Ziska and colleagues conducted a study of several rice cultivars (varieties) to determine whether changes of temperature and CO_2 levels affected seed yields. They also looked for visible traits that could signal whether a plant cultivar has the genetic potential for adapting successfully to elevated CO_2 levels.

For their study, the scientists included weedy red rice, a breed normally known as more of a pest than a food crop. Weedy red rice often infests cultivated rice cropland, pushing out the generally more desirable cultivars. Despite the plant's downside, previous assessments indicated that weedy rice growing under elevated CO_2 levels had higher seed yields than cultivated rice growing under the same conditions.

The scientists used environmental growth chambers to study genetically diverse rice cultivars at current and future projections of atmospheric CO_2 and a range of day/night air temperatures. They observed that all the rice cultivars put out more biomass at elevated CO_2 levels, although this diminished as air temperatures rose.

To farmers, biomass is less important than its seed yield. By this metric, which measures the amount of edible plant produced, only weedy rice and one other cultivar responded positively to elevated CO_2 levels when grown at today's normal air temperatures. The researchers were also intrigued that only weedy rice showed significant increases of biomass and seed yield under elevated CO_2 levels at the higher temperatures expected for rice-growing regions by the middle of the century.

When Ziska and colleagues analyzed the study data for the weedy rice, they observed that seed yield increases under elevated CO_2 resulted from an increase in seed head and tiller production. Tillers are stalks put out by a growing rice plant; as the plant matures, the seed heads—where the edible part of the rice grain is produced—develop at the end of the tillers.

Since rice tiller production is determined in part by a plant's genetic makeup, crop breeders might someday be able to use this weedy rice trait to develop commercial rice cultivars that can convert rising CO_2 levels into higher seed yields. In essence, they would be taking the advantageous traits of weedy rice and combining them with the favorable taste and size of other rice cultivars to make a type of rice that is perfectly suited to the future climate. To the researchers, these findings also suggest that the weedy, feral cousins of cultivated cereals could have other traits that would be useful in adapting to the environmental challenges that may come with climate change.

"We know that atmospheric CO_2 and air temperatures will increase together," says Ziska. "Ideally, we can develop plants that respond well, not just to elevated CO_2 levels, but also to higher temperatures and other effects of global climate change."

4.25

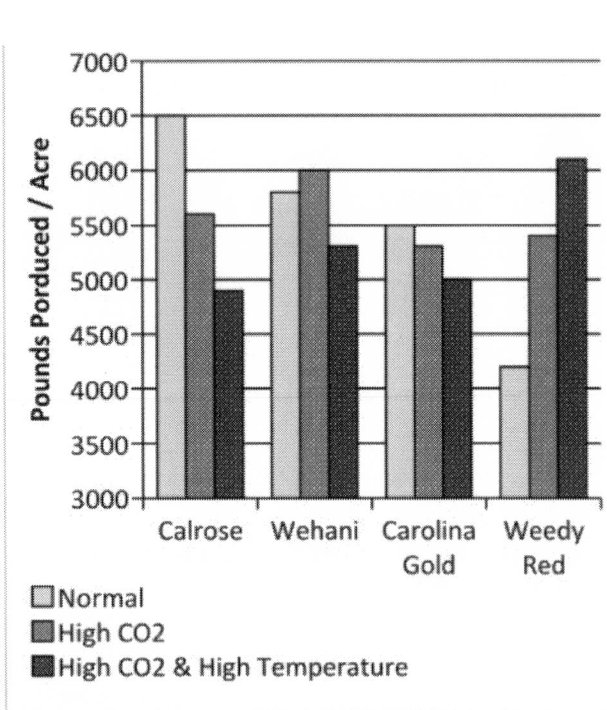

Figure 1: Average seed yields for four rice varieties grown under normal CO_2 and temperature conditions; high-CO_2, normal temperature conditions; and high-CO_2, high-temperature conditions.

1. Based on evidence in the passage, if Figure 1 showed the total biomass, rather than the seed yield, produced by the rice varieties, which of the following would most likely be true?

   A) The left bar would be higher than the middle and right bars for all four varieties.
   B) The left would be higher than the middle bar for only the Weedy Red variety.
   C) The middle bar would be higher than the left bar for all four varieties.
   D) The right bar would be higher than the middle bar for only the Weedy Red variety.

2. As used in line 3, "regimes" most nearly means

   A) conditions.
   B) schemes.
   C) governments.
   D) therapies.

3. How does the phrase "more of a pest than a food crop" in lines 22-23 affect the author's portrayal of the weedy red rice variety?

   A) It hints that any potential benefits of weedy red rice should be dismissed.
   B) It indicates that many people unfairly believe weedy red rice has no value.
   C) It foreshadows the damage that weedy red rice will cause as the climate changes.
   D) It emphasizes that rice is often grown for uses other than food.

4. It can be reasonably inferred from the passage that "biomass is less important than its seed yield" (lines 38-39) as a measure of rice production because

   A) fertilizer can be used to improve biomass but not seed yield.
   B) high-biomass crops are expensive to harvest.
   C) some farmers prefer low-biomass plants.
   D) not all of a rice plant's biomass is edible.

5. Which choice most effectively supports the answer to the previous question?

   A) Lines 17-20 ("They also… CO_2 levels.")
   B) Lines 25-29 ("Despite the… same conditions.")
   C) Lines 34-37 ("They observed… temperatures rose.")
   D) Lines 39-42 ("By this… air temperatures.")

6. Based on information in the passage and the figure, what is the "one other cultivar" referred to in line 40?

A) Calrose
B) Wehani
C) Carolina Gold
D) Weedy Red

7. As used in line 57, "makeup" most nearly means

A) temperament.
B) fiction.
C) cosmetics.
D) characteristics.

8. Information in the passage implies that the "advantageous traits of weedy rice" (lines 62) are

A) unlikely to be useful to future rice growers.
B) used to improve the size and flavor of other rice varieties.
C) largely related to tiller and seed-head production.
D) limited to current carbon dioxide and temperature levels.

9. Which choice provides the best evidence to support the answer to the previous question?

A) Lines 42-47 ("The researchers… the century.")
B) Lines 48-52 ("When Ziska… tiller production.")
C) Lines 61-65 ("In essence… future climate.")
D) Lines 73-76 ("'Ideally, we… climate change.'")

10. The passage's overall structure can best be described as

A) comparing and contrasting two alternative techniques.
B) describing a principle followed by several examples of that principle at work.
C) presenting a problem and one potential solution to that problem.
D) telling a chronological history of an innovation.

Practice Passage 2

This passage examines a unique approach to gathering data for scientific research.

It's the season of dramatic weather, when everyone from the National Weather Service to farmers and insurers monitors predictions of weather conditions—and assessments of where severe weather and its impacts are greatest. In this environment, a citizen science project called CoCoRaHS—the Community Collaborative Rain, Hail and Snow Network—is helpful. This program makes possible a detailed view of rainfall, snowfall, and hail in regions around the country. The organizers have found that precipitation is often highly variable; in extreme cases, it can vary by inches at locations just a few blocks from each other.

CoCoRaHS was first envisioned in 1997, after an intense rainstorm in Fort Collins, Colorado, caused massive flooding and more than $200 million in damage. Nothing in the forecast indicated that the storm would cause as much damage as it did. In addition, there was incredible variation in the amount of rainfall within the affected area—from less than 2 inches to more than 14 inches (which nearly equals that area's average *yearly* rainfall) over a distance of just 5 miles.

The unexpected severity of the storm and its uneven impacts suggested to researchers that enlisting individuals and families to report on precipitation from their locations could provide a more accurate and useful picture of rainfall and snowfall around the state and the country. Thus, in 1998, CoCoRaHS was born. Since the program started, 46,000 people, including participants from every state in the nation, have signed up through the CoCoRaHS website. To participate in the network, each citizen scientist must invest in a high-capacity 4-inch-diameter rain gauge (at a cost of about $30). All new participants in the CoCoRaHS network receive training in how to place their gauges and take accurate readings. Then, each time a rain, hail, or snow storm crosses their area, volunteers take measurements of precipitation.

Their reports are then recorded on the CoCoRaHS website. The data are displayed and organized for a range of end users—from the National Weather Service to the U.S. Department of Agriculture to emergency managers, hydrologists, farmers, ranchers, research scientists, educators, and the general public.

During 2014, there were more than 19,000 active users who set out rain gauges and sent in reports. More than 11,000 reports come in every day. Just as an image is sharper the more pixels it contains, having citizen scientists report precipitation data from thousands of locations provides a detailed picture valuable for predictions, emergency planning, insurance estimates, and a number of other uses.

Beyond its value to the consumers of the data, CoCoRaHS is engaging non-scientists in the kind of observation, reporting and analysis done by scientists. The educational aspects of their work are particularly important to members of the CoCoRaHS community. In addition to coordinating the volunteer reporting, CoCoRaHS sponsors webinars every month featuring experts discussing some aspect of weather or climate. Topics such as cloud formation, lightning, and atmospheric rivers of Pacific water vapor aiming at the west coast have been popular with the volunteers.

Many of the program's volunteers report being surprised that precipitation varies so much. This sort of learning is valuable to many of the volunteers for many reasons. Some enjoy returning to scientific topics that they have not studied since college. Others say that they wish they'd pursued a scientific career, and that the CoCoRaHS experience is giving them a scientific outlet. Still others just enjoy being a part of a communal project.

Being able to contribute scientific data to a network and see the impact of your observations is a powerful experience. The researchers are particularly excited to see volunteers from different age groups (including many high school students), different backgrounds, and different parts of the country taking part in the project. What volunteers are finding is fascinating, and it helps both scientists and ordinary people better understand rain, hail, and snow—phenomena that we've all experienced but that most of us take for granted.

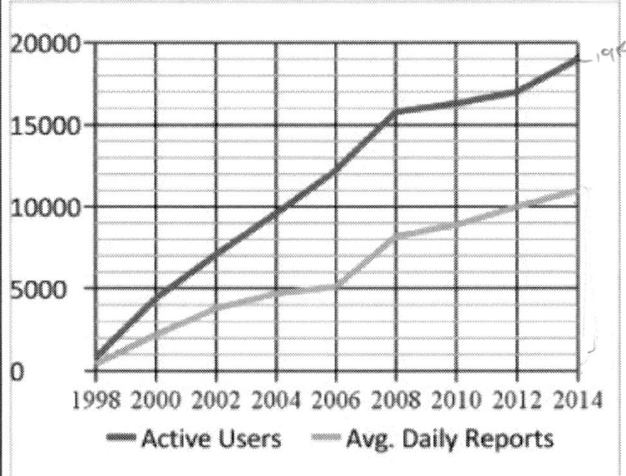

Figure 1: The number of active users and the average number of daily reports during each year of the CoCoRaHS program.

1. It can be reasonably inferred from the passage and the figure that which of the following is true regarding the "46,000 people" (line 33)?

   A) Nearly all are active users, although most of them do not submit daily reports.
   B) Many of them are not currently active users.
   C) Most signed up during the program's first two years.
   D) Nearly all of them provide daily reports on the precipitation in their areas.

2. Based on the figure, which of the following statements is accurate regarding CoCoRaHS?

   A) The program has grown in size during each year of its existence.
   B) The program experienced its largest increase in size between 2010 and 2012.
   C) The number of daily reports has little or no correlation with the number of active users.
   D) If trends continue, the average number of daily reports will reach 20,000 by 2016.

3. Information in the passage implies that the CoCoRaHS program was founded in large part to

   A) teach scientific concepts to students.
   B) better prepare for the impact of severe weather.
   C) help a city recover from a damaging flood.
   D) save money on the collection of weather data.

4. Which choice provides the most effective evidence to support the previous question's answer?

A) Lines 6-9 ("In this… is helpful.")
B) Lines 20-25 ("In addition… 5 miles.")
C) Lines 26-32 ("The unexpected… the country.")
D) Lines 46-51 ("The data… general public.")

5. The author uses which of the following to explain the significance of having thousands of daily precipitation reports?

A) A quote from an expert who uses the data
B) Examples from two contrasting ways of collecting data
C) An analogy to another topic
D) Profiles of several of the data collectors

6. As used in line 55, "sharper" most nearly means

A) harsher.
B) more sudden.
C) more intelligent.
D) clearer.

7. In the context of line 82, "outlet" most nearly means

A) release.
B) store.
C) exit.
D) stream.

8. Based on information in the passage, the CoCoRaHS volunteers can best be described as

A) professional.
B) youthful.
C) diverse.
D) selfish.

9. Which choice best supports the answer to the previous question?

A) Lines 61-64 ("Beyond its… by scientists.")
B) Lines 70-73 ("Topics such… the volunteers.")
C) Lines 79-82 ("Others say… scientific outlet.")
D) Lines 86-91 ("The researchers… the project.")

10. In the context of the passage's discussion of the CoCoRaHS program, the seventh paragraph (lines 74-83) primarily serves to

A) reveal the motivations of some of those involved with the program.
B) provide evidence that the program has helped advance weather prediction.
C) acknowledge an argument that some critics make against the program.
D) predict the ways that the program will change in the future.

11. The tone of the passage indicates that the relationship between the CoCoRaHS researchers and volunteers can best be characterized as

A) a fun way to teach volunteers, but not a scientifically valuable one.
B) a mutually beneficial collaboration.
C) an example of scientists taking advantage of non-scientists.
D) a well-intentioned failure for both groups.

Practice Passage 3

The following passage examines the history of a well-known political tradition.

On January 8, 1790, President George Washington delivered a speech at Federal Hall in New York City. This speech, called his first annual message to Congress (which we now refer to as the State of the Union), was short—in fact, it remains the shortest one ever.

In it, Washington touched on several subjects to which he recommended that Congress give its attention, including national defense, naturalization, uniform weights and measures, promotion of education, and support of the public credit.

The new leaders were fully aware of the enormity of the task in front of them. Washington's last sentence speaks to the heart of their endeavor: "The welfare of our country is the great object to which our cares and efforts ought to be directed.—And I shall derive great satisfaction from a co-operation with you, in the pleasing though arduous task of ensuring to our fellow citizens the blessings, which they have a right to expect, from a free, efficient and equal Government."

Washington gave this speech to fulfill the President's obligation outlined in Article II, Section 3, Clause 1, of the Constitution. It says that the President "shall from time to time give to the Congress Information of the State of the Union, and recommend to their Consideration such measures as he shall judge necessary and expedient."

The Constitution does not specify how frequently the President should share this information. As he did on so many other issues, Washington set the precedent that this message would be delivered to Congress once a year.

Washington's actions in another respect were not precedent-setting, however. Washington appeared before a joint session of Congress to deliver his annual messages in a speech. Second President John Adams followed suit. However, the Third President, Thomas Jefferson, set a new tradition when he sent his messages in writing and did not appear before Congress.

That precedent stuck until 1913, when President Woodrow Wilson addressed a joint session of Congress. Before Wilson, the annual messages were mostly a report to Congress of the activities of the Executive branch. After the increased attention Wilson's speech received, the State of the Union became a launching pad for Presidential initiatives and was used to raise support for the President's legislative agenda.

During Harry Truman's Presidency, the speech came to be widely known as the State of the Union address instead of the annual message.

President Abraham Lincoln was known for words that reverberate through the decades. His December 1, 1862, message became known as the "Fiery Trial" message, in which he acknowledged that "We of this Congress and this administration, will be remembered in spite of ourselves... The fiery trial through which we pass, will light us down, in honor or dishonor, to the latest generation."

This message was delivered exactly one month before the Emancipation Proclamation went into effect. Lincoln ended the message on the subject of slavery: "In giving freedom to the slave, we assure freedom to the free—honorable alike in what we give, and what we preserve. We shall nobly save, or meanly lose, the last best, hope of earth."

President Ronald Reagan's 1986 State of the Union address was originally scheduled for January 28, 1986. However, that day the Challenger space shuttle exploded. Reagan postponed his speech for a week in response to the accident. On February 4, Reagan began his message by paying tribute to "the brave seven" Challenger crew members. Later, he addressed the broader implications of the tragedy: "This nation remains fully committed to America's space program. We're going forward with our shuttle flights. We're going forward to build our space station."

These examples show the resilience of the State of the Union address. Since Washington's time, the Constitution's command that "from time to time" the President shall share information with Congress has meant, and continues to mean, the delivery of the State of the Union message once a year. This tradition is now firmly ensconced, and seems likely to continue as long as the union itself continues.

3:09

1. In the context of line 17, "object" most nearly means

A) recipient.
B) complaint.
C) article.
D) goal.

2. Information in the passage implies that which of the following is true regarding George Washington?

A) He referred to his annual speech as a "State of the Union address."
B) He tended to give longer and more elaborate speeches than later presidents.
C) Many of the actions that he took have since become presidential traditions.
D) He focused his speeches predominantly on the issue of slavery.

3. Which choice provides the best evidence to support the answer to the previous question?

A) Lines 3-6 ("This speech… one ever.")
B) Lines 13-14 ("The new… of them.")
C) Lines 24-26 ("Washington gave… the Constitution.")
D) Lines 34-36 ("As he did… a year.")

4. It can be reasonably inferred from information in the passage that Lincoln's words "reverberate through the decades" (lines 59-60) at least in part because he

A) was the first president to use the State of the Union to promote his initiatives.
B) emphasized cooperating with Congress rather than fighting with them.
C) was concerned with how his and others' actions would be remembered.
D) paid tribute to those who lost their lives in a tragedy.

5. Which choice provides the best evidence to support the answer to the previous question?

A) Lines 49-53 ("After the… legislative agenda.")
B) Lines 64-66 ("The fiery… latest generation.'")
C) Lines 77-80 ("However, that… the accident.")
D) Lines 88-89 ("These examples… Union address.")

6. One of the dominant themes of Lincoln's "'Fiery Trial' message" (line 61) was
   A) the need to create new traditions.
   B) the consequences of a moral choice.
   C) the importance of efficient government.
   D) the tragedy of a continuing war.

7. As used in line 73, "meanly" most nearly means

   A) shamefully.
   B) humbly.
   C) on average.
   D) as required.

8. The final paragraph of the passage is primarily focused on the State of the Union's

   A) influence on popular culture.
   B) enduring appeal.
   C) evolution over time.
   D) use of colorful language.

9. Which two presidents are cited in the passage for helping to evolve the State of the Union into its current form?

   A) Adams and Jefferson
   B) Jefferson and Obama
   C) Wilson and Truman
   D) Lincoln and Reagan

10. The passage's overall structure can best be characterized as moving from

   A) origins to current form.
   B) effects to causes.
   C) similarities to differences.
   D) broad trends to specific instances.

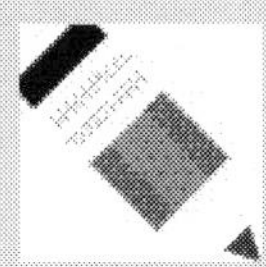

Practice Passage 4

These passages discuss issues related to diversity in computer science education.

Passage 1:

Meet Maddie, a Maryland high-school freshman who has a passion for computing. Eager to continue on her path, she hopes to take a computer science, or CS, course. However, her school no longer offers this course because it does not count toward students' graduation requirements.

According to computer science professor Marie desJardins, Maddie's story is all too common. A recent survey revealed several factors at play, including the lack of a unified curriculum and inadequate teacher certification programs. Furthermore, CS classes are less likely to be offered in rural and urban school districts than in suburban ones. Regardless of the reasons, the results are the same: A disproportionately low number of girls, students of non-white ethnicities, and persons with disabilities are taking CS classes.

DesJardins has been working to change the status quo by training of a wide swath of high school teachers to teach CS. She believes that CS should be included throughout the K-12 curriculum as a set of basic skills and knowledge for today's world. All citizens of the 21st century, especially the next generation of knowledge-based workers, will benefit greatly from learning about computational thinking, she says.

DesJardins' approach involves getting CS high-school teachers together to write a curriculum for a new Advanced Placement (AP) course called CS Principles. This differs from efforts that use professional curriculum writers since it integrates the perspectives, pedagogical expertise, and classroom experiences of a diverse group of teachers. The teachers are currently capturing the experiences of real teachers using the material so as to improve the course.

To scale up these efforts across the nation, desJardins says, we should be focusing on four immediate goals: creating appealing and engaging curricula, training teachers to deliver this material effectively to a diverse population, providing all students with access to these courses, and making sure that CS counts towards high school math or science requirements.

If desJardins' efforts succeed, computer science education will become much more accessible in schools across the country, making stories like Maddie's less common.

Passage 2:

The United States is in the middle of a vital time in computing. However, women are underrepresented, and diverse talent is needed to fill the 1.2 million U.S. computing job openings expected by 2022. At the current rate, U.S. computing undergraduates will only fill 39 percent of these jobs.

Girls represent a valuable, mostly untapped, talent pool, and their lack of participation has serious consequences for future technical innovation. According to the National Center for Women & Information Technology (NCWIT), if technology is designed by only half our population, we're missing out on the solutions and creations that the other 50 percent could bring.

Another obstacle: half of the United States doesn't allow computer science to count as a math or science graduation requirement, and the number of high schools offering Advanced Placement (AP) computer science (CS) is down 35 percent since 2005. This lack of informal introductions to CS impacts all students, especially girls and other underrepresented groups who have fewer occasions to gain experience.

Throughout the year, NCWIT members work to build a national female talent pipeline for computing. All of NCWIT's efforts are backed by researched-based practices for implementing change and raising awareness for women in technology.

The NCWIT Aspirations in Computing program is one exemplary effort that engages the rapidly growing coalition of NCWIT members and young women from 5th grade through graduate school. In the program, sponsors provide structured, long-term support for young women entering technical fields. They offer scholarships and internships, host award events, and more.

Additionally, NCWIT has recognized more than 3,300 young women with its Award for Aspirations in Computing since 2007. Award recipients consistently report greater confidence in their technical abilities, increased enthusiasm about computing, and greater awareness of career opportunities.

The power of ongoing encouragement shouldn't be underestimated. Research shows it is one of the most influential factors in girls' decisions to pursue computing education and careers. In a world where technology increasingly permeates every aspect of society, capitalizing on the benefits of women's participation results in innovation that is as broad as the population it serves.

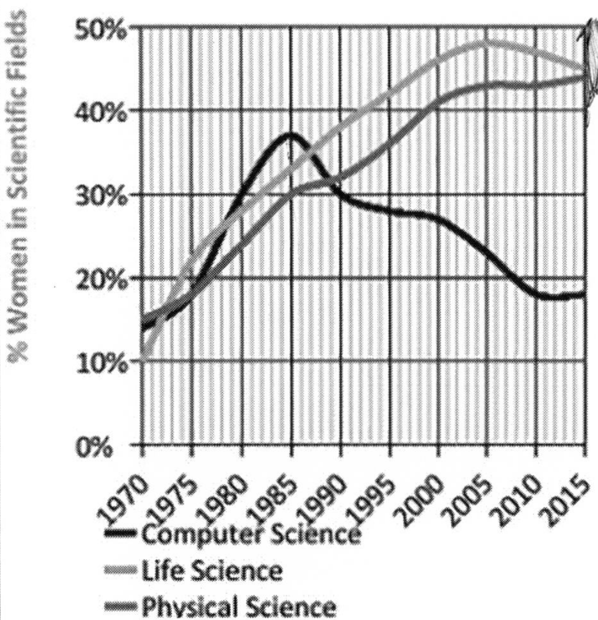

Figure 1: The percentage of graduate student positions held by women in three broad categories of science, according to national surveys.

1. In Passage 1, Maddie primarily functions as

   A) a person whose experiences contrast with those of Marie desJardins.
   B) proof that the methods described in the passage are effective.
   C) an expert whose opinions support the passage's arguments.
   D) an example of a trend that the passage argues should be reversed.

2. In the context of lines 44-45, "engaging" most nearly means

   A) appointing.
   B) engrossing.
   C) combating.
   D) interlocking.

3. Information in Passage 1 implies that most current high school CS texts

A) were written by developers with little classroom experience.
B) are too difficult for most high school students.
C) meet state high school graduation standards.
D) contain discriminatory language intended to appeal only to male students.

4. Which choice provides the best evidence for the answer to the previous question?

A) Lines 14-16 ("Furthermore, CS... suburban ones.")
B) Lines 23-26 ("She believes... today's world.")
C) Lines 34-38 ("This differs... of teachers.")
D) Lines 50-53 ("If desJardins'... less common.")

5. In context, the first three paragraphs of Passage 2 are primarily focused on

A) identifying a problem, several potential solutions for which are presented in the rest of the passage.
B) discussing specific examples that are then connected to draw broad conclusions later in the passage.
C) comparing two concepts that are contrasted in the rest of the passage.
D) providing background information on events that are described later in the passage.

6. As used in lines 77-78, "informal" most nearly means

A) off-the-record.
B) casual.
C) non-professional.
D) colloquial.

7. Information in Passage 2 implies that, without an increase in female participation in computer science, which of the following will occur?

A) Top technology firms leaving the United States
B) A shortage of qualified computing workers
C) An end to high school-level computer science courses
D) A corresponding drop-off in female participation in other scientific fields

8. Which choice provides the most effective support for the answer to the previous question?

A) Lines 57-60 ("However, women... by 2022.")
B) Lines 77-81 ("This lack... gain experience.")
C) Lines 84-87 ("All of... in technology.")
D) Lines 97-99 ("Additionally, NCWIT... since 2007.")

connects w/ rest of paragraph

9. The authors of both passages would most likely agree that which of the following techniques would improve diversity in computer science?

A) Giving awards to young female computer science students.
B) Eliminating Advanced Placement computer science courses.
C) Having active teachers create and test a new computer science curriculum.
D) Allowing more computer science courses to meet high school graduation requirements.

10. How do the approaches of Marie desJardins in Passage 1 and the NCWIT in Passage 2 differ?

A) DesJardins' work focuses more on teachers; the NCWIT's work focuses more on students.
B) DesJardins' work is based on proven research; the NCWIT's work is not.
C) DesJardins' work targets female college students; the NCWIT's work targets grade-school students.
D) DesJardins' work emphasizes computing; the NCWIT's work is broader, emphasizing several areas of the sciences.

11. According to information in the figure, the under-representation of women in computer science, as described in both passages, could potentially be improved upon by examining

A) the state of computer science before 1970.
B) female-dominated fields such as nursing and elementary education.
C) changes made in other scientific fields since 1970.
D) common practices used in computer science during the late 1980s.

Practice Passage 5

The following passage, adapted from Lucy Maud Montgomery's short story "The Finished Letter," describes the relationship between a young girl and an older woman.

She always sat in a corner of the west veranda at the hotel, knitting something white and fluffy, or pink and fluffy, or pale blue and fluffy—always fluffy, at least, and always dainty. When she finished one she gave it to some girl and began another. Every girl at Harbor Light that summer wore some distracting thing that had been fashioned by Miss Sylvia's slim, tireless, white fingers.

She was old, with that serene old age that is as beautiful in its way as youth. Her girlhood and womanhood must have been very lovely to have ripened into such a beauty of sixty years. It was a surprise to everyone who heard that she had never had children. She looked so like a woman who ought to have stalwart, grown sons and dimpled little grandchildren.

For the first two days after the arrival at the hotel she sat in her corner. There was always a circle of young people around her; old folks and middle-aged people would have liked to join it, but Miss Sylvia, while she was gracious to all, let it be distinctly understood that her sympathies were with youth. She sat among the boys and girls, young men and women, like a queen. Her dress was always the same and somewhat old-fashioned, but nothing else would have suited her half so well. She knitted continually and talked a good deal, but listened more. We sat around her at all hours of the day and told her everything.

When you were first introduced to her, you called her Miss Stanleymain. Her endurance of that was limited to twenty-four hours. Then she begged you to call her Miss Sylvia, and as Miss Sylvia you spoke and thought of her forevermore.

Miss Sylvia liked us all, but I was her favorite. She told us so frankly and let it be understood that when I was talking to her, we were not to be interrupted. I was as vain of her favor as any lovelorn suitor, not knowing, as I came to know later, the reason for it.

Although Miss Sylvia had an unlimited capacity for receiving confidences, she never gave any. We were all sure that there must be some romance in her life, but our efforts to discover it were unsuccessful. Miss Sylvia parried tentative questions so skillfully that we knew she had something to defend. But one evening, when I had known her a month, she revealed to me some of her story. The last chapter was missing.

We were sitting together on the veranda at sunset. Most of the hotel people had gone sailing. I was reading one of my stories to Miss Sylvia. In my own defense, I must allege that she tempted me to do it. I did not go around with manuscripts under my arm, inflicting them on defenseless people. But Miss Sylvia had discovered that I was a writer, and moreover, that I had shut myself up in my room that very morning and perpetrated a short story. Nothing would do but that I read it to her.

It was a rather sad little story. The hero loved the heroine, and she loved him. There was no reason he should not love her, but there was a reason he could not marry her. When he found that he loved her, he knew that he must go away. But might he not, at least, tell her his love? Might he not, at least, find out for his consolation if she cared for him? In the end, he went away without a word, believing it to be the more dignified course. When I began to read, Miss Sylvia was knitting, a pale green something this time. After a little her knitting slipped unheeded to her lap and her hands folded idly above it. It was the most subtle compliment I had ever received.

When I turned the last page of the manuscript and looked up, Miss Sylvia's soft brown eyes were full of tears. She lifted her hands, clasped them together and said in an agitated voice:

"Oh, no, no; don't let him go away without telling her—Don't let him do it!"

"But, you see, Miss Sylvia," I explained, flattered beyond measure that my characters had seemed so real to her, "that would spoil the story. It would have no reason for existence then. Its motif is his mastery over self. He believes it to be the nobler course."

"No, no, it wasn't—if he loved her he should have told her. Think of her—she loved him, and he went without a word and she could never know he cared for her. Oh, you must change it! I cannot bear to think of her suffering what I have suffered."

Miss Sylvia broke down and sobbed. To appease her, I promised that I would remodel the story, although I knew that doing so would leave it absolutely pointless.

1. According to the passage, Miss Sylvia's interactions with "the boys and girls" (lines 24-25) are

A) stern and judgmental.
B) generous and informal.
C) crude and rebellious.
D) personal and revealing.

2. Which example from the passage best supports the answer to the previous question?

A) Lines 15-17 ("She looked... little grandchildren.")
B) Lines 26-28 ("Her dress... so well.")
C) Lines 28-31 ("She knitted... her everything.")
D) Lines 39-41 ("She told... be interrupted.")

3. In the context of line 41, "vain" most nearly means

A) prideful.
B) idle.
C) insignificant.
D) futile.

4. As used in line 45, "confidences" most nearly means

A) scams.
B) self-assurances.
C) beliefs.
D) secrets.

5. It can be reasonably inferred from information in the passage that "the reason for" (line 43) Miss Sylvia's preference toward the narrator is that Miss Sylvia

A) hopes to convince the narrator to follow a profession other than writing.
B) feels comfortable revealing personal details to the narrator and no one else.
C) sees a similarity between her daughter and the narrator.
D) shares the narrator's belief that love is not necessary for young people.

6. Which choice most effectively supports the answer to the previous question?

A) Lines 50-52 ("But one... was missing.")
B) Lines 65-67 ("There was... marry her.")
C) Lines 81-83 ("She lifted... agitated voice.")
D) Lines 96-97 ("I cannot... have suffered.")

7. The author's use of the word "perpetrated" in line 62 is most likely intended to convey which of the following?

A) That the narrator's story was secretly written with Miss Sylvia in mind
B) That the narrator is not entirely confident in her writing abilities
C) That the story prominently features a famous real-life crime
D) That the narrator believes her story is immoral or even illegal

8. The passage's narrator agrees to "remodel" (line 99) her story primarily out of

A) pity and affection for a mentor figure.
B) a desire to make the story more likely to be published.
C) concern for the story's literary merit.
D) an intention to improve the story's realism.

9. The primary purpose of the passage is most nearly to

A) argue that all children should have older role models.
B) reveal a character to be more sinister than she at first appears.
C) compare and contrast two approaches to writing fiction.
D) subtly hint at the tragic past of a character.

10. The passage's tone when describing Miss Sylvia can best be characterized as

A) satirical.
B) defiant.
C) reverential.
D) disappointed.

Practice Passage 6

The following passage discusses several lines of research intended to help the United States' rainbow trout populations.

Each year, the rainbow trout industry suffers significant economic losses due to bacterial cold-water disease, caused by the bacterium *Flavobacterium psychrophilum.* The disease also affects salmon and other cold-water fish species. It first occurs when fish are small, often leading to rapid death. Larger fish can become chronically infected and consequently have lesions and impaired growth and yield.

At the Agricultural Research Service's National Center for Cool and Cold Water Aquaculture (NCCCWA) in Leetown, West Virginia, scientists have developed a new line of trout that is resistant to bacterial cold-water disease. They've also developed a susceptible line and a control line to use in studies of how breeding changes disease-resistance properties in trout. They have identified regions on several chromosomes that are responsible for disease resistance and have developed a test that detects *F. psychrophilum* after infection.

Molecular biologist Greg Wiens and geneticist Timothy Leeds recently completed a field performance evaluation in collaboration with industry and government stakeholders. In a 2013 study, Wiens measured performance of the control, disease-susceptible, and disease-resistant lines of fish under farm conditions before and after natural exposure to the pathogen.

After exposure, the disease-resistant line had a higher rate of survival than the control or susceptible lines. In addition, during the outbreak, fewer disease-resistant fish harbored the pathogen in their internal tissues, compared to the control and susceptible fish.

Wiens and fellow scientist David Marancik developed a highly sensitive real-time test that accurately measures small amounts of *F. psychrophilum* in fish tissue. The test recognizes a unique gene sequence that is only found in that pathogen. In the study, more than 200 different strains of *F. psychrophilum* were detected. These strains were all collected at farms where fish suffered from the disease.

No other species of environmental bacteria or fish pathogens were recognized by the test, which demonstrates its high specificity. At the conclusion of the farm trial, the test confirmed that the resistant-line fish did not harbor detectable levels of pathogen.

Scientists at NCCCWA are also investigating the mechanisms that cause fish to be disease resistant. After finding a correlation between disease resistance and larger spleen size in rainbow trout, Wiens and geneticist Yniv Palti searched for common genetic regions that influence both spleen size and disease resistance.

In their study, they mapped regions in the trout genome that determine spleen size and found links to chromosomes 19, 16, and 5. They also mapped disease resistance and found a closely linked region on chromosome 19 that had a major effect on bacterial cold-water disease resistance. This is the first study to identify a genetic link between a physical trait—spleen size—and specific disease resistance in fish. The researchers are now working to identify genes and mechanisms of resistance.

Based on the results of several field trials and laboratory-evaluation data, disease-resistant rainbow trout eggs were released in small numbers to stakeholders, who are propagating the line and continuing to evaluate its performance in large-scale trials in conjunction with NCCCWA scientists. If these evaluations continue to show results, the new trout line may soon appear at the seafood counter nearest you.

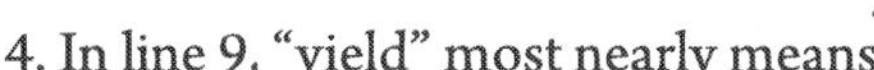

1. According to information in the passage, which of the following is most likely true regarding *Flavobacterium psychrophilum*?

A) It infects only rainbow trout.
B) It is found mainly in the spleens of infected fish.
C) It has different effects on older and younger fish.
D) It will soon be eliminated from fish farms.

2. Which choice best supports the answer to the previous question?

A) Lines 6-9 ("It first… and yield.")
B) Lines 18-21 ("They have… after infection.")
C) Lines 31-33 ("After exposure… susceptible lines.")
D) Lines 37-40 ("Wiens and… fish tissue.")

3. The "susceptible line" and "control line" (lines 15-16) primarily serve as

A) examples of what the resistant line could become.
B) other trout types that can be compared to the new disease-resistant line.
C) previous attempts to solve the problem that the resistant line is trying to solve.
D) evidence that the resistant line will have little effect.

4. In line 9, "yield" most nearly means

A) amount produced.
B) surrender.
C) investment.
D) explosive force.

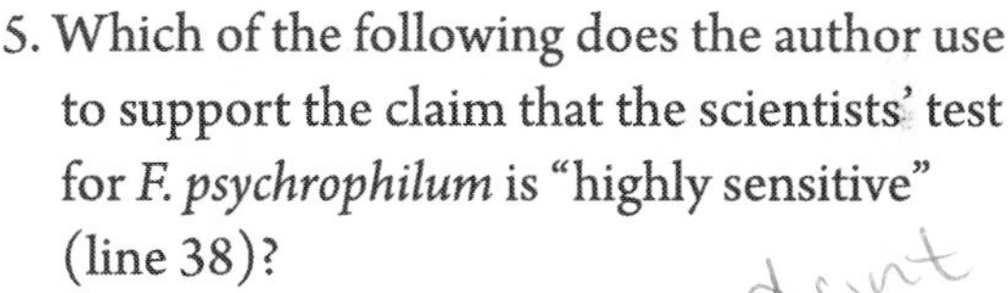

5. Which of the following does the author use to support the claim that the scientists' test for *F. psychrophilum* is "highly sensitive" (line 38)?

A) Data comparing the effectiveness of this test to that of other common tests
B) A quote from a famous scientist vouching for the test's efficacy
C) An extended explanation of how the test works on a molecular level
D) Evidence that the test identifies many strains of the bacterium—and nothing else

6. As used in line 44, "strains" most nearly means

A) tunes.
B) injuries.
C) exertions.
D) varieties.

7. Based on the passage, which of the following most accurately characterizes what scientists currently know about the link between large spleens and disease resistance?

    A) They have not yet identified which genes increase resistance or how the resistance is increased.
    B) They know which genes affect both spleen size and disease resistance in humans, but not in fish.
    C) They considered such a link, but data has so far shown there to be no correlation between spleen size and disease resistance.
    D) They have hypothesized that there is such a link but have yet to find any evidence to support it.

8. Which choice most clearly provides supporting evidence for the previous question's answer?

    A) Lines 46-48 ("No other… high specificity.")
    B) Lines 54-59 ("After finding… disease resistance.")
    C) Lines 69-70 ("The researchers… of resistance.")
    D) Lines 77-80 ("If these… nearest you.")

9. It can be reasonably inferred from information in the passage that the "stakeholders" in line 74 are

    A) genetic scientists.
    B) seafood eaters.
    C) trout farmers.
    D) government officials.

10. The passage's tone can best be described as

    A) whimsical.
    B) factual.
    C) argumentative.
    D) pessimistic.

Practice Passage 7

This passage discusses the development of SONAR technology and its use in marine biological research.

During the twentieth century, the use of acoustics to study life in the oceans was developed into a significant tool for research in marine biology. The general pattern was the development of acoustic technology for non-biological research uses, navigation and military operations to name two and then the application of that technology to the detection and study of marine life.

Many historians cite the sinking of the RMS Titanic as the immediate stimulus for the development of underwater acoustic ranging technology. In response to this event, Reginald Fessenden developed the "Fessenden oscillator" to detect icebergs and the sea floor. This device was first used on the US Coast Guard Cutter *Miami* in 1914. The threat of German submarines during the First World War led to significant advances in underwater acoustic technology.

The period from 1939 to 1945, World War II, saw an extremely rapid development of our understanding of the physics of sound propagation in the sea. The acronym, SONAR (SOund Navigation And Ranging), was proposed by F. V. (Ted) Hunt of Harvard University in 1942 and is the term most commonly applied to acoustic detection devices, both active and passive. This newfound knowledge was quickly applied to more peaceful enterprises, the commercial whaling and fishing industries in particular.

Following the end of World War II, 1946, surplus military SONAR units were fitted onto some whale catcher vessels of European nations and were used to hunt whales in the Southern Ocean. The use of this equipment greatly improved the efficiency of the whalers' efforts in killing whales. In the case of baleen whales, the SONAR pings frightened the whales, resulting in an escape behavior in which the animals swam at high speed near the surface in a straight line away from the sound source. This caused them to tire more quickly and made it easier to follow a whale and kill it.

During the "Cold War," 1948 to 1990, the reliance on passive acoustic methods to detect and track submarines gained favor and resulted in the expenditure of $15 billion over 40 years by the American defense establishment to develop and deploy the SOund SUrveillance System (SOSUS). During World War II, it had been discovered that, at the depth in the ocean where sound velocity is minimized, sound energy becomes trapped and can travel a great distance without dissipating. This "sound channel" or SOFAR level would allow a listener to hear sounds from great distances, tens of thousands of kilometers. In the 1950s, the US Navy began building a network of listening stations from which Soviet submarines could be located and tracked even if they were thousands of miles away.

In 1991, the navy largely decommissioned the SOSUS but left a small number of monitoring posts, three in the North Pacific Ocean, operational and made these available to the scientific community. The decommissioned SOSUS listening posts allowed biologists to track migrating whales in the North Pacific Ocean. Different marine mammals produce vocalizations which are characteristic of each species, allowing them to be tracked and identified at significant distances. An individual blue whale was tracked for 43 days using the SOSUS network.

The study of anthropogenic effects, wind farms, ship traffic, and military activity on marine mammals and fish is an increasingly important field of bioacoustic research. This is leading to an increased understanding of the role of acoustics in marine life as well as the effects of acoustic pollution in an increasingly noisy ocean. Of particular interest to scientists is the effect of acoustic pollution on whale foraging behavior and communication. Blue whales produce characteristic low-frequency (less than 100 Hz) "D-calls," believed to communicate the location of a food source to other whales. Anthropogenic noise has been shown to significantly disrupt whales' D-call patterns, although the long-term implications of this disruption for whale foraging and other behaviors are still unknown.

By the last quarter of the twentieth century, acoustic technology had become a significant tool in the study of marine life comparable in significance to molecular biology techniques and other leading-edge research technologies. Bioacoustics, by the end of the twentieth century, had become a mature independent discipline, thus setting the stage for significant new advances in this area of research in the twenty-first century.

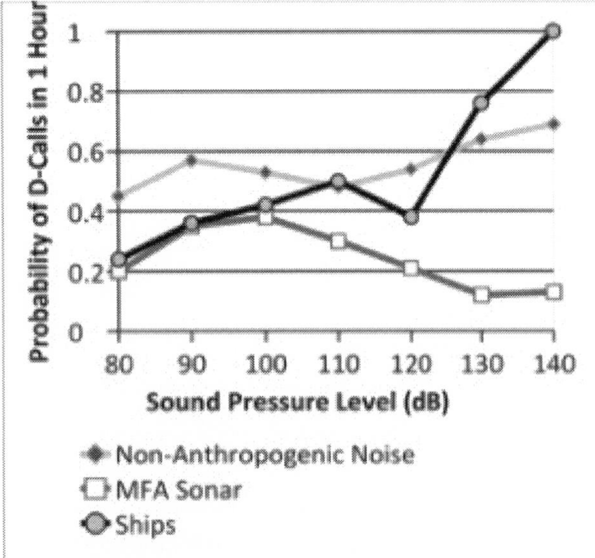

(Adapted from Mariana Melcón et al., "Blue Whales Respond to Anthropogenic Noise," PLOS ONE, *February 2012)*

1. As used in line 11, "stimulus" most nearly means

   A) catalyst.
   B) encouragement.
   C) instigation.
   D) subsidy.

2. The author indicates that the first efforts to invent underwater acoustic technology

   A) greatly aided the study of marine life.
   B) resulted from a desire to protect ships from natural hazards.
   C) were undertaken by the U.S. Coast Guard.
   D) quickly led to the invention of SONAR.

3. Which choice provides the best evidence for the answer to the previous question?

   A) Lines 1-4 ("During... marine biology.")
   B) Lines 10-13 ("Many historians... technology.")
   C) Lines 15-17 ("This device... in 1914.")
   D) Lines 21-29 ("The period... passive.")

4. The author of the passage would most likely agree that technology developed by the military

   A) is the primary source of scientific progress in the modern world.
   B) is extremely expensive and would be more lucrative if its development were left to the private sector.
   C) may become available for civilian applications in the years following the conclusion of major conflicts.
   D) should be restricted in its use on account of the risks it poses to marine wildlife.

5. Which choice provides the best evidence for the answer to the previous question?

   A) Lines 21-24 ("The period... in the sea.")
   B) Lines 46-50 ("During... defense establishment")
   C) Lines 64-68 ("In 1991... scientific community.")
   D) Lines 80-84 ("This is leading... noisy ocean.")

6. As used in line 85, "pollution" most nearly means

   A) contamination.
   B) corruption.
   C) disturbance.
   D) impurity.

7. The author most likely mentions "molecular biology techniques" (lines 98-99) in order to

   A) predict a likely area in which "significant new advances" (line 103) will be realized.
   B) favorably compare a technology that might wrongly be considered old-fashioned to one considered cutting-edge.
   C) identify molecular biology as an area of study in which acoustic sensing technologies are used.
   D) convey the relative importance of a set of research tools and methods.

8. Which of the following is an accurate statement based on the graph that follows the passage?

   A) Whales produce more D-calls in the presence of ship noise than in that of sonar regardless of the decibel level of the noise.
   B) Whales produce more D-calls in the presence of human-generated noise than in that of natural noise.
   C) Increasing the decibel level of sound pressure from SONAR can consistently be predicted to result in decreasing frequency of whale D-calls.
   D) Whales in the presence of a ship producing 140 decibels of noise can be predicted to average one D-call per hour.

9. Compared to the first five paragraphs (lines 1-63), the 6th, 7th, and 8th paragraphs constitute a shift toward emphasizing a technology's use

   A) for peaceful rather than violent ends.
   B) for research rather than commercial and military applications.
   C) for civilian rather than military purposes.
   D) in ways that are potentially harmful rather than strictly helpful.

10. Which of the following is a valid inference from information in both the passage and the graph?

   A) Blue whales emit fewer D-calls in the presence of SONAR because they are frightened by the sound.
   B) In the presence of SONAR, blue whale pods are entirely unable to forage effectively.
   C) Ships constitute the largest source of noise pollution in the ocean and the greatest threat to whales.
   D) The ability of whales to communicate with each other in the search for food is likely impaired by the presence of SONAR.

11. The author's primary purpose in writing this passage was most likely to

   A) evaluate the level of risk posed by the use of SONAR to marine mammals.
   B) defend the role of the military in inventing technologies later used for civilian research.
   C) provide a historical overview of how a technology has developed and become an important tool in a particular scientific field.
   D) weigh the beneficial and harmful effects of a major invention over the course of the twentieth century.

Practice Passage 8

This passage discusses the history of an unusual invented language.

Johann Schleyer was a German priest whose irrational passion for umlauts may have been his undoing. During one sleepless night in 1879, he felt a divine presence telling him to create a universal language. The result was Volapük. It was designed to be easy to learn, with a system of simple roots derived from European languages, and regular affixes which attached to the roots to make new words. Volapük was the first invented language to gain widespread success. By the end of the 1880s there were more than 200 Volapük societies and clubs around the world and 25 Volapük journals. Over 1500 diplomas in Volapük had been awarded. In 1889, when the third international Volapük congress was held in Paris, the proceedings were entirely in Volapük. Everyone had at least heard of it. President Grover Cleveland's wife even named her dog Volapük.

Though Schleyer was German, a large part of the Volapük vocabulary was based on English. "Volapük" was a compound formed from two roots, *vol* (from "world") and *pük* (from "speak"). However, it was often hard to spot the source of a Volapük word because of the way Schleyer had set up the sound system of the language. "Paper" was *pöp*, "beer" *bil*, "proof" *blöf* and "love" *löf*. He had rational reasons for most of the phonological choices he made. For simplicity, he tried to limit all word roots to one syllable. He avoided the 'r' sound, "for the sake of children and old people, also for some Asiatic nations." The umlauts, however, were there for *löf*.

"A language without umlauts," he wrote, "sounds monotonous, harsh, and boring." He decried the "endlessly gloomy u and o," the "broad a" and the "sharp i" of umlautless languages. Though many members of the growing Volapük community may have agreed with his aesthetic judgment, many others thought that for Volapük to have a serious chance at being a world language, the umlauts had to go.

Indeed, in the United States especially, those umlauts added a threatening and/or ridiculous air of foreignness to the language. Much fun was had at the expense of Volapük on account of those umlauts in local papers such as the *Milwaukee Sentinel:*

A charming young student of Grük
Once tried to acquire Volapük
But it sounded so bad
That her friends called her mad,
And she quit it in less than a wük.

By 1890 the Volapük movement was falling apart due to arguments about umlauts and other reforms. Meanwhile Esperanto, another language that had been rapidly growing since its introduction in 1887, was scooping up all the new recruits to the universal language idea.

Schleyer decried Esperanto as "an ugly-sounding hodgepodge." He criticized its use of "unnecessary" and "difficult to pronounce" sounds like "sh" and "ch." He scoffed at it for allowing diphthongs ("Ugly!"), "harsh sound combinations," and the "rattling, hard, bony 'r'". Also, it had no umlauts. According to Schleyer, if you compared Esperanto to Volapük it was clear that one "was created by a Pole" (the Bialystok-born Ludovic Zamenhof), and the other by "a music connoisseur, composer, and poet."

Every language has its lumpy bits, and beauty is in the ear of the beholder. You like potato; I like potahto, and Schleyer preferred *pötet.* It wasn't really the umlauts that killed Volapük, but a combination of factors, the most important probably being that the chances of any artificial language gaining a following are slim to none. There were hundreds of invented languages that came before Volapük and hundreds that came after, and almost no one has heard of any of them. Esperanto is the rare exception, but its success (relative as it is) has less to do with its linguistic features than with the luck of timing and circumstances.

Volapük didn't die out completely. It has a bit of life today; there are a few online lessons and discussion boards. There is even a Volapük Wikipedia with over 100,000 articles. And its name lives on in the Danish expression *det er det rene volapyk* – "It's pure Volapük," or, in other words "It's Greek to me."

1. According to the passage, the ease of learning Volapük resulted from its

   A) similarity to German.
   B) small vocabulary.
   C) pleasant, smoothly-flowing sound.
   D) systematic construction of words from simple building blocks.

2. Which choice provides the best evidence for the answer to the previous question?

   A) Lines 5-9 ("It was designed… new words.")
   B) Lines 20-27 ("Though Schleyer…. the language.")
   C) Lines 30-31 ("For simplicity…one syllable.")
   D) Lines 69-73 ("According to… 'and poet.'")

3. As used in line 16, "congress" most nearly means

   A) delegation.
   B) legislature.
   C) summit.
   D) union.

4. By this statement in lines 33-34 ("The umlauts, however, were there for *löf*."), the author most nearly means that

   A) Volapük's heavy use of umlauts was due to Schleyer's personal preferences rather than a rational, pragmatic motivation.
   B) Schleyer felt that umlaut-altered vowel sounds were easier for people of all ages to pronounce.
   C) Schleyer found himself unable to achieve the simplicity he desired for Volapük without the use of umlauts.
   D) the umlauts in Volapük provided a distinctly Germanic influence to an otherwise English-based language.

5. The author most likely included the *Milwaukee Sentinel's* poem (lines 51-55) to illustrate

   A) a common criticism of Volapük made by American linguistic scholars.
   B) the universal hostility with which Volapük was received by its intended audience.
   C) the apparent strangeness to an English speaker of Volapük's rules of pronunciation.
   D) how nineteenth-century Americans' prejudice against foreigners hindered the adoption of Volapük in America.

6. The author would most likely agree that, compared to Johann Schleyer, Ludovic Zamenhof was

   A) formally trained in music and poetry.
   B) more successful in creating a language of lasting popularity.
   C) far less interested in the aesthetic or musical qualities of language.
   D) inspired more by Romance languages than by Germanic ones in his creation of an invented language.

7. As used in line 85, "relative" most nearly means

   A) analogous.
   B) contingent.
   C) measured.
   D) pertinent.

8. The author would most likely agree that Volapük failed to attain greater popularity because of

   A) the inherent difficulty of achieving widespread adoption of an invented language.
   B) its ugly phonetic features.
   C) widespread ridicule by the mass media.
   D) its lack of appeal to non-English speakers.

9. Which choice provides the best evidence for the answer to the previous question?

   A) Lines 20-22 ("Though Schleyer... on English.")
   B) Lines 47-49 ("Much fun... *Sentinel.*")
   C) Lines 63-69 ("Schleyer decried... umlauts.")
   D) Lines 77-81 ("It wasn't really... to none.")

10. The author's overall attitude toward Schleyer is most nearly one of

    A) marked ambivalence.
    B) disillusioned admiration.
    C) dismissive ridicule.
    D) good-natured amusement.

Practice Passage 9

The following excerpt is from Vanity Fair, *by the English novelist William Makepeace Thackeray. It was first published in 1847.*

Cuff's fight with Dobbin, and the unexpected issue of that contest, will long be remembered by every man who was educated at Dr. Swishtail's famous school. The latter Youth (who used to be called Heigh-ho Dobbin, Gee-ho Dobbin, and by many other names indicative of puerile contempt) was the quietest, the clumsiest, and, as it seemed, the dullest of all Dr. Swishtail's young gentlemen. His father was a grocer in the city: and it was bruited abroad that he was admitted into Dr. Swishtail's academy upon what are called "mutual principles"—that is to say, the expenses of his board and schooling were defrayed by his father in goods, not money; and he stood there—most at the bottom of the school—in his scraggy corduroys and jacket, through the seams of which his great big bones were bursting—as the representative of so many pounds of tea, candles, sugar, mottled-soap, plums (of which a very mild proportion was supplied for the puddings of the establishment), and other commodities. A dreadful day it was for young Dobbin when one of the youngsters of the school, having run into the town upon a poaching excursion for hardbake and polonies, espied the cart of Dobbin & Rudge, Grocers and Oilmen, Thames Street, London, at the Doctor's door, discharging a cargo of the wares in which the firm dealt.

Young Dobbin had no peace after that. The jokes were frightful, and merciless against him. One boy would set a sum—"If a pound of mutton-candles cost sevenpence-halfpenny, how much must Dobbin cost?" and a roar would follow from all the circle of young knaves, usher and all, who rightly considered that the selling of goods by retail is a shameful and infamous practice, meriting the contempt and scorn of all real gentlemen.

"Your father's only a merchant, Osborne," Dobbin said in private to the little boy who had brought down the storm upon him. At which the latter replied haughtily, "My father's a gentleman, and keeps his carriage"; and Mr. William Dobbin retreated to a remote outhouse in the playground, where he passed a half-holiday in the bitterest sadness and woe. Who amongst us is there that does not recollect similar hours of bitter, bitter childish grief? Who feels injustice; who shrinks before a slight; who has a sense of wrong so acute, and so glowing a gratitude for kindness, as a generous boy? and how many of those gentle souls do you degrade, estrange, torture, for the sake of a little loose arithmetic, and miserable dog-Latin?

Now, William Dobbin, from an incapacity to acquire the rudiments of the above language, as they are propounded in that wonderful book the Eton Latin Grammar, was compelled to remain among the very last of Doctor Swishtail's scholars, and was "taken down" continually by little fellows with pink faces and pinafores when he marched up with his downcast, stupefied look, his dog's-eared primer, and his tight corduroys. High and low, all made fun of him. They sewed up those corduroys, tight as they were. They cut his bed-strings. They upset buckets and benches, so that he might break his shins over them, which he never failed to do. They sent him parcels, which, when opened, were found to contain the paternal soap and candles. There was no little fellow but had his jeer and joke at Dobbin; and he bore everything quite patiently, and was entirely dumb and miserable.

Cuff, on the contrary, was the great chief

and dandy of the Swishtail Seminary. He smuggled wine in. He fought the town-boys. Ponies used to come for him to ride home on Saturdays. He had a gold repeater and took snuff like the Doctor. He had been to the Opera, and knew the merits of the principal actors, preferring Mr. Kean to Mr. Kemble. He could knock you off forty Latin verses in an hour. He could make French poetry. What else didn't he know, or couldn't he do? They said even the Doctor himself was afraid of him.

Cuff, the unquestioned king of the school, ruled over his subjects, and bullied them, with splendid superiority. This one blacked his shoes: that toasted his bread, others would give him balls at cricket during whole summer afternoons. "Figs" was the fellow whom he despised most, and with whom, though always abusing him, and sneering at him, he scarcely ever condescended to hold personal communication.

1. The phrase "mutual principles" in line 12 refers to

   A) ideals of fairness.
   B) an exchange of favors or services.
   C) a prior agreement that must be honored.
   D) implied bribery.

2. Which choice provides the best evidence for the answer to the previous question?

   A) Lines 4-9 ("The latter… young gentlemen.")
   B) Lines 13-15 ("…that is... not money")
   C) Lines 32-34 ("One boy…must Dobbin cost?'")
   D) Lines 36-39 ("…who rightly considered… real gentlemen.")

3. According to the passage, which of the following is NOT a way in which Dobbin differs from most other students at his school?

   A) He is more intelligent and studious.
   B) He does not come from an upper-class background.
   C) He is quiet and reserved.
   D) He is teased and bullied because of his father's occupation.

4. Which choice provides the best evidence for the answer to the previous question?

    A) Lines 4-9 ("The latter… young gentlemen.")
    B) Lines 40-42 ("'Your father...upon him.")
    C) Lines 44-47 ("Mr. William… and woe.")
    D) Lines 56-61 ("Now, William… scholars")

5. The "Doctor" referred to throughout the passage is

    A) a physician.
    B) the head of a boys' school.
    C) the nickname of another boy who is bullied by Cuff.
    D) Dobbin's father.

6. The passage suggests that the first incident in which Dobbin is teased about his family background is especially unfair because

    A) no other student at the school is bullied.
    B) being a grocer is normally considered a respectable career.
    C) the boy teasing him is not upper-class either.
    D) his father provides much of the food that the boys at school eat.

7. In the context of the passage as a whole, lines 47-55 ("Who amongst us…dog-Latin?) serve to

    A) suggest the existence of a moral gray area.
    B) acknowledge the narrator's personal connection to the events of the story.
    C) clarify a character's motivation.
    D) directly encourage the reader to empathize with a particular character.

8. As used in line 74, "dumb" most nearly means

    A) foolish.
    B) incoherent.
    C) speechless.
    D) unintelligent.

9. The choice of the words "splendid superiority" (line 90) to describe Cuff is most likely intended to convey that Cuff is

    A) intimidating and impressive.
    B) narcissistic and delusional.
    C) charismatic and likable.
    D) deserving of his social status.

10. As used in line 96, "condescended" most nearly means

    A) acquiesced.
    B) agreed.
    C) consented.
    D) stooped.

Practice Passage 10

The following pair of passages presents two different viewpoints regarding the future of a federally funded particle physics laboratory near Chicago.

Passage 1:

Fermilab was once the pre-eminent facility for high energy physics. However, the Large Hadron Collider (LHC) on the border of France and Switzerland dwarfs the accelerator at Fermilab in terms of size, energy and ability to discover particles. It's only currently operating at half of its design energy, but has already set records. It is a dazzling facility.

We need to get beyond the "gee-whiz" and determine whether or not spending on Fermilab is prudent. There are two basic types of scientific research: theoretical and practical. In theoretical research, the scientists at Fermilab have introduced us to top quarks, bottom quarks, charm quarks, tao neutrinos and numerous others. The question to be asked is how the discovery of these particles will enhance our lives. Even if you could deliver a tangible answer to that question, how would Fermilab be able to do a better job than the LHC?

If you look at Fermilab's website or look for the answer to the question "What has high-energy particle physics done for us?", most of the answers are not so exciting. The "discoveries" most often mentioned are powerful instruments created for use at Fermilab, not as a result of discoveries made at Fermilab. The World Wide Web is also mentioned. Because scientists needed to transfer large amounts of data, they created the precursor to the Internet, and that is somehow justification for the particle accelerators. Because scientists needed to measure really small particles, they invented sophisticated instruments now used in medical imaging. But to say that medical imaging wouldn't have advanced otherwise is a dubious claim. I am guessing that if we had just put the money directly into research on supercomputers, medical imaging, etc., we could have come to the same discoveries at a fraction of the cost.

We could keep Fermilab going for a while. It could limp along for years doing minor research, but why? Are we going to make the case that budgets are tight right now and in a few years when we have more money we'll ramp back up? I don't see any hope in the medium or short range that we will get to big budget surpluses any time soon. If we think that Fermilab will have a big mission in a couple of years, we are only kidding ourselves. It's time to cut the cord.

Passage 2:

Particle physics research pushes the frontiers of knowledge and technology. The development and construction of particle accelerators, particle detectors and other research tools has led to many benefits to society.

The invention of the World Wide Web and contributions to the development of medical imaging techniques are among the better known particle physics innovations. But particle physics has myriad lesser-known impacts. For example, few people have probably heard that low-energy electron beams from particle accelerators provide an environmentally friendly way of sterilizing food packaging.

There are more than 30,000 particle accelerators in operation around the world today. They shrink tumors, make better tires, spot suspicious cargo, clean dirty drinking water, help design drugs, discover the building blocks of matter, and do much more.

Every major medical center in the nation uses accelerators producing x-rays, protons, neutrons or heavy ions for the diagnosis and treatment of disease. Positron emission tomography, the technology of PET scans, came directly from light-sensing detectors initially designed for particle physics experiments. Gamma-ray detectors designed by particle physicists now reveal tumors in dense tissue.

Biomedical scientists use the intense light emitted by synchrotron accelerators to decipher the structure of proteins, information that is key to understanding biological processes and healing disease. A clearer understanding of protein structure allows for the development of more effective drugs, such as Kaletra, one of the world's most-prescribed drugs to fight AIDS.

Cables made of superconducting material can carry far more electricity than conventional cables, with only nominal power loss. They offer an opportunity to meet increasing power needs in urban areas where copper transmission lines are near their capacity. Fermilab's partnership with industry to develop the mass production of superconducting wire for the Tevatron accelerator jump-started this industry.

Particle physicists developed the World Wide Web to share information quickly and effectively with colleagues around the world. Few other technological advances in history have more profoundly affected the global economy and societal interactions than the Web. In 1992, Fermilab launched the third web server in the United States. In 2001, revenues from the World Wide Web exceeded one trillion dollars, with exponential growth continuing.

1. The statement in lines 7-9 of Passage 1 ("It's only… dazzling facility.") is most likely included in order to

   A) acknowledge the technological feat of constructing a particle accelerator even while dismissing the practical value of ever doing so.
   B) indicate that a newer facility has rendered Fermilab obsolete.
   C) suggest that the author would support massive government investment in a particle accelerator if it were state-of-the-art.
   D) state a claim made by opponents of the author's position, with which the author does not actually agree.

2. Which choice provides the best evidence for the answer to the previous question?

   A) Lines 1-2 ("Fermilab was once… physics.")
   B) Lines 17-19 ("The question… our lives.")
   C) Lines 19-21 ("Even if... the LHC?")
   D) Lines 22-25 ("If you… not so exciting.")

3. The use of "gee-whiz" in quotation marks in line 10 suggests that the author of Passage 1

    A) is alluding to a previously stated opinion on Fermilab by a public figure.
    B) believes that less childish, more respectable arguments are needed to settle the debate at hand.
    C) hopes that the Large Hadron Collider's existence will not diminish general interest in the still-valuable, though less glamorous, technology available at Fermilab.
    D) believes some people are irrationally attached to Fermilab because of a sense of awe at the technology it represents.

4. As used in line 19, "tangible" most nearly means

    A) appreciable.
    B) concrete.
    C) palpable.
    D) physical.

5. The critique presented in paragraph 3 of Passage 1 (lines 22-41) is most nearly that Fermilab's defenders

    A) fail to make a distinction between the purpose of an invention and the reason that invention came to be.
    B) overstate the value beyond particle physics of technologies invented for use at Fermilab.
    C) advocate for research investments that are not likely to prove cost-effective.
    D) fail to demonstrate any direct benefit to society from particle physics itself.

6. In response to the assertion in lines 25-28 of Passage 1 ("The discoveries... at Fermilab."), the author of Passage 2 would most likely point out that

    A) particle accelerators are used directly in a wide variety of fields.
    B) the World Wide Web has contributed an enormous amount of value to the global economy since its creation.
    C) Calling these innovations "not so exciting" serves to demonstrate the clear bias of Passage 1's author.
    D) these discoveries are valuable whether or not they would have come to pass even without Fermilab.

7. Which choice provides the best evidence for the answer to the previous question?

    A) Lines 56-59 ("The development... society.")
    B) Lines 60-64 ("The invention... impacts.")
    C) Lines 69-74 ("There are... much more.")
    D) Lines 104-110 ("Few other... continuing.")

8. Which of the following is an example cited by Passage 2 of "powerful instruments created for use at Fermilab, not as a result of discoveries made at Fermilab" (lines 26-28)?

    A) "the World Wide Web" (line 60)
    B) "30,000 particle accelerators" (lines 69-70)
    C) "Positron emission tomography" (lines 78-79)
    D) "more effective drugs" (line 90)

9. As used in line 94, “nominal” most nearly means

   A) insignificant.
   B) ostensible.
   C) stated.
   D) symbolic.

10. Unlike Passage 1, Passage 2

   A) is supportive of extending government funding for Fermilab.
   B) does not explicitly advocate a course of action.
   C) asserts that technologies developed at Fermilab have provided economic and societal benefits.
   D) is likely written by a particle physicist.

11. With which of the following statements would the authors of Passage 1 and Passage 2 likely both agree?

   A) Fermilab is no longer suited for cutting-edge research, which can be done more effectively at the Large Hadron Collider.
   B) The World Wide Web likely would not have been developed if particle physicists had not needed to invent its precursor technology for their purposes.
   C) Theoretical research is of less value to society than practical research.
   D) Government-funded scientific endeavors have the potential to deliver broad benefits to society.

Practice Passage 11

The following report, from the research division of the U.S. Department of Education, addresses the gender gap in mathematical and scientific fields.

Although there is a general perception that men do better than women in math and science, researchers have found that the differences between women's and men's math- and science-related abilities and choices are much more subtle and complex than a simple "men are better than women in math and science." In fact, experts disagree among themselves on the degree to which women and men differ in their math- and science-related abilities. A quick review of the postsecondary paths pursued by women and men highlights the areas in math and science in which women are not attaining degrees at the same rate as men.

In 2004, women earned 58 percent of all bachelor's degrees. In general, women earn substantial proportions of the bachelor's degrees in math and the sciences, except in computer sciences, physics, and engineering. The pattern at the master's degree level is similar. At the doctoral level, however, gender imbalances become more prevalent, including in math and chemistry. Women earned 45 percent of all doctoral degrees, but they earn less than one-third of all doctoral degrees in chemistry, computer sciences, math, physics, and engineering. In contrast, women earn 67 percent of the doctoral degrees in psychology and 44 percent in other social sciences. This disproportionate representation in math and science graduate degrees is also reflected in math and science career pathways. While women make up nearly half of the U.S. workforce, they make up only 26 percent of the science and engineering workforce. The question many are asking is why women are choosing not to pursue degrees and careers in the physical sciences, engineering, or computer science.

An explanation for the observed differences in college and occupational choices may be that males and females have variant math and science abilities, as measured by standardized tests. Although girls generally do as well as, or better than, boys on homework assignments and course grades in math and science classes, boys tend to outscore girls when tested on the same content in high-pressure situations, such as standardized tests with time limits. These tests are typically not linked to instructed curriculum, and so can be understood to be measures of more general abilities in math and science. For example, on the 2005 NAEP math and science assessments, girls scored lower than boys when controlling for highest course completed at all levels, except the lowest level. Performance differences on timed standardized tests do not necessarily mean that girls are not as capable as boys in math or science. Researchers have found, for instance, that SAT math scores underpredict young women's performance in college math courses. This suggests that it is not ability, per se, that hinders girls and women from pursuing careers in math and science. If not ability, then what?

Areas where consistent gender differences have emerged are children's and adolescents' beliefs about their abilities in math and science, their interest in math and science, and their perceptions of the importance of math and science for their futures. In general, researchers have found that girls and women have less confidence in their math abilities than males do and that from early adolescence, girls show less interest in math or science careers. This gender difference is interesting, and somewhat puzzling, given that males and females generally enroll in similar courses and display similar abilities (at least as measured by course grades). In other words, girls, particularly as they move out of elementary school and into middle and high school and beyond, often discount their own abilities in mathematics and science. However, it is important to note that girls who have a strong self-concept regarding their abilities in math or science are more likely to choose and perform well in elective math and science courses and to select math- and science-related college majors and careers. This is noteworthy because it suggests that improving girls' beliefs about their abilities could alter their choices and performance. Theory and empirical research suggest that children's beliefs about their abilities are central to determining their interest and performance in different subjects.

Gender Disparities by Academic Degree (Bachelor's and Master's Degrees)

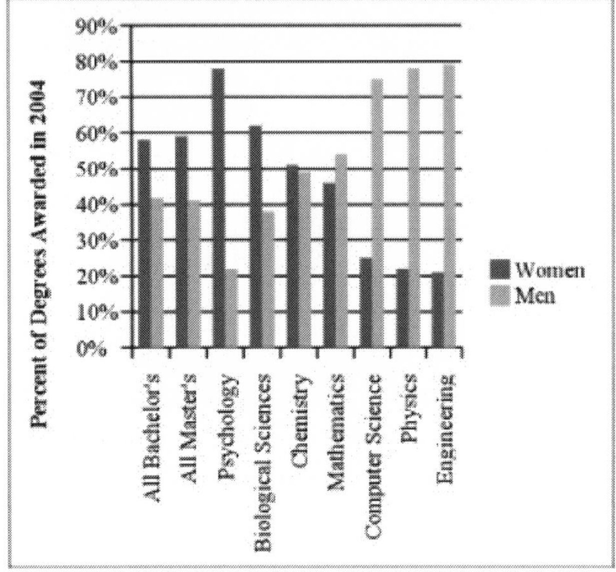

(Source: Diane Halpern et al., "Encouraging Girls in Math and Science", for the What Works Clearinghouse *initiative, Institute of Education Sciences, U.S. Department of Education)*

1. Which of the following observations, discussed in the passage, about the relationship between gender and math and science ability does NOT help support the authors' claim that this relationship is "subtle and complex" (line 6)?

    A) The size and nature of the gender gap varies at different ages and academic levels.
    B) The size and nature of the gender gap varies based on the type of evaluation used to measure it.
    C) Men and women obtain advanced degrees in computer science and engineering at dramatically different rates.
    D) There is a disparity between adolescent girls' self-assessments of their math and science ability and their performance in math and science classes.

2. Based on information in the passage and/or the associated graph, the percentage of doctoral degrees in psychology awarded to men is

   A) greater than the percentage of bachelor's and master's degrees in psychology awarded to men.
   B) greater than the percentage of bachelor's and master's degrees in mathematics awarded to women.
   C) greater than the percentage of bachelor's and master's degrees in biology awarded to men.
   D) less than the percentage of the science and engineering workforce that consists of women.

3. In context of the passage as a whole, the function of the third paragraph (lines 39-65) is most nearly to

   A) propose a novel interpretation of a familiar trend.
   B) summarize the existing data pertaining to an ongoing controversy.
   C) present and cast doubt upon a standard explanation for a sociological phenomenon.
   D) argue against the validity of a common measure of math and science ability.

4. As used in lines 54-55, "controlling for" most nearly means

   A) accounting for.
   B) instructing.
   C) manipulating.
   D) supervising.

5. The authors would most likely agree that standardized tests

   A) are intended to measure innate talent rather than book learning.
   B) do not produce meaningful or consistent predictions of students' performance in math and science.
   C) are an assessment format that is inherently biased in favor of male students.
   D) are an important but imperfect measure of math and science ability.

6. Which choice provides the best evidence for the answer to the previous question?

   A) Lines 43-49 ("Although... time limits.")
   B) Lines 49-52 ("These tests... math and science.")
   C) Lines 56-62 ("Performance differences... math courses.")
   D) Lines 62-65 ("This suggests... then what?")

7. It can be inferred from the passage that girls' "self-concept regarding their abilities in math or science" (lines 85-86)

   A) does not affect their actual performance in math and science classes or activities.
   B) tends to diverge increasingly from their actual abilities from adolescence onward.
   C) can be improved by choosing to take elective classes in math or science.
   D) is negatively influenced by poor performance on math and science tests.

8. Which choice provides the best evidence for the answer to the previous question?

    A) Lines 75-79 ("This gender... similar abilities")
    B) Lines 80-84 ("In other words... and science.")
    C) Lines 84-89 ("However... and careers.")
    D) Lines 90-92 ("This is... performance.")

9. As used in line 84, "discount" most nearly means

    A) forget.
    B) rebate.
    C) subtract.
    D) underrate.

10. Which of the following must necessarily be an accurate statement, according to information in the passage and/or the accompanying graph?

    A) More women received bachelor's degrees in 2004 than received doctoral degrees.
    B) In 2004, more bachelor's degrees were awarded to women in math than in computer science.
    C) Approximately 26 percent of women in the U.S. work force hold science and engineering jobs.
    D) More than three times as many women as men received bachelor's or master's degrees in psychology in 2004.

Practice Passage 12

This passage from the U.S. Department of Agriculture (USDA) focuses on investment in rural America in 2014.

These days, it seems like it's easier than ever to turn a good idea into reality. This is the era of Kickstarter, where entrepreneurs can connect with potential investors at the click of a button.

Of course, it takes more than money to grow an idea. It takes an atmosphere that fosters creativity and rewards innovation. And at a deeper, less obvious level, it requires strong, secure infrastructure—roads and bridges, but also internet access and community facilities like hospitals and schools—that improves connectivity and access to information, moves products to market, and makes communities competitive and attractive to new businesses and investments.

Part of the challenge we face in rural America is that in too many places, infrastructure is outdated and cannot support the same kinds of opportunities that are easily found in cities and larger towns.

USDA itself has a strong record of supporting rural infrastructure upgrades. Our Rural Development program has a loan portfolio of over $200 billion direct and guaranteed loans, representing the single largest increase in rural investment in recent decades. Yet there continues to be significant unmet demand for investment in rural America that exceeds our capacity.

We can't address this disparity alone, which is why this week, USDA, as part of the White House Rural Council, hosted the first-ever *Rural Opportunity Investment Conference.* This conference brought together key people from the investment community, rural areas and government to make the business case for investing in rural America.

In conjunction with the conference, we also announced a new $10 billion Rural Infrastructure Opportunity Fund. Supported entirely by private sector dollars with an initial investment from CoBank, a national cooperative bank and member of the Farm Credit System, and managed by Capitol Peak Asset Management, the Fund offers a sustainable platform for new kinds of investors to inject billions into rural infrastructure projects.

Up until now, we have faced a major hurdle when it comes to making the connection between the demand for investment in rural areas and the financial community. The new Fund serves as a proof point that rural America is a promising investment. The financial community should look at investing in rural America not just as a good thing to do—there is a huge opportunity for them to see a return on their investment in rural America as well.

The Fund represents a new approach to USDA's support for job-creating projects across the country. It allows us to act as a matchmaker between strong projects and potential private investors and expands our capacity to facilitate rural investment beyond what we can do alone.

Rural America needs strong, stable infrastructure in order to meet the current demand for food and farm products, as well as the growing demand in areas such as renewable energy, local and regional food, and the bioeconomy. To attract young people to rural America, prevent rural "brain drain," and ensure a stable rural workforce, we have to make sure that rural areas offer the same breadth of opportunity that cities can offer and that starts with strong, modern infrastructure.

These are high-potential areas that will

create jobs and stimulate growth, which makes rural infrastructure not just a rural issue—it's a national economic issue, too.

We believe that this Fund and the communities brought together for the first time at this week's conference are a key part of addressing the unmet demand for rural investment. If we can inject even a small portion of the enormous amount of available investment capital in the United States into rural projects, we can help to foster an environment that spurs rural innovation and ensures that rural America remains open for business.

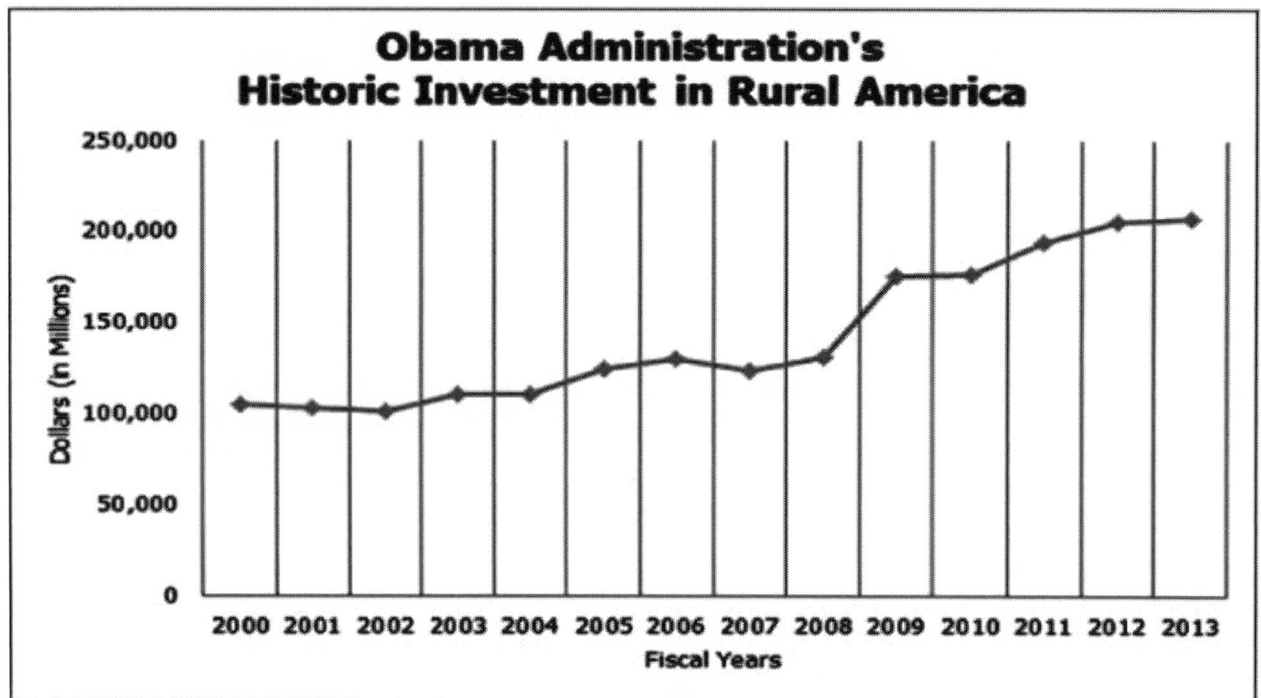

1. The primary purpose of this passage is to
   A) criticize a broken system.
   B) argue for investment in American businesses.
   C) describe the building of roads and other infrastructure.
   D) detail an organization's response to a concern.

2. Based on information in the passage, how would the author describe the state of agricultural investment?

   A) Unusually lucrative and supportive
   B) Promising but insufficient
   C) Plentiful but poorly directed
   D) Deficient and unnecessary

3. Which choice provides the best evidence for the answer to the previous question?

   A) Lines 1-5 ("These...button")
   B) Lines 6-8 ("Of...innovation")
   C) Lines 23-30 ("Our...capacity")
   D) Lines 54-58 ("The financial...well")

4. What is the primary purpose of lines 6-7 ("Of...idea")?

   A) To explain a situation
   B) To note an apparent inconsistency
   C) To detail the passage's main idea
   D) To qualify a previous statement

5. As it is used in line 31, "address" most nearly means

   A) solve.
   B) discuss.
   C) report.
   D) dispatch.

6. In the context of the passage as a whole, the function of the fifth paragraph is

   A) to present the problems facing rural investment.
   B) to transition from describing a current situation to providing ideas for fixing it.
   C) to discuss the future of farming in America.
   D) to contradict ideas presented earlier in the passage.

7. As it is used in line 63, "capacity" most nearly means

   A) bulk.
   B) volume.
   C) function.
   D) capability.

8. According to information in the passage, which of the following is NOT a program that the author would support?

   A) A rural job placement program that allows workers access to a variety of positions
   B) A costly government initiative to repair country roads
   C) A proposal to use agricultural technology to reduce the necessary number of farm workers
   D) A state plan to provide internet access to all of its citizens

9. Which of the following best describes the author's attitude in the final paragraph?

   A) emphatic
   B) inquisitive
   C) optimistic
   D) cynical

10. According to the chart and passage,

   A) over the past year, investments have plateaued without meeting the needed funding.
   B) investments have been largely successful and have fulfilled the funding demands.
   C) Obama's rural infrastructure upgrades have failed repeatedly.
   D) rural investment should continue its upward swing.

Practice Passage 13

This passage is adapted from "Oil for the Taking?" © 2011 by Achieve3000

A Spanish company called Repsol has discovered a huge amount of shale oil in Argentina, a find that could boost Argentina's potential to cash in on energy. However, some people are concerned about the cost—both financial and environmental—of extracting the oil.

The oil was discovered in the "Vaca Muerta," or "Dead Cow," formation of the arid Neuquén Basin in northern Patagonia, a region of rocky, treeless plains dotted with dry brush, with only two lakes in close proximity. According to Repsol, the discovery comprises almost 1 billion barrels of recoverable oil and natural gas, of which 741 million barrels are shale oil, and there may be even more than that—other areas of Argentina have yet to be explored and may also hold oil.

Oil is a widely used energy source and can be extremely valuable, so the find is big news—Argentina's economy stands to benefit from the export of oil.

Still, many people are not prepared to celebrate the discovery just yet. Experts say that the find is very promising, but they warn that the amount of time and financial resources needed to capitalize on the oil is still ambiguous.

"It must be proven, first of all, that [Repsol has found] commercially exploitable reserves," said Daniel Bosque, editor of the Argentina-based Web site Enernews. Bosque says a fundamental question is economic feasibility: whether there's a profit to be made from the shale oil. Unlike regular crude oil, which comes out of rock formations in liquid form, shale oil is drilled from rocks and is generally in solid form, making it more expensive to extract than normal crude oil.

Jason Schenker, an energy analyst, also had mixed emotions about the news because such oil discoveries "will be critical to meet rising global oil demand. Now the questions will be: How quickly can this oil be brought into production...and at what price?"

These are questions that Repsol wasn't immediately ready to answer with specific details. However, Repsol spokesperson Kristian Rix said that because 15 vertical wells have already been drilled and are producing 5,000 barrels of shale oil a day, developing the area "is uncomplicated from our point of view."

"It's [already an oil-producing] region, [and] all the infrastructure is there already, so putting new wells on line is very fast," Rix said. Typically, there is a lag time of five to seven years between oil exploration and oil production. "This is clearly not the case here, because we're already producing from wells."

Rix said it's still too early to comment on how long it would take or how much it would cost to get all of the oil from the area.

Some have also expressed apprehension about the environmental impact of getting the oil. The oil would be extracted by hydraulic fracturing, or "fracking," a technique that entails injecting water, sand, and chemicals into the rock, using high pressure to expel the fuel. It's not yet clear which water sources would be used for that process. In a recent report, the environmental group Greenpeace admonished that fracking puts considerable pressure on water supplies, particularly in arid regions.

Greenpeace also warned that chemicals used in the fracking process can taint underground aquifers and that little is known about other potential effects. The organization noted that up to 600 chemicals are used in fracking fluid, including known carcinogens and toxins such as lead, uranium, mercury, and formaldehyde. These chemicals have been found to leach into the groundwater, water that is stored underground in the soil, which can contaminate water used by local flora and fauna, as well as drinking water for any nearby towns.

Greenpeace opposes oil developments like the one in Argentina unless "it's shown that there's no [environmental] impact," said Ernesto Boerio, an energy and climate campaign coordinator for the organization in Argentina, adding, "More needs to be known about this project."

Speaking for Repsol, Rix said, "We operate to the highest standards of safety and environmental protection."

1. According to the passage, potential benefits of extracting the oil discovered in Patagonia include

   A) an increase in Spanish oil reserves.
   B) a significant boost to Argentina's economy.
   C) the creation of thousands of jobs in the oil industry.
   D) development in a previously under-developed region.

2. In lines 7-11 ("The oil...proximity"), what is the most likely reason the author noted that there are only two lakes nearby?

   A) To demonstrate that the location of the oil is very remote.
   B) To support the idea that marine wildlife would likely not be affected by oil extraction.
   C) To help pinpoint the exact location of the oil discovery.
   D) To suggest that a lack of available water may be a hurdle to extracting the oil.

3. Which choice provides the best evidence for the answer to the previous question?

   A) Lines 4-6 ("However...oil.")
   B) Lines 75-79 ("The organization ... formaldehyde.")
   C) Lines 67-71 ("It's not...regions.")
   D) Lines 84-86 ("Greenpeace...impact.")

4. The passage suggests that shale oil may be less desirable than crude oil because

   A) shale oil is often much more expensive to extract.
   B) crude oil is in greater demand in global markets.
   C) crude oil is a renewable resource, while shale oil is not.
   D) there are many more regulations governing the extraction of shale oil.

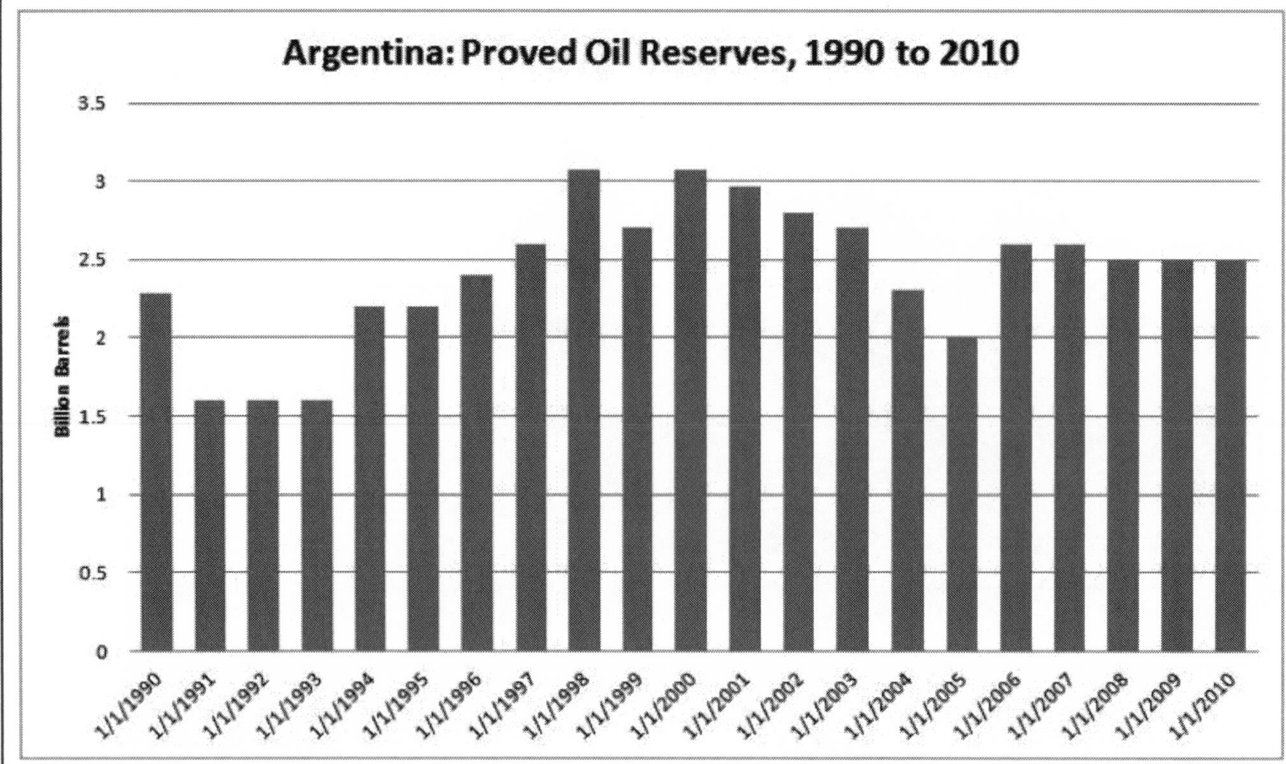

5. Which choice provides the best evidence for the answer to the previous question?

    A) Lines 18-20 ("Oil...news.")
    B) Lines 33-37 ("Unlike...oil.")
    C) Lines 38-41 ("Jason Scheker...demand.")
    D) Lines 58-60 ("Rix...area.")

6. As used in line 26, "ambiguous" most nearly means

    A) having several possible meanings.
    B) uncertain.
    C) obscure.
    D) having mixed feelings.

7. Which of the following statements most clearly expresses Jason Schenker's primary concern about the new oil discovery?

    A) That the environmental impact of extracting the oil may be too great
    B) That extracting the oil may cost too much time and money
    C) That the newly discovered oil may not be enough to meet rising global demand
    D) That shale oil is inferior to crude oil

8. As used in line 69, "admonished" most nearly means

    A) urged.
    B) scolded.
    C) cautioned.
    D) argued.

9. Assuming the discovery by Repsol is as large as is stated in the passage, about how high would you expect the next bar to be in the graphic?

   A) 2.25
   B) 2.5
   C) 3.0
   D) 3.5

10. On the map to the right, the Neuquen province is marked with a white arrow. Given the information in the passage, which of the following regions of the province would be least suited for hydraulic fracturing?

   A) The eastern region
   B) The southwestern region
   C) The northwestern region
   D) All regions are equally suited

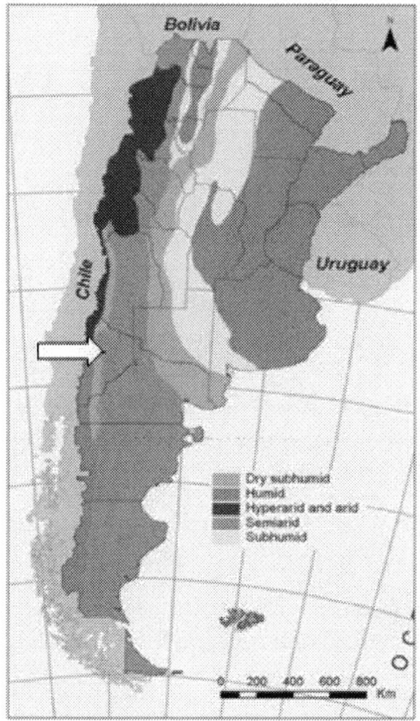

Practice Passage 14

When the Second Virginia Convention met in 1775, delegate Patrick Henry presented a proposal to organize a volunteer militia in every Virginia county, a direct contrast against the sentiments expressed by his fellow delegates, who still hoped for reconciliation with Britain. By custom, Henry addressed himself to the Convention's president, Peyton Randolph of Williamsburg.

Line

I have but one lamp by which my feet are guided; and that is the lamp of experience. I know of no way of judging of the future but by the past. And judging by the past, I wish to know what there has been in the conduct of the British ministry for the last ten years, to justify those hopes with which gentlemen have been pleased to solace themselves, and the House? Is it that insidious smile with which our petition has been lately received? Trust it not, sir; it will prove a snare to your feet. Suffer not yourselves to be betrayed with a kiss. Ask yourselves how this gracious reception of our petition comports with these war-like preparations which cover our waters and darken our land. Are fleets and armies necessary to a work of love and reconciliation? Have we shown ourselves so unwilling to be reconciled, that force must be called in to win back our love? Let us not deceive ourselves, sir. These are the implements of war and subjugation; the last arguments to which kings resort. I ask, gentlemen, sir, what means this martial array, if its purpose be not to force us to submission? Has Great Britain any enemy, in this quarter of the world, to call for all this accumulation of navies and armies? No, sir, she has none. And what have we to oppose to them? Shall we try argument? Sir, we have been trying that for the last ten years. Shall we resort to entreaty and humble supplication? What terms shall we find which have not been already exhausted? Let us not, I beseech you, sir, deceive ourselves. Sir, we have done everything that could be done, to avert the storm which is now coming on. We have petitioned; we have remonstrated; we have supplicated; we have prostrated ourselves before the throne, and have implored its interposition to arrest the tyrannical hands of the ministry and Parliament. Our petitions have been slighted; our remonstrances have produced additional violence and insult; our supplications have been disregarded; and we have been spurned, with contempt, from the foot of the throne. In vain, after these things, may we indulge the fond hope of peace and reconciliation. There is no longer any room for hope. If we wish to be free, if we mean to preserve inviolate those inestimable privileges for which we have been so long contending, if we mean not basely to abandon the noble struggle in which we have been so long engaged, and which we have pledged ourselves never to abandon until the glorious object of our contest shall be obtained, we must fight! I repeat it, sir, we must fight!

They tell us, sir, that we are weak; unable to cope with so formidable an adversary. Sir, we are not weak if we make a proper use of those means which the God of nature hath placed in our power. Three millions of people, armed in the holy cause of liberty, and in such a country as that which we possess, are invincible by any force which our enemy can send against us. Besides, sir, we shall not fight our battles alone. There is a just God who presides over the destinies of nations; and who will raise up friends to fight our battles for us. The battle, sir, is not to the strong alone; it is to the vigilant, the active, the brave. Besides, sir, we have no election. If we were base enough to desire it, it is now too late to retire from the contest. There is no retreat but in submission and slavery! Our chains are forged! Their clanking may be heard on the plains of Boston! The war is inevitable and let it come! I repeat it, sir, let it come.

It is in vain, sir, to extenuate the matter. Gentlemen may cry, Peace, Peace but there is no peace. The war is actually begun! The next gale that sweeps from the north will bring to our ears the clash of resounding arms! Our brethren are already in the field! Why stand we here idle? What is it that gentlemen wish? What would they have? Is life so dear, or peace so sweet, as to be purchased at the price of chains and slavery? Forbid it, Almighty God! I know not what course others may take; but as for me, give me liberty or give me death!

1. As it is used in line 23, the word "array" most nearly means

   A) display.
   B) series.
   C) group.
   D) attire.

2. Which of the following can NOT be inferred from the passage?

   A) Great Britain has already undertaken some threatening actions.
   B) Patrick Henry's fellow delegates are largely opposed to military action against Great Britain.
   C) The colonists have greater resources with which to fight a war than do the British.
   D) The delegates have repeatedly tried to resolve their differences with Britain through peaceful means without success.

3. Which of the following describes a counter-claim that Henry rebuts in his speech?

   A) Great Britain has established a military presence in the colonies.
   B) There is no longer any hope for a peaceful resolution with Britain.
   C) Other patriotic colonists are already fighting for freedom.
   D) The colonists are not strong enough to defeat the massive British military.

4. Which of the following provides the best evidence for the answer to the previous question?

   A) Lines 22-27 ("I ask...armies")
   B) Line 47 ("There is...hope")
   C) Lines 57-61 ("They...power")
   D) Lines 78-82 ("The next...field")

5. Which of the following best describes Henry's evidence in support of his claim that Britain's military presence in the colonies is intended to subjugate the colonists?

   A) He provides a detailed description of Britain's "war-like preparations" in order to establish the British threat to the colonists.
   B) He uses a rhetorical question to establish that since Britain has no enemies in this part of the world, there can be no other reason for the British military presence.
   C) He shares a personal anecdote to illustrate the "additional violence and insult" at the hands of the British.
   D) He uses metaphor to compare the colonists' subjugation by the British to slavery.

6. Which of the following best summarizes Henry's main claim?

   A) Since Britain has repeatedly rejected attempts at a peaceful resolution, war is the only option.
   B) If the colonists lose the war for freedom from the British, the colonists will be enslaved.
   C) The British are not worthy of controlling the colonies.
   D) The delegates hoping for peace are merely cowards.

7. Which of the following provides the best evidence for the answer to the previous question?

   A) Lines 4-10 ("And judging...received")
   B) Lines 20-27 ("Let us...none")
   C) Lines 47-55 ("There is...fight")
   D) Lines 70-75 ("Besides...Boston")

8. In relationship to the rest of the passage, the argument presented in lines 1-4 ("I...past.") serves to

   A) provide a counterclaim that Henry refutes in later paragraphs.
   B) create a metaphor that suggests that Henry's speech is intended to enlighten his listeners.
   C) establish Henry's authority in speaking about the long history between Great Britain and the American colonists.
   D) establish the basis for Henry's claim that since past efforts at reconciliation have been unsuccessful, future efforts are likely to be fruitless.

9. As it is used in line 71, the word "base" most nearly means

   A) foundational.
   B) established.
   C) immoral.
   D) worthless.

10. The author uses repeated references to slavery (lines 73 and 86) in order to

A) create fear in his listeners by suggesting that the British will literally enslave the colonists.
B) equate a refusal to fight with submission to slavery.
C) suggest that those who disagree with him are slaves to the British mindset.
D) vilify the practice of slavery in the colonies.

11. The structure of the passage can best be described as

A) a refutation of the arguments in favor of pursuing peaceful resolutions followed by arguments in favor of fighting the British.
B) a discussion of the past relations between the colonies and the British followed by an argument for severing that relationship.
C) a summation of the various resolutions that have been presented to the British followed by a denouncement of the British response.
D) a description of the British military presence in the colonies followed by a call for war.

Practice Passage 15

An Analysis of "Democracy"

Written in 1949, in the midst of civil rights tensions that had yet to form into a full-blown movement, Langston Hughes's poem "Democracy" argues that those without freedom should not wait for it. This worthy message is one few readers would argue with, and the fact that it comes from one of America's greatest poets endows it with even more weight. Yet, few readers would call "Democracy" the best poem Langston Hughes ever wrote. Just the opposite may be true, in fact. This is due mainly to two contrary approaches within the simple, twenty-one line poem. It is marred both by unsophisticated or even silly rhymes used to express high-minded ideals and by end rhyme that is mixed in a jarring way with free verse.

"Democracy" begins with a four-line stanza that says that freedom will not come "this year" by means of "compromise and fear." That is, the speaker, who clearly identifies as a person without freedom or democracy, dismisses the policy of accommodation that some African American leaders were advocating at the time the poem was written. Although the message of the four lines is exactly clear, the problems of the free-verse poem begin here. The four lines completely lack meter, yet they present the end rhymes "year" and "fear." These simple rhymes make serious ideas sound singsong and dilute the gravity of the message.

The same problem occurs in the second stanza. There the speaker says he has the right "to stand" and to "own the land." Again the idea is powerful, but the simple rhymes, this time embedded in a five-line stanza, sound silly in the service of such a noble idea—or at least inadequate to it. The cliché in this stanza about standing on one's own feet also diminishes the power of the message. Finally, there is the unpredictable rhyme, which also undercuts the stanza. Lines 3 and 5 rhyme; lines 1, 2, and 4 do not. This mixture of free verse and rhyme, for no apparent literary effect, is discordant. And while it might be argued that the mixing of free verse and exact rhyme is as contradictory as the coexistence of free and the not free within a so-called "democracy," the poem does not seem to be about such complexity. Instead, it says more simply, "No more waiting: I want freedom, now."

The third stanza, which consists of five lines, is more powerful because its rhymes seem less weak or contrived. Although Hughes uses yet another cliché, that tomorrow is another day, he strongly conveys the idea that waiting for tomorrow is tiring advice that ignores the needs of the present moment. Furthermore, it could be argued that Hughes incorporates clichés because the advice to wait for freedom had become a kind of cliché by 1949. Consistent with the cliché that might just work for that reason, the rhymes in this stanza, which has a final sophisticated last line, seem less forced and more appropriate to the message of refusing to wait for what is necessary and right. They also seem more appropriate to the overall message of wanting and deserving democracy.

The last two stanzas, which consist of four lines and three lines respectively, each line no longer than four words, also express strong ideas about freedom. Nevertheless, they again seem tossed off and singsong. Freedom is called a "strong seed," which does not make a lot of sense in the context, and, worse, seems to be used for the sake of rhyming with "need." As if to intensify the poem's problems, this stanza also switches suddenly, disturbingly, and just this once to regular meter. The last stanza, which calls for equality, also does so in a too-simple way. It uses three lines to rhyme "too" and "you." Perhaps this drives home the idea that freedom can, after all, be a simple matter. More likely, it leaves readers with a sense that this highly regarded poet, who most likely, like his speaker, cannot wait for democracy, unfortunately did not have the patience or take the time to make "Democracy" a better poem.

1. Which of the following is a claim the author makes early and supports throughout the passage?

    A) Langston Hughes uses rhyme and rhythm as metaphors for freedom and oppression.
    B) Although written by a superior American poet, "Democracy" is an inferior poem.
    C) The speaker in "Democracy" relies on common clichés to support a theme about common ground.
    D) Because the concept of democracy is such a simple idea, it demands a simple poem to do it justice.

2. Which choice provides the best evidence for the answer to the previous question?

    A) Lines 1–5 ("Written . . . wait for it")
    B) Lines 5–8 ("This worthy . . . more weight")
    C) Lines 11-13 ("This is due . . . poem")
    D) Lines 13-16 ("It is . . . free verse")

3. Which of the following best summarizes paragraph 2?

    A) The poem's shortcomings begin in the first verse.
    B) The principles of compromise and hope become the main ideas in the poem.
    C) African American leaders in 1949 wanted people to accommodate the laws of the time.
    D) The concept of democracy is naturally complex.

4. In paragraph 3, the author implies the claim that

    A) "Democracy" is ultimately a poem about impatience.
    B) grand ideas should be expressed in an appropriately grand manner.
    C) free verse creates a tone of discordance and contradiction.
    D) owning land was the goal of many African Americans in the mid-twentieth century.

5. Which choice provides the best evidence for the answer to the previous question?

   A) Lines 31-32 ("The same problem . . . stanza")
   B) Lines 32-33 ("There the . . . the land'")
   C) Lines 33-37 ("Again the . . . to it")
   D) Lines 39-42 ("Finally . . . do not")

6. As it is used in line 30, "gravity" most nearly means

   A) consequence.
   B) seriousness.
   C) attraction.
   D) pressure.

7. As it is used in line 55, "conveys" most nearly means

   A) makes.
   B) carries.
   C) transfers.
   D) communicates.

8. What claim does the author make in paragraph 4 about the line in the poem that states, "Tomorrow is another day"?

   A) The author most likely chose it because so many words rhyme with "day."
   B) "Tomorrow" would have been a better title for the poem because this is its most important line.
   C) Although it is a worn out expression, it adequately suggests that the fight for democracy had become tiresome.
   D) The line is the weakest and most unfortunate line in the poem because it is such a common saying.

9. Which of the following does the author imply in the last paragraph?

   A) Even great poets sometimes get impatient or careless.
   B) Great poetry can be surprising in its simplicity.
   C) The best lines of poetry are no longer than four words.
   D) Calling freedom a "strong seed" is a powerful metaphor.

10. Based on information in the passage, which of the following would you expect the author to admire?

   A) A haiku about world history
   B) A nursery rhyme about life and death
   C) A long, epic poem about a quest for power
   D) A free verse poem about the order of the universe

Evidence-Based Writing

What is the Evidence Based Writing Section?

What Is The Evidence Based Writing Section?
The Evidence Based Writing Section is designed to test your understanding of English grammar and conventions. You will be provided with several different passages from the following subjects: Careers, History/Social Studies, Humanities, and Science. Each passage will be written in a different style. One of the passages will have at least one graph which represents data that is pertinent to the passage. In each passage, you should expect to find at least one question on Command-of-Evidence and one question on Words-in-Context. Look at the "Writing By the Numbers" list to the right to get an idea of what the Evidence Based Writing Section will look like.

Writing By the Numbers:

- 35 minutes
- 4 passages with 400-450 words per passage
- 11 questions per passage
- 1 Non-Fiction passage
- 1-2 Argumentative passages
- 1-2 Informative/Explanatory passages
- 1 graph representing data pertinent to one passage

Your Evidence Based Writing Section will be scored on a scale from 10-40. This score will then be used to calculate your Evidence Based Reading and Writing Score on a scale from 200-800. In addition to the overall score from 10-40, you will get subscores in Expression of Ideas and Standard English Conventions. These subscores come solely from the Evidence Based Writing Section. Some questions in the Evidence Based Writing Section contribute to the subscores of Meaning of Words and Command of Evidence. Each of these subscores are scaled from 1 to 15.

How Should You Approach the Passages?
You can skim the four different passages and decide which one you like the best. If you have a clear favorite, read that first! Otherwise, go in the order of the passages. Work on each passage individually and finish it before moving on to the next passage. If you have a few questions where you aren't confident in your answer, circle them in the test booklet. You can go back and double-check them at the end if you have extra time. Remember, you don't want to leave anything blank. You don't get points deducted for wrong answers, so even a complete guess is better than nothing.

- You should answer grammar questions as you are reading the passage. For questions that ask for main ideas or thesis sentences, make sure you have read enough of the passage before answering them.

- Anticipate the answer before looking at the answer choices and find the answer choice that corrects the error. If there are multiple errors in an underlined portion of a sentence or sentences, correct one error at a time.
- Scan the answer choices and eliminate any choice that doesn't fix the first error, then go back to the remaining answer choices and determine which choice also fixes the second error. Avoid relying on, "hearing the error."
- Some things may sound wrong but be grammatically correct - standard written English is more formal than colloquial speech, so it may sound unfamiliar even when correct.
- Look at the answer choices for clues about what might be wrong with a section. For example, look at the following answer choices:
  - A) NO CHANGE
  - B) child; sharing meals; talking with them; or otherwise
  - C) child, sharing meals, talking with them, or otherwise
  - D) child, sharing meals (talking with them), or otherwise

  What do you notice about each choice? The words are the same, but the punctuation is different. So this question must be testing punctuation usage! You need to determine which choice is grammatically correct and adequately conveys the meaning of the sentence. Here is another example:
  - A) NO CHANGE
  - B) outcomes
  - C) events
  - D) consequences

  These are all different words with different meanings, so they are testing word choice. The question to ask is which choice is best supported by the context of the passage?

Helpful Tips:

- Don't be afraid to choose "NO CHANGE." That will be the answer just as often as any of the other answers.
- Answer everything! You don't get points off for wrong answers, and just like they say about the lottery, you can't win if you don't play!
- When in doubt, go with the shortest answer. Concise writing is the best writing.
- Check your answers! Go back to the underlined section in the passage and read the sentence encapsulating that underlined section. Read it silently in your head, but replace the underlined portion with your selected answer. Make sure it sounds right and matches the context of the surrounding sentences.
- Process of Elimination is critical. If you can't confidently pick the correct answer, start eliminating answer choices that you know do not fix the problem.
- If time is running out, guess aggressively and thoroughly. Do not leave any answer choices blank!

Step-by-Step Instructions for Attacking the Writing Passages

Actively read the passages. Some questions deal with logic and passage organization, so you need to have a good understanding of the main idea of each of the paragraphs and how they interact with each other.

Answer the underlined questions as you go through the passage. Anticipate an error, and pick the choice that corrects the error. If a question seems to be taking you too long, pick an answer and circle the question in your test booklet so you can go back and look at it if you have time.

Once you have finished reading the passage, go back and answer any questions that you may have left blank. Check over the answers on any questions that you circled. Make sure that you have answered every question for a passage before moving on to the next passage.

Subjects and Verbs

Concept & Strategy Lesson

All complete sentences must have a subject and a verb. The subject is the noun or pronoun performing the action. The verb is the action being performed.

SUBJECT-VERB AGREEMENT

One of the types of errors common to the SAT is subject-verb agreement. Subjects and verbs must agree in number – plural subjects get plural verbs, and singular subjects get singular verbs.

IDENTIFYING SUBJECTS AND VERBS

The first step to identifying a subject-verb agreement error is to identify the subject and the verb of the sentence. Let's use an example to help identify tricky subjects or verbs:

Step 1: Cross out phrases that are contained within sets of commas, parentheses, or dashes.

Each of the students, ~~including Annabelle~~, passed the final exam.

Step 2: Cross out prepositional phrases (phrases that begin with a preposition like *of, for, under,* etc.).

Each ~~of the students~~ passed the final exam.

Step 3: Of the remaining nouns and pronouns, determine which one is performing the action of the sentence.

Each Passed the final exam.

In this sentence, the pronoun "each" is performing the action. "The final exam" is an object rather than a subject.

Step 4: Identify the action taking place. If there is no action, look for helping verbs like *is/are, was/were,* or *has/have.* This is the verb.

In this sentence, the action is "passed," which is the verb of the sentence.

SUBJECT-VERB AGREEMENT ERRORS

There are several primary rules governing subject-verb agreement. Knowing these rules allows you to identify and correct subject-verb agreement errors.

Rule 1: Plural subjects take plural verbs, and singular subjects take singular verbs.

Each of the rivers *was/were* overflowing.

Rule 2: "Here" and "there" are not subjects. In sentences that begin with these words, the subject generally follows the verb.

There *is/are* sandbags along the riverbank.

Rule 3: Compound subjects connected by "and" take plural verbs.

Joanna and Grace *want/wants* to go see a movie.

Rule 4: Compound subjects connected by "nor" or "or" could require either a singular or a plural verb. The subject that is closer to the verb determines whether the verb should be singular or plural.

Either the students or the teacher *need/needs* to vacuum the classroom.

Rule 5: When the subject is an indefinite pronoun, a pronoun that does not refer to specific person, place, or thing, the subject might be singular or plural depending on the context. The chart below identifies indefinite pronouns as singular or plural.

All *is/are* well.

Singular Indefinite Pronouns		Plural Indefinite Pronouns	Variable Indefinite Pronouns
Somebody	Everybody	Both	Any
Something	Everything	A number	Some
Someone	Everyone	Fewer	More
Anybody	Each	Few	Most
Anything	Neither	Many	All
Anyone	Either	Several	None
Nobody	Much		
No one	One		
Nothing	The number		

Rule 6: Separate prepositional phrases from the rest of the sentence to see if the subject agrees with the verb. The words each, either, neither, anyone, and everyone are singular.

Neither of the baseball players *is/are* practicing on Wednesday.

Rule 7: If a sentence starts with a prepositional phrase, make sure that the verb agrees with the subject, as often there is a delayed subject.

Across the street from my house *live/lives* an old man and his wife.

Rule 8: If a sentence has a long prepositional phrase in it that includes the word "who," "which," or "that," then the subject that comes before the "who" "which" or "that" goes the verb. This is an exception to rule 6.

Either of the two actors who you are considering for the part *is/are* great performers.

Trigger: A verb is part of the underlined portion of the sentence, and the answer choices contain similar words with the verb changing in number and tense.

Response: Run through internal questions: Do the subject and verb agree? If not, fix that error, and cross out answer choices that do not correct the error.

KEY CONCEPTS

VERB TENSE, MOOD, AND VOICE

In addition to testing subject-verb agreement, the SAT will also test errors in verb tens, mood, and voice. A verb's tense tells us when an action occurs. A verb's mood tells us the attitude of the speaker. In addition, a verb's voice tells us the relationship between the verb and the participants in the action described by the verb.

VERB TENSES

Tenses tell us when the action of a verb occurs – past, present, or future. See the chart below for a detailed description of various verb tenses.

Past	Present	Future
Simple Past: Actions that took place at a specific time in the past. *I **rode** the bus home on Tues-day.*	Simple Present: Actions that take place at the present moment. *I **ride** the bus home every day.*	Simple Future: Actions that will happen at a point in time in the future. *I **will ride** the bus home on Friday.*
Past Progressive: Actions that occurred over a period of time in the past and were in-terrupted by another action. *I **was riding** the bus when it started snowing.*	Present Progressive: Actions that occur over a period of time that includes the present moment. *I **am riding** the bus.*	Future Progressive: Actions that will occur over a period of time in the future. *I **will be riding** the bus every day next week.*
Past Perfect: Actions that oc-curred before another event in the past. *I **had been riding** the bus be-fore my brother started driving me to school.*	Present Perfect: Actions that occurred in the past and in-clude the present moment. *I **have been riding** the bus all year.*	Future Present: Actions that will occur in the future but before another event in the future. *By the time I graduate, I **will have been riding** the bus for four years.*

On the SAT, it will be important to use context clues from the passage to determine the correct verb tense for a given sentence. Remember that sometimes the clues might come from sentences that come before or after the sentence in which the error has been underlined.

> **Rule:** Watch out for "time" words or phrases like "today" "yesterday" "last year," "later this afternoon." These indicate which tense (past, present, or future) needs to be used.

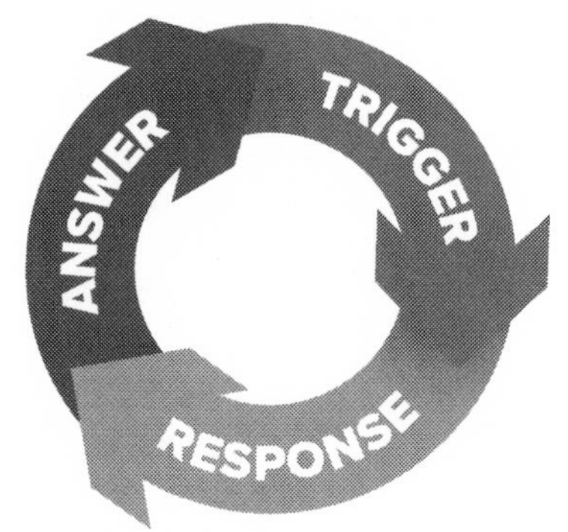

Trigger: The underlined portion of the sentence contains a verb, and the subject and verb agree.

Action: Ask yourself, "is the verb in the correct tense?" To determine tense, you need to look for clues, such as "time words" used in other parts of the sentence.

VERB MOODS

Most sentences us the indicative mood, including questions and statements of fact or opinion. The imperative mood is used to give commands. In these sentences, the subject is usually assumed to be "you," or the person being addressed by the sentence. Finally, the subjunctive mood expresses states of unreality, such as hypothetical situations, requests, hopes, and wishes.

Indicative Mood: I **will win** the lottery this week.
Imperative Mood: Please **go buy** a lottery ticket for me.
Subjunctive Mood: I wish I **would win** the lottery jackpot.

Rule: With the words "wish," "if" and "as though" use the plural verb "were" instead of the singular verb "was"

I wish I *was/were* a better singer.

VERB VOICE

Verb voice is either passive or active. A verb is in the active voice if the action is being performed by the subject. A verb is in the passive voice if a party other than the subject is performing the action.

Active Voice: I **watched** a movie last night.
Passive Voice: A movie **was watched** last night.

KEY CONCEPTS

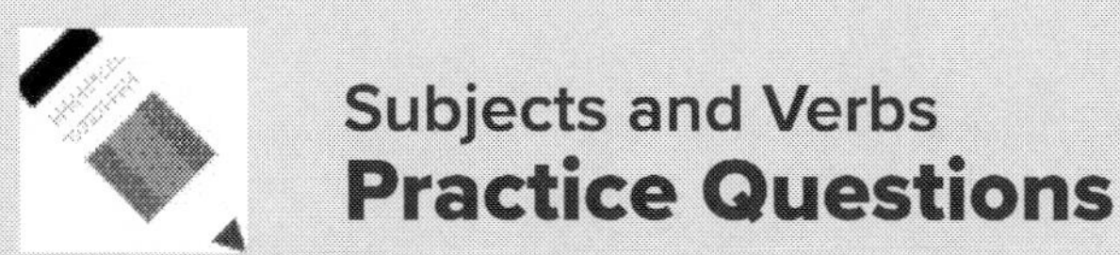

Subjects and Verbs
Practice Questions

PRACTICE EXERCISE 1

The most well-known of all ghost ship (1) stories are that of The Flying Dutchman. Although much of its story is mere legend, it is based on a real ship captained by Hendrick Vanderdecken, who set sail in 1680 from Amsterdam. According to legend, Vanderdecken's ship (2) encountered a severe storm as it was rounding the Cape of Good Hope. Vanderdecken ignored the dangers and kept sailing, but the ship sank, killing everyone on board. As punishment, the legend says, Vanderdecken and his crew are doomed to sail the waters near the Cape for all eternity. Sightings of the mysterious ship have continued for hundreds of years since the ship's sinking.

1. A) NO CHANGE
   B) stories is
   C) stories were
   D) stories was

2. A) NO CHANGE
   B) will have encountered
   C) will encounter
   D) encounters

PRACTICE EXERCISE 2

Directions: Identify the subject(s) of each sentence, then circle the correct verb(s) in parentheses. Remember that more complex sentences can have more than one subject and/or verb.

1. The most violent storms in nature (IS / ARE) tornadoes.

2. Thunderstorms or a tornado sometimes (CREATES / CREATE) large amounts of damage, but tornadoes (IS / ARE) much more violent weather events.

3. Spawned from a powerful thunderstorm, tornadoes often (CAUSES / CAUSE) fatalities and (DEVASTATES / DEVASTATE) whole communities.

4. There (IS / ARE) different types of tornadoes, but most tornadoes (APPEARS / APPEAR) as rotating, funnel-shaped clouds.

5. Although many tornadoes (IS / ARE) clearly visible, there (IS / ARE) others that are obscured by rain or nearby clouds.

PRACTICE EXERCISE 3

Directions: Each of the following sentences contains at least one error in verb tense, mood, or voice. Underline the verbs in each sentence, and then rewrite the sentence to correct the error.

1. I suggest that she seeks extra practice in math.

   ____

   ____

2. Concerts are often performed by stars to raise money for charities.

   ____

   ____

3. As Beebee looks for her glasses, her cell phone rang.

   ____

   ____

4. If we played better in the second half, we scored four additional baskets and won the game.

   ____

   ____

5. Tens of thousands of people have seen the exhibition before the museum closes.

   ____

   ____

Sentence Formation

Concept & Strategy Lesson

Complete sentences must have a subject and a verb, and they must express a complete idea. Sentences that don't meet these requirements are sentence fragments. Sentences that contain multiple subjects and verbs without being properly connect to each other are either run-on sentences or comma splices. It is important to know what makes a complete sentence and how to combine sentences in order to succeed on the SAT.

Sentences are made up of clauses. A clause is a series of words that includes a subject and a verb.

A *dependent clause* ____________________________________

An *independent clause* ____________________________________

FRAGMENTS, RUN-ONS, AND COMMA SPLICES

Sentence fragments are incomplete sentences. They are missing a subject or a verb, or they do not express a complete idea. In other words, a sentence fragment is a sentence that is missing an independent clause.

Fragment: After the movie is over.
Complete Sentence: The movie is over.

Run-ons and comma splices represent an opposite error to a sentence fragment. In these errors, too many clauses occur in the sentence without being properly connected.

Run-On: The movie is over so Lois went home.
Comma Splice: The movie is over, Lois went home.
Correct Sentence: ____________________________________

COMBINING SENTENCES

There are several ways to properly combine sentences: Coordination, subordination, semicolons, and colons.

Coordination

Coordination is used to combine two independent clauses with a comma and a coordinating conjunction. There are seven coordinating conjunctions that you can remember using the acronym FANBOYS: ____________________________________.

Incorrect: The movie is over, or Lois went home.
Correct: ____________________________________
Incorrect: The movie is over so Lois went home.
Correct: ____________________________________

There are two common errors when dealing with coordination. The first, as seen above, is to use a conjunction that doesn't properly communicate the relationship between the two clauses. In this case, "or" does not express any logical relationship between the first and second clauses. The second is to use a coordinating conjunction without a comma. Coordination requires both a comma and a conjunction.

Subordination

With subordination, one clause becomes a dependent clause while the other remains an independent clause. Dependent clauses can be formed by either omitting the subject or verb, or by adding a subordinating conjunction. There are many subordinating conjunctions, including:

Subordinating Conjunctions			
After	If	So that	Whenever
Although	In order that	Than	Where
As	Now that	That	Whereas
Because	Once	Though	Wherever
Before	Provided	Unless	Whether
Even	Rather than	Until	While
How	Since	When	

As with coordination, it is important to choose a conjunction that properly expresses the relationship between the two ideas. With subordination, we use a comma only when the clause with the subordinating conjunction comes first. If the clause with the subordinating conjunction comes second, no comma is needed.

Incorrect: Although the movie is over Lois has not yet gone home.
Incorrect: Lois has not yet gone home, although the movie is over.
Incorrect: Whether the movie is over, Lois has not yet gone home.

Correct: ______________________________
Correct: ______________________________
Correct: ______________________________

In the first sentence, the clause containing the subordinating conjunction "although" should have a comma after it. In the second sentence, the clauses should not be divided by a comma because the clause containing the subordinating conjunction comes last. In the third sentence, the subordinating conjunction "whether" does not describe a logical relationship between the two clauses.

SENTENCE FORMATION ERRORS

Sometimes, the SAT will specifically ask which of the following answer choices best combines two sentences. In this case, it is easy to tell that you will need to combine two sentences using punctuation, coordination, or subordination. The test may simply provide an underlined portion of one or two sentences, and the underlined portion will contain the part of the sentence that should be altered in order to correct a sentence formation error.

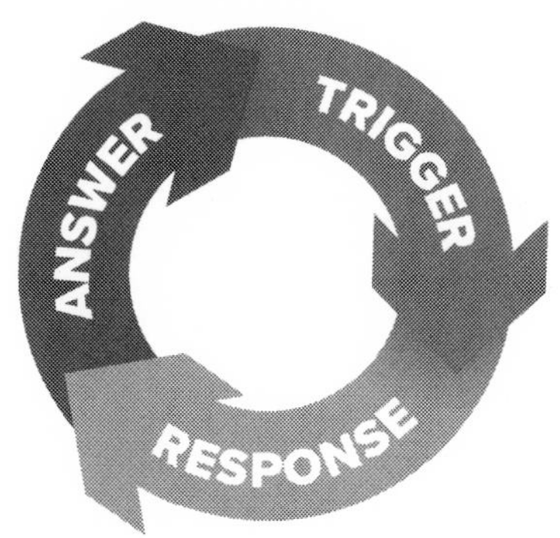

Trigger:

The question asks you how to best combine two sentences, or changes the words in a clause to change whether it is independent/dependent.

Response:

For any punctuation that you see and cannot change, run through the rules. Make sure that any conjunctions or subordinating phrases provide an appropriate connection.

KEY CONCEPTS

Sentence Formation
Practice Question

The Kinetoscope is an early motion picture exhibition device. It was designed for films to be viewed by one person at a time through a peephole window at the top of the device. The Kinetoscope was first described by Thomas Edison, but it was largely developed by his employee William Kennedy Laurie Dickson. (1) The device was very popular in the U.S., it had even greater influence abroad. Edison had chosen to patent the (2) device only in the U.S. so inventors abroad were free to alter and improve the technology.

1. A) NO CHANGE
   B) Unless the device was very popular in the U.S., it had even greater influenceabroad.
   C) The device was very popular in the U.S. but it had even greater influence abroad.
   D) Although the device was very popular in the U.S., it had even greater influence abroad.

2. A) NO CHANGE
   B) device. Only in the U.S., so inventors abroad were free
   C) device only in the U.S., so inventors abroad were free
   D) device only in the U.S.; so inventors abroad were free

Punctuation

Concept & Strategy Lesson

One of the frequent tested types of errors on the SAT Writing test is punctuation errors. Although there are a wide variety of possible punctuation errors, understanding the basic rules of punctuation will help you to address these questions.

NONESSENTIAL ELEMENTS

Nonessential elements are parts of a sentence that are unnecessary to the primary meaning of the sentence. To maintain the clarity of the sentence, nonessential elements have to be set off by punctuation.

Commas

To set off nonessential elements, the most commonly used punctuation marks are commas. Commas are generally used to set off information that feels like a natural part of the sentence.

Incorrect: The Food and Drug Administration, also known as the FDA, oversees products that include food, drugs, medical products, and dietary supplements.
Correct: The FDA, established in 1906, enforces a wide variety of federal laws that are intended to protect public health.

Parentheses

Parentheses are used to set off something that seems out of place in the sentence or that would otherwise interrupt the flow of the sentence. Parentheses must always be used in pairs.

Incorrect: The book (when read aloud to the class) took on new meaning.
Correct: The authors use of dialect (a regional form of a language) made the book ideal for reading aloud.

Dashes

Dashes are often used to add drama or emphasis to the information contained within them. Unlike parentheses, which minimize the information inside them, dashes highlight the information inside them.

Incorrect: My birthday—April 15—is an inauspicious day in history.
Correct: April 15 is the date on which Abraham Lincoln was killed, the Titanic sank, and the Boston Marathon was bombed—it's also my birthday.

OTHER USES OF COMMAS

Commas serve many functions in sentences. In addition to setting off nonessential elements, commas are commonly used to separate clauses within a sentence or to separate items in a series.

Commas with Coordination and Subordination

For a thorough overview of coordination and subordination, review the lesson on Basic Sentence Structure. Remember that the rules for comma usage with coordination and subordination are:

Rule One: When combining clauses using coordination, you must use a comma and a coordinating conjunction.

Incorrect: The 1938 Federal Food, Drug, and Cosmetic Act established the FDA but it has been amended many times since then.
Correct: The 1938 Federal Food, Drug, and Cosmetic Act established the FDA, but it has been amended many times since then.

Rule Two: When combining clauses using subordination, use a comma when the subordinating clause comes first.

Incorrect: Before the FFDCA was passed there were few regulations regarding the safety of new drugs.
Correct: Before the FFDCA was passed, there were few regulations regarding the safety of new drugs.

Rule Three: When combining clauses using subordination, do NOT use a comma when the subordinating clause comes second.

Incorrect: The new regulatory act was finally passed, after an improperly prepared medicine caused the deaths of more than 100 people.
Correct: The new regulatory act was finally passed after an improperly prepared medicine caused the deaths of more than 100 people.

Items in a Series

Commas are also used to separate items in a series when those items do not already contain commas. When the items in the series already contain commas or are particularly lengthy, semicolons are used to separate the items. Punctuation within a series of items must be consistent regardless of whether commas or semicolons are used.

Incorrect: On our vacation, we planned to visit London, England, Paris, France, and Berlin, Germany.
Correct: On our vacation, we planned to visit London, England; Paris, France; and Berlin, Germany.

Incorrect: On our vacation, we hope to ride a double-decker bus and tour the Tower of London, visit the Louvre and ride to the top of the Eiffel Tower, and see the Brandenburg Gate and tour Museum Island.
Correct: On our vacation, we hope to ride a double-decker bus and tour the Tower of London; visit the Louvre and ride to the top of the Eiffel Tower; and see the Brandenburg Gate and tour Museum Island.

SEMICOLONS

In addition to separating items in a series, semicolons can also be used to combine sentences. There are two important rules for combining sentences using semicolons:

Rule One: Semicolons can be used to combine two independent clauses when those clauses are closely and clearly related to one another.

Incorrect: We need to pick up some celery and carrots; we're out of apples.
Incorrect: We need to pick up some celery and carrots; because I need them to make soup.
Correct: We need to pick up some celery and carrots; I need them to make soup.

Rule Two: Semicolons should not be used with conjunctions, but they can be used with conjunctive adverbs (such as therefore or however) and with transitional phrases (such as for example).

Incorrect: There are many exceptions to grammar rules; and this makes English grammar difficult to master.
Correct: There are many exceptions to grammar rules; therefore, English grammar is difficult to master.

COLONS

Like semicolons, colons can also be used with items in a series and to combine sentences. Here are the rules for correct colon usage:

Rule One: Colons are used to introduce items in a series, but only when the clause preceding the colon is an independent clause.

Incorrect: When you go to the store, please get: apples, milk, and eggs.
Correct: When you go to the store, please pick up these items: apples, milk, and eggs.

Rule Two: Like semicolons, colons are only used to combine independent clauses, but unlike semicolons, colons are only used to combine sentences when the second sentence clarifies, explains, or otherwise expands upon the first sentence.

Incorrect: He got what he deserved: he can't wait to tell his wife.
Incorrect: He got what he deserved: because he really worked for that promotion.
Correct: He got what he deserved: he really worked for that promotion.

PUNCTUATION RULES

1. **Nonessential Elements:** Parentheses minimize information, dashes emphasize information, and commas are most commonly used to offset nonessential elements. Parentheses must always come in pairs, but dashes and commas can sometimes be used singly.
2. **Commas:** Use a comma with a coordinating conjunction when combining independent clauses. Only use a comma with a subordinating conjunction when the subordinating clause comes first. Use commas to separate items in a series when those items do not already contain commas.
3. **Semicolons:** Use semicolons to combine sentences when those sentences are clearly related. Semicolons should generally not be used with conjunctions. Semicolons are also used to separate items in a series when those items are lengthy or already contain commas.
4. **Colons:** Use colons to combine sentences when the second sentence expands upon the ideas in the first sentence. Colons can also introduce items in a series, but the clause before the colon must always be an independent clause.

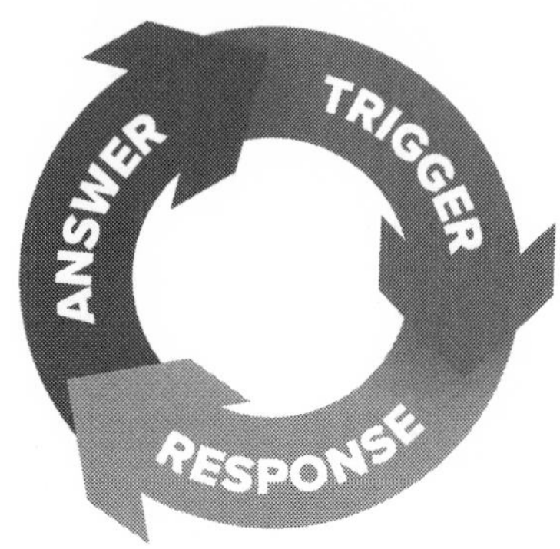

Trigger:
The answer choices involve adding, deleting, or moving pieces of punctuation around.

Response:
Run through the rules for each piece of punctuation that you see. Eliminate any answer choices that violate one of the rules. Look for the answer that fixes any problems that were in the initial sentence, but that does not introduce any new errors.

KEY CONCEPTS

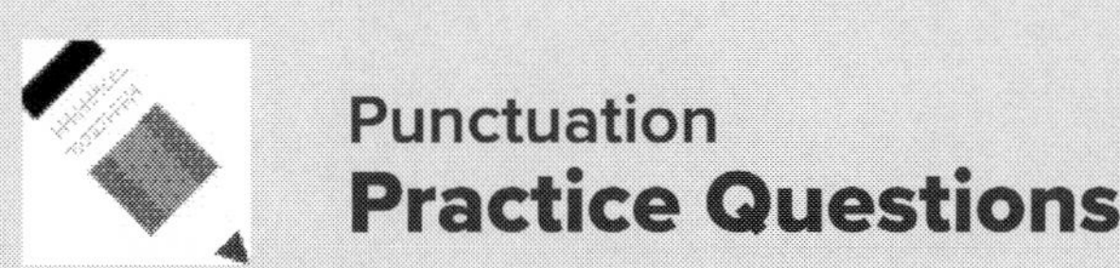

Punctuation
Practice Questions

PRACTICE EXERCISE 1

Although many people believe that *The Star-Spangled Banner* is about the (1)Revolutionary War the lyrics were actually written in 1814 following the Battle of Fort McHenry during the War of 1812. *The Star-Spangled Banner*(2) – which was officially used by the Navy beginning in 1889,became the official national anthem of the United States in 1931. Prior to that, several other songs were commonly used as anthems of (3) the U.S. including: *Hail Columbia; Yankee Doodle;* and *My Country, 'Tis of Thee.*

1. A) NO CHANGE
   B) Revolutionary War. The
   C) Revolutionary War; the
   D) Revolutionary War, the

2. A) NO CHANGE
   B) , which was used by the Navy beginning in 1889,
   C) which was officially used by the Navy beginning in 1889
   D) – which was officially used by the Navy beginning in 1889 –

3. A) NO CHANGE
   B) the U.S., including:
   C) the U.S.: these included
   D) the U.S. including;

PRACTICE EXERCISE 2

Directions: All of the following sentences are missing correct punctuation. Add the correct punctuation marks to each sentence. Keep in mind that some sentences may include more than one type of missing punctuation.

1. There were several very popular items on the menu figs wrapped in bacon apples stuffed with gruyere and polenta bites.

2. My father the man with the big white hat is the chef at this restaurant.

3. Although I am lactose-intolerant I love to cook with cheese cream and other dairy products.

4. My father cannot prepare shellfish dishes he is so allergic to seafood that even touching it causes a reaction.

5. My favorite dish at the restaurant is chicken under a brick my least favorite is the lobster bisque.

Pronouns

Concept & Strategy Lesson

Pronouns take the place of nouns in sentences to make writing less repetitive. The noun that a pronoun replaces is called its antecedent.

PRONOUN-ANTECEDENT AGREEMENT

Just as subjects and verbs must agree, so must pronouns and their antecedents. When a pronoun takes the place of singular noun, the pronoun must be singular; when a pronoun takes the place of a plural noun, the pronoun must be plural.

Each student must turn in *his or her/their* homework.

PRONOUN CASES

The case of a pronoun refers to whether the pronoun is acting as a subject or an object in the sentence. Look at the table below for information about pronoun cases:

Subjective	Objective	Possessive
I	me	my
You	you	your
He	him	his
She	her	her
It	it	its
We	us	our
They	them	their
Who	whom	whose
One	one	one's

When dealing with questions involving pronouns on the SAT, it is important to determine whether the pronoun is acting as a subject or an object in order to determine whether the appropriate pronoun is being used. Remember that the subject of the sentence performs the action, and the object is acted upon.

Determining pronoun case is often straightforward, but can be tricky with compound subjects and objects.

My dad will give the car to my sister and *I/me* when we graduate.

AMBIGUOUS PRONOUN REFERENCES

In good writing, it is important that pronouns and their antecedents must be clearly related. The reader should be able to tell what a pronoun refers to.

When we went to the museum, the guide told my sister that *she/my* sister knew a lot about art history.

Another common error with ambiguous pronoun references occurs when there is no antecedent at all.

If you want to work in a museum, *they/the management* require(s) that you have a degree in art history.

RELATIVE PRONOUNS

Relative pronouns introduce certain types of dependent clauses called relative clauses. The following chart lists relative pronouns:

<table>
<tr><th></th><th>Subject</th><th>Object</th><th>Possessive</th></tr>
<tr><td>Animate/Human restrictive</td><td>Who/that</td><td>Whom/that</td><td rowspan="2">Whose</td></tr>
<tr><td>Animate/Human nonrestrictive</td><td>Who</td><td>Whom</td></tr>
<tr><td>Inanimate/Nonhuman restrictive</td><td>Which/that</td><td>Which/that</td><td rowspan="2">Whose/of which</td></tr>
<tr><td>Inanimate/Nonhuman nonrestrictive</td><td>Which</td><td>Which</td></tr>
</table>

There are two types of relative clauses:

- restrictive (defining the antecedent and giving necessary information)
- non-restrictive (giving extra, unnecessary information)

Each type of clause has its own specific pronouns. In addition, when choosing relative pronouns, a distinction is made between human and non-human antecedents.

- People who
- Things that/which

PRONOUN RULES

1. When you encounter pronouns, always ask the question: "Which noun is the pronoun replacing?"

   Jill hit Jack, and she hit him on the head.

2. Singular nouns get replaced with singular pronouns and plural nouns get replaced with plural pronouns.

   When one player misses practice, *they/he* or she impact(s) the entire team.

3. Take out prepositional phrases to help see which noun the pronoun is replacing.

   Every one of the actors remembered *his or her/their* lines.

4. "his or her" is used on the SAT for singular nouns. The pronoun 'their' is still correct for plural nouns.

   Actors should never forget his or *her/their* lines.

5. Group words like "the horned owl," or "the rock band," or "the nation of China" are singular and need singular pronouns.

   The horned owl is a nocturnal predator, meaning they/it like(s) to hunt at night.

6. With a preposition (e.g. 'with') use an objective pronoun.

   Alex is coming to the game with Jesse and *I/me*.

7. The pronoun 'whom' is an objective pronoun, so it needs to be used with prepositions (e.g. with)

   The audience to *who/whom* she was writing did not appreciate her article.

8. In relative clauses, use "who" to refer to people and "that" or "which" to refer to things.

   The author *who/which* wrote this article needs to improve his or her grammar.

9. Watch out for ambiguous pronouns. Even when it seems clear what the pronoun "it" is referring to, the actual noun has to be established in the sentence before it can be replaced with a pronoun.

   The guitarist practices *it/his* or her guitar every day.

10. Don't switch back and forth between the pronoun "one" and the pronoun "you." Whichever one you start with, you need to use consistently throughout the sentence.

    If one can't attend the party this Saturday, *you/one* should at least let the host know.

11. Use a possessive pronoun with a gerund.

    I don't like *you/your* cutting to the front of the line.

Trigger:
A pronoun is part of the underlined portion of the sentence, and the answer choices contain similar words with the different pronouns.

Response:
Circle the pronoun and draw an arrow back to the word it replaces. Does it match in number? Is it clear what word it is replacing? If so, is the pronoun in the correct case?

KEY CONCEPTS

Pronoun
Practice Questions

PRACTICE EXERCISE 1

In early 2015, two probes that had spent the past year orbiting the moon on a NASA mission slammed into (1)<u>its</u> surface, destroying (2)<u>it</u>. This wasn't an accident. Such crash-landings are a typical method of bringing unmanned space missions to an end. As a result, (3)<u>us</u> and our space programs have littered our solar system with debris. In fact, the moon now hosts nearly 400,000 pounds of man-made material.

1. A) NO CHANGE
   B) the moon's
   C) their
   D) the probes'

2. A) NO CHANGE
   B) itself
   C) themselves
   D) ourselves

3. A) NO CHANGE
   B) we
   C) people
   D) ourselves

PRACTICE EXERCISE 2

Directions: Each of the following sentences includes a pronoun error. Underline all of the pronouns in the original sentence, and then rewrite each sentence to correct the error.

1. Each of the boys has his or her own savings account.

2. Neither Bill nor Alexandra could find their jacket.

3. Mike thought that his brother should see his doctor.

4. After the big boxing match between Alex and Rodriguez, he ran around the ring in a victory lap.

5. When I tried to pick up the dog's food dish, it bit me.

Frequently Confused Words

Concept & Strategy Lesson

The SAT will test your knowledge of frequently confused words, including possessive determiners and pairs or groups of words that are commonly confused.

Whenever you see answer choices that are spelled or pronounced very similarly, the question is likely a frequently confused words question, and you should pay careful attention to the minute differences between the answer choices.

POSSESSIVE DETERMINERS

Probably the most commonly tested category of frequently confused words is possessive determiners.

Possessive determiners tell us who possesses something. Examples include my and her. Some possessive determiners, like your, their, and its fall under the category of frequently confused words that might appear on the SAT.

Your vs. You're: "Your" is a possessive determiner, as in, "Your hair looks nice today." "You're" is a contraction that means "you are," as in, "You're going to the store."

Their vs. There vs. They're: "Their" is a possessive determiner, as in, "Their dog ran away." "There" is most frequently used to show the existence or position of something, as in, "There is a dog over there." "They're" is a contraction that means "they are," as in, "They're going on vacation."

Its vs. It's: "Its" is a possessive determiner, as in "The dog licked its injured foot." "It's" is a contraction that means "it is," as in, "It's cold in here."

The following is a list of some of the most commonly confused words that might appear on the SAT:

affect effect	**Affect** means "to influence": The temperature can *affect* the growth rate of plants. **Effect** is usually a noun meaning "a result": The temperature can have an effect on the growth rate of plants.
among between	**Among** is used for things that are not distinct or individuals: Gina is choosing *among* her top colleges. **Between** is used for things that are distinct or individual: She had trouble deciding *between* American College and U.S. University.
bare bear	**Bare** usually means "to reveal": When his private emails were leaked, the Senator was forced to *bare* his secrets to the world. **Bear** usually means "to carry": Now he must *bear* the burden of public shame.
complement compliment	**Complement** means "to make complete" or "to supplement": The upholstery *complements* the wall color by making it seem richer. **Compliment** means "to express admiration": My mom *compliments* my speaking abilities after every debate tournament.

assure ensure insure	**Assure** means "to guarantee": The doctor *assured* me that it was just a cold. **Ensure** means "to make sure": The medicine will *ensure* that I get over the cold quickly. **Insure** means "to provide insurance against loss or injury": Luckily, I am *insured,* so the doctor's bill will be small.
elicit illicit	**Elicit** means "to draw out": The knock on the door did not *elicit* a response. **Illicit** means "illegal or illegitimate": The locker search turned up no *illicit* materials.
perspective prospective	A **perspective** is a point of view: My sister shares my *perspective* on curfews. **Prospective** means "possible or likely to happen": I am going to visit my *prospective* colleges.
than then	**Than** is used to compare: This test is harder *than* any other test I've taken. **Then** is used to describe a time that is not now: Sharpen your pencil and *then* begin the test.

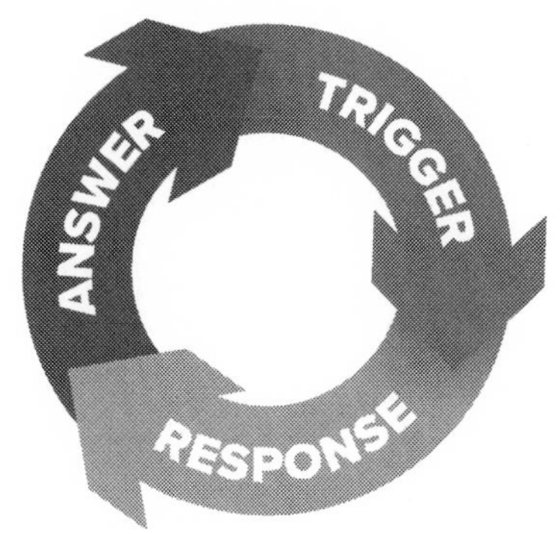

Trigger:
One or two words are underlined, and all of the choices use different words.

Response:
Check to see which answer choice most clearly matches the context clues in the rest of the sentence.

KEY CONCEPTS

Frequently Confused Words
Practice Questions

PRACTICE EXERCISE 1

Among all music formats, only online streaming and vinyl saw growth in 2014. Both digital downloads and CD sales declined. The resurgence of vinyl, a music format many have believed to be all but extinct, is surprising. The reason for its resurgence depends on one's (1) <u>prospective</u>. Some fans of vinyl believe that music simply sounds better on a record, but since many vinyl albums are reproduced from CDs, this is unlikely to be true. In truth, the resurgence of vinyl is likely about nostalgia and identity, as vinyl allows people to own and display (2) <u>there</u> musical tastes.

1. A) NO CHANGE
   B) prospect
   C) persecute
   D) perspective

2. A) NO CHANGE
   B) they're
   C) their
   D) your

PRACTICE EXERCISE 2

Directions: Each of the following sentences includes a misused commonly confused word. Underline the incorrect word and write the correct word on the line provided.

There were less customers than anticipated.

____

____

There going to the amusement park on Saturday

____

____

The chemical is terrible for the environment because it leeches into the ground.

____

____

My brother hurt his hand when he hit the wall in a fit of peak.

____

____

The dog keeps shaking its' head.

____

____

Parallelism

Concept & Strategy Lesson

Parallelism requires that elements in a sentence (or in related sentences) share the same form. This creates a better overall writing style by making writing clearer and preventing awkwardness.

PARALLELISM WITH COORDINATING CONJUNCTIONS

When elements of a sentence are joined by a coordinating conjunction, those elements must be in the same form.

Incorrect: I like to read and playing computer games.

Correct: ____

Correct: ____

PARALLELISM WITH ITEMS IN A SERIES

The same rules apply to items in a series: items in a series must be in the same form.

Incorrect: Today I need to go to the store, picking up the dry cleaning, and stop by the post office.

Correct: ____

PARALLELISM IN COMPARISONS

When two things are being compared, both items must be in the same form.

Incorrect: Driving across the country takes more time than to fly.

Correct: ____

Correct: ____

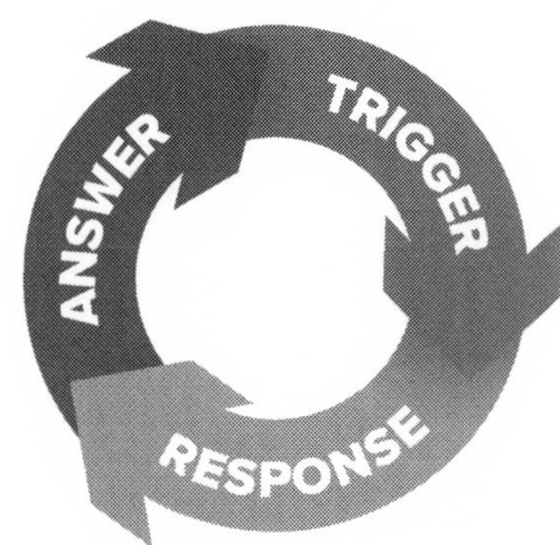

Trigger:
Either a list of items is underlined or the word “than” is underlined.

Response:
For a list, rewrite the list stacking each of the items on top of each other and then ask yourself, “are all the items of the list in the same form?” If the word than is underlined, ask yourself, “is the item before the “than” in the exact same form as the item after “than”?”

KEY CONCEPTS

Parallelism
Practice Questions

PRACTICE EXERCISE 1

New research shows that babies learn best before they sleep. The researchers tested 6- and 12-month old babies to see whether learning right before a nap would improve memory. During the experiment, researchers showed a baby (1) <u>how to remove a mitten from a puppet, ring a bell, and replacing the mitten</u>. They then tested whether the babies could perform those actions after 4 hours and after 24 hours. The 216 babies were split into groups. (2)<u>One group naps for at least 30 consecutive minutes</u>, one group did not nap during the four hour period following the demonstration, and one group did not receive a demonstration in order to act as a baseline. The babies who napped performed far better than those who didn't when compared to the baseline group, suggesting that sleep helps to improve learning in babies.

1. A) NO CHANGE
   B) how to remove a mitten from a pup pet, how to ring a bell, and replace the mitten
   C) how to remove a mitten from a pup pet, ring a bell, and replace the mitten
   D) removing a mitten from a puppet, ringing a bell, and replaced the mitten

2. A) NO CHANGE
   B) One group napped for at least 30 consecutive minutes
   C) One group had napped for at least 30 consecutive minutes
   D) One group has napped for at least 30 consecutive minutes

PRACTICE EXERCISE 2

Directions: Each of the following sentences contains a parallelism error. Rewrite the sentence to correct the error.

1. As the best player on his team, James often dunks, steals, and blocking the basketball.

   ____

2. Martin Luther King, Jr. is admired for his courage, his dedication, and being intelligent.

   ____

3. The ACT English section challenges students and frustration is found in them.

   ____

4. Alexander displays both a disregard for the rules and disrespecting his teachers.

   ____

5. The painter was complimented not only for his use of color but also about his technique.

   ____

Modifiers

Concept & Strategy Lesson

MODIFIER ERRORS

A modifier is a word or phrase that describes, clarifies, or otherwise modifies something else in a sentence. Modifier errors typically occur when the object being modified is either missing or does not appear immediately before or after the modifier. The SAT will test your ability to identify and correct modifier errors.

FIXING MISPLACED MODIFIERS

The first step is identifying the modifying word or phrase. Modifiers are usually adjectives, adverbs, or phrases such as prepositional phrases. They are often, but not always, set apart by commas. In the sample sentences below, the modifiers are underlined:

Sample 1: The woman <u>with brown hair</u> walked to her car.
Sample 2: Her <u>brand-new</u> car was cherry red.
Sample 3: <u>Parked crookedly</u>, the car was <u>already</u> dented.

The placement of modifiers can change the meaning of a sentence. Look at these sample sentences:

Sample 1: Miss Jones waved at Evan <u>just</u> as she came in.
Sample 2: Miss Jones waved <u>just</u> at Evan as she came in.
Sample 3: Miss Jones <u>just</u> waved at Evan as she came in.

These sentences are all virtually identical with the exception of the placement of *just.*

Since the placement of a modifier can change a sentence's meaning, misplaced modifiers can create unintended meanings. For example:

Incorrect: Thundering down the hill, Isaac was worried that the rocks would land on his campsite.

Correct: ____

The best way to fix a misplaced modifier is to ensure that the modifier is located as close to the intended object as possible.

SPOTTING AND FIXING DANGLING MODIFIERS

A similar type of error occurs when a modifier describes something that isn't actually mentioned in a sentence – this is called a dangling modifier. As with misplaced modifiers, it's important to first identify the modifier and then identify the thing being modified. Let's look at an example:

<u>Walking near the river</u>, the fish jumped.

In this sentence, the modifier, *walking near the river,* is modifying *fish.* This doesn't make logical sense. As an intelligent reader, we know that it is highly unlikely that the fish jumped while they were walking near the river; we can assume that the actual subject of the sentence is a person who was walking near the river. However, good writing never makes the reader assume something like that. To fix this dangling modifier, we need to rewrite the sentence to include the proper subject:

Walking near the river, *I watched as* the fish jumped.

Rule: If a sentence starts with a verb, make sure the word that follows the comma goes with that verb.

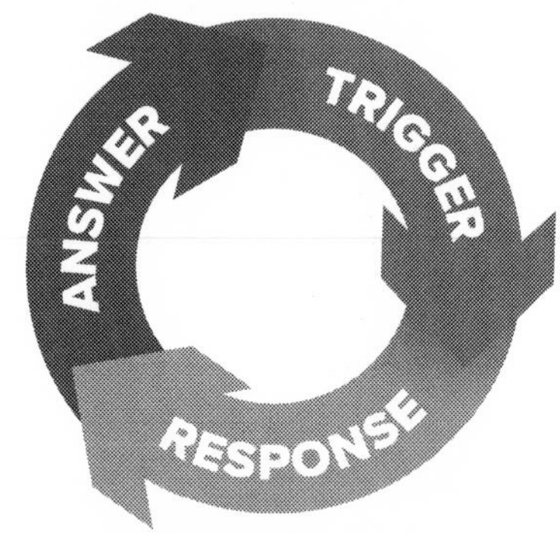

Trigger: A sentence starts with an -ed or -ing word.

Response: Make sure that the word that follows the comma goes with that "-ed" or "-ing" word. Make the opening phrase into a question. For example, using the sentence above, "Who was walking near the river?" If the answer isn't the word that follows the comma, the sentence needs to be fixed.

KEY CONCEPTS

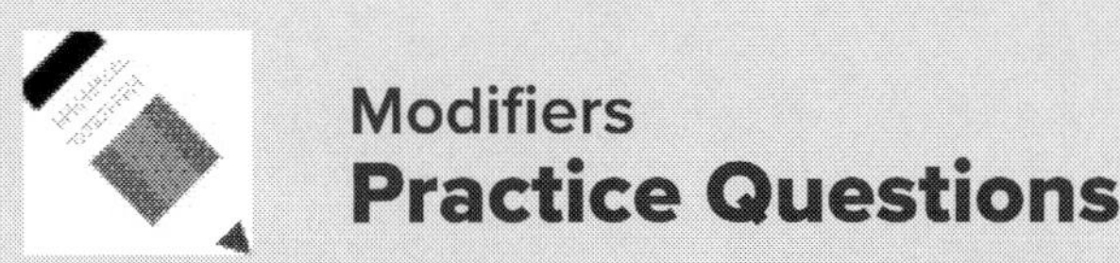

Modifiers
Practice Questions

PRACTICE EXERCISE 1

Growing cities have nowhere to go but up, leading to taller and taller buildings. The most efficient way to build new homes, skyscrapers cast long shadows, putting the people living and working below in near-permanent darkness. Attempting to solve the problem, (1) pairs of skyscrapers that work together to reflect sunlight in order to minimize shade have been designed by architects. (2) Using specially designed software, the buildings are curved to allow one building to reflect sunlight into the shade of the other building.

1. A) NO CHANGE
   a. working together to reflect sunlight in order to minimize shade, pairs of skyscrapers have been designed by architects
   b. architects have designed pairs of skyscrapers that work together to reflect sunlight in order to minimize shade
   c. architects, working together to reflect sunlight in order to minimize shade, have designed pairs of skyscrapers

2. A) NO CHANGE
   a. Architects designed curved buildings that use specially designed software
   b. The buildings are curved using specially designed software
   c. Using specially designed software, architects designed curved buildings

PRACTICE EXERCISE 2

Directions: Each of the following sentences contains a modifier error. Rewrite the sentence to correct the error.

Weighing more than 15,000 tons each, workers used massive tunnel boring machines to dig the tunnel.

Appointed as the nation's sole provider of telecommunications, widespread criticism about the Bell System proliferated.

Originally wanting to study biology, mathematics was the field in which she truly excelled.

Having finished his introduction, the slideshow was the first thing the presenter showed to the class.

Hiding in the dark, the cat's eyes glowed.

Logical Comparisons

Concept & Strategy Lesson

On the SAT, some questions test our ability to recognize and correct incomplete, inconsistent, or unclear comparisons. Problems with logical comparisons tend to fly under the radar – so be careful whenever you notice a comparison is being made.

INCOMPLETE COMPARISONS

For a comparison to be complete, at least two things have to be compared. Incomplete comparisons make the reader guess which two things are being compared. Let's look at an example:

Incorrect: That school has a longer waiting list this year.

Correct: That school has a longer waiting list this year than the school down the street does.
Correct: That school has a longer waiting list this year than last year.
Correct: That school has a longer waiting list this year than in any year prior.

Incorrect: Sue got a higher SAT score than anyone in her class.

Correct: Sue got a higher SAT score than anyone else in her class.

INCONSISTENT COMPARISONS

Not only must comparisons be complete, but they must also be consistent. This means that a comparison needs to compare apples to apples, not apples to oranges. For instance:

Incorrect: Sue's SAT score was not as high as the valedictorian.

Correct: Sue's SAT score was not as high as the valedictorian's SAT score.
Correct: Sue's SAT score was not as high as the valedictorian's.

UNCLEAR COMPARISONS

The last type of logical comparison error is an unclear comparison. For a comparison to be clear, the reader needs to be able to easily tell which items are being compared. For example:

Incorrect: I usually help my sister with her homework more than my brother.

Correct: I usually help my sister with her homework more than I help my brother with his.
Correct: I usually help my sister with her homework more than my brother does.

Tip: The word "than" becomes like the center of a see-saw. What comes before and after has to balance.

Trigger: The words "than," "more," or "most" are part of the underlined phrase, or words that end in "-er" or "-est."

Response: If the word than is underlined, make it the center of the seesaw. Does the sentence balance? Are you making a consistent comparison? Is it clear what is being compared? If words with "-er" or "-est" or the words "more" or "most" are underlined, then ask yourself, "Is it a clear comparison? Is it complete? Do the parts of the comparison balance each other?"

KEY CONCEPTS

Logical Comparisons
Practice Questions

PRACTICE EXERCISE 1

Tom Petty and Bruce Springsteen have something interesting in common: Although both are very well-known rock artists with decades' long careers, they are not known for their number one hits. Surprisingly, Bruce Springsteen has (1) <u>fewer number one hits</u>. In fact, he has never had a number one hit. In that regard, Tom Petty's musical career has been slightly more successful (2)<u>than Bruce Springsteen</u>. After a 38-year long career, Tom Petty finally landed his first number one album, yet he still has never had a number one hit song.

1. A) NO CHANGE
   B) fewer number one hits than Tom Petty does.
   C) fewer number one hits than any artist.
   D) fewer number one hits than Tom Petty's.

2. A) NO CHANGE
   B) than Bruce Springsteen has.
   C) than Bruce Springsteen's.
   D) than Bruce Springsteen's success.

PRACTICE EXERCISE 2

Directions: Each of the following sentences contains a comparison error. Rewrite the sentence to correct the error.

1. Students at these schools have a higher admission rate to tech schools such as CalTech and MIT than other states in the country.

   ____

2. New York has its share of excellent secondary schools, such as Stuyvesant High School, Brooklyn Latin School, and the Bronx School of Science, that have admissions rates to college that are much higher than other schools.

   ____

3. Measles, despite recent outbreaks, is a far lesser threat than it once was.

   ____

4. Like his later works, Claude Monet's early paintings demonstrated not only his astonishing level of artistic technique, but also he had masterful way of using color.

   ____

5. The pizza that we ordered from Papa's Pizza was far crispier and much more delicious than Gino's Pizza Parlor.

   ____

Organization

Concept & Strategy Lesson

LOGICAL SEQUENCE

Logical sequence questions ask you to put ideas in the most logical order, whether by rearranging sentences within a paragraph, deciding the most appropriate place to add a sentence, or rearranging paragraphs within a passage. Answering logical sequence questions requires that you pay close attention to context, relationships between ideas, and use of transitions in order to determine the most logical order of ideas.

LOGICAL SEQUENCE OF SENTENCES

- Rearrange the sentences within a paragraph or add a sentence in the most appropriate place in a paragraph.
- The most logical order of sentences in any given paragraph depends on the content of the individual sentences, so these questions require much closer reading than many other writing questions.
- Pay attention to transitional words and phrases, or places where transitions feel abrupt

LOGICAL SEQUENCE OF PARAGRAPHS

Logical sequence questions that focus on paragraphs require that you arrange the paragraphs within the passage in the most logical order. Often, these questions ask where a certain paragraph should be placed.

- Understanding the basic structure of a well-written passage is helpful when answering these questions.
- Remember that the first paragraph usually serves as an introduction and the final paragraph usually serves as a conclusion.
- The body paragraphs provide supporting information and should flow logically from one idea to the next.
- Transitions can be very helpful in determining the best order of the paragraphs.

INTRODUCTIONS AND CONCLUSIONS

Introduction questions usually ask you to either add a sentence to the beginning of the passage or to change a sentence that already appears in the beginning of the passage.

- A good introductory sentence will introduce the main topic of the passage
- A good conclusion should emphasize the main point of the passage
- Wait to answer these questions until after you have worked through the passage as a whole

KEY CONCEPTS

Transitions

Good transitions make for good writing. For these questions, focus on how to best connect ideas as they are presented in the passage.

TRANSITIONAL WORDS AND PHRASES

It is important to know the functions of different transitions so that you can identify the best transition to use in the context of the passage. For example:

> **Incorrect:** Animal welfare and human welfare are closely connected. *Nevertheless,* failure to embrace spay and neuter programs has led to animal overpopulation in many communities, causing the spread of certain diseases and a rise in minor car accidents.
>
> **Correct:** Animal welfare and human welfare are closely connected. *For example,* failure to embrace spay and neuter programs has led to animal overpopulation in many communities, causing the spread of certain diseases and a rise in minor car accidents.

The transition used in the first example incorrectly identifies the relationship between the two sentences as a contrasting relationship. But the information in the second sentence doesn't contrast with the information in the first sentence; instead it clarifies the information by providing an example. *For example* provides a transition that properly identifies this relationship.

- First read the sentences without any transition in place
- Then determine what function the transition needs to play to move you from the first sentence to the second
- Finally, use that function to eliminate incorrect answers.

The following is a table containing frequently used transitions and transitional phrases and the relationships they demonstrate.

Function	Transitional Words and Phrases		
Sequence	First Second Next Then	Finally After At last Before	Currently During Immediately Later
Conclusion	Finally In a word In brief In conclusion	In the end In the final analysis On the whole	Thus To conclude To summarize
Example	For example To illustrate	For instance Namely	Specifically
Position	Above Adjacent Below	Beyond Here There	In front In back Nearby

Function	Transitional Words and Phrases		
Cause/Effect	Therefore Accordingly	Consequently Thus	Hence So
Emphasis	Even Truly	Indeed	In fact Of course
Similarity	Also Just as	In the same way Similarly	Likewise Much as
Contrast	But Nonetheless Still	However Notwithstanding Yet	In spite of In contrast Nevertheless

TRANSITIONAL SENTENCES

Transitional sentences perform the same function as transitional words and phrases, but there are an infinite number of possible permutations of transitional sentences.

- Transitional sentences usually link paragraphs, so they can generally be found at the beginning or end of a paragraph.
- When a transitional sentence appears at the beginning of a paragraph, it is connecting that paragraph with the one preceding it.
- When a transitional sentence appears at the end of a paragraph, it is connecting that paragraph with the one following it.

As with introduction and conclusion questions, transitional sentence questions require that you pay close attention to the context of the passage, particularly the two paragraphs being linked.

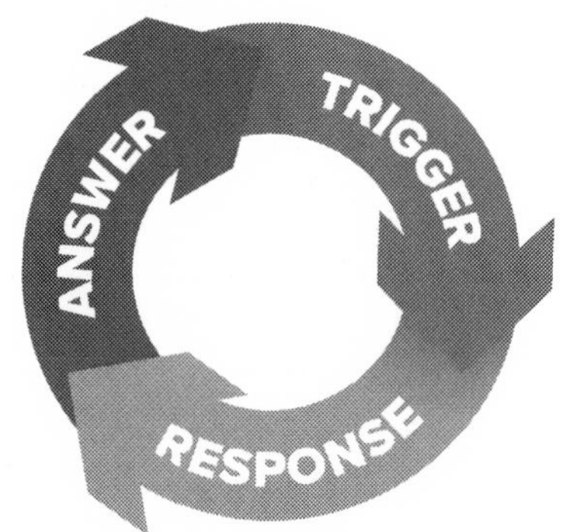

Trigger: The question mentions providing the best transition, or is a phrase underlined at the beginning of a sentence.

Response: First read the surrounding sentence with the underlined phrase or sentence removed. Think about what function the transition needs to serve. Then, eliminate any answer choices that do not perform that function.

KEY CONCEPTS

Style and Tone

Concept & Strategy Lesson

Authors use a specific style and tone to convey their intended meanings.

IDENTIFYING STYLE AND TONE

The author's purpose will often determine the tone of a passage. An author might be writing to explain, persuade, or tell a story. An author who intends to persuade an audience will often use a passionate tone, whereas an author writing simply to inform will often use an objective tone.

Style can sometimes be easier to determine simply by reading the passage. An author who uses slang and avoids high-level vocabulary is usually using an informal style, whereas an author who uses technical terms and high-level vocabulary is usually using a formal style. Style should generally remain consistent throughout a passage, so stylistically correct answer choices will generally suit the rest of the passage.

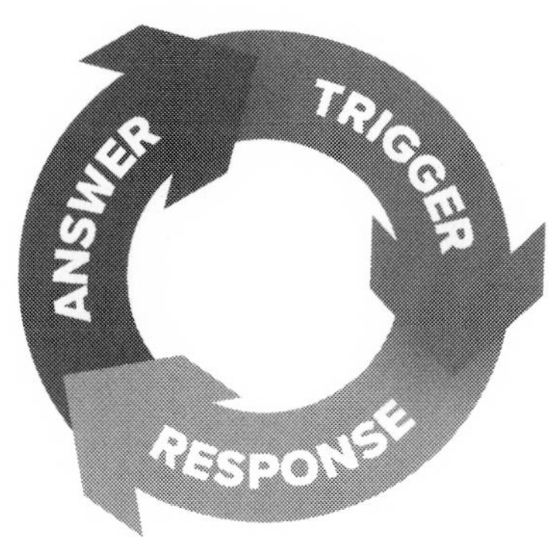

Trigger:
The main difference between the answer choices seems to be how formal or informal they are, or the question asks, "which of the following best fits the author's style and tone"

Response:
Think about what the overall style is before you look at the answer choices. Is it formal? Informal? Does the author use contractions? Use that information to help you to eliminate answer choices.

KEY CONCEPTS

Proposition, Support, Focus

Concept & Strategy Lesson

In addition to testing your knowledge of grammar and usage, the SAT will also test your ability to edit a passage to improve its content. The main question types used to test this skill are proposition, support, and focus questions.

PROPOSITION

- Identify the main idea of the paragraph
- Add or replace a sentence to provide a better thesis statement or topic sentence.
- Avoid answers that focus on a specific detail rather than the main idea
- Always keep an eye on style and tone

SUPPORT

- Identify appropriate evidence in support of a claim
- Add, remove, or revise supporting evidence to improve claims made in the text
- Make sure you understand the claim first before focusing on the support
- The correct answer must not only be true, but also support the claim

FOCUS

- Each paragraph should focus on a single main idea.
- Eliminate unnecessary information
- Make notes regarding the main ideas of the paragraphs in a passage.
- If you delete a sentence, make sure to read the paragraph once without the sentence in place to check for coherency

KEY CONCEPTS

Quantitative Information

Concept & Strategy Lesson

Each writing section will include at least one passage that is accompanied by a graphic such as a table, chart, graph, or map. Several questions will reference these graphics.

ADDRESSING QUANTITATIVE INFORMATION QUESTIONS

- Some ask you to add, remove, or revise information in the passage to reflect information in the graphic
- Others may ask you to provide a proposition or conclusion based on information in the graphic
- The graph is always correct – underlined portions of the text may not be
- Make sure to read all titles and axes carefully, paying attention to units of measurement

Trigger: The question refers you to the graphic.

Response: First, make sure that you fully understand what can be told from the graphic (and what cannot). Eliminate answers that are false based on the graphic.

KEY CONCEPTS

Words in Context

Concept & Strategy Lesson

The writing section tests your understanding of vocabulary and word choice through questions that require that you revise the passage for precision and concision. Precision questions test your ability to choose the most appropriate word or phrase for a particular context. Concision questions test your ability to recognize and correct wordiness and redundancy.

PRECISION

Precision questions may be presented in one of two ways:

- The question may ask you to choose the most precise word for a particular sentence.
- The question may simply offer an underlined word or phrase accompanied by three alternative choices.

Regardless of the question's presentation, precision questions require you to understand the slight differences in the meanings of similar words. There are a few basic concepts that must be understood in order to answer these questions:

- First, it is important to recognize the difference between an accurate word choice and a precise word choice. Consider this example:

  Accurate: She enjoys reading books, particularly those in the science fiction genres.
  Precise: She enjoys reading novels, particularly those in the science fiction genres.

- The second concept is the idea of connotation. A word's connotation is its implied meaning. For example, all of these words are synonyms for "smile": beam, grin, laugh, smirk, and simper. Some of these words suggest extreme happiness or joy (beam, grin, laugh), while others have more negative connotations (smirk, simper). It is important to use the context of the sentence or paragraph in which a given word appears in order to determine whether you should choose a word with a positive or negative connotation.

CONCISION

Conciseness questions require a thorough understanding of a couple of concepts: wordiness and redundancy.

Wordiness

When answering a conciseness question, you will usually choose the answer that includes the fewest words without losing any meaning. The most common mistakes that lead to wordiness include:

Passive Voice

It is usually best to use active voice in writing, in part due to the wordiness created by passive voice. For example:

> **Passive:** The race was won by the driver in the red car.
> **Active:** The driver in the red car won the race.

For more on passive voice, review the lesson on Verb Errors.

"There is," "There are," and "It is"
These often unnecessary phrases simply add word count. For example:

Wordy: There is a problem with this house.
Concise: This house has a problem.

This and That
Sentences can often be combined or shortened to reduce wordiness by eliminating words like "this," "that," and "which." For example:

Wordy: I like to go fishing, which is because I like being on the water.
Concise: I like to go fishing because I like being on the water.

Redundancy
Redundancy occurs when there is needless repetition of words, phrases, or ideas within a given sentence or paragraph. For example:

Redundant: Many uneducated citizens who never graduated from school continue to vote for education improvements.
Concise: Many uneducated citizens continue to vote for education improvements.

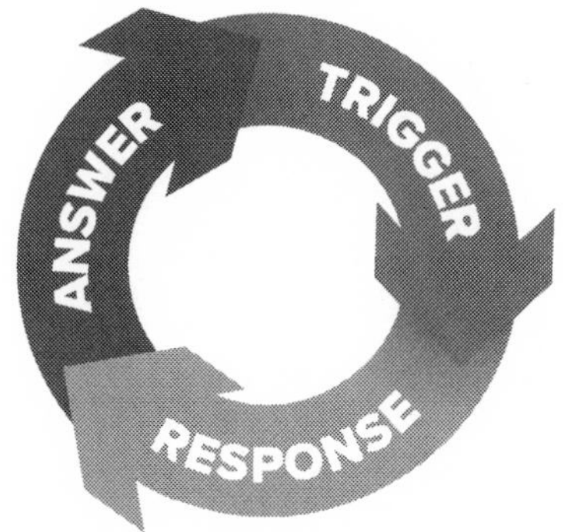

Trigger: The question contains the phrase, "the most precise..." or a word or phrase is underlined with three answer choices of varying lengths.

Response: First, ask yourself if one of the shorter answer choices conveys the same meaning. The most concise answer is frequently the best choice. Then, search the surrounding sentence for context clues as to whether you are looking for a positive or negative word and that hint at the connotation necessary for the correct choice.

KEY CONCEPTS

Words in Context
Practice Questions

Directions: Rewrite each sentence to eliminate wordiness or redundancy.

1. Trouble is caused when people disobey rules that have been established for the safety of all.

2. Angelina took me to a party that was a very fun time.

3. He has an affinity for The New York Times, this being the publication in which most of his early exposes had appeared.

4. She worked for thirty-three years as a teacher and librarian in the field of education in Los Angeles public schools.

5. Over several months, as time went by, his test scores improved.

Evidence-Based Writing

Practice Passage 1

Helping Small Farmers Cope with Climate Change

Last year, I served as a Peace Corps agribusiness (1) advisor in Bluefields a small farming and fishing village in Westmoreland parish in southwest Jamaica. I worked primarily with a group of organic farmers, (2) promoting sustainable agriculture and introducing climate change adaptation strategies through community engagement. I also conducted research on the vulnerability of local agricultural livelihoods to climate change.

(3) Despite the community integration and learning process, I facilitated an assessment with the Westmoreland Organic Farmers Society, a local organization engaged in production agriculture and home economics. The results of the assessment helped us to better understand factors affecting the economic and environmental sustainability of their livelihoods. Through informal discussions with farmers, I also (4) gained a sense of awareness of how changing weather patterns, such as variable rainfall, increased risk for these small-scale farm families.

In October 2012, Bluefields community organizations were given the opportunity to apply for small grants to support the development of livelihood opportunities more resilient to climate change. Designing a project and submitting a successful proposal (5) was easier because we had already collectively identified and prioritized the needs and interests of the organization.

Among other things, the funds went toward establishing an organic demonstration farm. {6} The farm was also used to host a Farmer Field School where community members learned about organic farming practices, (7) the potential impacts of climate change,

1. A) NO CHANGE
   B) advisor, in Bluefields a small farming and
   C) advisor in Bluefields, a small farming and
   D) advisor in Bluefields a small farming, and

2. Which choice most precisely conveys the intended meaning?

   A) NO CHANGE
   B) propagandizing
   C) demanding
   D) wishing for

3. Which transitional phrase is most appropriate here?

   A) NO CHANGE
   B) Without
   C) As part of
   D) Prior to

4. A) NO CHANGE
   B) sensed a gain in awareness
   C) gained awareness
   D) grew aware of

5. A) NO CHANGE
   B) were easier
   C) were more easy
   D) was more easy

plural → were

verb conj: look @ rules not sound

and possible adaptation and mitigation strategies. The group was also able to purchase improved processing equipment and receive food safety training, important steps toward establishing a formal agribusiness.

(8) The group continues to develop and improve the farm, as well as its processing capacity. More importantly, the Jamaican farmers are increasing resiliency by adapting new technology to their own cultural norms and practices. Working side-by-side with my Jamaican friends to establish the demonstration **(9)** farm, one of the joys of my life; it also showed me how difficult it is to cultivate marginal lands with simple hand tools—a reality for millions of men and women around the world.

[1] The data I collected can also be used to measure changes in vulnerability over time. [2] During my service, I designed a study to assess the vulnerability of local agricultural livelihoods to climate change. [3] My hope is that the results will illuminate areas where targeted programs can improve farmers' resiliency and increase incomes. **{10}**

I hope the change **(11)** we've seen in Bluefields will be that of more sustainable livelihoods through environmental stewardship and human empowerment. This is a very possible outcome if the Jamaican men and women I worked with in the farmers group are any indication.

6. Which true detail, if added here, best in the context of the passage?
   A) Groups in Chile and Malawi also received grant funds.
   B) The group's first addition was a structure to catch and store rain for irrigation.
   C) Organic farms do not use synthetic pesticides or fertilizers.
   D) In ten years, farmers hope to raise enough funds to build a larger demonstration farm.

7. A) NO CHANGE
   B) potentially impacted by
   C) impacting potentially by
   D) an impact potentially from

8. Which choice best states the paragraph's main theme?
   A) NO CHANGE
   B) Around the world, climates vary, but many challenges are shared.
   C) Scientists predict that sea levels will rise by at least 3 feet over the next century due to climate change.
   D) Most Jamaican farmers work on a small scale of 1 to 5 acres.

9. A) NO CHANGE
   B) farm; one
   C) farm, and one
   D) farm was one

10. The sentences in the preceding paragraph would be most logically placed in which order?
    A) As they are now
    B) 1, 3, 2
    C) 2, 3, 1
    D) 3, 1, 2

11. A) NO CHANGE
B) we'd seen
C) we're seeing
D) we'll see

Evidence-Based Writing

Practice Passage 2

Healthy Nails, Healthy Workers

(1) <u>There are hundreds of thousands of Vietnamese Americans living in the U.S.</u> After learning about the nail salon industry from friends in my English class, I became a manicurist. The work offered a flexible schedule for mothers of small children, like me, and the required training wasn't as long as for other professions. With determination, I was able to work my way up to eventually become the co-owner of Traci's Nails in Oakland, California. Last year, my business was officially recognized as a "Healthy Nail Salon" by Alameda County, California, for using safer practices and products in my salon. I've been able to do what is best for **(2)** <u>my health, the health of my co-workers, and my customers</u>.

[1] Like **(3)** <u>my industry</u>, I chose to become a manicurist to make women feel beautiful and to provide for my family. [2] Although there are many good things about the job—the glamour, the artistry, the beautiful colors, and the new **(4)** <u>designs—there</u> are also significant hazards. [3] Salon workers are exposed to toxic chemicals and **(5)** <u>repetitive, redundant</u> motions that can cause injuries and illnesses. [4] Many experience health symptoms like breathing difficulty, red and watery eyes, and skin reactions on a daily basis. [5] These symptoms also match with common allergic reactions. [6] We tell ourselves to accept these short-term health problems, but we worry about the possible long-term effects of chemical exposure: cancer, reproductive issues, and asthma. **{6}**

1. Which sentence best introduces the narrator?

   A) NO CHANGE
   B) My name is Chanh, and I am 5'2" tall.
   C) I immigrated to the United States, along with my young daughter, in 1992.
   D) I speak English much more fluently than I did 30 years ago.

2. A) NO CHANGE
   B) my health, my co-workers, and the health of my customers
   C) healthy me, my co-workers, and my healthy customers
   D) the health of myself, my co-workers, and my customers

3. A) NO CHANGE
   B) others in my industry
   C) my employment in the industry
   D) the industry's employment

4. A) NO CHANGE
   B) designs—and there
   C) designs; there
   D) designs, there

5. A) NO CHANGE
   B) repetitively excessive
   C) repetitive
   D) can also cause repetitive

6. Which sentence in the preceding paragraph can be deleted without losing information relevant to the passage?

   A) Sentence 3
   B) Sentence 4
   C) Sentence 5
   D) Sentence 6

The Occupational Safety and Health Administration (OSHA) has many useful resources for salon workers and owners like me, including a booklet called *Stay Healthy and Safe While Giving Manicures and Pedicures* **(7)** (which is 42 pages long). For the last several years, **(8)** they have been working to empower nonprofit organizations that offer safety training and resources to salon workers and employers. **(9)** OSHA in hair and nail salons also has special webpages about safety, the danger of chemicals like toluene, and how to transition to safer chemicals in the workplace. In California, thanks to the work of the California Healthy Nail Salon Collaborative, several areas have implemented Healthy Nail Salon Recognition Programs, awarding salons that use less-toxic products, improve ventilation, and participate in trainings that encourage healthier workplaces.

As an owner, I have gained greater control over the products and practices used in my workplace. I am hoping that other owners in the industry also adopt safer products and practices. That's why the collaborative work of OSHA, advocacy organizations like the California Healthy Nail Salon Collaborative, and local governments is so **(10)** lively to the lives of salon workers across the country.

(11) Nail salon workers and owners should not have to forego good health in order to make a living!

7. Given the narrator's background, which parenthesized detail fits best in the passage?
   A) NO CHANGE
   B) (available in Vietnamese, Korean, and Spanish as well as English)
   C) (unfortunately not useful for miners or farm workers)
   D) (a brochure I have read ten times)

8. A) NO CHANGE
   B) organizations have
   C) the booklet has
   D) OSHA has

9. A) NO CHANGE
   B) OSHA about safety in hair and nail salons also has special webpages
   C) OSHA also has special webpages in hair and nail salons about safety
   D) OSHA also has special webpages about safety in hair and nail salons

10. Which choice most precisely conveys the intended meaning?
    A) NO CHANGE
    B) alive
    C) vital
    D) vivid

11. Which statement best summarizes the passage's argument?
    A) NO CHANGE
    B) Nail salons should be banned from using toluene.
    C) Without OSHA, American workplaces would be much less safe.
    D) Immigrants, especially those with children, struggle to make ends meet.

Evidence-Based Writing

Practice Passage 3

What Women Want: Equal Pay

Fifty years ago, when President Kennedy signed the Equal Pay Act into **(1)** <u>law women</u> earned an average of 59 cents on the dollar compared to their male colleagues. At that time, as **(2)** <u>incredible</u> as it seems today, it really was legal to pay a woman less money to do the same work as a man. By signing the Equal Pay Act, Kennedy finally made it illegal to discriminate against women in the payment of wages.

We have seen progress over the past 50 years—but not enough. Today in America, for every dollar paid to a man, a woman is paid about 77 cents when the calculations are based on annual earnings, and more like 81 cents based on weekly wages. For women of color and women with disabilities, the wage gap is even larger. **{3}**

This reality has major implications for **(4)** <u>women's</u> ability to afford essentials like food, housing, and gas. Now more than ever, American families rely on the wages of women. **(5)** <u>In my city alone, there are thousands of single mothers supporting families</u>. Despite this, the wage disparity between women and men has persisted.

[1] In 2010, President **(6)** <u>Obama's creation</u>, the National Equal Pay Task Force to ensure that equal pay laws are vigorously enforced throughout the country. [2] As we in the task force chart the equal pay agenda for the next half-century, we look at strategies that empower each worker to know **(7)** <u>their</u> worth. [3] One of the biggest obstacles to combating pay discrimination is that so many women do not know they are being underpaid due to discrimination. [4] To address the policies and norms that result in pay secrecy, the task force continues to focus on the importance of collecting and publicizing better data on pay. **{8}**

1. A) NO CHANGE
   B) law—women
   C) law; women
   D) law, women

2. Which choice fits best with the tone of the passage?
   A) NO CHANGE
   B) spectacular
   C) favorable
   D) unique

3. Which statement, if added here, best supports the passage's argument with accurate information from the figure?
   A) The evidence shows, however, that white females are paid more than black men.
   B) Black females, for instance, earn less than 60 cents compared to each dollar a white male earns.
   C) One exception to this trend is Asian females, who typically earn about as much as white males.
   D) Hispanic females make less, on a per-dollar basis, than women of other ethnicities.

4. A) NO CHANGE
   B) womens'
   C) womens
   D) women

Closing the pay gap once and for all will help millions of women and their families right now, but it also has implications for the economic future of our country. We must enable government worker protection agencies to collaborate and coordinate more effectively, and we must encourage employers to take responsibility for **(9)** <u>the idea that they can offer</u> fair pay to all workers.

[5] Enforcement of existing civil rights laws, including the Equal Pay Act, will help. [6] Those laws, however, also leave gaps that must be filled. [7] That's why it is imperative that Congress address loopholes in existing law, strengthen remedies for pay discrimination, **(10)** <u>increased</u> outreach and education to working women, and provide additional research and resources to fight pay inequity. [8] Unfortunately, rampant gridlock in Congress has prevented any real progress from occurring. [9] Solutions to the problem of pay discrimination must also address the broader framework of practices that limit the full economic participation of women workers. **{11}**

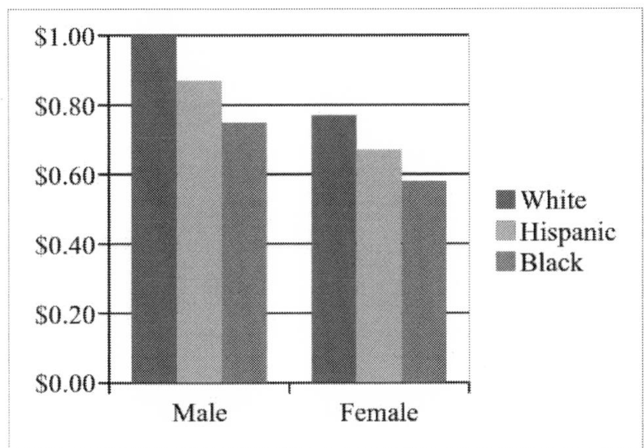

Figure 1: Annual earnings by gender and ethnicity on a per-dollar basis

5. Which true statement provides the most effective evidence to support the paragraph's claims?

   A) NO CHANGE
   B) Some women even earn higher wages than their male colleagues.
   C) American women today are better educated than they were even 20 years ago.
   D) Women make up nearly half of the U.S. labor force and a growing percentage of household breadwinners.

6. A) NO CHANGE
   B) Obama created
   C) Obama, who created
   D) Obama; he created

7. A) NO CHANGE
   B) your
   C) his or her
   D) its

8. The sentences in the preceding paragraph would be most logically placed in which order?

   A) As they are now
   B) 2, 3, 1, 4
   C) 3, 2, 4, 1
   D) 4, 1, 3, 2

9. A) NO CHANGE
   B) their duty to offer
   C) offering and granting
   D) offering

10. A) NO CHANGE
    B) increases in
    C) increasing
    D) increase

11. Which sentence in the preceding paragraph can most easily be deleted to improve the paragraph's focus?

A) Sentence 5
B) Sentence 6
C) Sentence 8
D) Sentence 9

Evidence-Based Writing

Practice Passage 4

The Birdman

[1] Bird artist John Gould captured the essence of his avian subjects with quick, bold lines, but his great success was due to more than a good drawing hand. [2] Just as important was his manner of production, which yielded an incredible fifty oversized volumes between 1830 and 1881. [3] First, Gould would make a rough sketch, jotting notes on the manuscript as to how to fill out the picture and which colors to add. [4] Then, he would pass the image on to other **(1)** <u>artists and colorists, including, his wife Elizabeth.</u> [5] She died in 1841, but John Gould continued producing drawings for another four decades. [6] Gould's beautiful drawings assured his popularity among a wealthy clientele, while the reliable scientific information in his tomes made for a wider commercial success. **{2}**

Born in Dorset in 1804, **(3)** <u>taxidermy was Gould's passion</u> as a child. He soon turned these skills into a lucrative career. By the time he was twenty, Gould was **(4)** <u>involved in</u> the booming trade and interest in taxidermy. This soon led to an appointment as curator and preserver to the Zoological Society of London's museum. **{5}**

1. A) NO CHANGE
   B) artists and colorists, including his wife, Elizabeth
   C) artists, and colorists including his wife, Elizabeth
   D) artists, and colorists including, his wife Elizabeth

2. Which sentence in this paragraph should be deleted because it consists entirely of information that is stated elsewhere in the passage?

   A) Sentence 2
   B) Sentence 3
   C) Sentence 4
   D) Sentence 5

3. A) NO CHANGE
   B) Gould became adept at taxidermy
   C) his taxidermy skills were evident
   D) Gould's father taught him taxidermy

4. Which choice most precisely matches the intended meaning?

   A) NO CHANGE
   B) adopted by
   C) capitalizing on
   D) running through

In 1829, Gould married Elizabeth Coxen, a well-bred governess. **(6)** As they raised a family, Elizabeth and John worked together to illustrate his books on birds. The first work John and Elizabeth collaborated on was the massive A Century of Birds from the Himalaya Mountains, which was issued in parts between 1830 and 1833. The two collaborated on two more tomes, **(7)** which were about the birds of Europe and Australia, before Elizabeth's death in 1841. Afterward, John Gould continued his work with other collaborators for another 40 years.

[7] More than an artist, Gould was a consummate entrepreneur, as the factory-like production of his art books attests. [8] During the hummingbird craze, which started with England's first glimpses of the unusual animal during the Great Exhibition of 1851, Gould collected well over five thousand hummingbird skins **(8)** in his personal collection. [9] Gould wrote about hummingbirds with admiration after seeing them for the first time: "With what delight did I examine its tiny body and feast my eyes on its glittering plumage." {9}

(10) Today, Gould's drawings are prized by art aficionados around the world. He helped identify species in the collection of 450 birds that Charles Darwin presented to the museum of the Zoological Society in 1837. This identification played a significant role in developing the theory of evolution. With Gould's help, Darwin was able to develop the concept of divergent evolution, whereby isolated populations can become new species. In addition to **(11)** aiding Darwin, Gould wrote more than three hundred scientific articles.

5. Which statement, if added here, best supports the paragraph's ideas about Gould's career?

   A) While in London, Gould witnessed many important events, including Queen Victoria's coronation.
   B) Many of the specimens Gould worked on can still be viewed at the museum today.
   C) Gould lacked a rigorous education; instead, he spent his teenage years working as a gardener.
   D) This prestigious position came with a salary of 100 pounds, a hefty income at the time.

6. A) NO CHANGE
   B) Because they raised
   C) And raising
   D) If raising

7. A) NO CHANGE
   B) they
   C) in which
   D) in that

8. A) NO CHANGE
   B) in the collection that he personally gathered
   C) for his own personal use
   D) DELETE the underlined portion

9. Where in the preceding paragraph would the following sentence be most logically added?
   However, he was not immune to the fascinations of his era.
   A) Before Sentence 7
   B) After Sentence 7
   C) After Sentence 8
   D) After Sentence 9

10. Which choice best articulates the paragraph's main idea?

A) NO CHANGE
B) Despite his many accomplishments, Gould remains little-known outside of ornithology circles.
C) In the course of his work, Gould also made notable contributions to science.
D) Gould's career in many ways parallels that of his American contemporary, John James Audubon.

11. A) NO CHANGE
B) the aid provided to Darwin by him
C) helping and giving aid to Darwin
D) being one of those who aided Darwin

Evidence-Based Writing

Practice Passage 5

Micro-Plastics: the New Pollution

[1] This is a relatively new but growing global problem, as is trash from plastic products in general. [2] As much as 80 percent of trash in the ocean comes from sources on land, and up to 60 percent of this trash is plastic. [3] Maybe you've heard of "micro-plastics." [4] **(1)** There created when plastic products eventually break down into tiny particles that drift in our ocean waters and can be eaten by fish and other wildlife. **{2}**

I got an offer from two conservation groups to tag along as they trawled **(3)** the upper Chesapeake Bay waters of plastics pollution to assess the extent. As an oceanographer, I always cherish the days that I get to take my off my tie and get back out on the bay, so I was eager to join them.

I predicted that we wouldn't find much. My theory was that the Chesapeake Bay is too **(4)** dynamic, with its constant tides, winds, and currents, to allow for large concentrations of micro-plastics. That environment contrasts strongly with the relatively quiet open-ocean circulation patterns that concentrate plastics pollution in the worst known instances, such as the **(5)** popular Great Pacific Garbage Patch.

{6} Unfortunately, my educated guess proved wildly inaccurate. The lead scientist for the sampling efforts was shocked at the amount of plastics that emerged from the sample net. The tiny specs of colored plastics scattered through all the leaves and organic debris captured by the net was among the highest amounts of plastic that he had seen in any ocean water sample.

1. A) NO CHANGE
   B) Their
   C) They're
   D) There's

2. The sentences in the preceding paragraph would be most logically placed in which order?

   A) As they are now
   B) 2, 1, 3, 4
   C) 3, 2, 4, 1
   D) 3, 4, 1, 2

3. A) NO CHANGE
   B) the upper Chesapeake Bay waters to assess the extent of plastics pollution
   C) the extent of plastics pollution to assess the upper Chesapeake Bay waters
   D) to assess the extent the upper Chesapeake Bay waters of plastics pollution

4. A) NO CHANGE
   B) dynamic with its constant tides, winds, and currents, to
   C) dynamic, with its constant tides, winds, and currents to
   D) dynamic with its constant tides, winds and currents to

5. Which choice fits best with the passage's context and tone?

   A) NO CHANGE
   B) conspicuous
   C) sleazy
   D) notorious

What we do on land, including how we **(7)** <u>dispose of our trash, impact</u> the quality of our waters and wildlife. As an oceanographer, I was taught that the oceans and coastal waters are the heartbeat of our planet. **{8}** In addition, seafood is a crucial source of nutrition for many cultures, and oceanic algae are among the top producers of atmospheric oxygen. In short, the oceans make our planet livable. That's why they deserve our respect and protection.

[5] **(9)** <u>Some</u> great efforts underway by government agencies and many dedicated outside organizations to stem the flow of trash into our waters. [6] In one of the more promising of these efforts, the Trash Free Waters program, the Environmental Protection Agency is developing projects **(10)** <u>to support efforts by groups to significantly reduce</u> trash entering our watersheds and oceans. [7] Such federal environmental programs are relatively new; the EPA was not even established until 1970. [8] Let's hope that these efforts are successful and that I see less plastic during future trips on the Chesapeake Bay. **{11}**

6. Which choice provides the most effective and accurate topic sentence for the paragraph?
   A) NO CHANGE
   B) Including me, there were 12 people on the expedition—most of them scientists.
   C) Scientists estimate that a single plastic soda bottle can break down into thousands of bits of micro-plastic.
   D) The ocean was beautiful that day, with no obvious signs of pollution.

7. A) NO CHANGE
   B) disposes of our trash, impact
   C) disposes of our trash, impacts
   D) dispose of our trash, impacts

8. Which true statement, if added here, adds the most effective evidence to support the paragraph's main ideas?
   A) They cover two-thirds of the Earth and control our planet's weather patterns, food production, and atmosphere.
   B) I have always particularly appreciated the enormous impact Chesapeake Bay has on the culture of the region.
   C) They have provided one of the most important means of transportation for humans over the last 2,000 years.
   D) Many millions of years ago, the distant ancestors of humans lived in the ocean.

9. A) NO CHANGE
   B) There are some
   C) With some
   D) And some

10. A) NO CHANGE
    B) to support a significant reduction in
    C) to significantly reduce
    D) with groups who support significantly reducing

11. Which sentence in the preceding paragraph should be deleted to improve the passage's focus?

A) Sentence 5
B) Sentence 6
C) Sentence 7
D) Sentence 8

Evidence-Based Writing

Practice Passage 6

Ending Deadlocks with the Seventeenth Amendment

When Congress opened its doors under the new Constitution for the first time on March 4, 1789, at Federal Hall in New York City, there were only eight senators present out of 22 expected. The senators from **(1)** the state of New York, which was hosting, were not among them. The day before, the New York state legislature had **(2)** adjourned without electing any senators.

In February and March, **(3)** the State Senate's Federalist controllers, and the State Assembly, controlled by the Anti-Federalists, fought bitterly over their preferred candidates for the U.S. Senate. Since both parties expected to win a majority in each house in New York's upcoming elections in **(4)** April, they were content to allow the state's Senate seats to remain vacant. Therefore, as the First Congress met in New York City, New York itself was not represented in the Senate. The state legislature remained in a deadlock for five months. It was not until July 16, 1789, that Federalists Rufus King and Philip J. Schuyler **(5)** had been chosen as New York's first senators.

[1] The issue of senatorial deadlocks did not end with the First Congress. [2] They are a consequence of the method of selection agreed upon by the Founders. [3] Article I, Section 3, of the Constitution states, "The Senate of the United States shall be composed of two Senators from each State, chosen by the Legislature thereof, for six Years." [4] Indeed, the only direct democracy outlined in the Constitution applies to members of the House of Representatives. **{6}**

Since most state legislatures are bicameral (with two houses), deadlocks frequently **(7)** rose when the two houses were controlled by different political parties and could not agree on a candidate. Instead of com-

1. A) NO CHANGE
   B) that very state, the host state, New York,
   C) the host state of New York
   D) New York, state of hosting,

2. In context, which choice most precisely conveys the intended meaning?

   A) NO CHANGE
   B) delayed
   C) divorced
   D) prolonged

3. A) NO CHANGE
   B) State Senate, controlled by the Federalists
   C) Federalists who controlled the State Senate
   D) the party that controlled the State Senate, the Federalists

4. A) NO CHANGE
   B) April; they were content
   C) April; content
   D) April, content

5. A) NO CHANGE
   B) were chosen
   C) were being chosen
   D) have been chosen

6. Which sentence in the preceding paragraph can be deleted without detracting from the passage's focus?

   A) Sentence 1
   B) Sentence 2
   C) Sentence 3
   D) Sentence 4

promising in these instances, state legislatures would simply not elect any senator for months, or even years. Between 1891 and 1905 alone, 45 deadlocks occurred in 20 different states; in 14 of those cases, no Senate election was held for an entire legislative session. **{8}**

[5] As support grew, it eventually led to the ratification of the 17th Amendment to the U.S. Constitution in 1913. [6] This amendment abolished the system of senatorial election by state legislatures and replaced it with direct popular election by citizens. [7] The issue of deadlocks, along with frequent allegations of corrupt senatorial **(9)** elections, and a push for more democratic participation contributed to a surge of support for a constitutional amendment to allow citizens to directly elect senators. [8] **(10)** One hundred and twenty-four years after the first deadlock in New York, the new method for selecting senators finally ensured an end to empty seats in the Senate. {11}

7. A) NO CHANGE
   B) razed
   C) arose
   D) raised

8. Which true statement, if added here, best characterizes the extent of the problem described in the paragraph?

   A) Today, senatorial seats can sometimes remain vacant for months, pending a special election.
   B) Many legislatures of the era were also corrupt, electing senators in exchange for money or favors.
   C) Many deadlocks were caused by inexperienced legislators in Western states; deadlocks soon became less frequent in these states.
   D) For instance, Delaware had only one senator in the 56th Congress (1899–1901) and no senators at all in the 57th Congress (1901–1903).

9. A) NO CHANGE
   B) elections and a push for more democratic participation contributed
   C) elections and a push, for more democratic participation, contributed
   D) elections and a push for more democratic participation, contributed

10. Which choice is most effective in the context of the passage as a whole?

   A) NO CHANGE
   B) Over a century ago
   C) Despite the dogged opposition of several states
   D) Whether this was a widespread problem or not

11. The sentences in the preceding paragraph would be most logically placed in which order?

A) As they are now
B) 6, 5, 7, 8
C) 7, 5, 6, 8
D) 7, 8, 5, 6

Evidence-Based Writing

Practice Passage 7

A Short-Sighted Speech?

The latest buzzword in the ever-shifting politics of American education is STEM. For the uninitiated, STEM is an acronym for Science, Technology, Engineering, and Math. **(1)** More relatedly, to hear many elected officials and well-meaning school reformers tell it, it's the only thing a young graduate can hope to get a decent job in anymore. An English major, you say? **(2)** You might as well get in line to apply at Burger King.

When it comes to STEM, Florida Governor Rick Scott is a true believer. In a 2011 interview published in the Sarasota Herald-Tribune, **(3)** it sparked controversy as Scott not only said Florida's public universities should devote more money to STEM programs and less to the humanities, but seemingly suggested that experts in less technical fields were not needed in Florida.

"We don't need a lot more anthropologists in the state," said Scott. "It's a great degree if people want to get it, but we don't need them here."

The governor's comments, to no one's surprise, didn't sit well with one group of **(4)** people in particular: anthropologists. Many quickly leapt to their profession's defense, accusing the governor of ignorance of **(5)** their many practical and profitable applications. Brent Weisman, chair of the Department of Anthropology at the University of South Florida (USF), retorted, "Anthropologists at USF work side by side with civil and industrial engineers, cancer researchers, specialists in public health and medicine, chemists, biologists, and others in the science, technology, and engineering fields that the governor so eagerly applauds." **{6}**

1. A) NO CHANGE
   B) The relevant part being
   C) More to the point
   D) To clarify what is truly meant

2. Which choice for the underlined sentence supports the author's characterization of the views of "many elected officials and... reformers"?

   A) NO CHANGE
   B) That would not qualify as a STEM field.
   C) You will probably need more years of schooling.
   D) Why would anyone want to study something so useless?

3. A) NO CHANGE
   B) Scott sparked controversy as he
   C) sparking controversy, it
   D) he sparked controversy as it

4. A) NO CHANGE
   B) people, in particular
   C) people, in particular,
   D) people in particular,

5. A) NO CHANGE
   B) one's many
   C) many of their
   D) its many

Students in Weisman's department prepared an online **(7)** presentation, in it various anthropologists describe their jobs. One helps doctors understand the cultural issues that complicate improving health care for migrant farm workers. Another advises businesses on cultural differences that affect international negotiations. Yet another, a forensic anthropologist, helps detectives reconstruct the events that led to a crime scene.

[1] **(8)** Accordingly, even within the field, not everybody is sold on the virtues of an anthropology degree. [2] And although there are jobs for anthropologists outside of academia, most are available to other social scientists as well. [3] As a practicing anthropologist, **(9)** Governor Scott might have a point, says Janice Harper. [4] She observes that the median age of an anthropology Ph.D. graduate is 36, higher than for any other field of study. [5] For these grads, finding a tenure-track job as a college professor can be a bit like finding a unicorn. **{10}**

Perhaps the governor's decision to single out the field for criticism above all other less-lucrative majors **(11)** was a personal issue. Critics of Governor Scott's remarks soon noted that his own daughter had recently graduated from a small liberal arts college. Her degree was in—what else?—anthropology.

6. Which addition to this paragraph would best support the claim that anthropology is a relevant and practical field of study?

   A) A criticism of low salaries for anthropologists
   B) An explanation of how anthropologists use math
   C) A statistic indicating an increasing number of jobs and professions requiring anthropological training
   D) A defense of the idea that anthropology is a valid science

7. A) NO CHANGE
   B) presentation; in which,
   C) presentation where
   D) presentation in which

8. Which choice for the underlined portion provides the most logical transition from the previous paragraph?

   A) NO CHANGE
   B) Still,
   C) In fact,
   D) In contrast,

9. A) NO CHANGE
   B) Janice Harper says Governor Scott might have a point
   C) says, Governor Scott might have a point, according to Janice Harper.
   D) Governor Scott, according to Janice Harper, might have a point.

10. In this paragraph, Sentence 2 would most logically and cohesively be placed

A) where it is now.
B) after Sentence 3.
C) after Sentence 4.
D) after Sentence 5.

11. Which choice for the underlined portion is clearest and most precise?

A) NO CHANGE
B) was his personal opinion.
C) had a more personal origin.
D) was a personal one.

Evidence-Based Writing

Practice Passage 8

Engineers at NASA's Marshall Space Flight Center in Huntsville, Alabama **(1)** has successfully tested the most complex rocket engine parts that it ever has created using additive manufacturing, or 3-D printing. NASA engineers pushed the limits of technology by designing a rocket engine injector – a highly complex part that sends propellant into the engine – with design features that took advantage of 3-D printing technology.

To make the parts, the design was entered into the 3-D printer's computer. The printer then built each part by layering metal powder and fusing it together using a laser, a process known as selective laser melting.

[1] This additive manufacturing process allowed rocket designers to create an **(2)** injector. [2] The injector had 40 individual spray elements, all printed as a single component rather than **(3)** manufactured. [3] The entire injector was created from just two **(4)** parts, had they used traditional manufacturing methods, engineers would have needed to make and then assemble 163 individual parts. [4] The 3-D printing technology saved time and money, and it allowed engineers to build parts that enhance rocket engine performance **(5)** and are less prone to failure. [5] The injector was similar in size to injectors that power small rocket engines and similar in design to injectors for large engines, such as the engine that will power NASA's Space Launch System (SLS) rocket, the heavy-lift, exploration class rocket under development to take humans beyond Earth orbit and to Mars. **{6}**

"We wanted to go a step beyond just testing an injector and demonstrate how 3-D printing could revolutionize rocket designs for increased system performance," said Chris Singer, director of Marshall's Engineering Directorate. "The parts performed exceptionally well during the tests."

1. A) NO CHANGE
   B) have successfully tested
   C) has been successfully testing
   D) is successfully testing

2. A) NO CHANGE
   B) injector with 40 individual
   C) injector, which having been constructed, had 40 individual
   D) injector of

3. A) NO CHANGE
   B) manufactured and produced as separate components
   C) manufactured individually
   D) manufactured individually as separate components

4. A) NO CHANGE
   B) parts had
   C) parts. Had
   D) parts, however, had

5. A) NO CHANGE
   B) or
   C) but
   D) yet

6. Which of the following sentences most effectively functions as the topic sentence of the paragraph?

   A) Sentence 1
   B) Sentence 3
   C) Sentence 4
   D) Sentence 5

(7) Additive manufacturing is more complicated than traditional manufacturing, yet it speeds up the entire design process. Using Marshall's in-house capability to design and produce small 3-D printed parts quickly, the propulsion and materials laboratories can work together to apply quick modifications to the test stand or the rocket component. "Having an in-house additive manufacturing capability allows us (8) to look at test data, to modify parts or the test stand based on the data, (9) materialize changes quickly, and get back to testing," said Nicholas Case, a propulsion engineer leading the testing. "This speeds up the whole design, development, and testing (10) process, allowing us to try innovative designs with less risk and cost to projects."

Marshall engineers have tested increasingly complex injectors, rocket nozzles and other components with the goal of reducing the time and cost of building and assembling future engines. {11}

7. Which of the following sentences would provide the best transition between the fifth and sixth paragraphs?

   A) NO CHANGE
   B) Additive manufacturing may have limited practicality now, but Marshall's engineers hope to expand its uses in the near future.
   C) Additive manufacturing not only helps engineers create better rocket parts, but also enables them to test faster and more intelligently.
   D) Additive manufacturing allows several teams to work together as part of the design process.

8. A) NO CHANGE
   B) look at the test data, and to modify
   C) to look at the test data, modifying
   D) to look at test data, modify

9. Which of the following is the most precise replacement for the underlined word?

   A) NO CHANGE
   B) implement
   C) actualize
   D) make good on

10. A) NO CHANGE
    B) process allowing
    C) process; allowing
    D) process: allowing

11. Which of the following, if added, would provide the best conclusion for the passage?

A) Additive manufacturing is a key technology for advancing this goal, and may one day enable missions into deep space.
B) Additive manufacturing is a key technology for enhancing industrial productivity.
C) Who knows what additive manufacturing will let us accomplish in the future?
D) Additive manufacturing may eventually have an impact on NASA's development process.

Evidence-Based Writing

Practice Passage 9

The Modesty in Women's Clothing in the 1910s. Modesty, as the word is commonly understood, is a distinctly human invention. While **(1)** you're understanding of the word may involve innocence, or inexperience, or even humility, these are not the case. It means **(2)** to be aware of your appearance and its appropriateness in the presence of the opposite gender. **{3}** It is one of the innumerable proofs of our peculiar psychic power to attach emotions to objects without a faintest shadow of real connection. The different levels of modesty vary most strongly not by a person's class or wealth, but by his or her gender.

Men's clothing–hats, shirts, shoes–**(4)** are most modified by physical conditions. On the other hand, the clothing that women wear is most modified by psychic conditions. As **(5)** there usually restricted to a very limited field of activity, and as **(6)** they're personal comfort was of no importance to most people, it was possible to maintain in their dress the influence of primitive conditions long considered inconsequential to men.

Over time, men have grown their scope and responsibilities in our society. We see at once why the dress of men has developed along the line of practical efficiency and general human distinction. As women are given **(7)** fewer roles, and the dress of women is still most modified by the separation of gender. Women's dresses are exactly that: labels for women to wear to seem more feminine.

1. A) NO CHANGE
   B) you are
   C) your
   D) yours

2. A) NO CHANGE
   B) being
   C) you are being
   D) you ought to be

3. Which of the following transitions, if inserted here, would most closely match the author's style and tone?

   A) A most variable thing is this modesty.
   B) Modesty a concept that many people have different opinions on.
   C) Most people agree that a woman should cover her legs when out in public.
   D) Clearly there are cultural differences that determine the suitability of dress.

4. A) NO CHANGE
   B) must be
   C) they are
   D) is

5. A) NO CHANGE
   B) theirs
   C) their
   D) they're

6. A) NO CHANGE
   B) there
   C) their
   D) they are

A man may run in a city's streets in scant clothes—a lack of clothes, even—women would be called grossly immodest wearing the same. He may bathe, publicly, and in company with women, so nearly bare as to shock even himself; while the women beside him are covered far more fully than in evening dress. **{8}**

Why should it be "modest" for a woman to exhibit her neck, arms, shoulders, and back, but "immodest" to go bathing without stockings? It is because we have attached sentiments of modesty to certain parts of the human frame, and not to **(9)** <u>others</u>—that is all.

These certain parts vary. In certain African tribes, women are forbidden to reveal even part of their faces. The British peasant woman is forced to " cover her hair, for to show **(10)** <u>its</u> an indecency.

We need not look for a reason where there never was one. These distinctions sprang from emotion or mere caprice, and vary with them. But whatever our notions of modesty in dress may be, we apply them to women for the most part and not to men. **{11}**

7. A) NO CHANGE
   B) fewer roles, the
   C) fewer roles, therefore the
   D) fewer roles, this is the reason that the

8. Which of the following facts would contradict the claims made in the previous paragraph?

   A) The rules of public decency have been applied in an unfair way since the beginning of the 20th century.
   B) A woman was arrested for public exposure when she left her house wearing a shirt which exposed her shoulders.
   C) The women's liberation movement has made great strides in achieving equality for women.
   D) A man was arrested for public exposure when he was picnicking with his family and removed his shirt.

9. A) NO CHANGE
   B) other
   C) other's
   D) others'

10. A) NO CHANGE
    B) it is
    C) its'
    D) it

11. Does the final sentence of this preceding paragraph effectively conclude the passage?

    A) No, because it does not address the main question of the passage, the inequalities between men and women.
    B) No, because it is does not address the specific issue discussed in the paragraph.
    C) Yes, because it summarizes the arguments made in the passage.
    D) Yes, because it defines what the rules of modesty should be.

Evidence-Based Writing

Practice Passage 10

The Measle Resurgence

Today, more than 1 in 20 children nationwide enter kindergarten without the recommended vaccines. The risks of going without vaccinations (**1**) are not isolated to unvaccinated children; as the number of unvaccinated children grows, the potential for disease outbreaks increases dramatically. (**2**) This is proven by facts. In 2000, it appeared that the U.S. had nearly eliminated the measles. Since then, we have experienced numerous troubling outbreaks. In 2008, (**3**) nearly 250 measles cases were confirmed in the U.S., the largest outbreak since 1997. That record was (**4**) beat in 2009 and again in 2010. In 2014, (**5**) more than 800 confirmed measles cases were reported, the highest number in more than 20 years. According to the CDC, the spread of these outbreaks was attributable to "pockets of persons unvaccinated because of philosophical or religious beliefs."

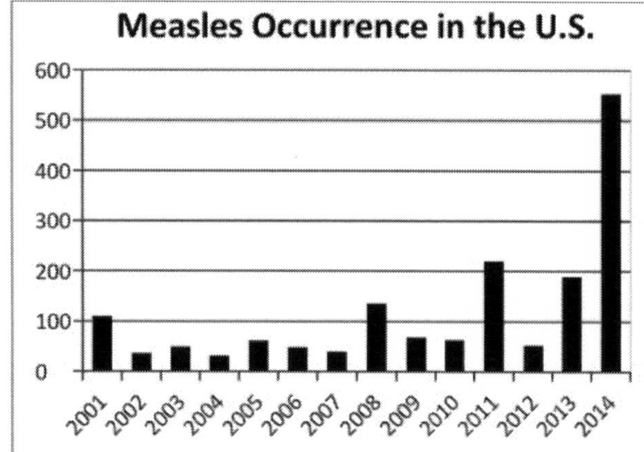

In the decades since vaccines were introduced, millions of lives have been saved. Vaccines are responsible for the elimination of several deadly diseases, including polio. While many other vaccine-preventable diseases have not yet been eliminated, morbidi-

1. A) NO CHANGE
   B) is not isolated to unvaccinated children
   C) are not isolated, to unvaccinated children
   D) were not isolated to unvaccinated children

2. Which of the following best fits the style and tone of the passage?

   A) NO CHANGE
   B) Don't believe it? Check this out.
   C) This is far from mere conjecture.
   D) Recent measles rates have been through the roof.

3. Which choice best completes the sentence with accurate data based on the graph provided?

   A) NO CHANGE
   B) nearly 550 measles cases were confirmed
   C) nearly 140 measles cases were confirmed
   D) nearly 80 measles cases were confirmed

4. Which of the following best fits the data provided on the graph?

   A) NO CHANGE
   B) beat in 2011 and again in 2013
   C) beat in 2010 and again in 2012
   D) beat in 2009 and again in 2013

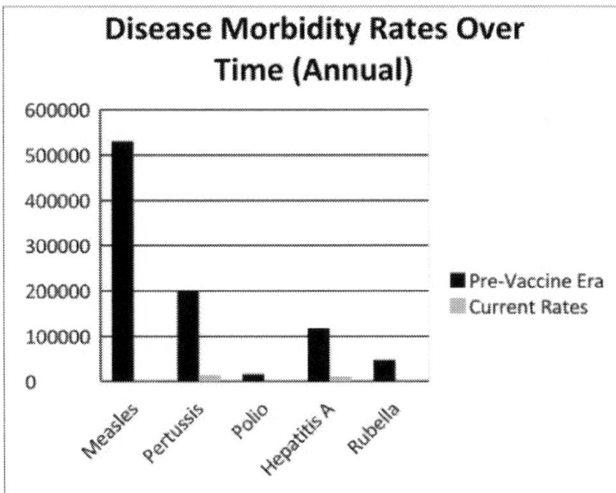

ty rates have dropped drastically since the introduction of vaccines. Measles, despite recent outbreaks, **(6)** <u>is a far lesser</u> threat than it once was. Prior to the widespread use of the measles vaccine, **(7)** <u>nearly one hundred thousand</u> people were infected each year. Today, even the most alarming outbreak seems minor by comparison. Pertussis (or whooping cough), another all-but-eliminated disease that has been making a slow resurgence as a result of the anti-vaccine movement, **(8)** <u>once affected more than 700,000 Americans each year</u>. Today that number is just 13,500, a 93% decrease. **(9)**

If vaccines are so important for public health, why are so many parents choosing not to vaccinate their children?

5. Which choice best completes the sentence with accurate data based on the graph provided?

   A) NO CHANGE
   B) more than 1000 confirmed measles cases were reported
   C) more than 260 confirmed measles cases were reported
   D) more than 550 confirmed measles cases were reported

6. A) NO CHANGE
   B) are a far lesser threat
   C) is far less than a threat
   D) is less than a threat than

7. Which choice best completes the sentence with accurate data based on the graph provided?

   A) NO CHANGE
   B) over one million
   C) more than half a million
   D) almost two hundred thousand

8. Which choice best completes the sentence with accurate data based on the graph provided?

   A) NO CHANGE
   B) once affected approximately 13,500 Americans each year.
   C) once affected 200,000 Americans every year.
   D) once affected more than 550,000 Americans every year.

The modern anti-vaccine movement stems, in large part, from a **(10)** paper which was deceitful and improperly vetted, by Andrew Wakefield in 1998. The paper claimed to have found that Measles-Mumps-Rubella (MMR) vaccines contributed to a spike in autism cases between 1988 and 1993. The media seized the story, inciting public fear of the MMR and of vaccines in general. In 2010, the paper was fully retracted after reviews by the CDC, the Institute of Medicine, the UK National Health Service, and others found absolutely no link between vaccines and autism, but by then, the damage had been done.

All efforts to negate the misconception about the link between vaccines and autism have proved ineffective. If public education is **(11)** deficient to address the growing problem of unvaccinated children, perhaps the only alternative is through public policy. In some states, opting out of vaccination requires little more than a onetime signature on a form. Tightening these policies may be considerably more helpful than trying to win the hearts and minds of skeptical parents.

9. Which of the following, if added to this paragraph, would add additional accurate data to the passage?

   A) Measles has been a greater threat than other diseases such as pertussis.
   B) This has not been the case for other diseases, such as rubella and hepatitis A.
   C) Vaccines have helped reduce measles as well as other diseases.
   D) Other diseases, such as hepatitis A and rubella, have seen similar declines thanks to vaccines.

10. A) NO CHANGE
    B) paper from 1998, written by Andrew Wakefield, who was deceitful and improperly vetted
    C) deceitful, improperly vetted paper written by Andrew Wakefield in 1998
    D) paper which was written by Andrew Wakefield, deceptive and improperly vetted, in 1998

11. Which of the following is the most precise replacement for the underlined word?

    A) NO CHANGE
    B) inefficient
    C) defiant
    D) insufficient

Evidence-Based Writing

Practice Passage 11

The Vietnam War: A Retrospective

Of all America's wars, the conflict in Vietnam (1) was perhaps the most controversial. Many protested America's involvement in Southeast Asia, questioning both motive and tactics. (2) Whether many dismissed the protestors in the early years of the war, their concerns seem quite prescient when viewed through the lens of retrospection. After all, the Vietnam War ultimately became one of America's deadliest wars (3). The impact of the Vietnam War was so great that, nearly half a century later, historians still debate whether American involvement in Vietnam was justified.

American involvement in Vietnam began with the assassination of South Vietnam's dictator (4) Ngo Dinh Diem in 1963. Anarchy swept the country, and John Kennedy's administration sent advisers in an attempt to restore order. North Vietnam, a Communist country under the leadership of dictator Ho Chi Minh, began training southern insurgents, infiltrating the South Vietnamese government, and (5) perpetuated propaganda against the U.S. The situation quickly escalated, and Kennedy's successor, Lyndon B. Johnson, reacted by scheduling bombings and committing troops to the conflict. In a speech to the American people, Johnson (6) declared that "around the globe, from Berlin to Thailand, are people whose well-being rests, in part, on the belief that they can count on us if they are attacked. To leave Vietnam to (7) its fate would shake the confidence of all these people in the value of America's commitment, the value of America's word."

1. A) NO CHANGE
   B) will have been
   C) were
   D) had been

2. A) NO CHANGE
   B) Also,
   C) In addition,
   D) Though

3. Which of the following, if added to the end of the sentence, would best support the sentence's main idea?

   A) , with American soldiers killing almost 1,100,000 North Vietnamese soldiers
   B) , much more deadly than the Korean War
   C) , third only to the American Civil War and World War II in casualties.
   D) , leaving many homeless and disabled veterans at the end of the war

4. A) NO CHANGE
   B) – Ngo Dinh Diem –
   C) (Ngo Dinh Diem)
   D) , Ngo Dinh Diem,

5. A) NO CHANGE
   B) had perpetuated propaganda
   C) perpetuating propaganda
   D) began perpetuating propaganda

6. Within the context of the passage, which of the following is the best replacement for the underlined word?

   A) NO CHANGE
   B) swore
   C) implied
   D) suggested

[1] Supporters of the Vietnam War argued that allowing South Vietnam to fall to communist forces would have led to a 'domino effect' in which more and more nations might fall under the yoke of communism. [2] After World War II, they argued, the United States was a moral force in the world, protecting countries that could not protect themselves against the larger menace of communism. [3] Johnson's speech says much to this regard. **{8}**

{9} Over 47,000 American soldiers died in the conflict, often as a result of being ill-trained to fight in the sweltering jungles of Vietnam against the guerilla tactics of the North Vietnamese. The financial costs were great, as well. **{10}** Had the United States stayed out of this conflict and allowed South Vietnam to surrender to the North Vietnamese, this could have been a minor passing incident in Southeast Asia's history. After all, once American troops withdrew from Vietnam in 1973, the North soon took over South Vietnam, rendering the conflict pointless. In the end, America can't act as the world's police – often it **(11)** <u>butts in</u> where it is not wanted, and besides, America has problems of its own to address before it starts sending young men five thousand miles away from home to die for an idea.

7. A) NO CHANGE
   B) it's
   C) their
   D) your

8. Which of the following sentences should be eliminated in order to improve the focus of the paragraph?

   A) Sentence 1
   B) Sentence 2
   C) Sentence 3
   D) NONE OF THE ABOVE

9. Which choice most effectively establishes the main topic of the paragraph?

   A) Was this a war that was worth fighting?
   B) Others argued that the war was not worth the effort and expense.
   C) The expense of the war, both financially and in terms of human life, proved that the conflict was not worth fighting.
   D) If you want to see whether the war was worth fighting, look at the expense.

10. Which of the following facts, if added, would best support the previous sentence?

   A) The war was enormously unpopular at home.
   B) The war cost approximately $111 billion, which by modern standards calculates to $700 billion.
   C) None of the soldiers knew what they were getting into.
   D) The war was continued by Richard Nixon.

11. A) NO CHANGE
   B) interferes
   C) goes places
   D) pries

Evidence-Based Writing

Practice Passage 12

The Paradoxes of Zeno of Elea

In the fifth century B.C.E., Zeno of Elea **(1)** had offered arguments that led to conclusions contradicting what we all know from our physical experience – that runners run, that arrows fly, and that there are many different things in the world. These arguments were paradoxes for the ancient Greek philosophers. Since most of the arguments turn crucially on the notion that space and time are infinitely divisible —for example, that for any distance there is such a thing as half that distance, and so on — Zeno was the first person in history to show that the concept of infinity is problematic.

{2} [1] In **(3)** his Achilles Paradox, Achilles races to catch a slower runner – for example, a tortoise that is crawling away from him. [2] Achilles was a mythical Greek hero who was one of the leaders of the Greek forces that invaded the city of Troy. [3] The tortoise has a head start, so if Achilles hopes to overtake it, he must run at least to the place where the tortoise presently is, but by the time he arrives there, it will have crawled to a new place, so then Achilles must run to this new place, but the tortoise meanwhile will have crawled on, and so forth. [4] Because of this, Achilles will never catch the tortoise, says Zeno. [5] Therefore, good reasoning shows that fast runners never can catch slow ones. [6] Zeno argued that this **(4)** invalidated the claim that motion really occurs. **{5}**

1. A) NO CHANGE
   B) has offered
   C) offered
   D) offers

2. Which choice most effectively establishes the main topic of the paragraph?

   A) According to Zeno, the Achilles Paradox proves that motion does not exist.
   B) Achilles will never catch the tortoise.
   C) Using good reasoning can lead to false conclusions.
   D) Achilles must run to at least to the place where the tortoise is before he can catch up to it.

3. A) NO CHANGE
   B) the
   C) Zenos'
   D) Zeno's

4. Which of the following is the most precise replacement for the underlined word?

   A) NO CHANGE
   B) disproved
   C) neutralized
   D) disqualified

5. Which of the following sentences should be eliminated in order to improve the focus of the passage?

   A) Sentence 1
   B) Sentence 2
   C) Sentence 3
   D) Sentence 4

Although no modern scholar would agree with Zeno's conclusion, one cannot escape the paradox by jumping up from **(6)** <u>your</u> seat and chasing down a tortoise, nor by saying Achilles should run to some other target place ahead of where the tortoise is at the moment. **{7}**

[1] Although many of Zeno's ideas may seem outlandish, he has had a marked influence on Western thinking. [2] Let's begin with his influence on the ancient Greeks. [3] Zeno also drew new attention to the idea that the way the world appears to us is not how it is in reality. [4] Before Zeno, philosophers expressed their philosophy in **(8)** <u>poetry, and</u> he was the first philosopher to use prose arguments. [5] This new method of presentation **(9)** <u>destined</u> to shape almost all later philosophy, mathematics, and science. [6] Awareness of Zeno's paradoxes made Western intellectuals more aware that **(10)** <u>illusions</u> can be made when thinking about infinity, continuity, and the structure of space and time, and it made them wary of any claim that a continuous magnitude could be made of discrete parts. **{11}**

6. A) NO CHANGE
   B) our
   C) its
   D) one's

7. Which of the following sentences would provide the best transition into the next paragraph?

   A) Logical paradoxes cannot be addressed so easily because they require irrefutable reasoning to be solved.
   B) Having suitably demonstrated the fallacies in the paradox, Zeno's influence in modernity has greatly diminished.
   C) In the same manner, one cannot deny that simply because his paradoxes have been solved does not mean that Zeno has lacked for influence.
   D) After all, a paradox is by definition unsolvable.

8. A) NO CHANGE
   B) poetry; and
   C) poetry,
   D) poetry and

9. A) NO CHANGE
   B) has been destined
   C) had been destined
   D) was destined

10. Which of the following is the most precise replacement for the underlined word?

    A) NO CHANGE
    B) delusions
    C) corrections
    D) mistakes

11. For the sake of the coherence of this paragraph, sentence 3 should be placed

A) where it is now.
B) before sentence 2.
C) after sentence 5.
D) after sentence 6.

Evidence-Based Writing

Practice Passage 13

The Year of the Barricades

The uprising of May 1968 in France resulted from years of social upheaval throughout the late **(1)** <u>1960s; what began as a student protest, but</u> ballooned into a general strike involving two-thirds of the French work force. Talk of revolution filled the air. But even at the time, what sort of revolution this might be was elusive to its participants **(2)** <u>equally to</u> the rest of the world.

For months prior, conflict had been brewing between students and administrators at the Sorbonne, Paris's premier university. **(3)** <u>Echoing similar protests in America at such colleges as the University of California</u>, the French students wanted a greater say in the administration of the university, and an end to what they perceived as an authoritarian teaching model that did not encourage intellectual inquiry. In response to protests, the Sorbonne shut its doors on May 2nd. Angry students took to the streets.

[1] By May 10th, the police, against an estimation of 20,000 student demonstrators, took to the streets to restore order. [2] **(4)** <u>They responded aggressively with</u> tear gas and beatings. [3] Soon a huge cross-section of French society poured into the streets in solidarity with the students and in outrage at the brutality. [4] For Communists and anarchists, the strike's endgame was **(5)** <u>revolution</u>; whereas for the more moderate Socialist party, new elections and the resignation of President Charles de Gaulle was the goal. [5] By the 17th of May, a general strike involving millions of workers had paralyzed the country. **{6}**

1. A) NO CHANGE
   B) 1960s that had begun as a student protest, while it
   C) 1960s, for it began as a student protest, but
   D) 1960s. What began as a student protest

2. A) NO CHANGE
   B) as equally as to
   C) the same as
   D) every bit as much as to

3. Which choice for the underlined portion would provide the least relevant, informative detail in the context of the paragraph as a whole?

   A) NO CHANGE
   B) Frustrated by an outdated curriculum and rigid classroom expectations
   C) In a year of widespread unrest over such global events as the Vietnam War
   D) Disdainful of institutional authority and espousing a commitment to democracy

4. A) NO CHANGE
   B) The police responded aggressively to the protests with
   C) Their aggressive response led to
   D) It responded aggressively with

5. A) NO CHANGE
   B) revolution
   C) revolution, whereas
   D) revolution:

(7) In the end, de Gaulle turned the tables. In a May 30th address to the nation, de Gaulle suggested that the military would be sent in to forcibly end the protests and orchestrated a large counter-demonstration in support of his presidency, while also scheduling new elections. Despite de Gaulle's unpopularity, his gambit proved successful: France was even less inclined to unite behind any of the fragmented leftist **(8)** movements, that sought to claim ownership of the uprising, and de Gaulle's conservative nationalist party won a stunning victory.

The remarkable thing about the May 1968 movement is that it almost wholly lacked leaders or a coherent agenda. The **(9)** basic idea of the protests was anti-capitalist but hardly pro-communist. The movement sought a broad decentralization of economic and political power. **(10)** To this end, committees had seemed to emerge spontaneously to discuss how to restructure not just higher education but the news media, the film industry, the industrial workplace, and ultimately, French society itself.

6. Sentence 5 of this paragraph would most logically be placed

   A) where it is now.
   B) after Sentence 1.
   C) after Sentence 2.
   D) after Sentence 3.

7. Which choice for the underlined portion would provide the most logical and appropriate sentence to introduce this paragraph?

   A) NO CHANGE
   B) President de Gaulle was opposed to the protests.
   C) The protest movement's agenda was unclear.
   D) President de Gaulle prepared a speech to give to the people of France.

8. A) NO CHANGE
   B) movements, sought to claim ownership of the uprising
   C) movements, sought to claim ownership of the uprising,
   D) movements that sought to claim ownership of the uprising,

9. Which choice for the underlined portion is clear and consistent with the style and tone of the passage?

   A) NO CHANGE
   B) general vibe to
   C) prevailing sentiment of
   D) predominant philosophical and ideological persuasion of participants in

One of the slogans of May 1968 was "Be realistic: Demand the impossible!" This was the most dramatic expression of the utopian spirit of the 1960s counterculture—the belief that the world could, in fact, be changed; that something altogether new might happen. **(11)** In the end, May 1968 may also have been the moment at which it became clear that the world ultimately would not change very much at all.

10. A) NO CHANGE
    B) To this end, committees seemed to emerge
    C) To this end, committees emerging
    D) Toward the end, committees had seemed to emerge

11. Which of the following alternatives for the underlined portion would NOT be acceptable?

    A) NO CHANGE
    B) Given its failure
    C) Looking back
    D) In addition

Evidence-Based Writing

Practice Passage 14

Spinal Cord Injury

Until World War II broke out, a serious spinal cord injury (SCI) (1) usually meaning certain death. Anyone who survived such injury relied on a wheelchair for mobility in a world with few accommodations and faced an ongoing struggle to survive (2) the many various other secondary complications such as breathing problems, blood clots, kidney failure, and pressure sores. By the middle of the twentieth century, new antibiotics and novel approaches to preventing and treating bed sores and urinary tract infections (3) had revolutionized care after spinal cord injury. This greatly expanded life expectancy and required new strategies to maintain the health of people living with chronic paralysis. Now there are more than a quarter of a million Americans currently living with spinal cord injury of some kind. Though most are caused by vehicular accidents, (4) fewer people are injured in sports or violence related incidents than most would expect. [5]

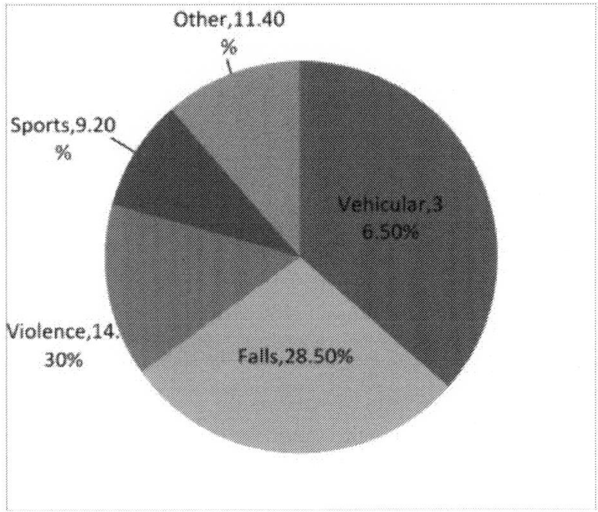

1. A) NO CHANGE
   B) usually meant
   C) usually means
   D) could mean

2. Which of the following changes would create the most concise version of this sentence?

   A) NO CHANGE
   B) the many other
   C) the various other
   D) Remove this phrase from the paragraph

3. A) NO CHANGE
   B) have revolutionized
   C) revolutionizing
   D) revolutionize

4. A) NO CHANGE
   B) fewer persons suffer in sports and violence related incidents
   C) less people are injured in sports or violence related incidents
   D) fewer injuries are caused by sports or violence related incidents

5. Based on the graph what fact should be added into the above paragraph?

   A) "Other" causes of spinal cord injury occur more often than sports-related causes.
   B) The second most common cause of spinal cord injury is falling, not sports or violence.
   C) Sports-caused injuries happen fewer times than violence related injuries.
   D) The most common cause of spinal cord injury is vehicular accidents.

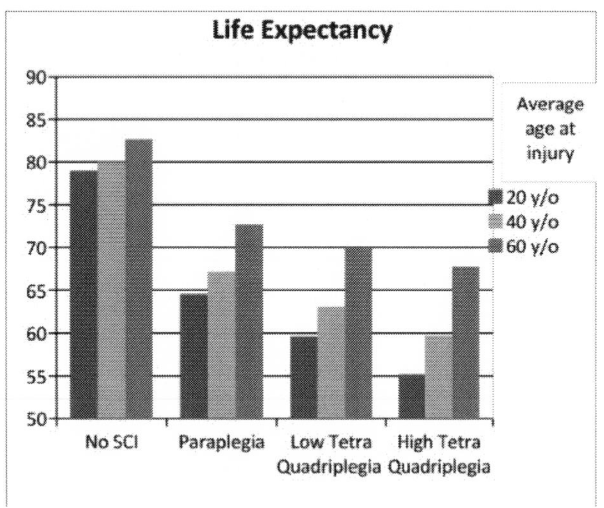

Note: In the figure above, there were 100 people surveyed in each age group

Today, (6) improved emergency care by people with spinal cord injuries, antibiotics to treat infections, and aggressive rehabilitation can minimize damage to the nervous system and restore function to varying degrees. Thanks to these modern innovations, (7) patients with paralysis regularly live pretty long; some of these patients are still able to find employment after their injuries [8]. Current advances in spinal cord injury research (9) is giving doctors and people living with SCI (10) hope that these injuries will eventually be repairable. With new surgical techniques and developments in spinal nerve regeneration in mind, (11) the future for spinal cord injury survivors looks brighter than ever.

6. A) NO CHANGE
   B) improved emergency care for people with spinal cord injuries
   C) improved emergency care with people with spinal cord injuries
   D) improved emergency care from people with spinal cord injuries

7. Using the above graph, what is the best way to improve this sentence?

   A) patients with paraplegia regularly live longer than patients with quadriplegia
   B) patients with quadriplegia regularly live to at least 55
   C) patients with paraplegia and quadriplegia regularly live an average of 30 more years after injury
   D) patients without spinal cord injury regularly live over 75

8. Given the context of the passage, which of the following facts would best support the claim made in this sentence?

   A) More than half of the patients with SCI were employed at the time of their injury.
   B) 80% of all SCI patients are men.
   C) 34.9% of patients eventually find employment
   D) 87.1% of patients discharged from the hospital go back to regular life.

9. A) NO CHANGE
   B) is given
   C) has given
   D) are giving

10. A) NO CHANGE
    B) hopes
    C) are hoping
    D) hoping

11. A) NO CHANGE
    B) the future for spinal cord injury survivors looks bright.
    C) spinal cord injury survivors have a brighter future to look forward to than ever.
    D) spinal cord injury survivors have a brighter future than ever.

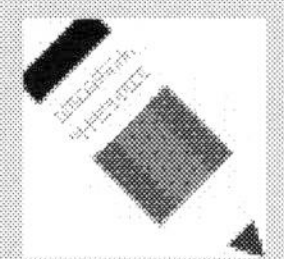

Evidence-Based Writing

Practice Passage 15

The Rise and Fall of the Red Delicious

The archetypal apple is glossy, red, and beautiful. It is a feast for the eyes. Yet all throughout the nation, the Red Delicious is ignored at the bottom of lunch bags, left untouched on hospital trays, forlorn in the fruit bowl at hotel breakfast buffets, and the lone **(1)** legacy of a holiday gift basket. This is the paradox of the Red Delicious: alluring, yet **(2)** undesirable, the most produced and arguably the least popular apple in the United States.

The story of this unlikeable apple began in the 1870s, when Iowan farmer Jesse Hiatt discovered a mutant seedling among his Yellow Bellflower trees. He chopped it down twice, but it grew back each time. "If thee must grow," he told the intrepid sprout, "thee may." Ten years later, the tree bore apples with red-and-gold striped **(3)** skin, crisp flesh, and an enjoyable flavor that quickly drew attention.

In 1893, Stark Brothers' Nursery of Missouri secured the rights to Hiatt's apple, later named the Red Delicious. The nursery embarked on an aggressive marketing campaign over the next two decades: traveling salesmen were dispatched to farms across the country, and the apple was exhibited at the 1904 World's Fair. The Red Delicious was soon a favorite from coast to coast; but as its commercial success grew, so did its distance from the original Hiatt fruit.

{4} [1] In 1923, a New Jersey orchardist reported that a single limb of a tree from the Stark nursery was producing prematurely crimson apples with a deep, **(5)** uniform color. [2] Growers sought to turn this random genetic mutation into profit. [3] Apples that reddened before fully ripening could be picked earlier and stored longer, and skins with more red pigment tended to be thicker, which extended shelf life and hid bruises. [4] Unfortunately, selective breeding that

1. A) NO CHANGE
   B) remnant
   C) vestige
   D) aftermath

2. A) NO CHANGE
   B) undesirable, they are both
   C) undesirable, existing as both
   D) undesirable, it is both the

3. A) NO CHANGE
   B) skin and crisp flesh to help enjoy the flavor
   C) skin, crisp flesh, and a flavor able to be enjoyed by all
   D) skin and crisp flesh, an enjoyable flavor

4. Which choice most effectively establishes the main topic of the paragraph?

   A) Apple growers hailed the prematurely red apples, but shoppers were suspicious.
   B) For thousands of years, selective breeding techniques have allowed people to manipulate crops.
   C) Scientific advances now ensure that apples are crisp and fresh upon arrival to supermarkets.
   D) A genetic anomaly would soon enhance the fruit's looks but harm its flavor.

5. A) NO CHANGE
   B) stable
   C) orderly
   D) rigid

favored looks over taste eventually resulted in apples with tough, bitter skins and mushy, sugar-soaked flesh. [5] Customers clamored for a taste of the beauties. [6] By the 1940s, the Red Delicious had become the country's most popular apple. [7] Shoppers ended up routinely throwing purchases of Red Delicious into the trash. **{6}**

Then in the 1990s, new and tastier apple varieties—including the Gala and the Fuji— **(7)** <u>begun</u> to edge into the market. Shoppers had their taste buds awakened, and since then, Red Delicious production has declined by 40 percent. The Washington Apple Commission— **(8)** <u>which growers produce</u> the majority of apples in the United States—recently recommended that up to two-thirds of the state's Red Delicious yield this year be **(9)** <u>exported; a larger</u> portion than **(10)** <u>ever before in history</u>. The international success of the Red Delicious may depend on targeting places where the fruit is unfamiliar. Meanwhile, in the United States, consumers are slowly returning to apples they can believe in. **{11}**

6. For the sake of cohesion of this paragraph, Sentence 4 should be placed

   A) where it is now.
   B) before Sentence 3.
   C) after Sentence 3.
   D) after Sentence 6.

7. A) NO CHANGE
   B) had began
   C) began
   D) was beginning

8. A) NO CHANGE
   B) has growers producing
   C) whose growers produce
   D) with growers which produce

9. A) NO CHANGE
   B) exported with a larger
   C) exported, a larger
   D) exported as part of a larger

10. A) NO CHANGE
    B) had been exported ever
    C) earlier on
    D) ever before

11. Which of the following facts would best support the ideas presented in this paragraph?

    A) Between 1997 and 2000, growers lost close to $800 million due to unsold Red Delicious apples.
    B) American growers originally developed the Gala and the Fuji for overseas markets.
    C) China has increased its production to become the world's top producer of apples.
    D) In some communities, the Red Delicious has maintained its popularity because the color red stands for good luck.

Math

Math Introduction

What Does the Math Section Look Like?

The math portion of the test consists of two different sections. One section allows the use of a calculator, and the other section does not. The first section is shorter and will be the one where the use of a calculator is not permitted. Both sections will include multiple choice and grid-in type questions.

The overall math section is scored on a scale from 200-800. However, questions in the math section contribute to the cross-test subscores for Analysis in Science and Social Studies. In addition to contributing to the cross-test subscores, there are 3 subscores specifically for the math section. These are Heart of Algebra, Problem Solving and Data Analysis, and Passport to Advanced Math. Each of these subscores is evaluated on a scale from 1 to 15.

Math By the Numbers:

- Non-Calculator Section
    - 25 minutes
    - 20 total questions
    - 15 multiple choice
    - 5 grid-in questions
- Calculator Section:
    - 55 minutes
    - 38 total questions
    - 30 multiple choice questions
    - 8 grid-in questions
- 9 Heart of Algebra questions
- 17 Problem Solving and Data Analysis Questions
- 16 Passport to Advanced Math Questions
- 6 Additional Topics in Math Questions.

How should you approach the math section?
Time is critical. On the math non-calculator, especially, approximate and cross out wrong answers. Since all questions are worth one point, make sure that you get all the easy and hard questions correct. If you are on a hard multiple choice question, you may want to skip it to get to an easy grid-in question.

Plug In. The first strategy is to work backwards or plug in answer choices. We know that one of the answers has to be correct. If you don't know what to do with an equation, try "Plugging In." Plug the numbers from each of the answer choices into the problem and see which one makes sense. Sometimes this strategy can be faster than trying to solve a long or confusing equation.

Note: When you see the words "of the following" then it is a process of elimination question and you need to work backwards by plugging in the answer choices. Most people would naturally start with answer choice A and work their way down. This is a waste of time because on the problems where you need to plug in, the test makers will often make the correct answer choice C, or D. When you have to plug in answers, start with answer D and work your way up. This will save you time.*

Pick Numbers. Some problems will be much easier if you choose your own numbers. By picking numbers for the variable, you are often able to solve the problem much more quickly and easily. About 20% of the math questions can be solved by choosing numbers. Remember to pick numbers that make sense in the context of the question. For instance, if the problem says "x is a non-zero integer" don't choose zero for x. Make smart choices when picking your numbers - choose easy numbers! Most of the time the easiest numbers to work with are small numbers like 1 and 2, but when working with questions about time try choosing 60, and when working with percent questions try choosing 100, etc.

Multiple percent change questions are one of the types of problems that can often be solved by choosing numbers. Don't add percentages together in these kinds of problems! This will give you the wrong answer - and it'll probably be one of the answer choices. You have to do these problems one step at a time. Let's look at an example.

A radio announcer says "30% off everything in the store, and this weekend only, take an additional 20% off items as marked." What is the total percentage discount?

Most people would try to shortcut this problem by thinking "30% plus 20% off? That's a 50% discount!" Don't make this mistake! Solve the problem one step at a time. If you are not given the original cost of the merchandise and the question asks you to calculate the total percentage of the multiple discounts, choose a starting price. The easiest starting price to choose when working with percentages is $100.

Helpful Tips:

- **Dive Right In.** On many problems, you might look at the problem and tell yourself that you can't solve it. However, there may be steps that you know you need to take. If that is the case, just look at all the information that is given to you, and start taking small steps with that information. Sometimes, the complete path to solving a problem doesn't become evident until after you have started working on the problem.
- **Use Your Calculator** (at least on the calculator section!) Remember, you are allowed to use a calculator on some parts of the SAT. All the problems are designed so that a calculator is not necessary to solve them, but it may be helpful in finding common denominators, dividing fractions into decimals and translating percents to use one. Don't overuse your calculator though, it can't do the test for you. Use the calculator to make long computations or conversions faster and more accurate, that way you can focus on the process of solving the problems. It's good to practice without your calculator, especially since you know there will be a section where you can't use it.
- **Use the shape.** If a picture says "Not Drawn to Scale," then you can't tell anything from how it is drawn. However, if it doesn't say, "Not Drawn to Scale" then you can assume that it is drawn to scale, and you can use the shape to guesstimate lengths and angle measures.

Pre–Algebra Review

Concept & Strategy Lesson

The following reminders, tips, and tricks review many of the topics covered in Pre–Algebra. Carefully read each topic and then try the problems on the next pages for extra practice.

Operations on Integers

- Change subtraction signs to addition signs and change the sign of the second number
- Multiplying or dividing two numbers with the same signs: ________________
- Multiplying or dividing two numbers with different signs: ________________

Fractions

- To add/subtract fractions: ________________
- To multiply fractions: ________________________
- To divide by fractions: ________________________

Decimals

- Decimal to percentage: ______________________________
- Percentage to a decimal: _____________________________
- Fraction to decimal: __________________________________
- Decimal to fraction: ___________________________________

Percentages

- Per cent: out of 100
- To calculate: $\frac{\text{part}}{\text{whole}} \times 100 = \%$
- Percent change: $\frac{\text{part}}{\text{whole}} \times 100 = \%$

Exponents and Radicals

- $g^5 = g \times g \times g \times g \times g$.
- $a^2 \times a^3 = a^5$.
- $\frac{b^8}{b^6} = b^2$
- $(c^5)^7 = c^{35}$.
- $x^1 = x$
- $x^0 = 1$
- $d^{-1} = \frac{1}{d}$
- $\sqrt[5]{x^3} = x^{\left(\frac{3}{5}\right)}$
- $j^m k^m = (jk)^m$

Order of Operations

PEMDAS

Absolute Value

Distance to zero on a number line

Treat absolute value bars as parentheses for the purpose of PEMDAS

After performing all of the operations inside the absolute value bars, change the final answer to a positive number. $|5-8|=|-3|=3$

Coordinate Geometry

Midpoint formula: $\left(\frac{x_1+x_2}{2}, \frac{y_1+y_2}{2}\right)$.

Distance formula: $d = \sqrt{(x_2 - x_1)^2 + (y_2 - y_1)^2}$

Slope formula: Rise/Run = (y2-y1)/(x2-x1)

Pre-Algebra Review Practice Problems

1. The temperature in Lincoln, Nebraska, is currently –19°F. If the temperature decreas-es by another 8°F tonight, what will be the temperature be tomorrow?

   A) –27°F
   B) –11 °F
   C) 11°F
   D) 27°F

2. A grocery store takes a loss of 25 cents every time it sells a gallon of milk. If the grocery store currently is projected to make$1054.50 before accounting for milk sales, what will its profit be after selling 340 gal-lons of milk?

   A) –$969.50
   B) –$85.00
   C) $969.50
   D) $1139.50

3. Which of the following numbers is closest to 16/25?

   A) 0.60
   B) 0.65
   C) 0.70
   D) 0.75

4. Before driving to work, Marcel completely filled his 20–gallon fuel tank. On his way to work, Marcel used 1/4 of his gasoline. On his way home, Marcel used 1/3 of the remainder of his fuel, then used 2 gallons of gasoline to go to his friend's place and back home. How many gallons of gasoline will Marcel need to buy to re–fuel his tank after returning home?

   A) 7
   B) 8
   C) 10
   D) 12

5. Which of the following numbers is not equal to the other three?

   A) 0.03
   B) 3/100
   C) 0.03%
   D) 3%

6. After a chemical reaction, the amount of sulfur dioxide in a beaker decreased from 24.6 mg to 12.3 mg. What was the percent decrease in mass of sulfur dioxide in the beaker?

   A) 50%
   B) 100%
   C) 150%
   D) 200%

7. Jonathan wants to leave a 20% tip on the post–tax price of his family's meal. If the meal cost him \$80.00 and the sales tax is 8%, how much did Jonathan pay for the meal in all?

   A) \$69.12
   B) \$88.32
   C) \$102.40
   D) \$103.68

8. A jacket in a retail clothing store is on sale for 30% off. Because of a coupon, an additional 10% is taken off the sales price of the jacket at the register. If the jacket normally costs \$*j*, what is the price of the jacket, in dollars, after both the sale and the coupon are taken into account?

   A) $0.4j$
   B) $0.6j$
   C) $0.63j$
   D) $0.67j$

9. 36.4% of 12.8 is equivalent to 1.28% of

   A) 0.364
   B) 3.64
   C) 36.4
   D) 364

10. The price of a house increases from \$125,000 to \$150,000. By what percentage did the price of the house increase?

   A) $16\frac{2}{3}$%
   B) 20%
   C) 25%
   D) $83\frac{1}{3}$%

Linear Equations and Inequalities

Concept & Strategy Lesson

Linear equation problems may ask you to solve for a variable or deal with a straight line.

Solving Linear Equations

- To find the value of the variable, isolate it
- Simplify both sides of the equation – distribute, eliminate fractions, combine like terms
- Golden rule of algebra: what you do to one side of the equation, do to the other.

Solving Linear Inequalities

- Linear inequalities can be solved just like linear equations.
- Whenever you multiply or divide both sides of the inequality by a negative number, you MUST flip the inequality sign (so $<$ becomes $>$, or $\geq$ becomes $\leq$).

Example 1:

$$\frac{3(y-2)+7}{5}=\frac{2-(2-y)}{7}$$

In the equation above, what is the value of y?

A) $-\frac{35}{26}$

B) $-\frac{7}{16}$

C) $\frac{3}{20}$

D) $\frac{7}{16}$

Creating and Interpreting Equations and Inequalities

- Linear equations will show up in many word problems
- The SAT will usually tell you which quantity you are solving for and assign it a variable – if they don't, then you should.
- Occasionally, the SAT will ask you to interpret the meaning of part of an equation. The best way to handle these types of questions is to test numbers.
- One of the first steps to solving a word problem is to translate the words into equations.

Steps for Solving a Word Problem

1. Read the problem carefully, and make sure that you know what you are being asked.
2. Break the problem into parts.
3. Translate each of the parts into equations.
4. Use the equations to solve the problem.
5. Double check that you answered the question that was being asked.

Algebraic Term	Key Words
$+$	more than, increased by, greater than, additional, exceeds, sum
$-$	less than, decreased by, fewer than, difference
$\times$	of, each, product
$\div$	per, ratio of, for every
$=$	is, equals, is equivalent to
$<$	less than, fewer than
$>$	more than, greater than
$\leq$	at most, no more than, no greater than
$\geq$	at least, no less than, no fewer than

Example 2:

A sheep farmer needs to make at least \$115,000 per year to remain profitable. Currently, each of his 2,500 sheep produces enough wool to make him \$40 per year. Which of the following inequalities can be solved to find the number of sheep, *s*, that the sheep farmer needs to acquire to make his farm profitable?

A) $40(2500-s)\geq 115000$
B) $40(2500+s)\geq 115000$
C) $40(2500-s)\leq 115000$
D) $40(2500+s)\leq 115000$

Linear Equations and Inequalities Practice Problems

$$\frac{3(2-y)+3}{5} = \frac{2(y-3)+2}{3}$$

1. In the equation above, what is the value of y?

A) $\frac{32}{19}$
B) $\frac{23}{11}$
C) $\frac{47}{19}$
D) $\frac{47}{13}$

$$\frac{1}{2}(5x-2) = \frac{1}{4}(10x-15)$$

2. In the equation above, what is the value of x?

A) $-\frac{11}{20}$
B) 0
C) All real numbers.
D) No real solution exists.

$$0.85(a-3) - 0.75 = 3.25a$$

3. In the equation above, what is the value of a?

A) −1.5625
B) −1.375
C) −0.9375
D) 0.9375

$$s = 117 + 2t$$

4. The equation above is used to model the relationship between the number of surfboards, s, rented per day at a beach and the average daily temperature, t, in degrees Fahrenheit. According to the model, what is the meaning of the 2 in the equation?

A) For every increase of 1°F, two more surfboards will be rented.
B) For every decrease of 1°F, two more surfboards will be rented.
C) For every increase of 2°F, one more surfboard will be rented.
D) For every decrease of 2°F, one more surfboard will be rented.

$$5m-8(-7m-1)=8$$

5. In the equation above, what is the value of m?

6. If $3t - 1 > \frac{16}{7}$, then

A) $t > \frac{3}{7}$
B) $t > \frac{5}{7}$
C) $t > \frac{17}{21}$
D) $t > \frac{23}{21}$

$$\frac{3}{4}u - \frac{1}{2} \geq \frac{1}{3}u$$

7. In the inequality above, which of the following is a possible value of u?

A) $\frac{1}{2}$
B) 1
C) $\frac{11}{10}$
D) $\frac{3}{2}$

8. If $-5x + 15 \leq -3x - 5$, then

A) $x \geq -10$
B) $x \leq -10$
C) $x \geq 10$
D) $x \leq 10$

9. If $-3 < 4h + 5 \leq -1$, which of the following is NOT a possible value of h?

A) -2.0
B) -1.9
C) -1.7
D) -1.5

10. If $j \geq 3$ and $k \leq -4$, which of the following is a possible value of jk?

A) -10.5
B) -11.0
C) -11.5
D) -12.0

$-5x + 15 \leq -3x - 5$

Solving Systems of Linear Equations and Inequalities

Concept & Strategy Lesson

- There are three common ways to solve a system of equations: Substitution, Elimination, and Graphing.
- Substitution requires you to solve one of the two equations for a variable, then to plug that variable's value into the second equation.

$$\begin{matrix}(1)3x - y = 2 \\ (2)y - x = 12\end{matrix} \rightarrow \begin{matrix}(1)3x - y = 2 \\ (2)y = x + 12\end{matrix} \rightarrow \textit{Substitute } (2) \textit{ into } (1)\text{: } 3x - (x + 12) = 2$$

$$\textit{Solve for } x\text{: } 2x - 12 = 2 \rightarrow x = 7$$
$$\textit{Solve for } y\text{: } y - (7) = 12 \rightarrow y = 19$$

Solution: (7, 19)

- Elimination requires you to multiply one of the two equations by a constant (if necessary), then to add the two equations together to eliminate a variable. Elimination is the fastest method when variables are easily eliminated.

$$\begin{matrix}(1)3x - y = 2 \\ (2)y - x = 12\end{matrix} \rightarrow \textit{Add the equations: } 3x - x = 14$$

$$\textit{Solve for } x\text{: } 2x = 14 \rightarrow x = 7$$
$$\textit{Solve for } y\text{: } 3(7) - y = 2 \rightarrow y = 19$$

Solution: (7, 19)

- Graphing requires you to graph each of the two equations then find the point of intersection of the two lines. Graphing is the most time consuming of the three methods, especially if you do not get to use a calculator, and you should avoid using it if at all possible.

- Sometimes, two equations never intersect. In this situation, the system has no solution. These systems of equations occur when the two lines are parallel

- Sometimes, two equations graph the same line. In this situation, the system has an infinite number of solutions. You should be able to manipulate the two equations so that all the coefficients and constants match

Example 1:

$$\frac{3}{5}x - uy = 12$$
$$6x - 120 = 10y$$

In the system of linear equations above, u is a constant. If the system has an infinite number of real solutions, what is the value of u?

A) –10
B) –1
C) 1
D) 10

Example 2:

A parking lot can admit no more than 300 vehicles each day. The parking lot charges $3.50 for each car it admits and $1.50 for each motorcycle it admits. If the parking lot needs to make at least $900 today, which of the following systems of inequalities can be used to yield the number of cars, *c*, and motorcycles, *m*, that can be let in today?

A) $c + m \geq 300$
$3.50c + 1.50m \geq 900$

B) $c + m \leq 300$.
$3.50c + 1.50m \geq 900$

C) $c + m \geq 900$
$3.50c + 1.50m \leq 300$

D) $c + m \leq 900$
$3.50c + 1.50m \leq 300$

Systems of Linear Equations and Inequalities Practice Problems

$$x - y = 19$$
$$x - 3y = 12y + 5$$

1. Based on the system of equations above, what is the value of the quotient $\frac{x}{y}$?

   A) -20
   B) $-\frac{1}{20}$
   C) $\frac{1}{20}$
   D) 20

$$3x - 6y = -12$$
$$28 - 3y = qx$$

2. In the system of equations above, q is a constant. If the system has no real solutions, what is the value of q?

   A) $-\frac{7}{3}$
   B) $-\frac{3}{2}$
   C) $\frac{3}{2}$
   D) $\frac{7}{3}$

$$b > 2a - 4$$
$$a = 3a - 12$$

3. Based on the equation and inequality above, what is a possible value of b?

   A) 6
   B) 7
   C) 8
   D) 9

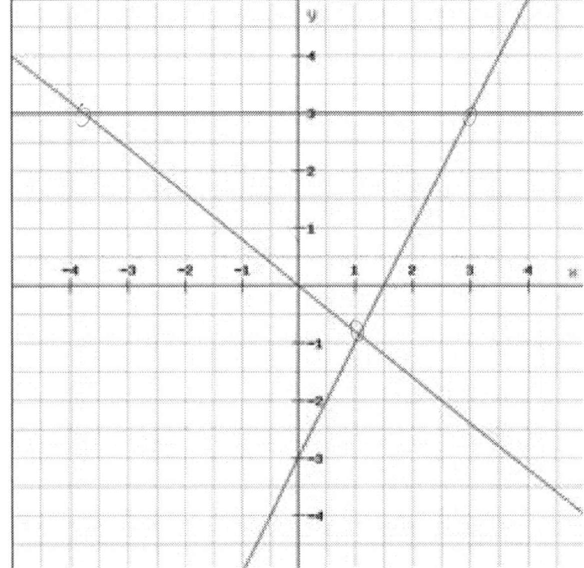

4. A system of three equations and their graphs in the xy–plane are shown above. How many solutions does the system have?

   A) 0
   B) 1
   C) 2
   D) 3

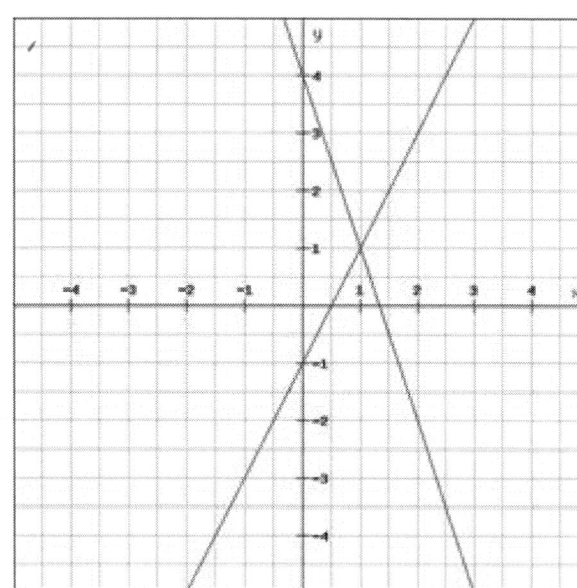

5. Which of the following points is a solution to the system of equations shown above?

A) $(-1, -1)$
B) $(-1, 1)$
C) $(1, -1)$
D) $(1, 1)$

6. A company sells two different types of math textbooks. The cost, C, of producing n copies of its Algebra book is $C = 12n + 3500$, while the cost of producing n copies of its Chemistry book is $C = 10n + 4000$. If the company wants to split costs evenly between the two books, how many copies of each book should it produce?

A) 125
B) 250
C) 375
D) 500

7. A local aquarium has two enclosures of otters. One enclosure has 36 members. Every year, one of the members dies, while two are born. The other enclosure has 24 members. Every year, two of the members die, while four are born. After how many years will the two enclosures have the same number of otters?

A) 6
B) 12
C) 18
D) 48

$$3x - y = 2y - 9$$
$$y - 3 = 2x - 7$$

8. Based on the system of equations above, what is the value of the sum of x and y?

A) -3
B) 7
C) 10
D) 17

9. If $\frac{1}{2}x + \frac{1}{2}y = 12$ and $2x + 2y = 48$, then $x + y =$

A) 6
B) 24
C) 36
D) It is impossible to determine.

Question 10 refers to the following information.

The toll rates for a new highway are \$2.50 for a truck and 75 cents for a car. During a three–hour period, a total of 212 trucks and cars crossed the tollbooth, and the total amount of money collected in tolls was \$334.

10. Solving which of the following systems of equations yields the number of cars, c, and the number of trucks, t, that crossed the bridge during the three hours?

A) $c + t = 334$
$2.5t + 0.75c = 212$

B) $c + t = 212$
$2.5t + 75c = 334$

C) $c + t = 212$
$2.5t + 0.75c = 334 \times 2$

D) $c + t = 212$
$2.5t + 0.75c = 334$

Ratios and Percentages

Concept & Strategy Lesson

Solving Ratios, Proportions, Rates, and Scale Drawing Problems

- A ratio is a relationship between two or more values and can generally be written as a fraction:

$$3 \text{ boys for every } 5 \text{ girls} = 3 \text{ boys:}5 \text{ girls} = \frac{3 \text{ boys}}{5 \text{ girls}}$$

- There are several ways to solve a ratio word problem.
-
- Proportions occur when ratios are set equal. They can be solved by cross multiplying:

$$\frac{3}{5} = \frac{2}{x} \rightarrow$$

- There are three typical types of proportion problems: Rate, Recipe, Scale

- The most basic rate questions involve the equation below:

$$\text{distance} = \text{rate} \times \text{time}$$

- Rates are used to show a "distance" that happens over a period of time. One example is miles per hour. However, the "distance" does not have to be a physical distance. A pay rate, such as dollars per hour, is another common rate.

Example 1:

While Aqucer is working his paper route, he can deliver 48 newspapers per half hour. As he delivers papers, he travels at a rate of 3 miles per hour. If Aqucer starts his day with 720 newspapers, how many miles will he travel to deliver all of them?

A) 22.5
B) 25
C) 45
D) 50

Solving Percentage Problems

- The most common types of percentage problems will be word problems.
- *Tax* and *Tip* are percentages added to the cost of a purchase
- *Commission* is a percentage used in calculating how much money certain salespeople make
- Some problems will ask you to add a percent while some ask you to subtract – there are some significant differences

Example 2:

Cameron is going to a go–kart track that charges \$1.25 per lap plus tax to drive the go–kart. The state's sales tax is 10%, and an additional fee of \$6.95 is charged by the track for insurance before tax is applied. Which of the following represents the total charge, in dollars, if Cameron takes c laps around the track?

A) $(1.25 + 0.10c) + 6.95$
B) $1.10(1.25c + 6.95)$
C) $1.10(1.25c) + 6.95$
D) $1.10(6.95 + 1.25)c$

Ratios and Percentages Practice Problems

1. In 1998, the price of a two–bedroom condominium in Charlotte, North Carolina, was $125,000. In 2008, the price of the condominium was $150,000. In 2013, the price of the condominium decreased by the same percentage that it increased between 1998 and 2008. What was the price of the condominium in 2013?

   A) $120,000
   B) $125,000
   C) $140,000
   D) $180,000

2. In a molecule of sucrose, the atoms carbon, hydrogen, and oxygen appear in the ratio of 12:22:11, respectively, and no other atoms are present. If a lab technician prepares an amount of sucrose that contains 3,600 total atoms, how many hydrogen atoms does it contain?

   A) 880
   B) 960
   C) 1,760
   D) 1,840

3. At Central High School, there are currently 23 teachers and 414 students. The school's principal knows that 180 new students will be added next semester because of a merger with another school and that no students are currently expected to leave the school. How many teachers should the principal hire to keep the student to teacher ratio consistent?

   A) 5
   B) 10
   C) 18
   D) 23

Questions 4 and 5 refer to the following information.

A 10,000 gallon swimming pool is currently one–fourth full. Two hosepipes are being used to fill it: one hosepipe fills the pool at a rate of 6 gallons per minute, while the other fills the pool at a rate of 4 gallons per minute.

4. How long will it take to fill the pool completely?

   A) 4 hours and 10 minutes
   B) 8 hours and 20 minutes
   C) 12 hours and 30 minutes
   D) 16 hours and 40 minutes

5. After some time, the pool develops a leak that causes water to pour out of the pool at a rate of 1 gallon per minute. Approximately how long will it take to fill the pool completely if it currently is half full?

A) 6 hours and 15 minutes
B) 7 hours and 30 minutes
C) 9 hours and 15 minutes
D) 11 hours

6. A map of a subway system is set up so that every mile of the subway's route is equivalent to 8 inches on the map. Which of the following equations could be used to find the length of a route in miles, x, that is 15 inches long on the map?

A) $\frac{1}{8} = \frac{15}{x}$
B) $\frac{8}{1} = \frac{x}{15}$
C) $8 = 15x$
D) $\frac{1}{8} = \frac{x}{15}$

7. A 30–ounce solution of water and vinegar is currently 10% vinegar. How many ounces of vinegar need to be added to the solution so that is becomes 20% vinegar?

A) 3
B) 3.25
C) 3.5
D) 3.75

8. Two students, Jon and Rob, are working together to finish a science project. If Jon can finish the project alone in j hours and Rob can finish the project alone in r hours, how long will it take them to finish the project working together, in terms of r and j?

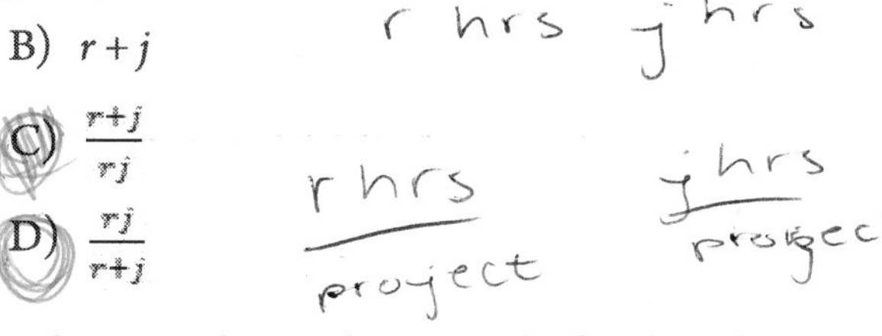

A) $\frac{1}{r+j}$
B) $r+j$
C) $\frac{r+j}{rj}$
D) $\frac{rj}{r+j}$

9. A furniture factory has recently developed a process that lets the factory improve the rate at which it can produce couches. Previously, the factory could produce 300 couches per hour; however, the new process improves that rate by 12%. How many more couches can the factory produce in a 12–hour shift at the new rate as opposed to the old rate?

A) 96
B) 336
C) 432
D) 4032

10. A barbeque restaurant charges $12.25 per pound for its smoked beef and 25 cents each for buns. The state's food sales tax is 6%. Which of the following represents the total charge, in dollars, to order y pounds of smoked beef and z buns?

A) $1.06(12.25y + 25z)$
B) $1.06(12.25y + 0.25z)$
C) $1.06(12.25y) + 0.25z$
D) $1.06(12.25y) + 25z$

Unit Conversions

Concept & Strategy Lesson

Unit conversions are helpful – especially for word problems. This method is also known as dimensional analysis. Unit Conversion Problems

- The easiest way to convert one unit to another unit is to use a table like the one below.

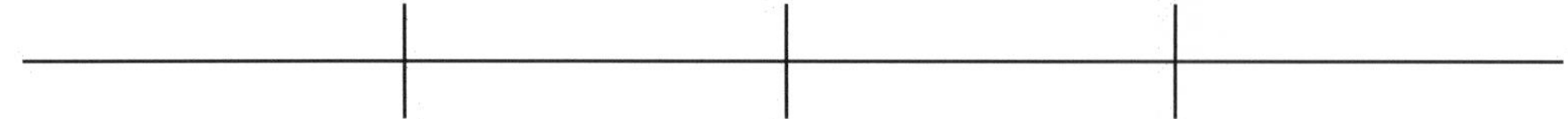

- Put your initial term (it will probably be a constant, rather than a rate) in the top left scorner. Then place unit conversions in subsequent columns in such a way that units cross out. Look at the example below:

Example 1:

A 30,000 gallon pool is being drained at a rate of 12 gallons per minute. However, due to city sewage ordinances, pools can only be drained for 4 hours per day. How much water will be left in the pool after 1 week of draining?

A) 2,880 gallons
B) 9,840 gallons
C) 20,160 gallons
D) 27,120 gallons

Density Problems

- The density of a substance is its mass per unit volume.
- The formula to find density, ρ, is $\rho = mV$.
- Density problems can most easily be solved using a combination of the formula and the table above.

Unit Conversions Practice Problems

1. The density of an iron ingot is 7.87 grams per cubic centimeter. What is the mass, in kg, of an iron ingot with a volume of 3 cubic meters?

   A) 2.361
   B) 23.61
   C) 2,361
   D) 23,610

2. The ideal gas law, $PV = nRT$, relates the pressure (P in atm), volume, (V in L), amount of substance (n in moles), and temperature (T in Kelvin) of a substance. R is a constant. In order for the units of both sides of the ideal gas law equation to balance, what must be units of R?

   A) atm · L · K · mol
   B) $\frac{\text{atm}\cdot\text{L}}{\text{K}\cdot\text{mol}}$
   C) $\frac{\text{K}\cdot\text{mol}}{\text{atm}\cdot\text{L}}$
   D) $\frac{1}{\text{atm}\cdot\text{L}\cdot\text{K}\cdot\text{mol}}$

3. The acceleration of an object can be found by dividing the change in velocity of an object by the time it takes for that change to occur. The velocity of an object increases from 32 m/s to 45 m/s over the course of 26 seconds. What is the acceleration of that object to the nearest hundredth of a km/min^2?

   A) 0.03
   B) 0.3
   C) 0.5
   D) 1.8

$$V_{Au} = \frac{M_j \times \frac{kt}{24}}{19.32}$$

4. To find the volume of pure gold in a piece of gold jewelry, jewelers use the above formula, where V_{Au} is the volume of gold present, in mL, M_j is the total mass of the piece of jewelry in grams, and kt is the carat purity of the jewelry. To the nearest hundredth of a mL, what is the volume of pure gold present in a 22–carat golden ring that weighs 3.8 grams?

   A) 0.18
   B) 7.19
   C) 67.30
   D) 80.09

5. The gas mileage for Eugene's snowmobile is 32 miles per gallon when the snowmobile travels an average speed of 40 miles per hour. The snowmobile's gas tank has 15 gallons of gas at the beginning of the trip. If Eugene's snowmobile travels at an average speed of 40 miles per hour, which of the following functions f models the number of gallons of gas remaining in the tank t hours after the trip begins?

   A) $15 - \frac{4}{5t}$
   B) $15 - \frac{5t}{4}$
   C) $\frac{15-32t}{40}$
   D) $\frac{15-40t}{32}$

6. A typical photograph taken of a comet is 6.8 gigabits in size. A satellite near Earth can receive the data from the photograph at a data rate of 2.5 megabits per second for a maximum of 16 hours each day. If 1 gigabit equals 1,024 megabits, what is the maximum number of typical images that the tracking station could receive from the camera each day?

   A) 1
   B) 2
   C) 20
   D) 21

7. An online flooring company sells wood flooring by the box. Each box holds 34.69 square feet of flooring, and each box costs \$155.11. If Jan and Kim need to refinish their 20 × 18 square foot living room with wood flooring, how much will they pay?

   A) \$80.51
   B) \$1494.66
   C) \$1609.67
   D) \$1706.21

8. The battery life of a popular cell phone decreases from 100% to 45% in 165 minutes of use. If the phone's battery drains at that rate over the course of a day, how long will it take the battery to go from 100% to 0%, to the nearest second?

   A) 300 s
   B) 5,445 s
   C) 15,231 s
   D) 18,000 s

9. The length of a marathon is approximately 26.2 miles. Rachelle wishes to run a marathon; however, she knows her pace for the first half of the length of the marathon will be slightly faster than her pace for the second half. If her pace for the first half of the marathon is 8 minutes per mile, and her pace for the second half is 20% slower than that, how long will it take her to finish the marathon, to the nearest minute?

   A) 3 hours and 9 minutes
   B) 3 hours and 30 minutes
   C) 3 hours and 51 minutes
   D) 4 hours and 3 minutes

10. The acceleration due to gravity on Earth is approximately 32.2 feet per second squared. The acceleration due to gravity on the moon is approximately one–sixth of that value. What is the acceleration due to gravity on the moon, to the nearest hundredth, in miles per minute squared? (There are 5280 feet in 1 mile.)

   A) 3.66
   B) 5.37
   C) 131.73
   D) 283.36

Graphs of Equations

Concept & Strategy Lesson

Graphing Linear Equations

- The **slope**, m, of an equation represents the rate at which the y–values of the equation change as the x–values change
- **Slope:** given two points (x_1, y_1) and (x_2, y_2) $m = \frac{y_2 - y_1}{x_2 - x_1}$
- The **y–intercept**, b, of an equation represents the initial point of the equation: the value of y when x equals 0.
- You can obtain the equation of a linear graph when you have either two of the points that lie on that line, or one of the points and the y–intercept.
- $y = mx + b$
- $y - y_1 = m(x - x_1)$

Example 1:

If k is a positive constant different from 1, which of the following could be the graph of $x - y = \frac{x-y}{k}$ in the xy–plane?

A) 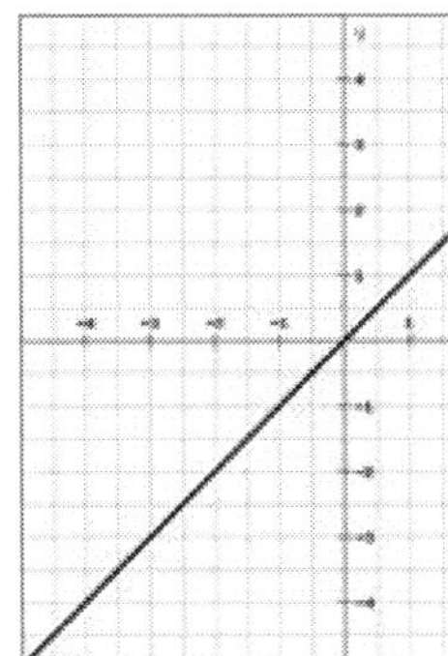

B) 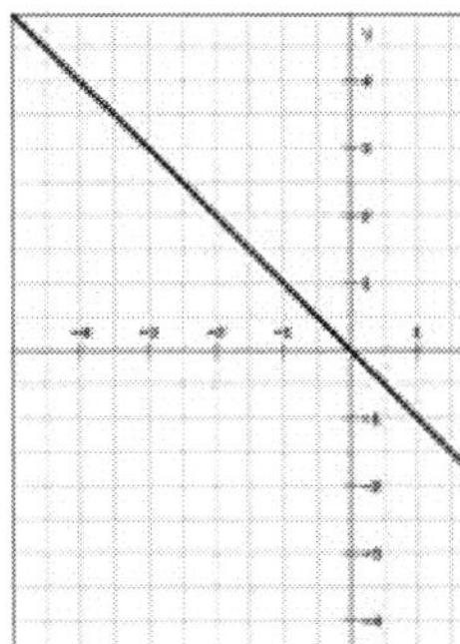

C) 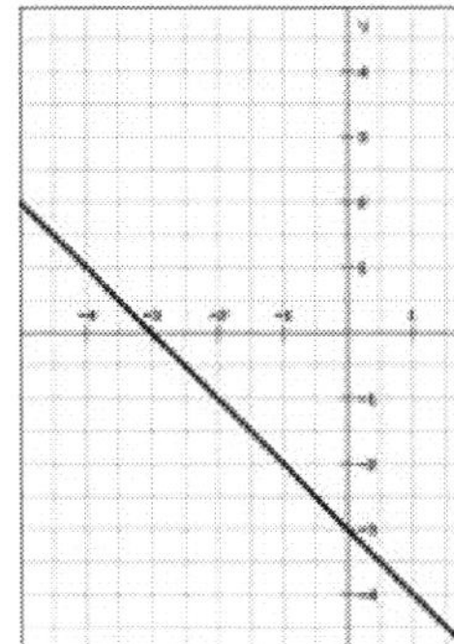

D) 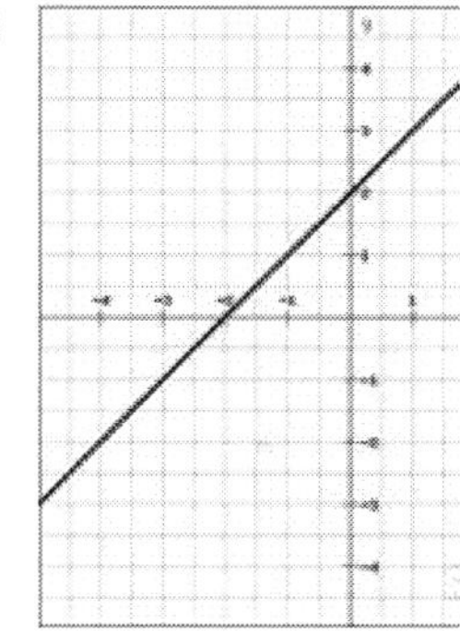

Graphing Quadratic and Exponential Equations

- The highest term of a quadratic equation is x^2. The graphs of these functions are symmetric – thus, they increase and then decrease, or decrease and then increase, as shown below:
- The most common scenario modeled by a quadratic equation is projectile motion.

Example of a quadratic equation:

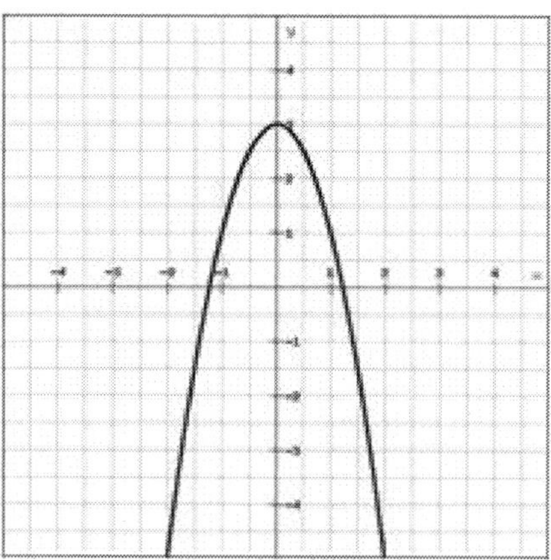

- Exponential equations are of the form $a \cdot b^x$, where a and b are both nonzero numbers.
- Exponential equations usually model situations that involve continuous increases or decreases over time, such as a changing population or the amount of money in a bank account that is accruing interest.

Example of an exponential equation:

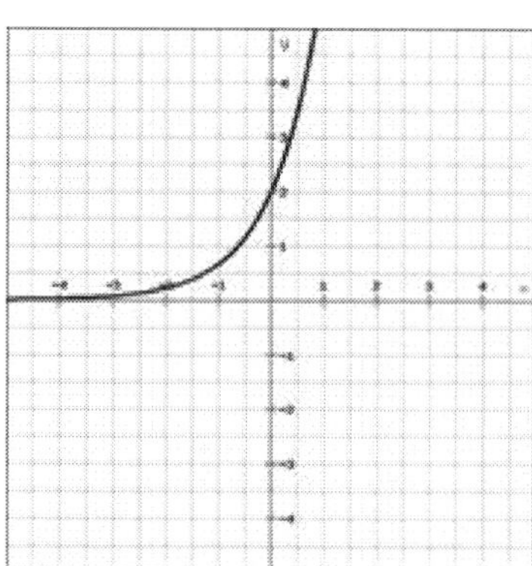

Example 2:

An object is launched at a velocity of 7.9 m/s from a height of 2.4 m above the surface. The height of the object, $f(t)$, at time t can best be modeled by which of the following types of equations?

A) Linear
B) Quadratic
C) Exponential
D) None of the above

Graphs of Equations Practice Problems

1. Line l is graphed in the xy–plane below.

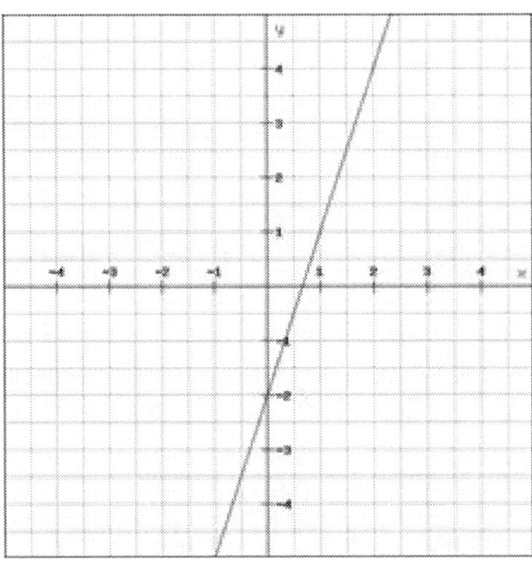

If line l is translated up 3 units and left 4 units, then what is the slope of the new line?

A) -3
B) -2
C) $\frac{6}{5}$
D) 3

Questions 2 and 3 refer to the following information.

The mean number of students per faculty member, y, at a university can be estimated using the equation $y = 0.13x + 13.6$, where x represents the number of years since 2005 and $0 \le x \le 10$.

2. Which of the following statements is the best interpretation of the number 0.13 in the context of this problem?

A) The estimated mean number of students per faculty member in 2005
B) The estimated mean number of students per faculty member in 2015
C) The estimated yearly decrease in the mean number of students per faculty member
D) The estimated yearly increase in the mean number of students per faculty member

3. Which of the following statements is the best interpretation of the number 13.6 in the context of this problem?

A) The estimated mean number of students per faculty member in 2005
B) The estimated mean number of students per faculty member in 2015
C) The estimated yearly decrease in the mean number of students per faculty member
D) The estimated yearly increase in the mean number of students per faculty member

4. A deep–sea diver is exploring the sunken ruins of an ocean liner. When he dives to a depth of 350 feet below the surface, the pressure is 170.2 psi. As the diver descends, the pressure increases linearly. At a depth of 500 feet, the pressure is 236.9 psi. If the pressure increases at a constant rate as the scientist's depth below the surface increases, which of the following linear models best describes the pressure p in psi at a depth of d feet below the surface?

   A) $p = 0.44d + 0.92$
   B) $p = 0.44d + 16.2$
   C) $p = 2.2d - 1.1$
   D) $p = 2.2d - 600$

Questions 5 and 6 refer to the following information.

The mean age of the population of India, y, can be estimated using the equation $y = 0.03x + 27.6$, where x represents the number of years since 1990 and $x > 0$.

5. What would be the estimated mean age of the population of India in 1980?

   A) 27.3
   B) 27.6
   C) 27.9
   D) It is unable to be determined

6. Which of the following statements is the best interpretation of the number 27.6 in the context of this problem?

   A) The estimated mean age of the population of India in 1990
   B) The estimated mean age of the population of India after 1990
   C) The estimated yearly decrease in the mean age of the population of India
   D) The estimated yearly increase in the mean age of the population of India

Questions 7 and 8 refer to the following information.

A mountain climber is climbing Mt. Everest. When she is 10,000 feet up the mountain, the pressure is 69.7 kPa. As the climber ascends, the pressure decreases linearly. As she approaches the summit, the pressure is 37.6 kPa at 25,000 feet.

7. If the pressure decreases at a constant rate as the scientist's height above the surface increases, which of the following linear models best describes the pressure p in kPa at a height of h feet above the surface?

   A) $p = -467.29h + 7429.9$
   B) $p = -467.29h + 22570.1$
   C) $p = -0.00214h - 15.9$
   D) $p = -0.00214h + 91.1$

8. The height of Mt. Everest is approximately 29,000 feet. What is the approximate pressure at this height?

   A) 19 kPa
   B) 29 kPa
   C) 79 kPa
   D) 99 kPa

Questions 9 and 10 refer to the graph of line *l* below.

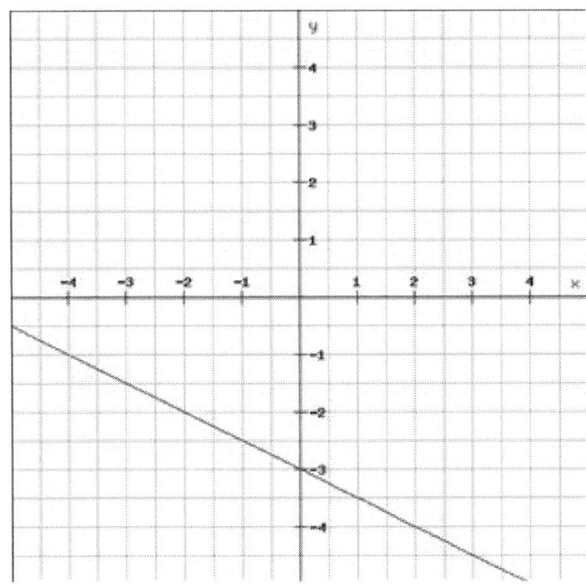

9. What is the sum of the x– and y–intercepts of the graph of the linear function above?

A) –18
B) –9
C) 3
D) 9

10. Line k is perpendicular to line l and intersects it at the point (–2,–2). Which of the following is the equation of line k?

A) $y = 2x - 2$
B) $y = 2x + 2$
C) $y = -2x + 6$
D) $y = -2x - 6$

Scatterplots

Concept & Strategy Lesson

Students will be given scatterplots and be asked to select the equation of the line or curve of best fit, interpret the line in the context of the situation, and use the line or curve to make predictions.

Scatterplots

- A scatterplot shows the relationship between two sets of values

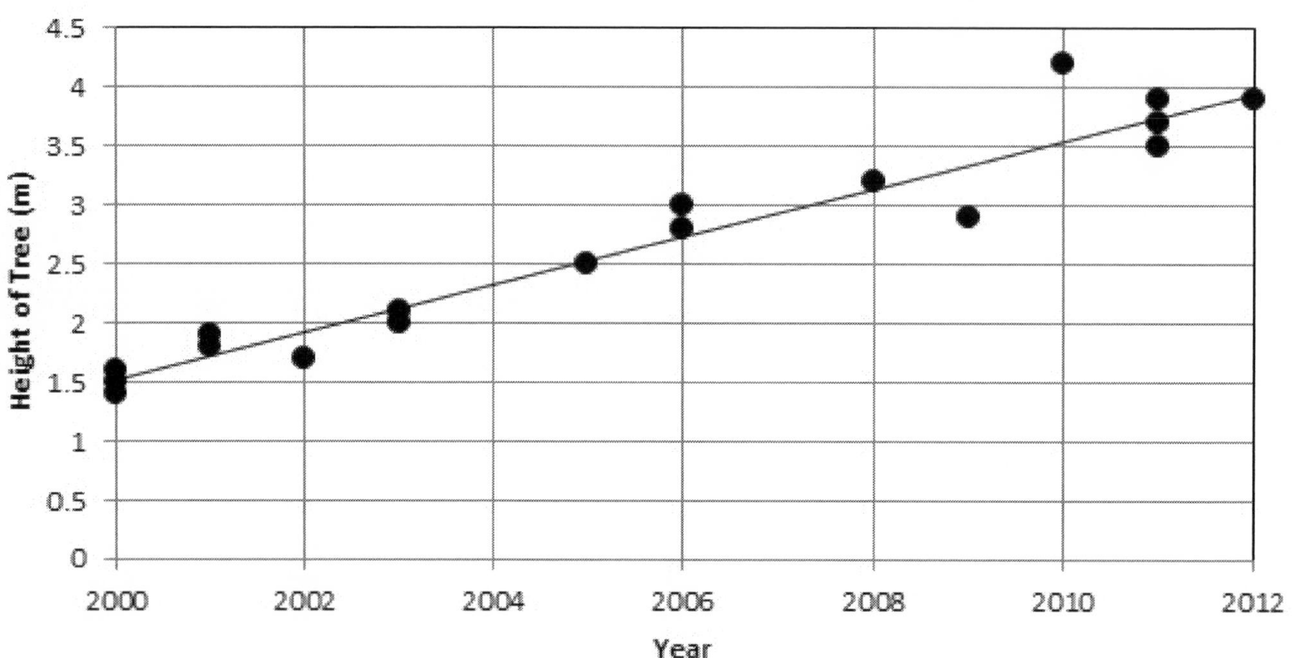

What is shown on this graph?

- X–axis: ________________
- Y–axis: ________________
- Line of best fit: ______________________
- Title: ______________________
- Most of the lines of best fit will be linear, though you will see the occasional quadratic or exponential line of best fit as well.
- To predict another data point that is not given, you should expand the line of best fit to points beyond those given. If the line of best fit is linear, plug the point (x or y) into the line of best fit that you have found.

Example 1:

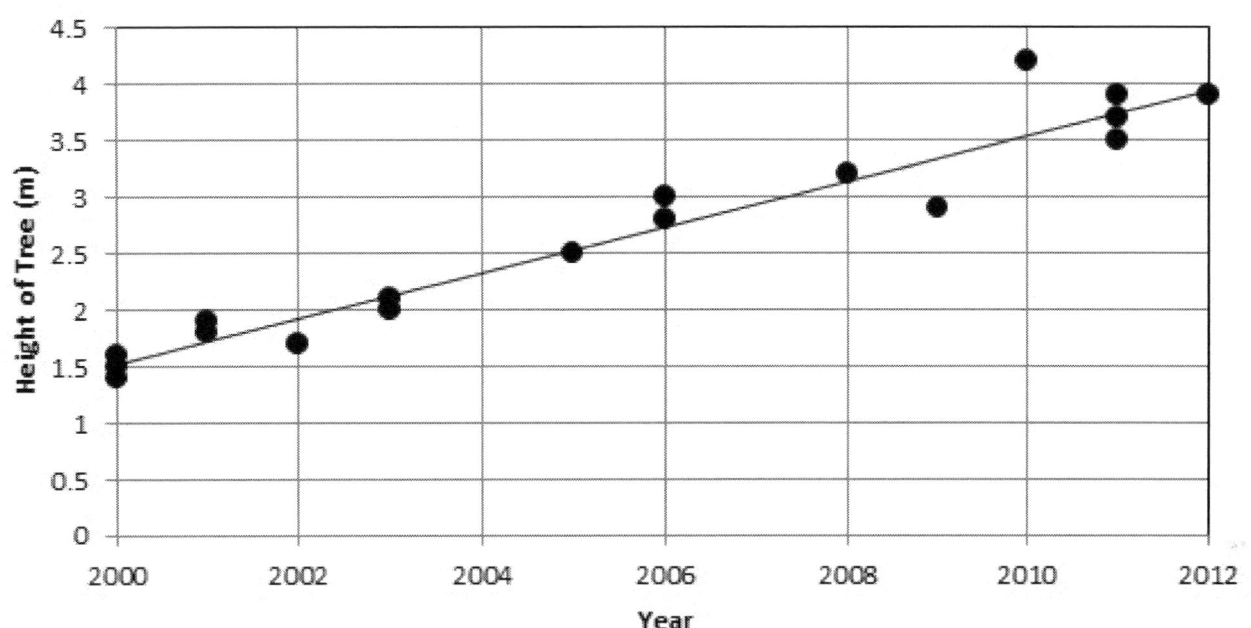

The scatterplot above shows heights of randomly selected pine trees from a commercial pine tree farm in Georgia. Based on the line of best fit to the data shown, which of the following values is closest to the average increase in the height of a randomly selected pine tree from this farm per year?

A) 0.15 feet
B) 0.30 feet
C) 0.60 feet
D) 1.20 feet

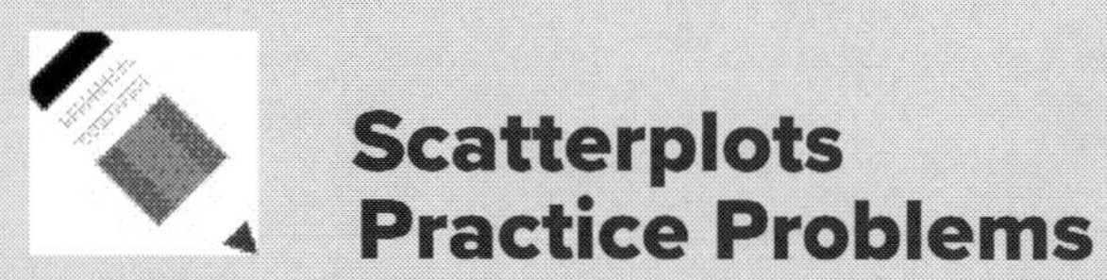

Scatterplots Practice Problems

Questions 1 – 3 refer to the following information.

Armspan is the physical measurement of the length from one of an individual's arms (measured at the fingertips) to the other end when raised parallel to the ground at shoulder height. The scatterplot below shows the relationship between the height and armspan of 9 people. The line of best fit is also shown

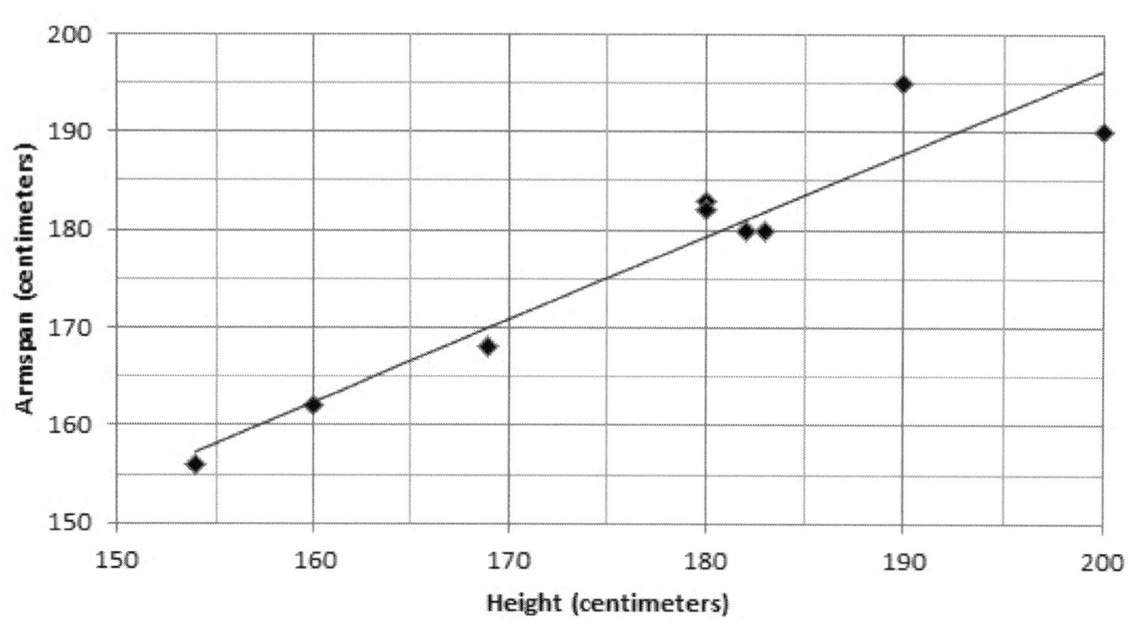

1. How many of the nine people have an actual height that differs by more than 5 centimeters from the height predicted by the line of best fit?

   A) 0
   B) 1
   C) 2
   D) 3

2. Which of the following is the best interpretation of the slope of the line of best fit in the context of this problem?

    A) The predicted length of armspan increase in centimeters for every centimeter increase in height.
    B) The predicted height increase in centimeters for every centimeter increase in length of arm-span.
    C) The predicted height in centimeters of a person with a length of armspan of 0 centimeters.
    D) The predicted length of armspan in centimeters of a person with a height of 0 centimeters.

3. Based on the line of best fit, what is the predicted length of armspan for someone with a height of 185 centimeters?

    A) 180 centimeters
    B) 183.5 centimeters
    C) 187 centimeters
    D) 192.5 centimeters

Questions 4 – 6 refer to the following information.

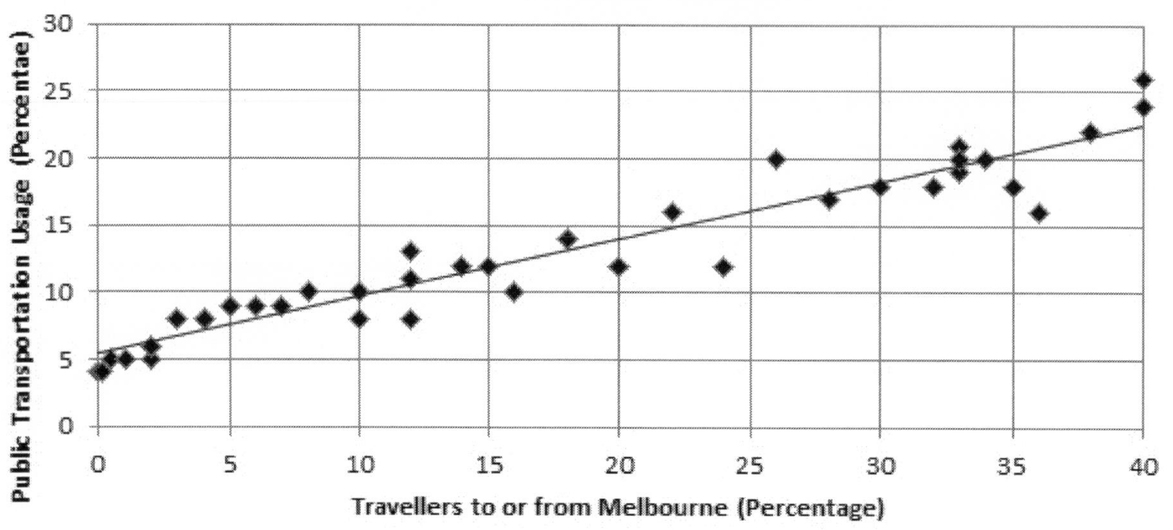

4. On a day in which 22.5% of Melbourne workers travel to or from Melbourne, what percentage of workers is expected to use public transportation?

   A) 10%
   B) 15%
   C) 22.5%
   D) 40%

5. Which of the following data points, if added to the scatterplot on the previous page, would create the largest positive change in the slope of the line of best fit to the data?

   A) (5,20)
   B) (15,15)
   C) (30,20)
   D) (35,30)

6. The slope of the line of best fit to the data above is approximately

   A) 0.2
   B) 0.4
   C) 0.6
   D) 0.8

Questions 7 – 9 refer to the following information.

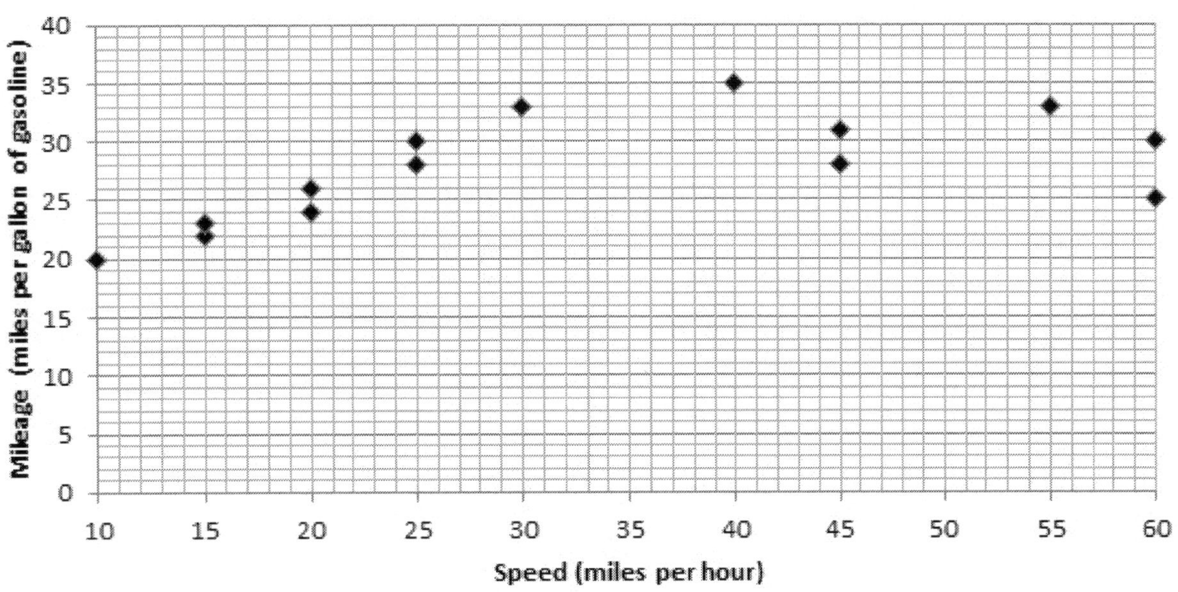

7. Which type of line of best fit best matches the data points in the scatterplot above?

A) Constant
B) Linear
C) Quadratic
D) Exponential

8. At a speed of 25 miles per hour, the expected mileage of the car model is

A) 20 miles per gallon
B) 30 miles per gallon
C) 40 miles per gallon
D) 50 miles per gallon

9. An increase in speed of 10 miles per hour equates to what change in mileage?

A) –5 miles per gallon
B) +5 miles per gallon
C) +10 miles per gallon
D) It is impossible to determine

Two–Way Tables

Concept & Strategy Lesson

Students will summarize categorical data and use that data to calculate relative frequencies, conditional probabilities, association of variables, and independence of events.

Two–Way Tables

- Two–way tables show data from one group that pertains to two distinct categories.
- Below is an example of a two–way table:

	VOTED YES	VOTED NO	DID NOT VOTE	TOTAL
18– to 39–year–olds	356	123	562	1,041
40– to 59–year–olds	562	453	203	1,218
People 60 years–old and over	392	476	135	1,003
Total	**1,310**	**1,052**	**900**	**3,262**

- Notice that each cell in the final row and final column is a total amount.
- The **relative frequency** of a value is the fraction or proportion of times the value occurs. So, the relative frequency of people 60 years–old and over in the survey above is $\frac{1003}{3262}$.
- **Conditional frequency** is the ratio of a subtotal to the value of a total. In the two–way table above, the conditional frequency of 18– to 39–year olds who voted no is $\frac{123}{1041}$. The conditional frequency of people who voted no who are 18 to 39 years–old, on the other hand, is $\frac{123}{1052}$.
- **Conditional probability** is the probability that an event occurs, given that another event has already occurred. The probability of a person voting no provided that he or she is 18 to 39 years–old is also $\frac{123}{1052}$.
- Two events are **independent** if the occurrence of one event does not affect the probability of the occurrence of the other event.

Example 1:
A survey was conducted among a randomly chosen sample of Wyoming residents about whether or not they voted for a proposition in a recent election. The table below displays a summary of the survey results.

	VOTED YES	VOTED NO	DID NOT VOTE	TOTAL
18– to 39–year–olds	356	123	562	1,041
40– to 59–year–olds	562	453	203	1,218
People 60 years–old and over	392	476	135	1,003
Total	**1,310**	**1,052**	**900**	**3,262**

According to the table, which of the following groups had the highest relative frequency?

A) 18– to 39–year–olds who did not vote
B) 18– to 39–year–olds who voted yes
C) 18– to 39–year–olds who voted no
D) 40– to 59–year–olds who voted no

Example 2:
Of the people 60 years–old and over who reported voting, 200 were selected at random to do a follow–up survey in which they were asked to choose from among 3 candidates for governor. The results of the follow–up survey are included below. Using the data from both the initial survey and the follow–up survey, which of the following is most likely to be an accurate statement?

	CANDIDATE A	CANDIDATE B	CANDIDATE C	NO PREFERENCE
# of Voters	86	53	46	15

A) About 225 people over the age of 60 in the initial survey would choose to support Candidate A.
B) About 375 people over the age of 60 in the initial survey would choose to support Candidate A.
C) About 375 people over the age of 60 in the initial survey would choose to support Candidate B.
D) About 275 people over the age of 60 in the initial survey would choose to support Candidate B.

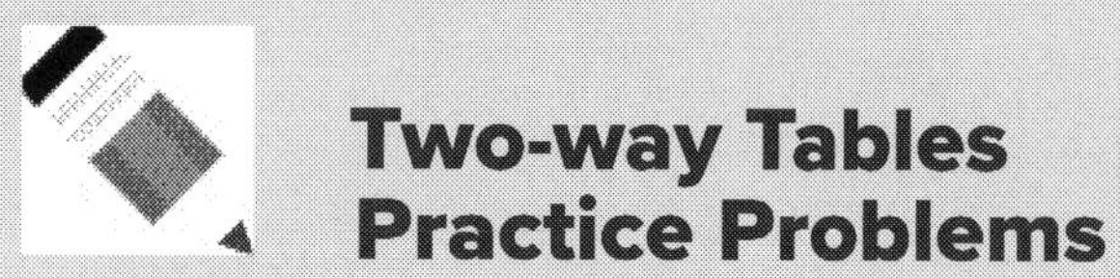

Two-way Tables Practice Problems

Questions 1 – 3 refer to the following information.

The table below classifies the number of visitors to several Caribbean islands in February based on their continent of origin.

	Grenada	Jamaica	Puerto Rico	Total
North America	82	156	180	418
South America	168	46	26	240
Europe	71	24	123	218
Total	321	226	329	876

1. What fraction of all visitors from South America went to either Jamaica or Puerto Rico?

2. Which of the following conditional probabilities is greatest?

   A) The probability that a visitor from Europe vacationed in Jamaica.
   B) The probability that a visitor from South America vacationed in Puerto Rico.
   C) The probability that a visitor from South America vacationed in Jamaica.
   D) The probability that a visitor from North America vacationed in Grenada.

3. Of the people who visited Grenada, 200 were surveyed and asked whether or not they would visit again. 45% of those surveyed answered yes, 40% answered no, and the remainder were unsure. Based on those results, approximately how many of the 321 people who visited Grenada would definitely visit Grenada again?

   A) 90
   B) 120
   C) 144
   D) 193

Questions 4 – 6 refer to the information below.

A survey was conducted among a randomly chosen sample of Georgia residents about voter participation in the 2014 Senate election.

Reported Voting by Age (in hundreds)

	Voted	Did Not Vote	No Response	Total
18– to 34–year–olds	595	3,658	346	4,599
35– to 54–year–olds	923	1,171	378	2,472
55– to 74–year–olds	796	1,278	200	2,274
People 75 years old and over	248	1,235	113	1,596
Total	2,562	7,342	1,037	10,941

4. According to the table, for which age group did the smallest percentage of people report that they had voted?

   A) 18– to 34–year–olds
   B) 35– to 54–year–olds
   C) 55– to 74–year–olds
   D) People 75 years old and over

5. Of the people 75 years old and over who reported voting, 350 were selected at random to do a follow–up survey in which they were asked which candidate they voted for. 150 people in this survey voted for Candidate A, 175 voted for Candidate B, and the rest voted for someone else. Using the data from both the follow–up survey and the initial survey, which of the following is most likely to be an accurate statement?

   A) About 10,000 of the people 75 years old and over would report voting for Candidate A in the election.
   B) About 68,400 of the people 75 years old and over would report voting for Candidate A in the election.
   C) About 109,800 of the people 75 years old and over would report voting for Candidate A in the election.
   D) About 468,900 of the people 75 years old and over would report voting for Candidate A in the election.

6. The initial survey was very thorough – nearly 10% of all of the people of voting age in Georgia were surveyed. Approximately how many people in the state of Georgia are 55 years old or over?

   A) 1.25 million
   B) 1.75 million
   C) 2.25 million
   D) 3.87 million

Questions 7 – 8 refer to the information below.

The table below lists all four types of hits compiled by four members of a baseball team.

	Singles	Doubles	Triples	Home Runs	Total
Player A	110	43	4	18	175
Player B	88	34	2	29	153
Player C	116	27	0	10	153
Player D	115	26	3	11	155
Total	429	130	11	68	638

7. A player's Batting Average is calculated by taking his total hits and dividing that number by his number of At Bats. Each of the four player's At Bats is listed below. Which player has the highest Batting Average?

	At Bats		At Bats
Player A	607	**Player C**	582
Player B	566	**Player D**	573

A) Player A
B) Player B
C) Player C
D) Player D

8. Which player has the greatest ratio of Doubles to Home Runs?

A) Player A
B) Player B
C) Player C
D) Player D

Questions 9 – 10 refer to the information below.

A survey was conducted among a randomly chosen sample of U.S. residents about their income.

	Below \$30,000	Between \$30,000 and \$100,000	Above \$100,000	Total
Southeast	623	879	687	2,189
Northeast	486	1,171	952	2,609
Southwest	698	1,089	852	2,639
Northwest	532	599	423	1,554
Total	2,339	3,738	2,914	8,991

9. The proportion of people who earn below \$30,000 is greatest among the people of which region?

A) Southeast
B) Northeast
C) Southwest
D) Northwest

10. The proportions of people surveyed from each area are indicative of their proportion of the adult U.S. population. If the population of U.S. adults is 242 million, approximately how many adults live in the Southwest?

A) 41 million
B) 59 million
C) 71 million
D) 78 million

Measures of Center and Spread

Concept & Strategy Lesson

Students will calculate measures of center and spread, including mean, median, mode, and range, for a set of data. Students must use given statistics, including standard deviation, to compare two different sets of data.

Measures of Center

- Mean: ______________________________
- Median: ______________________________
- Mode: ______________________________
- If there is an even number of points in the data set, the median is the mean of the two middle points.
- When can you have more than 1 mode? ______________________________

Measures of Range

- Range: ______________________________
- Standard deviation: ___________+______________
- The more spread out the data points are from the mean of a set, the greater the standard deviation. The closer the data points are to the mean of a set, the smaller the standard deviation.
- If all of the data points in a data set are the same, its standard deviation is 0.

Softball Player Heights (inches)		Basketball Player Heights (inches)	
61	61	65	68
62	62	70	70
63	63	70	71
65	68	71	72
69	69	73	
69	70		
71	71		

The data above show the heights of Somerville High School's girls' softball and girls' basketball teams.

Example 1:

Based on the information in the data sets above, which of the following statements is true?

A) The mean height of the girls' softball team is larger than the mean height of the girls' basketball team.

B) The mean height of the girls' basketball team is larger than the mean height of the girls' softball team.

C) The median height of the girls' softball team is larger than the median height of the girls' basketball team.

D) The range of heights on the girls' basketball team is larger than the range of heights on the girls' softball team.

Example 2:

The standard deviation of the heights of the girls' softball team is 3.903, while the standard deviation of the heights of the girls' basketball team is 2.345. Based on his information and the information in the data sets above, which of the following statements is true.

A) The player heights for the softball team are less spread apart than the player heights for the bas-ketball team.
B) The average player height for the softball team is greater than the average player height for the basketball team.
C) The player heights for the basketball team are less spread apart than the player heights for the softball team.
D) Every player on the basketball team is taller than every player on the softball team.

Measures of Center and Spread Practice Problems

Questions 1 – 3 refer to the following information.

College Football Player Weights (pounds)		High School Football Player Weights (pounds)	
256	261	165	268
150	196	170	136
180	162	136	182
178	182	156	209
210	196	136	212
223	146	182	200
276	187	156	199

The data above show the weights of randomly selected football players from one college team and one high school team.

1. Based on the information in the data sets above, which of the following statements is true?

   A) The mean weight of the high school football team is larger than the mean weight of the college football team.
   B) The mean weight of the college football team is larger than the mean weight of the high school football team.
   C) The median weight of the high school football team is larger than the median weight of the college football team.
   D) The range of weights on the college football team is larger than the range of weights of the high school football team.

2. In comparison to the median weight of the players selected from the high school football team, the median weight of the players selected from the college football team is

   A) approximately 20 pounds heavier.
   B) approximately 15 pounds heavier.
   C) approximately 15 pounds lighter.
   D) approximately 20 pounds lighter.

3. In comparison to the range of weights of the players selected from the high school football team, the range of weights of the players selected from the college football team is

   A) approximately 2 more
   B) approximately 16 more
   C) approximately 16 less
   D) approximately 2 less

Questions 4 – 7 refer to the following information.

The cost of a ferry at a local company is dependent on both the weather conditions and the number of passengers. Each **x** below represents one instance of that cost in the last 3 weeks.

Cost of Ferry									
			x		x				
			x	x	x				
	x	x	x	x	x	x	x		
x	x	x	x	x	x	x	x		x
$20	$22	$24	$26	$28	$30	$32	$34	$36	38

4. To the nearest integer, what is the mean ferry cost over the previous 3 weeks?

   A) $26
   B) $28
   C) $29
   D) $30

5. Adding which of the following data sets to the Cost of the Ferry data above will increase the median of the data set by the largest amount?

   A) {26, 26, 28}
   B) {28, 28, 30}
   C) {30, 30, 32}
   D) {26, 36, 36}

6. Which of the following statements about the data above is true?

   A) The distribution of data points is symmetric.
   B) The mean of the data set is greater than at least one of its modes.
   C) The median of the data set is greater than its mean.
   D) The ferry will never cost less than $20 or more than $36.

7. The standard deviation of the data above is 4.5. Adding which of the following data sets to the Cost of the Ferry data on the previous page will increase the standard deviation by the largest amount?

A) {26, 28}
B) {22, 34}
C) {22, 30}
D) {28, 34}

Questions 8 – 10 refer to the following information.

Two chemistry classes taught by the same teacher each took the same test. The grades of each student in each class are listed below.

Class A Grades		Class B Grades	
36	80	60	72
65	80	60	75
65	82	65	75
68	85	65	78
70	88	68	82
75	92	72	85
75	95	72	100

8. Which class performed better on the exam?

A) Class A because it had a higher mean exam score.
B) Class A because it had a higher median exam score.
C) Class B because its extreme values are larger than Class A's extreme values.
D) Class B because its range of exam scores is lower.

9. What is the difference in the median scores of the two classes above?

A) 1.93
B) 3.00
C) 5.50
D) 8.00

10. Halfway through grading Class B's exams, the teacher discovered the key had a mistake. Thus, half of the grades listed above for Class B are 5 points too low. What is the new mean exam score for Class B?

A) 73.5
B) 76
C) 78.5
D) It is impossible to determine.

Population Parameters and Data Collection

Concept & Strategy Lesson

Population Parameters

- Sample: ________________________
- Parameter: ________________________
- Confidence interval: ________________________
  A 95% confidence interval states that the population mean of the weights of males in Volusia County, Florida is 181 ± 1.9 pounds. We can expect 95% of estimates of the weights of males of that county are between 179.1 and 182.9 pounds. The 1.9 pounds on either side of the mean is known as our margin of error.
- Measurement error: ________________________

Data Collection

- Data should be collected in as non–biased a way as possible. Ideally, all subgroups of a population should be equally represented within the sample.
- Convenience sample: ________________________
- Voluntary sample: ________________________
- Simple random sample: ________________________
- Stratified random sample: ________________________

A survey was conducted among a randomly chosen sample of 3,000 New York City football fans about their favorite football team. The table below displays a summary of the survey results.

	NEW YORK OGRES	NEW YORK COPTERS	BOSTON NATIONALISTS	OTHER TEAM	TOTAL
Poll Results	1,236	1,069	365	330	3,000

Example 1:

The population of New York City is 8.406 million people and approximately 50% of those residents have a favorite football team. Assuming that the data above are representative of the city as a whole, how many New York City residents cite the New York Copters as their favorite team?

A) 1.498 million
B) 1.732 million
C) 2.995 million
D) 3.463 million

Example 2:

The population of the United States as a whole is approximately 320 million people, and approximately 40% of those are football fans with a favorite team. How many Americans like a team besides the Ogres or the Copters?

A) 14.1 million
B) 29.6 million
C) 98.3 million
D) The answer cannot be obtained from the information given.

Population Parameters and Data Collection Practice Problems

1. A statistician randomly selected 100 employees from the list of all the salaried employees of a company. She asked each of the 100 employees, "How many hours do you typically work per week?" The mean number of working hours in the sample was 45.8 and the margin of error for this estimate was 2.4 hours. Another statistician intends to replicate the survey and will attempt to get a smaller margin of error. Which of the following samples will most likely result in a smaller margin of error for the estimated mean number of weekly working hours of salaried employees in the company?

   A) 50 randomly selected salaried employees of the company
   B) 50 randomly selected employees of the company
   C) 500 randomly selected salaried employees of the company
   D) 500 randomly selected employees of the company

Questions 2 and 3 refer to the following information.

A researcher wants to know if there is an association between height and speed of long–distance runners in Canada. He obtained survey responses from a random sample of 3000 Canadian long–distance runners
and found convincing evidence of a positive association between height and speed.

2. Which of the following conclusions is well supported by the data?

   A) There is a positive association between height and speed for long–distance runners in Canada.
   B) There is a positive association between height and speed for long–distance runners in the world.
   C) Using height and speed as defined by the study, an increase in height is caused by an increase in speed for long–distance runners in Canada.
   D) Using height and speed as defined by the study, an increase in speed is caused by an increase in height for long–distance runners in Canada.

3. Canadian long–distance runner Jay is 183 cm tall, while Canadian long–distance runner Kim is 172 cm tall. Based on the information above, you can tell that

   A) Kim definitely runs faster than Jay does.
   B) Kim most likely runs faster than Jay does.
   C) Jay most likely runs faster than Kim does.
   D) Jay definitely runs faster than Kim does.

Questions 4 and 5 refer to the following information.

A researcher wants to know if there is an association between height and wingspan of college men's basketball players. He obtained survey responses from a random sample of 1,000 college men's basketball players and found convincing evidence of a positive association between height and wingspan.

4. One of the players surveyed had a height of 192 cm and a wingspan of 191 cm. Another player had a height of 187 cm. His wingspan is most likely

   A) 185 cm
   B) 186 cm
   C) 187 cm
   D) It cannot be determined from the information provided.

5. Which of the following conclusions is well supported by the data?

   A) There is a positive association between height and wingspan for college basketball players.
   B) There is a positive association between height and wingspan for basketball players
   C) Using height and wingspan as defined by the study, a taller men's college basketball player will generally have a longer wingspan.
   D) Using height and wingspan as defined by the study, more wingspan equates to more height.

Questions 6 and 7 refer to the following information.

A survey was conducted among a randomly chosen sample of 2,845 students of a particular university in regards to what region of the country they are from. The results are shown below.

	Southeast	Northeast	Southwest	Northwest	TOTAL
Poll Results	896	536	790	623	2,845

6. The university has 23,596 enrolled students. Assuming the results of the survey are consistent with the university as a whole, approximately how many of the university's students are not from the Southwest?

   A) 7,501
   B) 8,508
   C) 15,088
   D) 16,095

7. The following year, the university is concerned that too many of its students are from the Southeast and wants to decrease the number of students from that region by 10%, assuming that an equal number of students from the other three regions will take their places. If the university wants to increase its enrollment to 25,000 people, how many people should it expect to have from the Northwest?

   A) 5,694
   B) 6,569
   C) 7,169
   D) 8,113

8. Which of the following methods should be used to obtain the most accurate data about the mean income of the population of a certain state?

   A) Use voluntary sampling; people in the state will self–select to provide the most accurate income information.
   B) Ask 100 random people from each county in the state to provide income information.
   C) Simple random sampling; ask 10,000 random people from a list of every person in the state as a whole to provide income information.
   D) Determine the population of each county in the state, then ask a number of random people from each county, in proportion with the population of that county, to provide income information.

Questions 9 – 10 refer to the following information.

A survey was conducted among a randomly chosen sample of nation–wide voters about their preferred presidential candidate. The table below displays a summary of the survey results.

	Candidate A	Candidate B	Candidate C	TOTAL
Poll Results	13,523	14,569	1,897	29,989

9. The surveyors have determined that each value is accurate to within 5%; that is, the number of voters for each candidate can be either 5% higher or 5% lower than the numbers shown above. Based on that information, which candidate is most likely to win the election?

   A) Candidate A
   B) Candidate B
   C) Candidate C
   D) It is impossible to determine.

10. In an election in which 100,000 people vote and the ratio above is maintained, approximately how many people will vote for Candidate B?

A) 20,584
B) 45,093
C) 48,581
D) 63,257

Functions

Concept & Strategy Lesson

Students must be able to create and solve quadratic and exponential functions that model situations.

Functions

- A **function** is a relationship between a set of inputs and a set of outputs wherein each input is related to exactly one output.
- Domain: ______________________________
- Range: ______________________________
- The ordered pair (x, y) is a solution to the function $f(x)$.
- Roots, or zeros, of a function are the points where the function crosses the x–axis

Quadratic Functions

- $f(x) = ax^2 + bx + c$.
- Every quadratic function has either a maximum or a minimum
- This maximum or minimum is always located at the vertex of the function
- The x–coordinate of the vertex always has the value of $-\frac{b}{2a}$
- The y–coordinate of the vertex can be found by plugging this x–value into the function.
- A quadratic function will always have at most 2 real roots.

Example 1:

The function f is defined by $f(x) = 2x^2 - hx - 3$, where h is a constant. In the xy–plane, the graph of f intersects the x–axis at the two points $(-3,0)$ and $(j,0)$. What is the value of $h - j$?

A) –5.5
B) –4.5
C) 4.5
D) 5.5

Exponential Functions

- Exponential functions are typically of the form $f(x)= a \cdot b^x + c$, where b is a positive constant not equal to 1.
- Every exponential function has a vertical asymptote, which can be found at $y = c$. If $a > 0$, then every point on the function will be greater than this asymptote. If $a < 0$, then every point on the function will be less than this asymptote.
- An exponential function will have at most 1 real root.

Example 2:

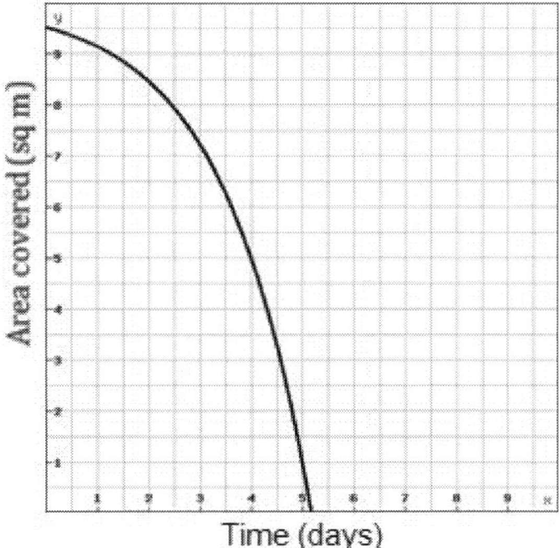

A researcher studies a large mat of moss that has been invaded by a particular fungus. After initially measuring the area that the moss covers, the research measures and records the area covered by living moss every 6 hours and records her results. The data for the moss were fit by a smooth curve, as shown above, where the curve represents the area of living moss as a function of time, in days. Which of the following is a correct statement about the data above?

A) After 2 hours, only 8.5 square meters of living moss remained.
B) At time $t = 2.5$ days, 25% of the initial mat of moss had already died.
C) At time $t = 4$ days, 50% of the initial mat of moss had already died.
D) The moss is dying at a greater initial rate for the first 2 days than the final 2 days.

Functions Practice Problems

1. The surface area of the Aral Sea shrunk by approximately 3% each year from 1960 to 2004. Its surface area in 1960 was approximately 68,000 km^2. If $A(t)$ represents the area of the Aral Sea t years after 1960, then which of the following equations represents the model of the lake's surface area over time?

   A) $A(t) = 68000(-0.03)^t$
   B) $A(t) = 68000(0.03)^t$
   C) $A(t) = 68000(-0.97)^t$
   D) $A(t) = 68000(0.97)^t$

2. Every five years, the amount of money in a savings account increases by 12%. If F represents the current amount of money in the savings account and $f(t)$ represents the amount of money in the savings account t years later, then which of the following equations represents the model of the amount of money in the savings account over time?

   A) $f(t) = F(0.12)^{\frac{t}{5}}$
   B) $f(t) = F(0.12)^{\frac{t}{5}}$
   C) $f(t) = F(1.12)^{\frac{t}{5}}$
   D) $f(t) = F(1.12)^{5t}$

Questions 3 and 4 refer to the following information.

A cannonball is launched at 19.6 meters per second from a platform that is 2.3 meters tall. The equation for the cannonball's height s at time t seconds after launch is $s(t) = -4.9t^2 + 19.6t + 2.3$.

3. At what time does the cannonball reach its maximum height?

   A) 1 *s*
   B) 2 *s*
   C) 3 *s*
   D) 4 *s*

4. What is the maximum height, $s(t)$, that the cannonball reaches?

   A) 2.3 m
   B) 17 m
   C) 19.6 m
   D) 21.9 m

Questions 5 – 7 refer to the following information.

$$y = 3x^2$$
$$y = 2^x - 1$$

A business chooses to model its growth power, y, based on the number of months it's been in operation, x, with the two simple models shown above.

5. The business starts in January, 2014 ($x = 0$). After how many months will the growth power expected by the exponential growth model overtake the growth expected by the quadratic growth model?

   A) 6
   B) 8
   C) 10
   D) 12

6. In what month will the growth power predicted by the quadratic growth model exceed 50?

   A) March, 2014
   B) April, 2014
   C) May, 2014
   D) June, 2014

7. In January, 2015, the business discovered that its growth power was 450. Which model most accurately predicted the grow power?

   A) The quadratic model
   B) The exponential model
   C) Both models worked equally well.
   D) It is impossible to say which model worked better.

Questions 8 and 9 refer to the function below.

$$f(x) = -3(2)^{x-2} + 6$$

8. What is the domain of the function above?

   A) $(-6,\infty)$
   B) $(6,\infty)$
   C) $(-\infty,2)$
   D) $(-\infty,\infty)$

9. What is the range of the function above?

   A) $(-6,\infty)$
   B) $(6,\infty)$
   C) $(-\infty,6)$
   D) $(-\infty,\infty)$

10. If $f(x) = \frac{3x-2}{x-2}$, what value does $f(x)$ approach as x gets infinitely larger?

   A) -2
   B) -1
   C) $\frac{3}{2}$
   D) 3

Operations on Polynomials

Concept & Strategy Lesson

Students must be able to add, subtract, multiply, and simplify the results of polynomial expressions.

Operations on Polynomials

- Expressions with **like terms** have the same exact variables raised to the same powers.
- You can only add or subtract like terms. Thus, $3xy^2 + 9xy^2 = 12xy^2$, but $6ab^2 + 7a^2 b$ cannot be combined.
- To multiply terms, follow the rules we showed in **Chapter 1**. However, you should only add the exponents of like variables. Thus, $(3x^2 y^6)(-6xy^{-1}) = -18x^3 y^5$.

Distributive Property

- $3x(x-5) = 3x(x) + 3x(-5) = 3x^2 - 15x$

FOILing

- When multiplying two binomials, remember the mnemonic device **FOIL:** **F**irst, **O**uter, **I**nner, **L**ast.
- To multiply $(2x - 5)(4x - 9)$, first multiply the first terms, then the outer terms, then the inner terms, then the last terms. Finally, simplify by combining like terms:

$$2x(4x) + 2x(-9) + -5(4x) + -5(-9) = 8x^2 - 38x + 45$$

Example 1:

$$3x(2x - y) + (x^2 - y)(x + 3)$$

Which of the following expressions is equivalent to the expression above?

A) $x^3 + 7x^2 - 4xy + 3$
B) $x^3 + 9x^2 - 4xy - 3$
C) $x^3 + 7x^2 - 4xy - 3y$
D) $x^3 + 9x^2 - 4xy - 3y$

Operations on Polynomials Practice Problems

1. If a = $3c^2 + c - 8$ and b = $3c^3 - 4c^2 + 8$, what is $b - a$ in terms of c?

   A) $3c^3 - 7c^2 - c$
   B) $3c^3 - c^2 - c + 16$
   C) $3c^3 - 7c^2 - c + 16$
   D) $3c^3 + 7c^2 - c - 16$

2. Which of the following expressions is equivalent to $3x^3 - 12x^2 + 9x$?

   A) $3x(x - 3)(x - 1)$
   B) $(3x + 3)(x - 3)$
   C) $3x(x + 3)(x - 1)$
   D) $3(x^2 - 3)(x - 1)$

3. If $f = 3g + 3$ and $h = g + 1$, what is $-\frac{h}{f}$ in terms of g?

   A) -3
   B) $-\frac{1}{3}$
   C) 3
   D) $\frac{1}{3}$

Questions 4 – 6 refer to the following information:

$$A = 19 - 3x$$
$$B = 11 + 2x$$
$$C = 3 - 5x$$

4. $Ax + Bx + Cx =$

   A) $33x$
   B) $33 - 6x^2$
   C) $33x - 6x^2$
   D) $627x - 60x^2$

5. $ABC =$

   A) $30x^3 - 43x^2 - 1030x + 627$
   B) $30x^3 - 7x^2 + 1030x + 627$
   C) $30x^3 + 7x^2 - 1060x + 627$
   D) $30x^3 - 43x^2 - 1060x + 627$

6. $Ax^2 - Bx - C =$

   A) $-3x^3 + 17x^2 - 6x - 3$
   B) $-3x^3 + 21x^2 - 6x - 3$
   C) $-3x^3 + 17x^2 - 16x - 3$
   D) $-3x^3 + 21x^2 - 16x - 3$

Questions 7 – 9 refer to the following information:

$$A = xy^2 - xyz$$
$$B = xz + xyz^2$$
$$C = x - xy - xyz$$

7. What is the greatest common factor of A, B, and C?

   A) 1
   B) x
   C) xz
   D) xy

8. The value of B–A is equivalent to

   A) $xz + xyz^2 - xy^2 + xyz$
   B) $xz + xyz^2 - xy^2 - xyz$
   C) $xz + xyz^2 + xy^2 + xyz$
   D) $xz + xyz^2 + xy^2 - xyz$

9. If $x = 3$, $y = 2$, and $z = -3$, what is the value of $A - C$?

10. If $(h + 8)(h + 2) = 100$, then $(h + 4)(h + 6) =$

Radicals and Exponents

Concept & Strategy Lesson

Students must be able to solve and create equivalent expressions involving radicals and rational exponents, including those with extraneous solutions.

Radicals and Exponents

- Know the exponent rules
- Do the opposite
- Example: $x^2 = 9$ ____________________
- Example: $\sqrt[3]{x} = \frac{2}{3}$ ____________________
- Check for **extraneous solutions**

Example 1:

$$\sqrt{(x+2)^3} = 8$$

Which of the following is a solution to the equation above?

A) –2
B) 0
C) 2
D) No solution exists.

Example 2:

$$T = 2\pi\sqrt{\frac{L}{g}}$$

The formula above is used to solve for the length of the swing of a pendulum, T, given L, the length of the pendulum, in meters, and g, the acceleration of gravity, in $\frac{m}{s^2}$. Which of the following expressions relates the length of the pendulum in terms of g and T?

A) $L = \frac{T^2 g}{4\pi^2}$
B) $L = \frac{T^2 g^2}{4\pi^2}$
C) $L = \frac{T^2 g}{4\pi}$
D) $L = \frac{T^2 g^2}{4\pi}$

Radicals and Exponents Practice Problems

1. Which of the following is the set of all real solutions to the equation $(3x-2)(2x-1)^2=0$?

   A) $x=-\frac{3}{2},-2$
   B) $x=-\frac{1}{2},-\frac{2}{3}$
   C) $x=\frac{3}{2},2$
   D) $x=\frac{1}{2},\frac{2}{3}$

2. The equation $KE=\frac{1}{2}mv^2$ relates the kinetic energy, *KE*, of an object to its mass, *m*, and velocity, *v*. Which of the following expressions relates the velocity of an object in terms of its mass and kinetic energy?

   A) $v=\pm\sqrt{\frac{2KE}{m}}$
   B) $v=\pm\sqrt{\frac{KE}{2m}}$
   C) $v=\pm2\sqrt{\frac{KE}{m}}$
   D) $v=\pm\frac{1}{2}\sqrt{\frac{KE}{m}}$

3. Which of the following is a solution to the equation $3=\sqrt[5]{\frac{3}{x}}$?

   A) $-\frac{1}{3}$
   B) $-\frac{1}{9}$
   C) $\frac{1}{9}$
   D) $\frac{1}{3}$

$$T=2\pi\sqrt{\frac{L}{g}}$$

4. The formula above is used to solve for the length of the swing of a pendulum, *T*, given *L*, the length of the pendulum, in meters, and *g*, the acceleration of gravity, in $\frac{m}{s^2}$. Which of the following expressions relates the acceleration of gravity in terms of *L* and *T*?

   A) $g=\frac{T^2L}{4\pi^2}$
   B) $g=\frac{4\pi^2L}{T^2}$
   C) $g=\frac{T^24\pi}{L}$
   D) $g=\frac{4\pi L^2}{T^2}$

5. The equation $x^4-x^2=0$ has how many distinct, real solutions?

   A) 1
   B) 2
   C) 3
   D) 4

6. $$v=\sqrt{\frac{F}{m/L}}$$

   Which of the following contains all of the excluded values of the equation above?

   A) $m\leq0$
   B) $L\leq0$
   C) $m\leq0, L\leq0, F<0$
   D) $m\leq0, L\leq0, F\leq0$

Questions 7 and 8 refer to the following information.

$$f(x) = -\left(\sqrt{1-x} + 2\right)^3$$

7. What is the domain of $f(x)$?

A) $[-1,\infty)$
B) $[1,\infty)$
C) $(-\infty,1]$
D) $(-\infty,\infty)$

8. What is the range of $f(x)$?

A) $[-8,\infty)$
B) $[8,\infty)$
C) $(-\infty,-8]$
D) $(-\infty,\infty)$

9. If $\sqrt{2x^2 - 7} = 3 - x$, then $x =$

A) $-8, 2$
B) $-2, 8$
C) $-8, -2$
D) $2, 8$

10. If $\sqrt{x-3} - \sqrt{x} = 3$, then $\sqrt{x} =$

A) -4
B) -2
C) 2
D) There is no real solution.

Quadratic Expressions

Concept & Strategy Lesson

Students must be able to solve quadratic equations and systems of one linear and one quadratic equation.

Solving Quadratic Expressions

$$x = \frac{-b \pm \sqrt{b^2 - 4ac}}{2a}$$

- Factoring ______________________

Example 1:

If $s^2 + 2s = 35$ and $s < 0$, what is the value of $s + 15$?

Systems of Equations with Quadratic Expressions

- Sometimes, the SAT will include systems of equations that feature one linear expression and one quadratic expression.
- If one of these two expressions features only one variable, solve that one first.
- Otherwise, the substitution method will usually be the easiest way to solve these.
- Some of these systems will have one or two solutions; others will have zero. If a graphing calculator is available to you, try to graph the expressions to check your answers.
- Remember that sometimes systems of equations have no solutions, so always plug your answer back into both expressions to make sure that it is valid.

Example 2:

$$x^2 - y^2 = 90$$
$$x = 19y$$

If (x, y) is a solution to the system of equations above, what is the value of $2y^2$?

A) $\frac{1}{4}$
B) $\frac{1}{2}$
C) $\frac{361}{4}$
D) $\frac{361}{2}$

Quadratic Expressions Practice Problems

Questions 1 – 3 refer to the following information.

A cellphone company sells its new cell phone for $400 and manages to sell 30,000 in the first month. After some research, the company decides that for every $10 decrease in the price, it can sell 1,000 more phones, but for every $10 increase in the price, it sells 1,000 fewer phones.

1. Which of the following equations shows the revenue, R(x), the company obtains by decreasing the price by x instances of $10.

A) $R(x) = 400(30000 + 1000x)$
B) $R(x) = (400 + 10x)(30000 + 1000x)$
C) $R(x) = 400x + 1000x$
D) $R(x) = (400 - 10x)(30000 + 1000x)$

2. What cellphone price maximizes the company's monthly revenue?

A) $450
B) $350
C) $50
D) $5

3. What is the maximum amount of revenue that the company can make in a month from celling this cellphone?

A) $350
B) $450
C) $12,250,000
D) $15,750,000

4. For which values of x is $6 - x^2 \geq 4 - x$ true?

A) $x \leq 2$
B) $x \geq -1$
C) $-1 \leq x \leq 2$
D) $-2 \leq x \leq 1$

$$x^2 - 6x = y$$
$$y = x - 10$$

5. Which of the following points is a solution to the system of equations above?

A) $(-2, -12)$
B) $(2, 8)$
C) $(5, -5)$
D) $(15, 5)$

Questions 6 and 7 refer to the following information.

A farmer plans to use a 500–foot roll of metal fencing to construct a rectangular chicken pen.

6. What is the area of the largest chicken pen that can be constructed from the fencing?

A) 500 square feet
B) 10,000 square feet
C) 15,000 square feet
D) 15,625 square feet

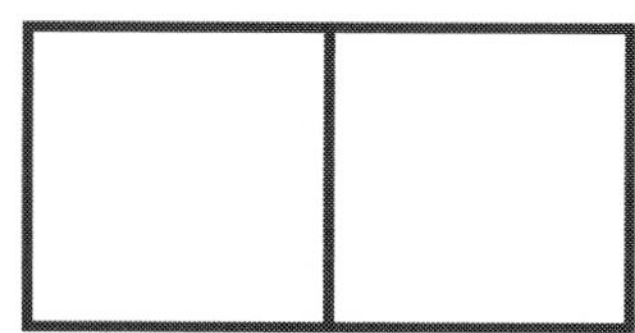

7. The farmer decides to make two pens of equal size, as shown in the image above. What is the approximate area of the largest chicken pen that can be constructed from the fencing?

   A) 7,500 square feet
   B) 8,666.66 square feet
   C) 10,416.66 square feet
   D) 15,625 square feet

Questions 8 and 9 refer to the following information.

The quadratic function $y = ax^2 + bx + c$ crosses the y–axis at $(0, -3)$ and passes through the points $(1, 2)$ and $(-1, 2)$.

8. Which of the following is the value of a?

   A) –5
   B) 0
   C) 5
   D) 10

9. Which of the following is the value of b?

   A) –5
   B) 0
   C) 5
   D) 10

10. Which of the following quadratic functions does NOT have a real solution?

    A) $y = t^2 - 3t - 4$
    B) $y = t^2 - 3t - 2$
    C) $y = t^2 - 3t + 2$
    D) $y = t^2 - 3t + 4$

Rational Functions

Concept & Strategy Lesson

Students must be able to rewrite and solve rational expressions in one variable and recognize extraneous solutions.

Rational Functions

- **Common Denominators** – combine like terms
- **Polynomial Long Division**
- **Synthetic Division**
- There are workarounds for both of these methods

Example 1:

What is one possible solution to the equation $x - 13 = -\frac{42}{x}$?

Rational Function Word Problems

- The most common rational function word problems are those that involve rates of work.
- Remember that *distance* = *rate* × *time* can be rewritten as $rate = \frac{distance}{time}$.
- When two people work together on a project, you should add their rates of work together: $rate_1 + rate_2 =$ *total rate*

Example 2:

Julian is trying to fill his pool using two different garden hoses. One of the garden hoses fills the pool 3 times as fast as the other one does. Together, the garden hoses can fill the pool in 32 hours. Which of the following equations can be used to solve for *t*, the number of hours needed for the slower garden hose to fill the pool?

A) $\frac{1}{t} + \frac{3}{t} = \frac{1}{32}$
B) $t + 3t = 32$
C) $\frac{32}{t} + \frac{96}{t} = \frac{1}{t}$
D) $\frac{3}{t} - \frac{1}{t} = 32$

Rational Functions Practice Problems

1. What is one possible solution to the equation $\frac{6}{x-3} - \frac{4}{x-2} = 1$?

2. Which of the following is the set of all possible solutions to the equation $\frac{x}{x-2} + \frac{1}{x-4} = \frac{2}{x^2-6x+8}$?

   A) $x = -1$
   B) $x = 4$
   C) $x = -1$ and 4
   D) $x = 2$ and 4

3. For all values of $x \neq \frac{1}{2}, x \neq 3,$ the expression $\frac{2x^2-5x-3}{(x-3)^2} \cdot \frac{x^2-5x-6}{2x+1} =$

   A) $\frac{(2x-1)(x-2)}{2x+1}$
   B) $\frac{x-2}{x-3}$
   C) $x - 2$
   D) $x - 3$

4. If $\frac{1}{x} + \frac{1}{x^2}$, then $x =$

   A) 1
   B) ± 1
   C) $\frac{1 \pm \sqrt{3}}{2}$
   D) $\frac{1 \pm \sqrt{5}}{2}$

$$\frac{x^3 - x^2 - 6x}{x^2 + 5x + 6}$$

5. Which values are excluded from the domain of the function above?

   A) –3 only
   B) –3 and –2
   C) –3 and 0
   D) –3, –2, and 0

Questions 6 and 7 refer to the following information.

Jimmy and Randy are sorting a crop of cabbages by weight. Randy can sort twice as fast as Jimmy, and together they can sort all of the cabbages in 6 hours.

6. How long would it take Randy to sort all of the cabbages by himself?

   A) 2 hours
   B) 4 hours
   C) 9 hours
   D) 18 hours

7. How long would it take Jimmy to sort all of the cabbages by himself?

   A) 2 hours
   B) 4 hours
   C) 9 hours
   D) 18 hours

Questions 8 – 9 refer to the following information.

The cost per ton, $C(x)$, to build a dock that weighs x tons is $C(x) = \frac{350{,}000}{x+625}$.

8. What is the approximate difference in price between a 100-ton and a 125-ton oil platform?

   A) $16
   B) $5,000
   C) $10,000
   D) $15,000

9. A dock that cost $437.50 per ton would cost approximately how much to build?

   A) $450
   B) $800
   C) $76,500
   D) $273,500

Equivalent Forms of Expressions

Concept & Strategy Lesson

Students must be able to choose and produce equivalent forms of expressions to reveal and explain properties of a quantity, especially by using structure.

Equivalent Forms of Expressions

- Simplify what you see
- Factoring or FOILing – do the opposite of what is there
- Choose numbers

Example 1:

$$\frac{1}{1-x}-\frac{1}{x+1}$$

For all real values of x not equal to 1 or -1, which of the following expressions is equivalent to the expression above?

A) -2
B) $-2x$
C) $-\frac{2}{x^2-1}$
D) $-\frac{2x}{x^2-1}$

Example 2:

If the expression $\frac{9x^2}{3x+1}$ is written in the equivalent form $\frac{1}{3x+1}+G$, what is G in terms of x?

A) $3x - 1$
B) $3x + 1$
C) $9x^2$
D) $9x^2 - 1$

Equivalent Forms of Expressions Practice Problems

1. If the expression $\frac{3x+3}{3x+1}$ is written in the equivalent form $\frac{2}{3x+1} + A$, what is the value of A?

$$x^3 - 3x^2 + 3x - 9$$

2. Which of the following expressions is NOT equivalent to the expression above?

A) $(x - 3)(x^2 + 3)$
B) $(x + 3)(x^2 - 3)$
C) $(x - 1)^3 - 8$
D) $x(x(x - 3) + 3) - 9$

3. For all real values of x in the domain of both $f(x)$ and $g(x)$, $f(g(3x))$ is equivalent to which of the following expressions?

A) $3(f(g(x))$
B) $3f(x)g(x)$
C) $g(f(3x))$
D) It is unable to be determined by the given information.

4. Which of the following equations is not equivalent to the other three, for all nonzero real values of n, R, T, P, and V?

A) $RT = \frac{PV}{n}$
B) $\frac{VP}{T} = Rn$
C) $\frac{1}{V} = \frac{P}{nRT}$
D) $n = \frac{RT}{PV}$

$$\frac{d^{-\frac{1}{2}}c^{\frac{1}{2}}}{d^{-2}c^{3}}$$

5. Which of the following expressions is equivalent to the expression above?

A) $\sqrt{\frac{d^5}{c^5}}$
B) $\sqrt{\frac{c^5}{d^5}}$
C) $\sqrt{\frac{d^3}{c^5}}$
D) $\sqrt{\frac{c^5}{d^3}}$

$$\left(g^{-\frac{1}{2}}\right)^{-4} \times g \times \frac{1}{g^{-1}}$$

6. Which of the following expressions is equal to the expression above?

A) 0
B) 1
C) $\frac{1}{g^4}$
D) g^4

7. Which of the following expressions is not equivalent to $3x^3 - 6x^2 - 144x$?

A) $-x(24 - 3x)(x + 6)$
B) $x(3x - 24)(6 + x)$
C) $x(3x - 8)(x + 18)$
D) $3x(x - 8)(x + 6)$

$$\frac{x-3}{15-2x-x^2} + \frac{3x-6}{2x^2+6x-20}$$

8. The expression above is equivalent to which of the following expressions?

A) $\frac{-1}{2(x+5)}$
B) $\frac{1}{2(x+5)}$
C) $\frac{3}{2(x+5)}$
D) $\frac{5}{2(x+5)}$

$$g(x) = \frac{f(x+h) - f(x)}{h}$$

9. Given that $f(x) = 3x - 7$ and $h \neq 0$, $g(x)$ is equivalent to

A) -11
B) 0
C) 3
D) $3h$

10. For all nonzero real values of U, q_1, q_2, k, and r, which of the following expressions is not equal to the other three?

A) $Ur = kq_1q_2$
B) $\frac{Ur}{kq_1q_2} = 0$
C) $\frac{Ur}{q_1q_2} = k$
D) $U = k\frac{q_1q_2}{r}$

Analysis of Graphs

Concept & Strategy Lesson

Students must be able to interpret the variables and constants in linear and non-linear expressions and understand the connections between algebraic and graphical representations.

Analysis of Graphs

- Review the kinds of graphs in previous lessons
- **Solution or Zero:** ____________________
- Use a table of values to quickly tell if a graph matches a given expression.
- **Points of Intersection:** ______________________________

Example 1:

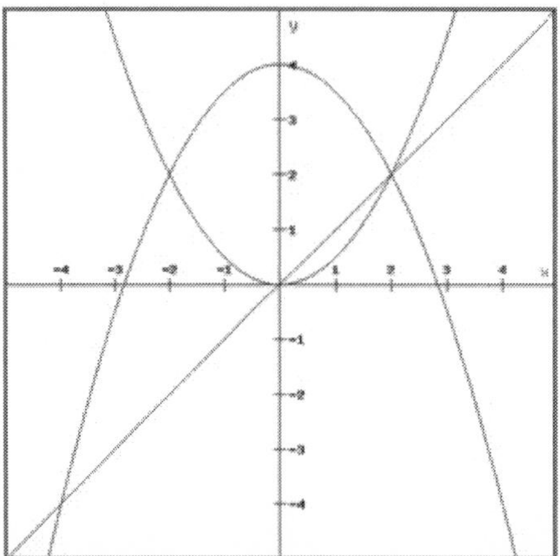

A system of three equations in the xy-plane is shown above. How many solutions does the system have?

A) One
B) Two
C) Three
D) Four

Analysis of Graphs Practice Problems

Questions 1 – 3 refer to the following information.

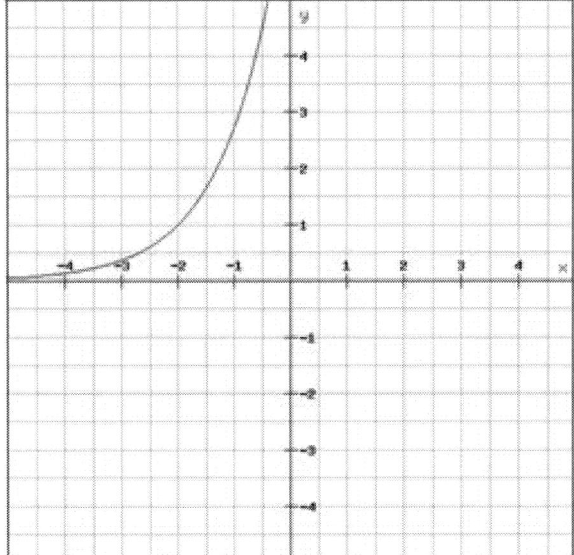

$y = e^{x+2}$

1. To obtain the graph of $y = e^x$, the line above must be

A) shifted two units to the right.
B) shifted two units to the left.
C) shifted two units up.
D) shifted two units down.

2. The horizontal asymptote of the graph above is located at

A) $y = -2$
B) $y = 0$
C) $x = -2$
D) $x = 0$

3. The vertical asymptote of the graph above is located at

A) $y = -2$
B) $y = 0$
C) $x = 0$
D) A vertical asymptote does not exist.

Questions 4 – 5 refer to the following information.

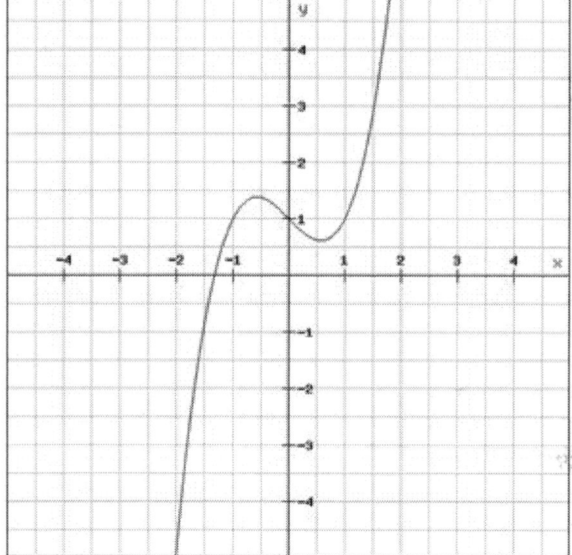

$f(x)$

4. Which of the following is the most likely equation of $f(x)$?

A) $x^3 - x + 1$
B) $x^3 + x^2 + x + 1$
C) $x^3 + x - 1$
D) $x^3 - x^2 + x - 1$

5. The graph of f(-x) is equivalent to which of the following?

   A) $f(-x)$
   B) $-f(-x)$
   C) $-f(x)$
   D) None of the above

6. The graph of $-f(x) + 3$ intersects the y-axis at

   A) $(0, 4)$
   B) $(0, -2)$
   C) $(0, -3)$
   D) $(0, -4)$

Questions 7 and 8 refer to the following information.

$$y = -\frac{1}{2}x^2 - \frac{5}{2}x - 3$$

7. The graph of the function above intersects the x-axis at which points?

   A) $(-2, 0)$ and $(-3, 0)$
   B) $(-2, 0)$ and $(3, 0)$
   C) $(2, 0)$ and $(-3, 0)$
   D) $(2, 0)$ and $(3, 0)$

8. The graph of $y = 1$ intersects the function above in how many points?

   A) Zero
   B) One
   C) Two
   D) Three

Questions 9 – 10 refer to the following information.

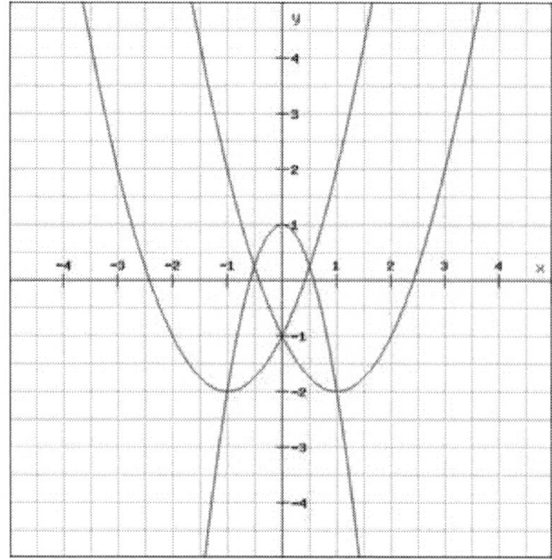

$$f(x) = x^2 - 2x - 1$$
$$g(x) = x^2 + 2x - 1$$
$$h(x) = -3x^2 + 1$$

9. A system of three equations and their graphs in the xy-plane are shown above. How many solutions does the system have?

   A) Zero
   B) One
   C) Two
   D) Three

10. The sum of the y-coordinates of the vertices of each of the functions above is

    A) -3
    B) -1
    C) 0
    D) 1

Graphs of Polynomials

Concept & Strategy Lesson

Students must understand the relationship between zeros and factors of polynomials and use that relationship to sketch graphs.

Properties of the Graphs of Polynomials

To match the sketch of a graph to a polynomial, remember these key points:

- **Zero:** ________________________________
- **Degree:** ____________________________________
- **Leading Coefficient:** __________________________________
- **Even degree** and a **positive leading coefficient:** __________________________
- **Even degree** with a **negative leading coefficient:** __________________________
- **Odd degree** and a **positive leading coefficient:** ____________________________
- **Odd degree** and a **negative leading coefficient:** _________________________________
- You can always use a table of values

Example 1:

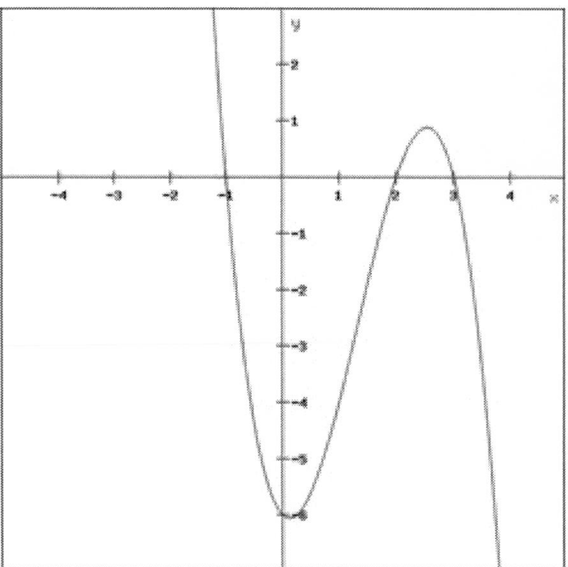

Which of the following expressions matches the graph in the *xy*-plane shown above?

A) $-x^3 + 4x^2 - x - 6$
B) $x^3 - 4x + x + 6$
C) $-x^4 - 3x^3 - 3x^2 + 7x + 6$
D) $x^4 + 3x^3 + 3x^2 - 7x - 6$

Graphs of Polynomials Practice Problems

1. The graph of $y = (4x - 8)(x - 8)$ is a parabola in the xy-plane. In which of the following equivalent equations do the x- and y-coordinates of the vertex of the parabola appear as constants or coefficients?

   A) $4x^2 - 40x + 64$
   B) $4x(x - 10) + 64$
   C) $4(x - 5)^2 - 36$
   D) $(x - 2)(4x - 32)$

Questions 2 – 4 refer to the following information.

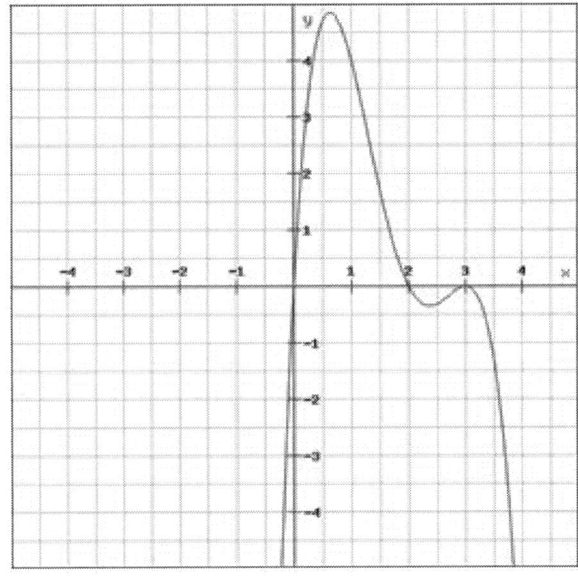

2. Which of the following expressions matches the graph of $f(x)$ in the xy-plane shown above?

   A) $-x(x - 2) (x - 3)$^2
   B) $x(x - 2) (x - 3)$^2
   C) $-x(x - 2)(x - 3)$
   D) $x(x - 2)(x - 3)$

3. Which of the following best describes the end behavior of $f(-x)$?

   A) As x decreases, $f(-x)$ increases. As x increases, $f(-x)$ increases.
   B) As x decreases, $f(-x)$ increases. As x increases, $f(-x)$ decreases.
   C) As x decreases, $f(-x)$ decreases. As x increases, $f(-x)$ increases.
   D) As x decreases, $f(-x)$ decreases. As x increases, $f(-x)$ decreases.

4. Which of the following best describes the end behavior of $-f(x)$?

   A) As x decreases, $-f(x)$ increases. As x increases, $-f(x)$ increases.
   B) As x decreases, $-f(x)$ increases. As x increases, $-f(x)$ decreases.
   C) As x decreases, $-f(x)$ decreases. As x increases, $-f(x)$ increases.
   D) As x decreases, $-f(x)$ decreases. As x increases, $-f(x)$ decreases.

Questions 5 and 6 refer to the following information.

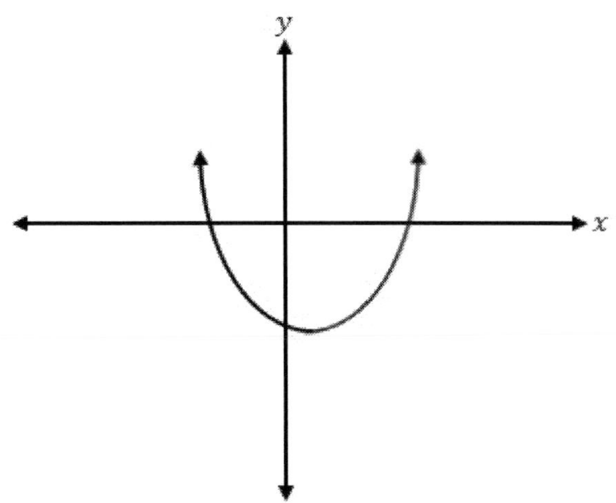

Figure not drawn to scale.

5. The parabola above has a vertex at $(1, -4)$ and intersects the line y=4 at $(5, 4)$. Which of the following could be equation of the parabola, f(x)?

A) $y = \frac{1}{2}x^2 + x - \frac{7}{2}$
B) $y = \frac{1}{2}x^2 - x - \frac{7}{2}$
C) $y = x^2 + 2x - \frac{7}{2}$
D) $y = x^2 - 2x - \frac{7}{2}$

6. The vertex of $-f(-x)$ is located at which of the following points?

A) $(-1, -4)$
B) $(-1, 4)$
C) $(1, -4)$
D) $(1, 4)$

Questions 7 and 8 refer to the following information.

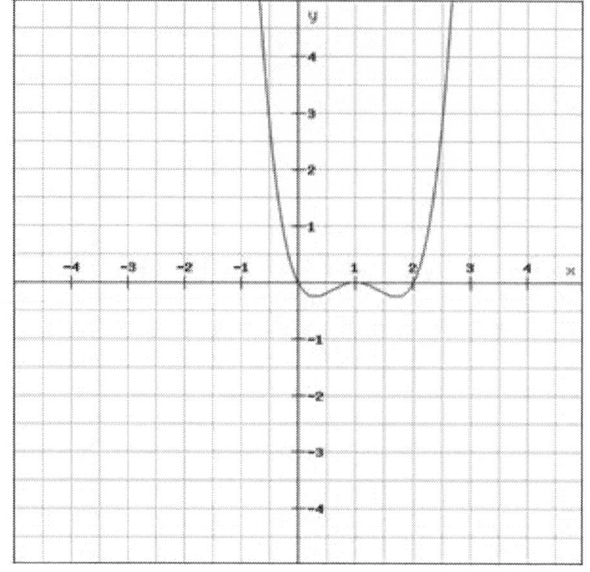

7. Which of the following expressions matches the graph of $f(x)$ in the xy-plane shown above?

A) $f(x) = x(x - 1)^2 (x - 2)$
B) $f(x) = x(x + 1)^2 (x + 2)$
C) $f(x) = x(x - 1)(x - 2)$
D) $f(x) = x(x + 1)(x + 2)$

8. What is the maximum value of the function graphed on the xy-plane shown above, for $0 \leq x \leq 2$?

A) 0
B) 1
C) 2
D) ∞

9. The graph of $y = -2(x + 2)^2 + 2$ is a parabola in the xy-plane. In which of the following equivalent equations are the roots of the parabola most easily identified?

A) $y = -2(x^2 + 4x + 4) + 2$
B) $y = -2x(x - 2) + 6$
C) $y = 2x^2 + 8x + 6$
D) $y = -2(x + 1)(x + 3)$

10. The y-value of which of the following polynomials would increase as its x-value approaches ∞?

A) $y = -2(-x - 5)^2 + 3$
B) $y = -(x + 1)^3 - 2$
C) $y = \frac{1}{2}(3 - x)^2 - 2$
D) $y = \frac{1}{3}(5 - x)^5 - 6$

Isolating and Identifying Terms

Concept & Strategy Lesson

Students must be able to use structure to isolate or identify a quantity of interest in an expression or equation.

Isolating and Identifying Terms

- Often times, the SAT will ask you to solve for a quantity such as $x + 2$ or $3x$ instead of simply solving for x.
- Adjust the initial expression
- Watch out for trick answers – only choose the value of x if the problem wants to know what x is!

Example 1:

If $\frac{3}{4}c - \frac{2}{3}d = -12$, what is the value of $8d - 9c$?

Example 2:

$$3x - 6y = 178.5$$
$$5y - 2x = 161.5$$

For the system of equations above, what is the value of $x - y$?

Isolating and Identifying Terms Practice Problems

1. If $\frac{3}{1-c} = -\frac{9}{d}$ where $c \neq 1$ and $d \neq 0$, what is d in terms of c?

A) $d = 3c - 3$
B) $d = 3 - 3c$
C) $d = \frac{1}{3}c - 3$
D) $d = 3 - \frac{1}{3}c$

2. If $x^{-\frac{1}{4}} = y$, where y > 0 and x > 0, which of the following equations gives x in terms of y?

A) $x = \frac{1}{\sqrt[4]{y}}$
B) $x = \frac{1}{y^4}$
C) $x = \sqrt[4]{y}$
D) $x = -x^4$

3. If $F = \frac{1}{4\pi\epsilon_0}\frac{q_1q_2}{r^2}$, $F \neq 0$, $r \neq 0$, and $\epsilon_0 \neq 0$, then $r^2 =$

A) $\frac{1}{4\pi\epsilon_0}\frac{q_1q_2}{\sqrt{F}}$
B) $\frac{1}{4\pi\epsilon_0}\frac{q_1q_2}{F}$
C) $4\pi\epsilon_0\frac{F}{q_1q_2}$
D) $4\pi\epsilon_0\frac{\sqrt{F}}{q_1q_2}$

4. In right triangle ABC, where C is a right triangle, a, b, and c are all side lengths of the triangle, with c being its hypotenuse. Which of the following represents b in terms of a and c?

A) $b = a - c$
B) $b = c - a$
C) $b = \sqrt{a^2 - c^2}$
D) $b = \sqrt{c^2 - a^2}$

5. If $\sin^2 x + \cos^2 x = 1$, then $\sin x =$

A) $\sqrt{\cos^2 x - 1}$
B) $\sqrt{1 - \cos^2 x}$
C) $\sqrt{\cos^2 x + 1}$
D) $\sqrt{1 + \cos^2 x}$

$$8\left(\frac{x^2}{y}\right) = y$$

6. If (x, y) is a solution to the equation above and $x \neq 0, y \neq 0$, what is the ratio of $\frac{y}{x}$?

A) 2
B) $2\sqrt{2}$
C) 4
D) 64

7. The volume of a cone can be found by using the formula $V = \frac{\pi r^2 h}{3}$. If the height of a cone is twice the length of its radius, what is the height of the cone in terms of its volume?

A) $h = \sqrt[3]{\frac{12\pi}{V}}$
B) $h = \sqrt[3]{\frac{\pi V}{12}}$
C) $h = \sqrt[3]{\frac{12V}{\pi}}$
D) $h = \sqrt[3]{\frac{\pi}{12V}}$

Questions 8 – 10 refer to the following information.

$f = \frac{\omega}{2\pi}$ $T = \frac{1}{f}$ $\omega = \omega_0 + at$

8. Which of the following represents ω_0 in terms of f, a, and t?

A) $\omega_0 = \frac{2\pi f}{at}$
B) $\omega_0 = \frac{at}{2\pi f}$
C) $\omega_0 = 2\pi f - at$
D) $\omega0 = 2\pi f + at$

9. Which of the following represents ω in terms of T?

A) $\omega = \frac{2\pi}{T}$
B) $\omega = 2\pi T$
C) $\omega = 2\pi - T$
D) $\omega = \frac{T}{2\pi}$

10. Which of the following represents ω_0 in terms of t, a, and T?

A) $\omega_0 = \frac{2\pi - atT}{T}$
B) $\omega_0 = \frac{atT - 2\pi}{T}$
C) $\omega_0 = \frac{2\pi T - at}{T}$
D) $\omega_0 = \frac{at - 2\pi T}{T}$

Complex Numbers

Concept & Strategy Lesson

While these sound scary to many students, it can be very easy if you simply remember the basics of working with imaginary numbers.

The Imaginary Number

- The imaginary number, i, is a variable that always has the same value on the SAT.
- i is equivalent to $\sqrt{-1}$. This lets us work with it to find values we can work with, unlike true variables. Try working with it to be able to memorize the relationships below:
  - $i = \sqrt{-1}$
  - $i^2 = i \times i =$ __________
  - $i^3 = i \times i^2 =$ __________
  - $i^4 = i^2 \times i^2 =$ __________
- To quickly simplify an imaginary number raised to an integer power, use long division to divide the exponent by 4.
  - Ex: $i^{27} =$ ____________________

Adding, Subtracting, Multiplying, and Simplifying Complex Numbers

- **Complex Number:** $a + bi$
- **Adding and Subtracting:**
  - Example: $(3 - 2i) - (2 + 8i) = 1 - 10i$.
- **Multiplying:**
  - Example: $3i(9 - 2i) = 27i - 6i^2 = 27i + 6$.

Example 1:

The expression $(i - 3)(5 - 2i) - (11i - 13)$ is equivalent to what? (Note: $i = \sqrt{-1}$)

Dividing Complex Numbers

- **Division:** To simplify these, you must multiply both the numerator and the denominator by the conjugate of the denominator.
    - **Conjugate:** ___________________________

Example 2:
Which of the following is equal to $\frac{3-2i}{2-5i}$? (Note: $i = \sqrt{-1}$)

A) $\frac{11}{10}$

B) $-\frac{16+11i}{21}$

C) $\frac{4+11i}{29}$

D) $\frac{16+11i}{29}$

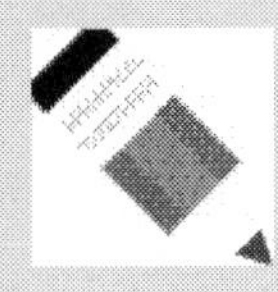

Complex Numbers Practice Problems

(Note: $i = \sqrt{-1}$)

1. Which of the following is equal to $(7 - 6i)(3 + 15i)$?

   A) $-69 + 87i$
   B) $21 - 90i$
   C) $111 - 90i$
   D) $111 + 87i$

2. Which of the following is equal to i^{675}?

   A) $-i$
   B) -1
   C) 1
   D) i

3. Which of the following is equal to $\frac{19-8i}{i}$?

   A) $-8 - 19i$
   B) $-8 + 19i$
   C) $8 - 19i$
   D) $8 + 19i$

Questions 4 and 5 refer to the following information.

$$y = x^4 - 81$$

4. Which of the following is not a root of the above polynomial?

   A) -3
   B) 3
   C) $3i$
   D) $1 - 3i$

5. Which of the following is not a factor of the above polynomial?

   A) $x^2 - 9$
   B) $x^2 - 3$
   C) $x + 3$
   D) $x^2 + 9$

6. $(-i^2)^2 \times i^5 =$

   A) -1
   B) $-i$
   C) i
   D) 1

7. Which of the following quadratic functions does not have any imaginary roots?

   A) $y = 2x^2 + 3x + 3$
   B) $y = 5x^2 + 5x + 1$
   C) $y = 5x^2 + 6x + 7$
   D) $y = 8x^2 + 14x + 12$

8. Which of the following quadratic functions only has imaginary roots?

   A) $y = 5x^2 + 10x + 4$
   B) $y = 2x^2 + 5x + 2$
   C) $y = 3x^2 + 4x + 7$
   D) $y = 8x^2 + 10x + 3$

9. Which of the following answer choices lists the terms in ascending order?

   A) $i^8 < 2i^{10} < 2i^{12} < i^{14}$
   B) $i^8 < i^{14} < 2i^{10} < 2i^{12}$
   C) $2i^{10} < i^8 < i^{14} < 2i^{12}$
   D) $2i^{10} < i^{14} < i^8 < 2i^{12}$

10. $\frac{3-i}{i-3} =$

A) -8
B) -1
C) 1
D) 8

Lines, Angles, Triangles

Concept & Strategy Lesson

Students must be able to use concepts and theorems about congruence and similarity to solve problems above lines, angles, and triangles.

Lines and Angles

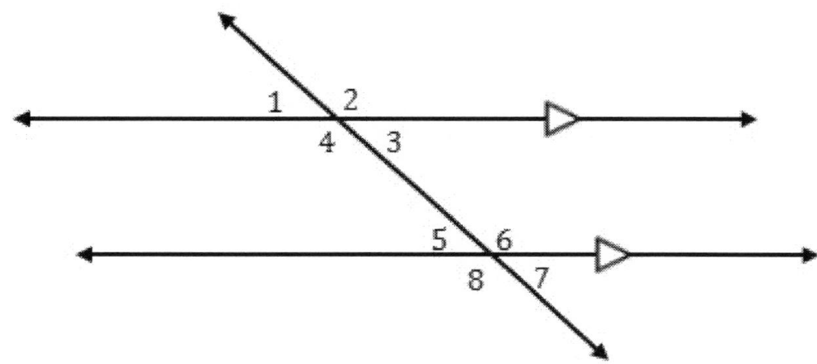

- **Transversal** ______________________________
- **Vertical Angles** __________________________
- **Congruent** _______________________________
- **Supplementary** ___________________________
- **Which angles are congruent?** _________________________________

Triangles

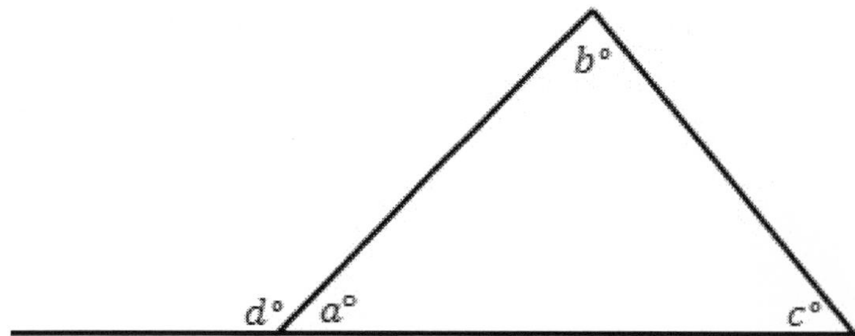

- The measures of the interior angles of a triangle add up to: __________
- The measure of an exterior angle of a triangle is equal to the sum of the two interior angles of the triangle that are not adjacent to that exterior angle ($d = b + c$).
- The longest side of a triangle is always opposite the largest interior angle of the triangle, the shortest side of a triangle is always opposite the smallest interior angle, and If two of the interior angles of a triangle have equal measures, then the sides opposite those two angles have equal lengths.
- The lengths of any two sides of a triangle must add up to more than the third side of the triangle.

- **Isosceles triangle:** __________________________

- **Equilateral Triangle:** __________________________

Congruence in Triangles

Two triangles are congruent if they have exactly the same 3 side lengths and the same 3 angle measures

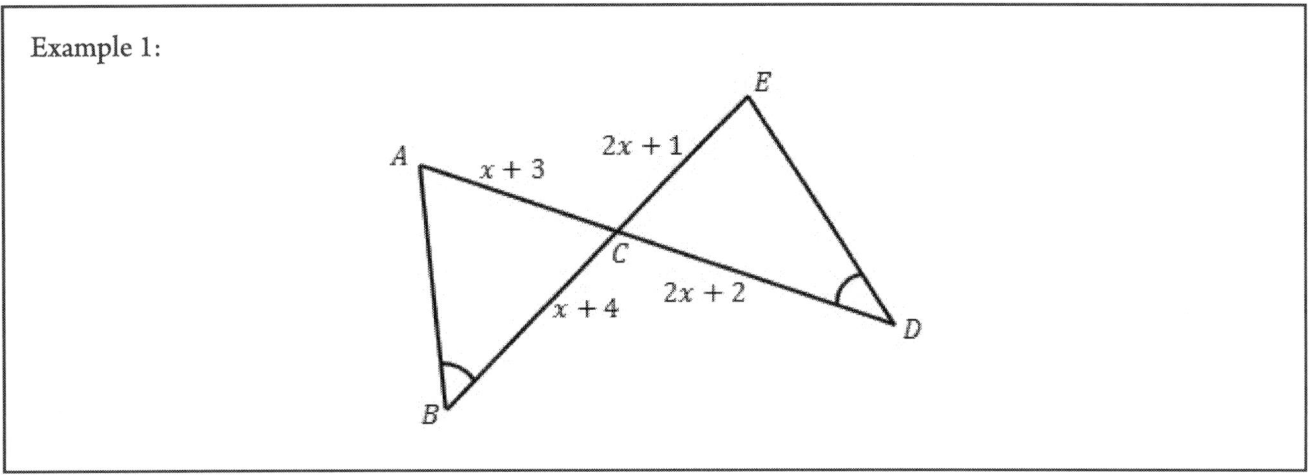

Symbols to Remember

The SAT will use some of the following symbols to represent geometric relationships, so it is important to know the meanings:

- $\sim$ denotes similarity
- $\cong$ denotes congruence
- $\perp$ denotes perpendicular lines
- $||$ denotes parallel lines

Lines, Angles, Triangles Practice Problems

Questions 1 and 2 refer to the following information.

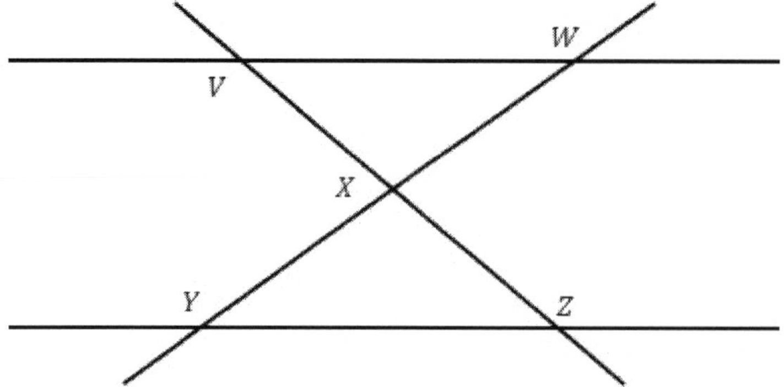

Note: Figure not drawn to scale.

In the figure above, $\Delta VWX \sim \Delta ZYX$.

1. Which of the following must be true?

   A) (VZ) ⊥ (WY)
   B) (VW) ⊥ (ZY)
   C) (VZ) || (WY)
   D) (VW) || (ZY)

2. If $m\angle XZY$ is 50° and $m\angle VWX$ is 45°, what is $m\angle VXW$?

   A) 75°
   B) 85°
   C) 95°
   D) 105°

3. Which of the following could not be the set of lengths of the sides of a triangle?

   A) 6, 7, 8
   B) 10, 12, 22
   C) 15, 16, 30
   D) 1, 98, 98

Questions 4 and 5 refer to the following information.

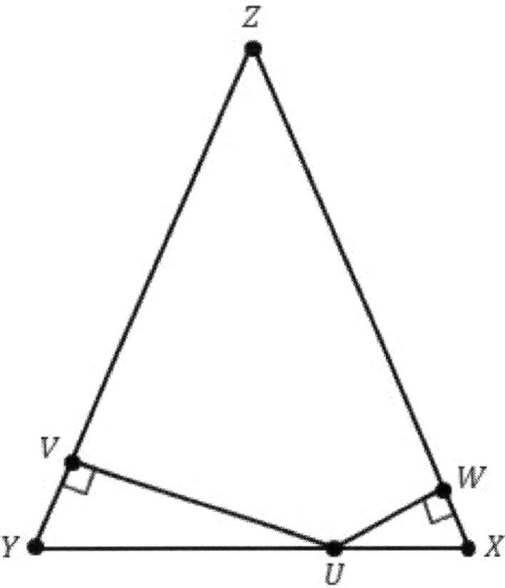

Note: Figure not drawn to scale.

4. Triangle XYZ above is isosceles with $YZ = XZ$ and $YX = 52$. The ratio of UW to UV is $4 : 9$. What is the length of UY?

A) 13
B) 14
C) 26
D) 36

5. What of the following is equivalent to $\frac{\angle VUY}{\angle WUX}$?

A) $\frac{4}{9}$
B) 1
C) $\frac{13}{9}$
D) $\frac{9}{4}$

Questions 6 and 7 refer to the following information.

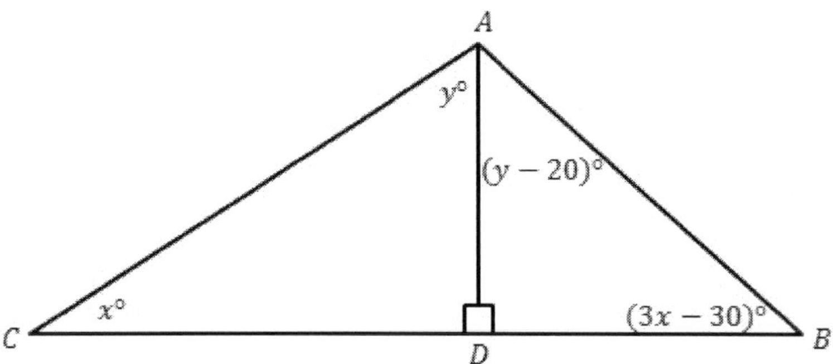

Note: Figure not drawn to scale.

6. What is the value of $y - x$?

   A) 15
   B) 25
   C) 40
   D) 65

7. What is the measure of $\angle$ BAC?

   A) 25°
   B) 45°
   C) 90°
   D) 110°

Questions 8 – 10 refer to the following information.

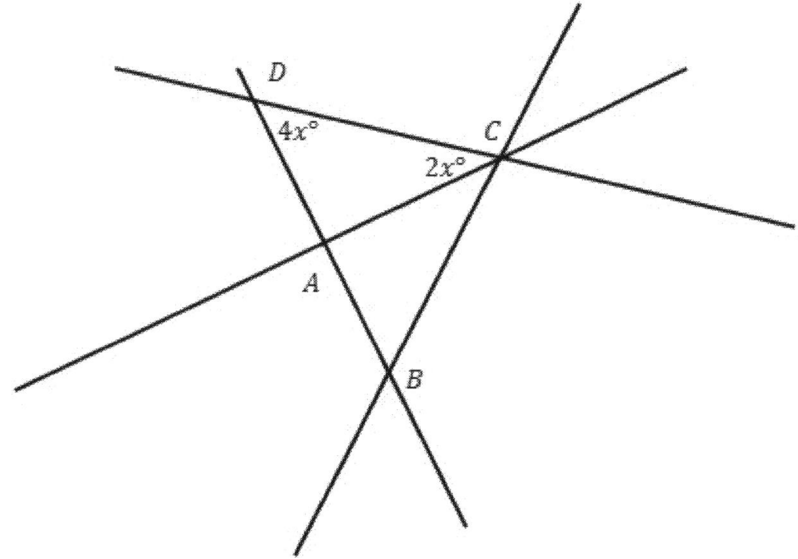

Note: Figure not drawn to scale.

8. If CA bisects both DB and $\angle BCD$ and $CB = DC$, what is the measure of $\angle BCD$?

A) 20°
B) 40°
C) 60°
D) 80°

9. Based on the information obtained in Question 17, what is the measure of $\angle DAC$?

A) 30°
B) 60°
C) 90°
D) 120°

10. Which of the following side lengths is longest?

A) AB
B) BC
C) AC
D) It is impossible to determine.

Right Triangles

Concept & Strategy Lesson

Similarity

In review:

- Same shape, different sizes
- Set up a proportion to solve

Pythagorean Theorem

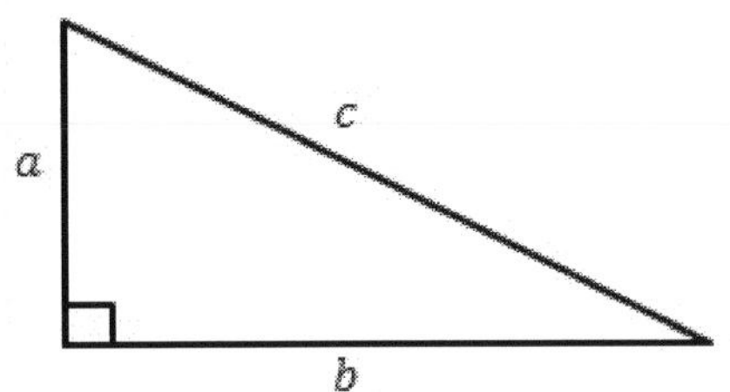

$a^2 + b^2 = c^2$

Common ratios: 3:4:5

5:12:13

Special Right Triangles

- 45-45-90
- 30-60-90

Trigonometric Ratios

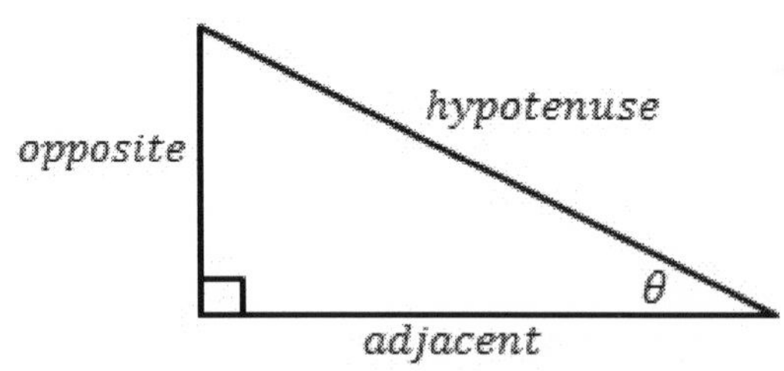

- SOH CAH TOA: $\sin\theta = \frac{opposite}{hypotenuse}$ $\cos\theta = \frac{adjacent}{hypotenuse}$ $\tan\theta = \frac{opposite}{adjacent}$
- $\sin\theta = \cos(90 - \theta)$ and $\cos\theta = \sin(90 - \theta)$
- $\frac{\sin\theta}{\cos\theta} = \tan\theta$

Example 1:

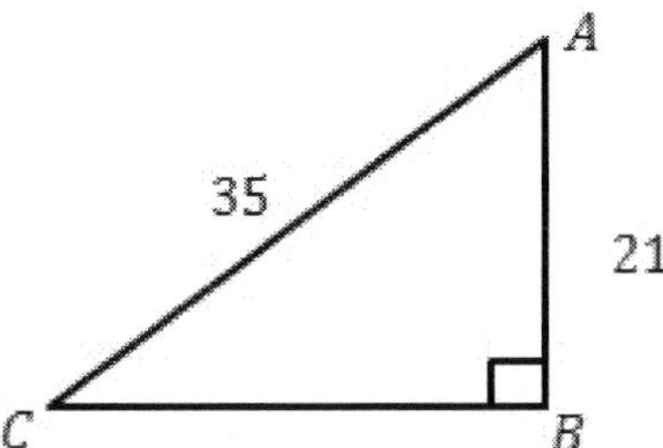

Given triangle ABC above, what is the value of $\cos C$?

A) $\frac{3}{5}$
B) $\frac{3}{4}$
C) $\frac{4}{5}$
D) $\frac{4}{3}$

Example 2:

Joe is looking up to the top of an 85-foot vertical cliff with an angle of elevation, from the ground, of 45°. If he walks towards the cliff until his angle of elevation to the top of the cliff is 60°, how far, to the nearest tenth of a foot, did he walk?

Right Triangles Practice Problems

Questions 1 – 4 refer to the following information.

An architect drew the sketch below while designing a house roof. The dimensions shown are for the interior of the triangle.

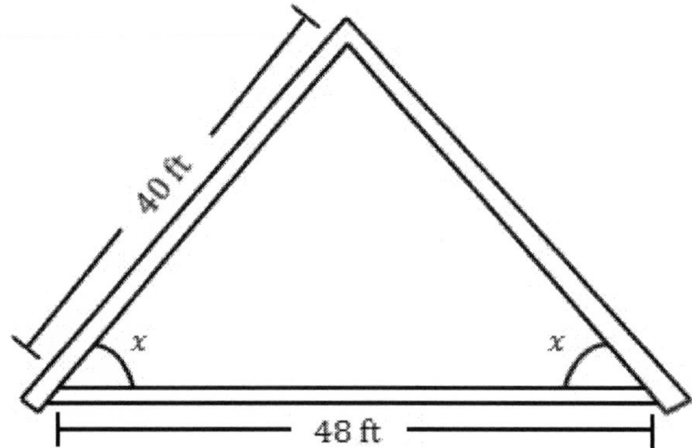

1. What is the value of cos x?

2. What is the value of sin x?

3. What is the value of tan x?

4. What is the height of the roof above, to the nearest foot?

5. A right triangle has legs of length x and $x\sqrt{3}$. What is the angle measure of the smallest angle of the right triangle?

   A) 15°
   B) 30°
   C) 45°
   D) It is unable to be determined.

6. The lengths of the three legs of a right triangle exist in the ratio of $x : x + 7 : x + 8$. What is the area of the triangle?

   A) 30
   B) 32.5
   C) 60
   D) 65

7. The diagonal of a rectangle measures 20 inches. If the length of the rectangle is 4 inches longer than its width, what is the area, in square feet, of the rectangle?

   A) $\frac{2}{3}$
   B) $1\frac{1}{3}$
   C) 96
   D) 192

Questions 8 and 9 refer to the following information.

Samir is facing a 200-foot tower and stands 150 feet away from the base of it.

8. To the nearest degree, what is Samir's angle of elevation when he looks at the top of the tower?

   A) 31°
   B) 37°
   C) 51°
   D) 53°

9. Samir turns around 180° and, using the same angle of elevation, views the top of a 300-foot tower. To the nearest foot, how far away is he from the tower?

   A) 136 feet
   B) 226 feet
   C) 239 feet
   D) 398 feet

10. The side lengths of four triangles are given below. Which is not a right triangle?

   A) 6, 8, 10
   B) $4, 4\sqrt{2}, 4\sqrt{2}$
   C) $6, 6\sqrt{3}, 12$
   D) 8, 15, 17

Circles

Concept & Strategy Lesson

Degrees to Radians

$360° = 2\pi$ radians; you can always set up a proportion to convert back and forth

Circles

Circles have basic equations and proportions that help us solve for missing information:

- **Circumference** ____________________
- **Area** ________________
- The ratio of the **arc length** of a circle to the circumference of the circle is equal to the ratio of the central angle of the circle to 360° (or 2π).

$$\frac{arc\ length}{2\pi r} = \frac{central\ angle\ measure}{360°}$$

- The ratio of the **area of a sector** of a circle to the area of the circle is also equal to the ratio of the central angle of the circle to 360° (or 2π).

$$\frac{sector\ area}{\pi r^2} = \frac{central\ angle\ measure}{360°}$$

- **Inscribed angle** ________________________

Example 1:

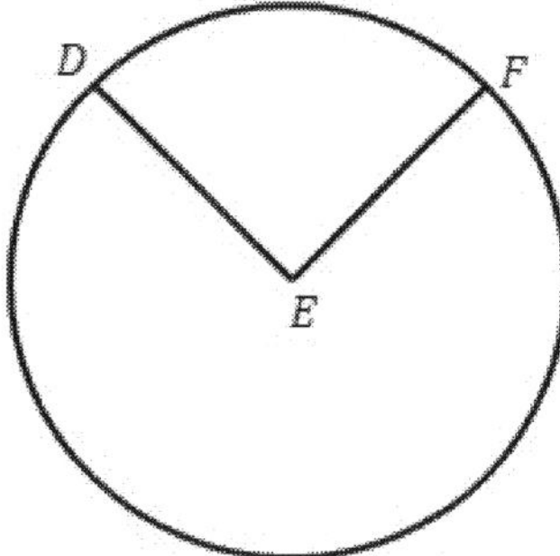

Circle E above has diameter of length d and $\angle DEF$ is a right angle. What is the length of chord $\overline{DF}$ in terms of d?

A) $\frac{d\sqrt{2}}{4}$
B) $\frac{d}{2}$
C) $\frac{d\sqrt{2}}{2}$
D) $d\sqrt{2}$

The Unit Circle

If you find it useful, you can memorize the unit circle to save time when solving questions involving trigonometric ratios. The first number in each set of parentheses is the cosine of the angle measurement; the second number is the sine of the angle measurement.

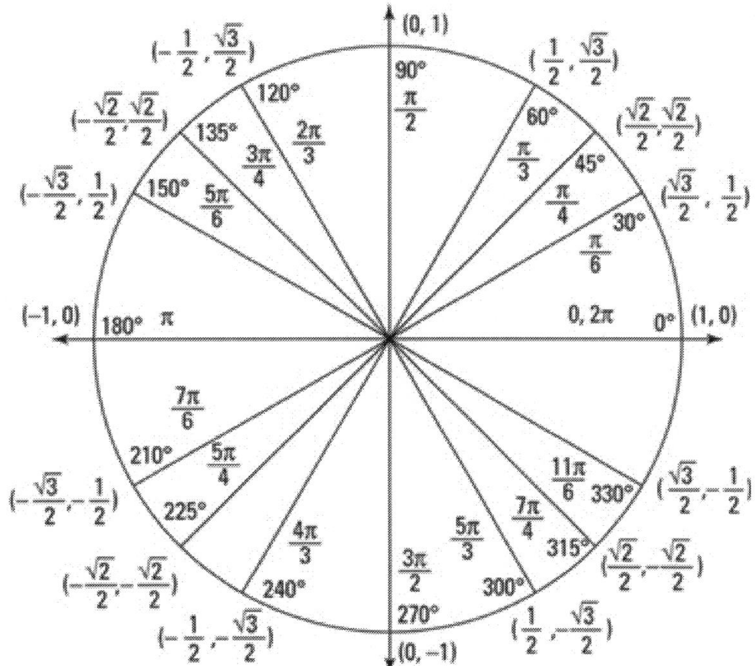

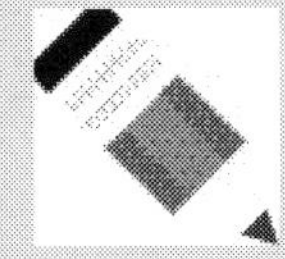

Circles Practice Problems

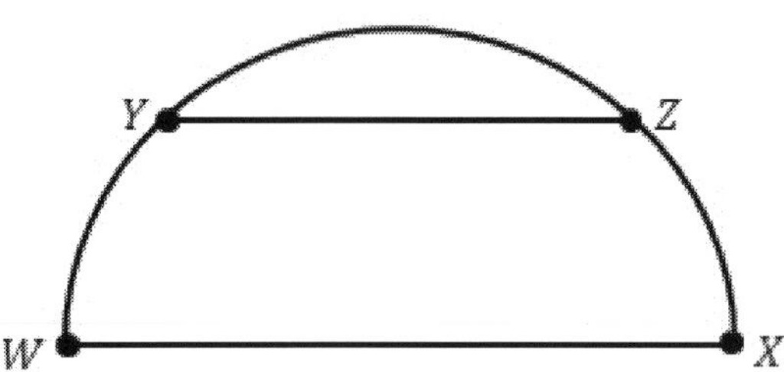

1. The semicircle above has a radius of r inches, and chord $\overline{YZ}$ is parallel to the diameter $\overline{WX}$. If the length of $\overline{YZ}$ is $\frac{1}{2}$ of the length of $\overline{WX}$, what is the distance between the chord and the diameter in terms of r?

   A) $\frac{r}{4}$
   B) $\frac{3}{4}r$
   C) $\frac{r\sqrt{3}}{2}$
   D) $\frac{\sqrt{15}}{4}r$

2. A circle has a sector with arc length of 10π and radius of 25. How large is the central angle of that sector, in radians?

   A) $\frac{\pi}{5}$
   B) $\frac{2\pi}{5}$
   C) $\frac{3\pi}{5}$
   D) $\frac{4\pi}{5}$

3. A circle has a sector with area of 10π and diameter of 10. How large is the central angle of that sector, in radians?

   A) $\frac{\pi}{5}$
   B) $\frac{2\pi}{5}$
   C) $\frac{3\pi}{5}$
   D) $\frac{4\pi}{5}$

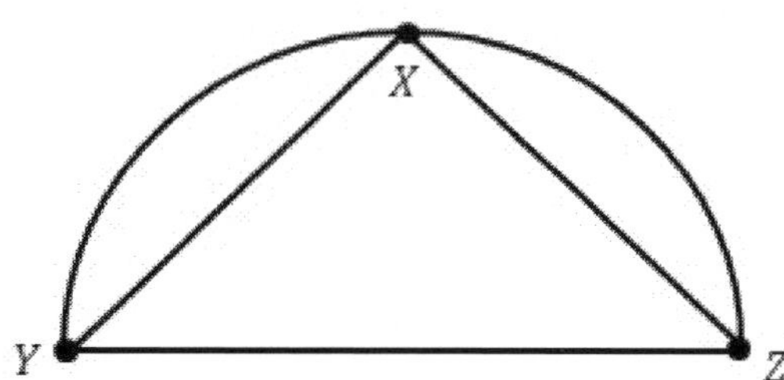

Isosceles right triangle *XYZ* is inscribed in the semicircle with radius *r* above.

4. In terms of *r*, what is the length of minor arc *XY* above?

   A) $\frac{\pi r}{2}$
   B) πr
   C) $\frac{\pi r^2}{4}$
   D) $\frac{\pi r^2}{2}$

5. $\sin\frac{\pi}{2}$ is equivalent to which of the following?

   A) -sin 270°
   B) -sin 90°
   C) sin (-180°)
   D) sin 270°

6. In 1 mile, a tire makes exactly *a* complete rotations. What is the radius of the tire, in feet, in terms of *a*?

   A) $\frac{1}{2\pi a}$
   B) $\frac{1}{\pi a}$
   C) $\frac{2640}{\pi a}$
   D) $\frac{5280}{\pi a}$

7. If the area of a circle is increased by 50%, its radius is increased by approximately

   A) 22.5%
   B) 25.0%
   C) 50.0%
   D) 61.2%

8. A circle is inscribed within a trapezoid and tangent to the trapezoid at both of its bases. If the bases of the trapezoid measure 10 and 16 and the trapezoid has an area of 130, what is the area of the inscribed circle?

A) 25π
B) 50π
C) 75π
D) 100π

9. $\sin \frac{9\pi}{4}$ is equivalent to all of the following except

A) $\sin 45°$
B) $\cos -45°$
C) $\sin 315°$
D) $\cos 315°$

10. If the circumference of a circle is decreased by 30%, the length of its radius is decreased by what percent?

Volume

Concept & Strategy Lesson

Students must be able to use given information about figures to calculate missing information. All required volume formulas will be provided to students in the reference section of the SAT.

Reference Equations
(Put volume ref. equations here?)

Volume

- Density: ______________________________

Example 1:

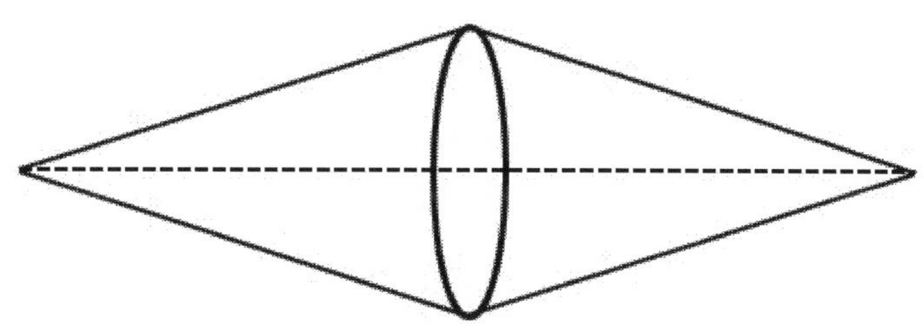

The solid figure above consists of two congruent metal cones attached at their bases. The diameter of the base of each cone is 10 cm and the density of the metal is 6.4 grams per cubic cm. If the mass of the figure is 5.094 kg, what is the length of the figure, to the nearest cm, as marked by the dashed line above? (Density is mass divided by volume.)

Volume Practice Problems

Questions 1 – 3 refer to the following information.

Density of common metals (lb/in3)	
Zinc	0.258
Iron	0.284
Steel	0.292
Copper	0.324

1. To the nearest tenth of a pound, how many more pounds does a zinc sphere of radius 4 inches weigh than a copper sphere of radius 3 inches?

2. To the nearest tenth of a pound, how many more pounds does a zinc cube of side length 7 inches than a steel sphere of radius 4 inches weigh?

3. To create a metal engine part, a factory worker must fill a hollow mold (Volume: 0.694 ft^3) with one of the above four metals. The mass of the engine part must be between 340 and 352 pounds. Which of the metals can be used?

   A) Zinc and Iron
   B) Iron and Steel
   C) Zinc, Iron, and Steel
   D) Iron, Steel, and Copper

4. A cube of volume 512 cm^3 is inscribed within a sphere. What is the volume of the sphere, to the nearest cm^3?

   A) 1,045
   B) 1,393
   C) 2,660
   D) 11,144

Questions 5 and 6 refer to the following information.

Object:	Prism A	Prism B	Prism C
Length	3 cm	1.5 m	50 cm
Width	2 cm	1.0 m	1 m
Height	4 cm	2.0 m	75 cm
Mass	25 g	3145 kg	348 kg

5. An object will float if its density is less than the density of the substance that it is submerged in. Which of the above objects will float in water (Density = 1 g/cm^3)?

A) Prism A
B) Prism B
C) Prism C
D) None of the above

6. The density of a salt water solution is equivalent to $1 + \frac{x}{100}$ g/cm^3, where x is the salt percentage of the salt water. Of the following salt water solutions below, which has the lowest salt concentration but can be used to float all 3 prisms?

A) 4% salt water solution
B) 5% salt water solution
C) 6% salt water solution
D) 7% salt water solution

7. How many books (6 in × 4 in × 3 in) will fit inside of a cubic box with side length of 1 foot?

A) 12
B) 18
C) 24
D) 72

8. The volume of a square pyramid is 108 m^3. Which of the following are not possible dimensions of the pyramid?

A) $4 \times 9 \times 9$
B) $3 \times 3 \times 36$
C) $6 \times 6 \times 9$
D) $3 \times 4 \times 27$

9. The trapezoid that makes the base of a trapezoidal prism has a height of 10 inches and base heights of 6 and 8 inches. If the height of the prism is 10 inches what is the volume of the prism, in square inches?

10. Ten cubic boxes, each of side length 3 feet, are inserted into an empty trailer of dimensions 6 feet by 8 feet by 8 feet. To the nearest percentage point, what percentage of the trailer's space is still free?

Circles in the Coordinate Plane

Concept & Strategy Lesson

Students must be able to create an equation or use properties of an equation of a circle to demonstrate or determine a property of the circle's graph.

Circles in the Coordinate Plane

The equation of a circle of center (h, k) and radius r in the xy-coordinate plane is given by the formula $(x - h)^2 + (y - k)^2 = r^2$.

Example 1:

In the xy-plane, a circle with the equation $(x - 3)^2 + (y + 5)^2 = r^2$ passes through the point (0,-1). What is the length of the diameter of the circle?

Completing the Square

Circle equations are sometimes given in the general format of $ax^2 + by^2 + cx + dy + e = 0$. For circle problems where equations are not already in the $(x - h)^2 + (y - k)^2 = r^2$ format, the SAT may require us to "complete the square".

Example: Find the center and radius of the circle with equation $4x^2 + 4y^2 - 16x - 24y + 51 = 0$
Steps to solve: (Insert A PICTURE)

- Move number to other side of equation: $4x^2 + 4y^2 - 16x - 24y = -51$
- Group variables: $4x^2 - 16x + 4y^2 - 24y = -51$
- Divide the coefficient on the squared terms (will almost always be the same for SAT problems): divide by 4 to get $x^2 - 4x + y^2 - 6y = -\frac{51}{4}$
- Now we need to create the square terms to make our classic circle equation make space for the square term: $(x^2 - 4x \quad) + (y^2 - 6y \quad) = -\frac{51}{4}$
- Take the x-term coefficient, multiply it by $\frac{1}{2}$, square it, and add to both sides of the equation; do the same with the y-term: $x: (-4 \times \frac{1}{2})^2 = 4$ and $y: (-6 \times \frac{1}{2})^2 = 9$
- So now we have $(x^2 - 4x + 4) + (y^2 - 6y + 9) = -\frac{51}{4} + 4 + 9$
- This can be converted to squared form: $(x - 2)^2 + (y - 3)^2 = \frac{1}{4}$
- and now we have our solutions: center at (2, 3) and radius $= \sqrt{\frac{1}{4}} = \frac{1}{2}$

Circles in the Coordinate Plane Practice Problems

1. Which of the following is the equation of a circle in the xy-plane?

    A) $x^2 + 2x + y^2 - 6y = 18$
    B) $x^2 + 2x - y^2 - 6y = 18$
    C) $-x^2 + 2x - y^2 - 6y = 18$
    D) $x^2 + 2x + y^2 - 6y = -18$

$$x^2 + 8x + y^2 + 4y = 16$$

2. What is the length of the diameter of the circle in the xy-plane described by the equation above?

$$2x^2 - 4x + 2y^2 + 4y = 16$$

3. What is the center of the circle in the xy-plane described by the equation above?

    A) (-2,2)
    B) (-1,1)
    C) (1,-1)
    D) (2,-2)

$$(x + 4)^2 + (y + 4)^2 = 18$$
$$y - x = 0$$

4. Which of the following lists all of the solutions to the system of equations above?

    A) (-1,-1)
    B) (-1,-1),(-6,-6)
    C) (1,1)
    D) (1,1),(6,6)

Questions 5 and 6 refer to the following information.

A circular metal tin 1.5-inches thick is graphed in the *xy*-plane. On this xy-plane, each 1 unit is equivalent to 1 inch. The equation of the circle is $\left(x-\frac{2}{5}\right)^2+\left(y+\frac{4}{7}\right)^2=5$

5. What is the volume of the metal tin?

   A) 7.5 cubic inches
   B) 20.4 cubic inches
   C) 23.6 cubic inches
   D) 117.5 cubic inches

6. The density of the metal used in the question above is 0.38 pounds/in^3. What is the mass, in ounces, of the metal tin?

   A) 9.0 ounces
   B) 45.6 ounces
   C) 62.0 ounces
   D) 143.5 ounces

7. Which of the following equations describes a circle in the xy-plane with a center of $(-3, 0)$ and a diameter length of 12?

   A) $(x-3)^2+y^2=36$
   B) $(x-3)^2+y^2=144$
   C) $(x+3)^2+y^2=36$
   D) $(x+3)^2+y^2=144$

Questions 8 and 9 refer to the following information.

The diameter of a circle in the *xy*-plane passes through the points (–4,-5) and (3,2).

8. What is the equation of the circle above?

   A) $\left(x-\frac{1}{2}\right)^2+\left(y-\frac{3}{2}\right)^2=\frac{7\sqrt{2}}{2}$
   B) $\left(x-\frac{1}{2}\right)^2+\left(y-\frac{3}{2}\right)^2=\frac{49}{2}$
   C) $\left(x+\frac{1}{2}\right)^2+\left(y+\frac{3}{2}\right)^2=\frac{7\sqrt{2}}{2}$
   D) $\left(x+\frac{1}{2}\right)^2+\left(y+\frac{3}{2}\right)^2=\frac{49}{2}$

9. What is the circumference of the circle?

A) $\frac{7\pi\sqrt{2}}{2}$

B) $7\pi\sqrt{2}$

C) $\frac{49\pi}{2}$

D) 49π

$$x^2 + (y - 1)^2 = 4$$

10. Which of the lines below is not tangent to the equation of the circle above in the xy-plane?

A) $y = 3$
B) $y = -2$
C) $x = -2$
D) $x = 2$

Writing the Essay

Essay Grading
Approaching the Essay
Step-By-Step
Evaluating your Essay
Practice Essay Prompts

Essay Grading

How the New SAT Essay Is Graded

THE SAT ESSAY

- It's optional – however, it is strongly recommended that you take it at least once
- 50-minutes total
- 650-750 word persuasive passage which you will evaluate
- Remember – it's not about whether or not you agree with the author's position on the topic

THE ESSAY PROMPT

Although the passage will differ from test to test, the prompt itself will always look the same:

As you read the passage below, consider how [the author] uses

- evidence, such as facts or examples, to support claims.
- reasoning to develop ideas and to connect claims and evidence.
- stylistic or persuasive elements, such as word choice or appeals to emotion, to add power to the ideas expressed.

The passage will appear here.

Write an essay in which you explain how [the author] builds an argument to persuade his or her audience that [author's claim]. In your essay, analyze how [the author] uses one or more of the features listed above (or features of your own choice) to strengthen the logic and persuasiveness of his or her argument. Be sure that your analysis focuses on the most relevant aspects of the passage.

Your essay should not explain whether you agree with [the author's] claims, but rather explain how the author builds an argument to persuade his or her audience.

THE SAT ESSAY SCORE

- It will not affect your overall SAT score – it will be given as a separate score
- The essay will be graded on a scale of 1 to 4 by two separate essay graders, resulting in a total possible score of 8 for each category

  READING – Score out of 8
  - Was the passage fully understood?
  - Does the essay demonstrate understanding of the complex and nuanced ideas in the passage?

  ANALYSIS – Score out of 8
  - Does the essay go beyond what is explicitly stated in the passage to draw reasonable inferences?
  - Does the essay go beyond a superficial analysis?
  - Is evidence from the passage included and used effectively to support the claims made in the essay?

  WRITING
  - Does the essay focus on one clearly stated central claim?
  - Does the essay utilize a variety of transitional strategies to create a smooth and logical flow of ideas?
  - Is the essay's style formal and informative?
  - Is the use of language precise, high level, and appropriate to the task?
  - Is the essay free of grammar and spelling errors?

Approaching the Essay

ACTIVE READING

- Use active reading – take notes and mark up the important parts
- Read the prompt before you jump into the passage – read with a purpose
- Look for evidence, reasoning elements, and stylistic elements
- Reasoning to develop ideas and to connect claims and evidence.

KINDS OF EVIDENCE

Different kinds of evidence can be more or less compelling, and also operate differently in an argument

- Hypothetical examples
- Anecdotal evidence
- Expert testimony
- Research

REASONING

- How does the author link his claim to his evidence?
- Does the author's reasoning make strong logical sense?

ORGANIZATION

- Have a strong thesis
- Clear structure is important – introduction and conclusion, topic sentences
- Progress your ideas in a logical manner
- Use transitional sentences and phrases

STYLE AND TONE

- Formal, informative tone
- Avoid the use of contractions, slang
- Utilize varied sentence structures
- Include higher-level vocabulary where appropriate

Step By Step

Putting it All Together

TIMING YOUR ESSAY

Read and annotate the passage: *15-20 minutes*
Remember to read the last part of the prompt before reading the passage so that you know the main claim in advance. Take note of evidence, reasoning, and persuasive elements.

Plan the essay: *3-5 minutes*
Identify the items you plan to discuss in the essay and sketch out a brief outline for your essay. Taking the time to plan makes your writing more organized.

Write the essay: *20-25 minutes*
Remember to include an introduction and conclusion. Utilize transitional strategies to improve the flow of the essay.

Review the essay: *Remaining time*
Use your remaining time to review the essay in order to make corrections, revisions, and improvements. The editing step is important to your score.

Evaluating Your Essay

Here are a series of questions that you can use to help you evaluate example essays and other practice essays that you write. While Reading and Analysis sub-scores are contained within one category each, Writing sub-scores will be composed of three smaller components: Focus and Organization, Written Expression, and Conventions.

READING COMPREHENTION

Was the passage fully understood? Does the essay go beyond what the passage explicitly says in order to draw reasonable inferences from the passage?

4 – Essay presents an accurate interpretation of what the text says explicitly and inferentially.
3 – Essay presents a mostly accurate interpretation of what the text says explicitly and inferentially.
2 – Essay presents a generally accurate interpretation of what the text says explicitly, though inferences may be somewhat inaccurate.
1 – Essay presents a minimally accurate interpretation of what the text say explicitly, but makes little or no attempts to present inferences from the text.
0 – Essay presents an inaccurate interpretation of the text or does not present an interpretation of the text at all.

Does the essay demonstrate understanding of the more complex and nuanced ideas from the passage?

4 – Essay demonstrates the student's full comprehension of complex ideas in the source text.
3 – Essay demonstrates the student's extensive comprehension of the complex ideas expressed in the text.
2 – Essay demonstrates the student's basic comprehension of the complex ideas in the text.
1 – Essay demonstrates the student's minimal comprehension of the complex ideas expressed in the text.
0 – Essay demonstrates that the student has little or no comprehension of the complex ideas expressed in the text.

ANALYSIS AND USE OF EVIDENCE

Does the essay analyze the passage in depth or is the analysis superficial?

4 – Response analyzes source text in substantial depth and specificity.
3 – Response analyzes source text in some depth and specificity, but is predominantly general.
2 – Response provides an uneven, cursory analysis that achieves little depth.
1 – Response provides minimal analysis of the source text.
0 – Response provides a wholly inaccurate or incomplete analysis.

Is evidence from the passage included to support claims made in the essay, and is that evidence used properly and integrated smoothly into the essay?

4 – Use of evidence is integrated, comprehensive, relevant, and concrete.
3 – Adequate evidence is included in the response, but citations may be imprecise and evidence may not be well integrated.
2 – Some evidence is included, but it is not properly cited or integrated into the response.
1 – Use of evidence is minimal, absent, incorrect, or irrelevant.
0 – No evidence is provided.

FOCUS AND ORGANIZATION

Does the essay have one clearly stated central claim? Does the essay as a whole focus on that claim?

4 – Central claim is clearly stated, focused, and strongly maintained.
3 – Central claim is clear and mostly maintained, though some loosely related material may be present.
2 – Central claim may only be somewhat clear or partially focused. If the central claim is clear, it may not be sufficiently maintained.
1 – Central claim may be confusing or ambiguous. If the central claim is somewhat clear, it is poorly maintained.
0 – Central claim may be inappropriate to task, purpose, and/or audience or completely off-topic.

Does the essay include a strong introduction and conclusion?

4 – Essay includes a strong introduction and conclusion.
3 – Essay includes an adequate introduction and conclusion.
2 – Essay includes a weak introduction and conclusion.
1 – Essay may be lacking either an introduction or a conclusion.
0 – Essay does not include an introduction or a conclusion.

Does the essay flow logically and smoothly from one idea to the next?

4 – Essay is written in a manner that creates a logical progression of ideas from beginning to end. Essay exhibits consistent use of a variety of transitional strategies.
3 – Essay is written in a manner that creates an adequate progression of ideas from beginning to end. Essay exhibits adequate use of transitional strategies with some variety.
2 – Essay is written in a manner that creates an uneven progression of ideas from beginning to end. Essay exhibits inconsistent use of transitional strategies with little or no variety.
1 – Essay is written in a manner that creates an unclear progression of ideas. Essay exhibits few or no transitional strategies.
0 – Essay is written in a manner that lacks any coherence, clarity, or cohesion. Essay may be illegible.

WRITTEN EXPRESSION

Is the style formal and informative?

4 – Establishes and maintains a formal and informative style.
3 – Establishes and maintains an effective style.
2 – Establishes and mostly maintains an appropriate style.
1 – Fails to maintain an appropriate style or establishes a style that has limited effectiveness.
0 – Establishes inappropriate style.

Is the use of language precise, high level, and appropriate?

4 – Uses precise language consistently, including descriptive words and phrases, linking and transitional words, and words to indicate tone.
3 – Uses mostly precise language, including descriptive words and phrases, linking and transitional words, and words to indicate tone.
2 – Uses some precise language, though language use may be inconsistent.
1 – Includes limited descriptions, details, linking or transitional words, or words to indicate tone.
0 – Uses no precise language.

PRACTICE ESSAY PROMPTS

There are three practice essay prompts listed on the next few pages. Try them out to get a preview of the types of passages you will see on the new SAT.

Practice Essay 1

As you read the passage below, consider how Kristof uses

- evidence, such as facts or examples, to support claims.
- reasoning to develop ideas and to connect claims and evidence.
- stylistic or persuasive elements, such as word choice or appeals to emotion, to add power to the ideas expressed.

Adapted from "Where's the Empathy?" by Nicholas Kristof, published January 24, 2015 in The New York Times.

We hear a lot about wealth gaps, wage gaps, and opportunity gaps, but perhaps we are ignoring a more important gap: an empathy gap. We have a tendency to judge others too harshly, labelling others as lazy or unworthy.

This was made clear to me by the recent death of my high school friend Kevin Green. The doctors say he died at age 54 of multiple organ failure, but the deeper truth is that he died of inequality and a lack of good jobs. Many would have seen Kevin – obese, surviving on disability and food stamps – as a moocher. They would have been harshly judgmental about Kevin's life choices – he should have taken better care of himself, should have made better decisions.

This condescension reflects the delusion on the part of many affluent Americans that those like Kevin are lazy or living the high life. A recent Pew Research Center poll found that more than half of those in the top wealth levels agree that "poor people today have it easy because they can get government benefits without doing anything in return."

It's easy to judge Kevin without knowing him. It becomes harder when you learn more about him. Kevin grew up on a small farm a couple of miles from my family's, and we both attended the same small rural high school. We both ran cross country, took welding and agriculture classes, and joined Future Farmers of America.

The Greens may not have lived the American dream, but they certainly embodied solid upward mobility. Kevin's father, Thomas, had only a third-grade education and couldn't read. But he had a good union job as a cement finisher, paying far above the minimum wage, and he worked hard and made sure his kids did, too. Kevin and his sister both earned high school diplomas. Kevin was sunny, cheerful, and amazingly helpful: At the slightest hint that something needed to be fixed, he was there with a hammer. But then the dream began to disintegrate.

The local glove factory closed, followed by the feed store; in reaction, other blue-collar employers cut back. Good union jobs became hard to find. For a while, Kevin held a low-wage nonunion job with a construction company. When that company went under, he worked as shift manager making trailer homes.

Kevin's life wasn't easy, but he found happiness. He fell in love and had twin boys that he doted on. But because he and his girlfriend struggled financially, they never married. About 15 years ago, that happiness disappeared. Kevin hurt his back and was laid off, making hard times worse. Soon afterward, his girlfriend moved out, took the boys, and asked for child support. The loss of his girlfriend, kids, and job was a huge blow.

"It knocked him to the dirt," says his younger brother, Clayton. "It destroyed his self-esteem."

Depressed and hopeless, Kevin began to fall apart. His weight ballooned to 350 pounds, and he developed diabetes and had a couple of heart attacks. Kevin eventually got disability benefits, but by that time, he was so far behind in child support that he was punished by losing his driver's license. Between health problems and a lack of transportation, getting a job in a town where jobs were scarce was an impossible task.

It's absurd to think that people like Kevin are somehow living it up. After child support deductions, he was living on about $180 a month plus food stamps. He supplemented this by growing a huge vegetable garden and fishing in the Yamhill River.

It's difficult to diagnose just what went wrong in that odyssey from sleek distance runner to his death at 54, but the lack of good jobs was central to it. Kevin surely made mistakes, but his father had opportunities for good jobs that Kevin never had.

Today's young adults face these same difficulties – and more. Kevin did not have a college degree; if he had, he may have had greater opportunities. Today, that no longer holds true. In 2010, the unemployment rate among young people hit 18%, and over the past five years, real wages have fallen for millennials – and only for millennials. Experts expect this generation to be the first generation to experience a shorter lifespan than their parents.

Will we judge this generation as harshly as Kevin has been judged? Will we continue to disparage those who lack opportunity? Or, as more and more people experience hardship, will we learn to embrace empathy?

Write an essay in which you explain how Nicholas Kristof builds an argument to persuade his audience that empathy is a necessity when confronting hardship. In your essay, analyze how Kristof uses one or more of the features listed in the box above (or features of your own choice) to strengthen the logic and persuasiveness of his argument. Be sure that your analysis focuses on the most relevant features of the passage.

Your essay should not explain whether you agree with Nicholas Kristof's claims, but rather explain how Kristof builds an argument to persuade his audience.

Practice Essay 2

As you read the passage below, consider how Newton uses

- evidence, such as facts or examples, to support claims.
- reasoning to develop ideas and to connect claims and evidence.
- stylistic or persuasive elements, such as word choice or appeals to emotion, to add power to the ideas expressed.

Adapted from "Higher Education Is Not a Mixtape" by Derek Newton, published Jan. 27, 2015, in The Atlantic

Will higher education follow the paths of music albums and cable television? Is it inevitable that the college degree will be broken apart by the Internet?

Some entrepreneurs think so. Fortunately, they're wrong.

Technology has unbundled both cable television and record albums. By providing individual songs and shows, the Internet has offered consumers lower prices and greater options. Some entrepreneurs hope to push college in the same direction – unbundling degrees online.

One of these entrepreneurs is Martin Smith, who argues for a future in which colleges separate their courses from their related degrees, much as individual songs have been separated from their albums. Smith argues that the music industry suffered from a lack of foresight into the implications of technology. To avoid the same fate, Smith says that colleges must embrace the idea of "unbundling" their services. In Smith's vision, someone could build a degree, one course at a time, from all of the best professors at schools across the country.

Smith is correct in that higher education is dominated by institutions that have failed to keep up with technology. And, like cable television and record companies, colleges don't produce the content they sell. Colleges are also under unprecedented pressure to reform at a time when technology allows education content to be delivered cheaply and efficiently even as traditional delivery methods – classrooms and campuses – are becoming prohibitively expensive.

Despite the apparent logic behind Smith's arguments, they are based on inaccurate analogies that ignore the reality of higher education.

The parallels between higher education and the entertainment industry are limited. Consumers of music and television are shopping for pieces of content – one song, one show. Consumers of higher education – students and parents – shop for schools, not for classes or for professors. The consumer choice is for the bundler – the brand or, in this case, the school – not for individual course content.

College data proves this. For example, the 2012 UCLA annual survey of incoming college freshmen found that nearly two-thirds said that the school's reputation was "very important" in their decision on which college to attend.

Moreover, the very concept of comparing a 99 cent song to the six-figure cost of a four-year private college education is almost insulting. A music purchase is an entertainment indulgence with minimal investment and limited risk. Choosing the right college, on the other hand, often involves years of research and planning.

If you buy a song you don't like, the consequences are practically nonexistent. The same cannot be said for online college courses. And, in fact, most students fail to succeed in online courses. In 2011, a Columbia University's Teachers College study found that students in online courses were significantly more likely to fail those courses and drop out of school than those in traditional courses. Another study from the University of Pennsylvania found that only about half of students enrolled in massive open online courses, or MOOCs, view even a single online lecture and that the average completion rate is just 4 percent.

If colleges move towards unbundling courses, students will fail to thrive. How long will students and parents be willing to invest in a product that simply doesn't work?

As for the argument that rising college costs have created demand for unbundled content, such arguments ignore the fact that the economics of college dictate that the most expensive products are the most in demand. According to the U.S. News and World Report's annual rankings, the top 25 universities in the country are also some of the most expensive at an average of $46,600 per year – yet they remain the most in demand schools in the country, with an average of 36,500 applications per year per school, more than double the number received by colleges in the next highest ranked group.

Even if unbundling were on the horizon for higher education, more problems would be created than solved. If colleges begin rewarding professors based on who gains a larger online audience, treating them like rock stars, the line between professor and performer would blur. There is a reason that educators aren't rewarded based on popularity; doing so would necessarily undercut educational substance, turning educators into edu-tainers.

Proponents of unbundling the college degree fail to understand the economics of higher education. Of greater concern, they fail to understand the purpose of higher education. If we want higher education to provide valuable knowledge and experiences, then basing education on student choice is the wrong way to go. The unbundling of education simply won't happen – and more importantly, it shouldn't happen.

Write an essay in which you explain how Derek Newton builds an argument to persuade his audience that unbundling college courses will be more harmful for than beneficial to students. In your essay, analyze how Newton uses one or more of the features listed in the box above (or

features of your own choice) to strengthen the logic and persuasiveness of his argument. Be sure that your analysis focuses on the most relevant features of the passage.

Your essay should not explain whether you agree with Derek Newton's claims, but rather explain how Newton builds an argument to persuade the audience.

Practice Essay 3

As you read the passage below, consider how Bogard uses

- evidence, such as facts or examples, to support claims.
- reasoning to develop ideas and to connect claims and evidence.
- stylistic or persuasive elements, such as word choice or appeals to emotion, to add power to the ideas expressed.

Adapted from Paul Bogard, "Let There be Dark." ©2012 by the Los Angeles Times. Originally published December 21, 2012.

At my family's cabin on a Minnesota lake, I knew woods so dark that my hands disappeared before my eyes. I knew night skies in which meteors left smoky trails across sugary spreads of stars. But now, when 8 of 10 children born in the United States will never know a sky dark enough for the Milky Way, I worry we are rapidly losing night's natural darkness before realizing its worth. This winter solstice, as we cheer the days' gradual movement back toward light, let us also remember the irreplaceable value of darkness.

All life evolved to the steady rhythm of bright days and dark nights. Today, though, when we feel the closeness of nightfall, we reach quickly for a light switch. And too little darkness, meaning too much artificial light at night, spells trouble for all.

Already the World Health Organization classifies working the night shift as a probable human carcinogen, and the American Medical Association has voiced its unanimous support for "light pollution reduction efforts and glare reduction efforts at both the national and state levels." Our bodies need darkness to produce the hormone melatonin, which keeps certain cancers from developing, and our bodies need darkness for sleep.

Sleep disorders have been linked to diabetes, obesity, cardiovascular disease and depression, and recent research suggests one main cause of "short sleep" is "long light." Whether we work at night or simply take our tablets, notebooks and smartphones to bed, there isn't a place for this much artificial light in our lives.

The rest of the world depends on darkness as well, including nocturnal and crepuscular species of birds, insects, mammals, fish and reptiles. Some examples are well known—the 400 species of birds that migrate at night in North America, the sea turtles that come ashore to lay their eggs—and some are not, such as the bats that save American farmers billions in pest control and the moths that pollinate 80% of the world's flora. Ecological light pollution is like the bulldozer of the night, wrecking habitat and disrupting ecosystems several billion years in the making. Simply put, without darkness,

Earth's ecology would collapse . . . .

In today's crowded, louder, more fast-paced world, night's darkness can provide solitude, quiet and stillness, qualities increasingly in short supply. Every religious tradition has considered darkness invaluable for a soulful life, and the chance to witness the universe has inspired artists, philosophers and everyday stargazers since time began. In a world awash with electric light. . . how would Van Gogh have given the world his "Starry Night"? Who knows what this vision of the night sky might inspire in each of us, in our children or grandchildren?

Yet all over the world, our nights are growing brighter. In the United States and Western Europe, the amount of light in the sky increases an average of about 6% every year. Computer images of the United States at night, based on NASA photographs, show that what was a very dark country as recently as the 1950s is now nearly covered with a blanket of light. Much of this light is wasted energy, which means wasted dollars. Those of us over 35 are perhaps among the last generation to have known truly dark nights. Even the northern lake where I was lucky to spend my summers has seen its darkness diminish.

It doesn't have to be this way. Light pollution is readily within our ability to solve, using new lighting technologies and shielding existing lights. Already, many cities and towns across North America and Europe are changing to LED streetlights, which offer dramatic possibilities for controlling wasted light. Other communities are finding success with simply turning off portions of their public lighting after midnight. Even Paris, the famed "city of light," which already turns off its monument lighting after 1 a.m., will this summer start to require its shops, offices and public buildings to turn off lights after 2 a.m. Though primarily designed to save energy, such reductions in light will also go far in addressing light pollution. But we will never truly address the problem of light pollution until we become aware of the irreplaceable value and beauty of the darkness we are losing.

Write an essay in which you explain how Paul Bogard builds an argument to persuade his audience that natural darkness should be preserved. In your essay, analyze how Bogard uses one or more of the features listed in the box above (or features of your own choice) to strengthen the logic and persuasiveness of his argument. Be sure that your analysis focuses on the most relevant features of the passage.

Your essay should not explain whether you agree with Bogard's claims, but rather explain how Bogard builds an argument to persuade his audience.

Section 6
Full-Length Practice Tests

Reading Test

65 MINUTES, 52 QUESTIONS

Mark your responses on this test. Use the "How to Calculate Your Scores in the back of this book to determine your scores.

DIRECTIONS

Each passage or pair of passages below is followed by a number of questions. After reading each passage or pair, choose the best answer to each question based on what is stated or implied in the passage or passages and in any accompanying graphics (such as a table or graph).

Questions 1-10 are based on the following passage.

The following passage is adapted from an article originally published in Scientific American *in 2012. The article explores water-saving measures that were tested in the state of Georgia.*

Fifteen gasoline-powered augers will soon drill 100 holes in the corn, cotton, and peanut fields of the Lower Flint River Basin in southwest Georgia. Scientists from the University of Georgia (UGA) will then slip half-meter-long PVC pipes into these holes. The pipes are filled with sensors for soil moisture and temperature; they are topped by a flexible antenna that can handle being run over by a tractor while still being able to relay information to a computer. Over a two-year time span, these sensors will provide readings on soil conditions from 20, 40, and 60 centimeters deep. Combined with more accurate weather forecasts, the data will help farmers decide when and where to best use their irrigations systems.

"The biggest problem we've got with irrigation is we [have to] use old wives' tales to decide when to irrigate," says farmer Marty Tabb, who will host the probes in a field at his 1,050-he-ctare Bushwater Farm near Colquitt, Ga., to help him irrigate corn, cotton, and peanut crops. This technology can help to save water by producing more crop per drop. "Using the simplest soil monitor and a computer program, my peanut yields jumped 20 percent," Tabb reports. "I know, just from that, that if we learn how to water corn, cotton, wheat, we can save water because we tend to overwater."

Overwatering is a major problem, particularly in the Lower Flint River Basin, which lies in a region gripped by drought. The area produces the most peanuts and pecans in the nation, in addition to huge amounts of cotton and corn. Perhaps more importantly, the Lower Flint River Basin is the major recharge zone for the Floridian Aquifer, which provides water to Florida, Mississippi, Alabama, South Carolina, and Georgia.

Farmers in the region have a direct impact on this vital groundwater. Waters on the surface and below ground are directly linked: a downpour can replenish the aquifer, but excessive pumping of underground water to irrigate fields can deplete nearby rivers and streams. When there is plenty of surface water, the groundwater is also plentiful, but when one begins to dry up, so does the other. "Because of the drought and because of us irrigating, we have pulled water down, and the springs don't pump anymore," Tabb says.

In an attempt to cut down on water use while still maintaining the $2 billion in corn, cotton, peanuts, and other crops grown in the region, the Nature Conservancy and the U.S. Department of Agriculture, along with UGA and the University of Florida, have teamed up with more than 1,000 local farmers. They began by switching some irrigation systems from high pressure mists to a low pressure system, thus saving both water and energy. This relatively simple switch can reduce water use by more than 22 percent.

Next, they helped some local farmers install so-called variable-rate irrigation, which varies water application rather than simply dumping water equally across an entire field. "Last year that system at my farm, we saved two to three million gallons of water by having that system cut off over wasteland," Tabb notes. In fact, variable-rate irrigation systems save 15 percent of water use on average. As a result, the technology has begun to spread across the region and is now being offered as an option for new irrigation systems worldwide.

Despite the success of variable-rate irrigation, it has its drawbacks. It relies on a static map of a given field and does not take soil type or field conditions into consideration. The new UGA sensor probes, which allow farmers to monitor soil moisture in real time, will help to address this shortcoming. With specific data in hand, farmers will be able to better target water where it is most needed.

The new technology won't just help farmers in the Lower Flint River Basin; it may also help all those who rely on the water from the Floridian Aquifer. Not only do tens of thousands of residents of Savannah, Orlando, and other nearby cities rely on the Floridian Aquifer for much of their water, but the Lower Flint River Basin is also home to the largest concentration of amphibian and reptile species in the entire U.S., many of which are threatened or endangered. When farmers like Tabb conserve water, more of it flows in the region's waterways, providing water for humans and animals alike.

1

As it is used in line 10, "relay" most nearly means

A) hand over.
B) race.
C) communicate.
D) spread.

2

The author most likely included the quotes from Marty Tabb in the second paragraph (lines 18-30) in order to

A) provide expert testimony to establish the benefits of the new sensors.
B) offer a statistical study to establish the necessity of the new sensors.
C) engage the reader by including colloquial language in the passage.
D) suggest that the sensors may not work since the only available evidence is a mere personal anecdote.

3

Based on information in the third paragraph (lines 31-40), it can be reasonably inferred that

A) without the Lower Flint River Basin, the nation would not have access to peanuts and pecans.
B) the Lower Flint River Basin has never experienced a worse period of drought.
C) the biggest problem faced by residents of the Lower Flint River Basin is overwatering.
D) the Lower Flint River Basin is vital to many residents in several states.

4

The relationship between surface water and groundwater (lines 42-43) is most similar to

A) a predatory relationship in which one species hunts another species.
B) a parasitic relationship in which one species lives off of the other without giving anything in return.
C) a symbiotic relationship in which two species are dependent on one another to thrive.
D) a cooperative relationship in which two species choose to work together for a short time.

5

According to the passage, the Lower Flint River Basin is important because it

A) provides all of the peanuts and pecans grown in the U.S.
B) is the site of a major scientific experiment.
C) is the only source of water for the entire southeast.
D) adds $2 billion to Georgia's agriculture each year.

6

Which of the following provides the best evidence to support the previous question?

A) Lines 1-4 ("Fifteen...Georgia")
B) Lines 33-35 ("The area...nation")
C) Lines 36-40 ("the Lower...Georgia")
D) Lines 53-56 ("In an...region")

7

As it is used in line 67, "application" most nearly means

A) industry.
B) coverage.
C) demand.
D) operation.

8

Which of the following is a widespread impact of the partnership among the Nature Conservancy, the U.S. Department of Agriculture, UGA, and the University of Florida?

A) UGA will install sensors in every field in the region.
B) New, water-saving options are being offered for new irrigation systems worldwide.
C) Residents of cities that rely on the Floridian Aquifer will never have to worry about water supplies.
D) Drought is no longer a concern for farmers in the Lower Flint River Basin.

9

Which of the following provides the best evidence to support the answer to the previous question?

A) Lines 1-4 ("Fifteen...Georgia")
B) Lines 31-33 ("Overwatering...drought")
C) Lines 73-76 ("the technology...worldwide")
D) Lines 87-89 ("it may...Aquifer")

10

Which of the following describes the purpose of the sensors in relation to the other water-saving measures discussed in the passage?

A) To allow farmers to target their improved water systems to the areas that need it most
B) To allow tractors to still traverse the fields among the new watering systems
C) To provide soil readings from multiple depths in order to improve weather forecasts
D) To allow more water to flow through the region's waterways

Questions 11-20 are based on the following passage.

This is an excerpt from Three Men in a Boat *a humorous account of a boating holiday written by Jerome K. Jerome and published in 1889.*

I remember going to the British Museum one day to read up the treatment for some slight ailment of which I had a touch—hay fever, I fancy it was. I got down the book, and read all I came to read; and then, in an unthinking moment, I idly turned the leaves, and began to indolently study diseases, generally. I forget which was the first distemper I plunged into—some fearful, devastating scourge, I know--and, before I had glanced half down the list of "premonitory symptoms," it was borne in upon me that I had fairly got it.

I sat for awhile, frozen with horror; and then, in the listlessness of despair, I again turned over the pages. I came to typhoid fever—read the symptoms--discovered that I had typhoid fever, must have had it for months without knowing it—wondered what else I had got; turned up St. Vitus's Dance—found, as I expected, that I had that too—began to get interested in my case, and determined to sift it to the bottom, and so started alphabetically—read up ague, and learnt that I was sickening for it, and that the acute stage would commence in about another fortnight. Bright's disease, I was relieved to find, I had only in a modified form, and, so far as that was concerned, I might live for years. Cholera I had, with severe complications; and diphtheria I seemed to have been born with. I plodded conscientiously through the twenty-six letters, and the only malady I could conclude I had not got was housemaid's knee.

I felt rather hurt about this at first; it seemed somehow to be a sort of slight. Why hadn't I got housemaid's knee? Why this invidious reservation? After a while, however, less grasping feelings prevailed. I reflected that I had every other known malady in the pharmacology, and I grew less selfish, and determined to do without housemaid's knee. Gout, in its most malignant stage, it would appear, had seized me without my being aware of it; and zymosis I had evidently been suffering with from boyhood. There were no more diseases after zymosis, so I concluded there was nothing else the matter with me.

I sat and pondered. I thought what an interesting case I must be from a medical point of view, what an acquisition I should be to a class! Students would have no need to "walk the hospitals," if they had me. I was a hospital in myself. All they need do would be to walk round me, and, after that, take their diploma.

Then I wondered how long I had to live. I tried to examine myself. I felt my pulse. I could not at first feel any pulse at all. Then, all of a sudden, it seemed to start off. I pulled out my watch and timed it. I made it a hundred and forty-seven to the minute. I tried to feel my heart. I could not feel my heart. It had stopped beating. I have since been induced to come to the opinion that it must have been there all the time, and must have been beating, but I cannot account for it. I patted myself all over my front, from what I call my waist up to my head, and I went a bit round each side, and a little way up the back. But I could not feel or hear anything. I tried to look at my tongue. I stuck it out as far as ever it would go, and I shut one eye, and tried to examine it with the other. I could only see the tip, and the only thing that I could gain from that was to feel more certain than before that I had scarlet fever.

I had walked into that reading-room a happy, healthy man. I crawled out a decrepit wreck.

I went to my medical man. Rather than bore him with my list of complaints, I felt it easier to tell him what was *not* the matter. "I have not got housemaid's knee. Everything else, however, I *have* got."

And I told him how I came to discover it all.

Then he opened me and looked down me, and hit me over the chest when I wasn't expecting it—a cowardly thing to do, I call it — and immediately afterwards, he sat down and wrote out a prescription.

It read: "Don't stuff up your head with things you don't understand."

I followed the directions, which the happy result that my life is still going on.

11

The author can best be described as

A) A layperson learning more about human anatomy and health.
B) A doctor familiarizing himself with new developments in medicine.
C) Someone who is easily convinced of things he reads.
D) A skeptic who is attempting to disprove medical science.

12

The author went to the library in order to research

A) hay fever.
B) cholera.
C) housemaid's knee.
D) scarlet fever.

13

What is the central theme of the passage?

A) Everyone is in poorer health than they expect.
B) It can be easy to convince yourself that you are sick.
C) Medical science is often untrustworthy.
D) The great amount of medical knowledge available can be overwhelming for patients.

14

The word "acute" in line 24 most nearly means

A) sharp.
B) severe.
C) important.
D) perceptive.

15

As it is used in line 42, "malignant" most nearly means

A) spiteful.
B) cancerous.
C) dangerous.
D) unkind.

16

The narrator's response to his self-diagnosis can best be described as

A) proud.
B) horrified.
C) jocular.
D) indifferent.

17

Which of the following gives the best evidence for the answer to the previous question?

A) Lines 13-15 ("I… pages.")
B) Lines 25-28 ("Bright's… years.")
C) Lines 34-35 ("I… slight.")
D) Lines 48-51 ("I... class!")

18

What role does the fourth paragraph play in the passage?

A) It communicates the narrator's disdain for hospitals.
B) It suggests a new method for medical students to learn about disease.
C) It humorously overstates the narrator's medical problems.
D) It communicates the author's despair at his medical condition.

19

When he shares them with others, the author begins to see his ailments as

A) the results of an overactive imagination.
B) the signs of his impending demise.
C) an overdramatic response to some real but solvable problems.
D) a complicated medical dilemma.

20

Which of the following gives the best evidence for the answer to the previous question?

A) Lines 7-12 ("I forget…got it.")
B) Lines 48-51 ("I sat…class!")
C) Lines 78-80 ("Rather…matter.")
D) Lines 85-91 ("Then…understand.")

Questions 21-31 are based on the following passage.

The following passages are excerpted from a pair of National Science Foundation articles. The first is from an article titled "Snails in the Waters, Disease in the Villages." The second is from an article titled "'Defective' Virus Leads to Epidemic of Dengue Fever."

Passage 1

Watch where you jump in for a swim or where your bath water comes from, especially if you live in Africa, Asia, or South America. Snails that live in tropical fresh water in these locations are intermediaries between disease-causing parasitic worms and humans. The worms' infectious larvae emerge from the snails, cruise in shallow water, easily penetrate human skin, and mature in internal organs. The result is schistosomiasis, the second most socioeconomically devastating disease after malaria.

People in developing countries who don't have access to clean water and good sanitation facilities are often exposed to the infected snails, and thus the parasitic worms. Over 70 developing nations have identified significant rates of schistosomiasis in human populations.

There has been much debate about how long treatment should last once someone has schistosomiasis. Current guidelines focus on suppressing the disease's effects by limiting the infection during childhood, but that may not be enough to cure it or to prevent re-infection, leaving children still at risk for stunted growth and anemia.

Schistosomiasis is usually treated with a single dose of the oral drug praziquantel. World Health Organization (WHO) guidelines recommend that when more than 10 percent of the children in a village have parasite eggs in their urine or stool—a clear sign of schistosomiasis—everyone in the village should receive treatment. In addition, school-age children should receive additional treatments every two years.

However, because of the long-term health effects of schistosomiasis, many scientists are critical of this plan. They now argue instead for regular yearly treatment, saying that current WHO recommendations cannot achieve full suppression of schistosomiasis. In higher-risk villages, repeated annual treatment is necessary for an indefinite period—until the eco-social factors that foster the disease, such as poor wastewater treatment, are removed. Fixing the water treatment problem can reduce human diseases much more effectively and at a lower cost than simply focusing on disease treatment.

To achieve the goal of the complete elimination of schistosomiasis, scientists need to determine what makes a "wormy village," how often therapy is needed to prevent disease in such locations, and what can be done to change the environment so that a high-risk village becomes a low-risk one. There is a long way to go before this goal is reached.

Passage 2

It's 2001 in Myanmar (formerly known as Burma), a country in Southeast Asia. Almost 200 people have died, and more than 15,000 are ill—all having contracted dengue fever. Dengue is a disease transmitted by mosquitoes and caused by four types of the dengue virus. Infection may not result in symptoms; it may cause mild, flu-like illness; or it may result in potentially deadly hemorrhagic fever.

Dengue virus infects some 50-100 million people annually in Southeast Asia, South America, and parts of the United States. In Myanmar, dengue is endemic. The disease has occurred there in three- to five-year cycles since the first recorded outbreak in 1970. Each one has been more deadly than the last.

What caused the widespread infection in Myanmar in 2001, a disease that resulted from one type of dengue virus, DENV-1? For more than a decade, researchers have been working to solve the puzzle.

One potential explanation involves so-called "defective" viruses. A defective virus results from genetic mutations or deletions that eliminate essential functions. They're generated in viruses with high mutation rates. These defective viruses were once considered unimportant.

However, in a recent study, scientists reported a significant link between one such defective virus and the high rate of transmission of DENV-1 in Myanmar in 2001. They found that the normal, functional virus is actually helping the defective virus. While defective viruses can't complete their life cycle on their own, if they're able to get into the same cell with a non-defective virus, they can "hitchhike" with the non-defective one and propagate.

Pathogens can depend on the presence of other species to spread, or, as in this case, other varieties of the same species. Understanding these interactions is critical for predicting when the next epidemic might occur—and how to prevent it.

Why would a defective virus increase transmission of a disease? One hypothesis is that the defective virus may be interfering with the disease-causing virus, making the disease less intense. People then have a milder infection, and because they don't feel as sick, they're more likely to go out of their homes and spread the disease.

The biologists believe that their work will help turn the tide of the next deadly outbreak of dengue in Myanmar—and in other tropical countries around the globe.

21

The primary goal of the scientists in Passage 1 is to

A) eliminate schistosomiasis.
B) kill off the snails in tropical waters.
C) change the WHO guidelines.
D) identify at-risk populations.

22

Which of the following best supports the answer to the previous question?

A) Lines 13-16 ("People...worms")
B) Lines 16-18 ("Over...populations")
C) Lines 21-26 ("Current...anemia")
D) Lines 50-56 ("To achieve...one")

23

According to the passage, why does schistosomiasis typically only impact people in developing nations?

A) Because people in developing nations lack access to adequate healthcare facilities for early treatment of the illness.
B) Because people in developing nations often lack access to the clean water and sanitation facilities that can eliminate the parasite.
C) Because the WHO guidelines in place in developing nations are inadequate.
D) Because villages in developing nations have a large percentage of vulnerable populations like children.

24

As it is used in line 39, "critical" most nearly means

A) serious.
B) crucial.
C) demanding.
D) disparaging.

25

According to the first passage, which of the following is the best way to reduce diseases?

A) Improving water treatment, particularly in developing countries
B) Focusing research on developing cost-effective treatment options
C) Treating patients regularly for an unspecified period of time
D) Identifying the means by which diseases are spread

26

The purpose of the information in lines 58-61 ("It's...fever") is to

A) explain how quickly dengue virus spreads.
B) convince the reader to take action to solve the dengue virus endemic in Myanmar.
C) establish the severity of the dengue virus endemic in Myanmar.
D) show that the dengue virus endemic in Myanmar is not as bad as it is in other areas.

27

Which of the following best establishes the primary idea of the second passage?

A) Lines 58-66 ("It's...fever")
B) Lines 67-70 ("Dengue...endemic")
C) Lines 70-73 ("The disease...last")
D) Lines 74-78 ("What...puzzle")

28

As it is used in line 82, "essential" most nearly means

A) requisite.
B) underlying.
C) crucial.
D) cardinal.

29

Which of the following describes the effect of the author's use of the term "hitchhike" in line 94?

A) To use a common term to illustrate a complex process
B) To create imagery through descriptive words
C) To suggest that defective viruses engage in risky behavior similar to hitchhiking
D) To personify the virus in order to better explain its motives

30

Based on evidence in the passage, the authors of both passages would likely agree that

A) scientists must determine how to change the environment in order to reduce the risk of disease.
B) diseases typically occur in three-to five-year cycles.
C) diseases impacting developing nations require yearly treatment.
D) pathogens can depend on other organisms to spread.

31

The scientists in both passages hope to

A) cure parasitic diseases.
B) reduce infections.
C) determine how long treatment should last.
D) test people in developing nations for contagious diseases.

Questions 32-42 are based on the following passage.

The following is an excerpt from a speech delivered by U.S. Supreme Court Justice Stephen G. Breyer to lawyers and judges at a meeting of the American Bar Association.

Three weeks ago, when Justice O'Connor and I were at the Ninth Circuit Judicial Conference, a judge asked us whether we thought judges should participate in community affairs. Justice O'Connor and I agree about many things—not everything—and we certainly agreed about the answer to that one. Of course they should. Yet more important—so should lawyers. After all, Roscoe Pound once defined our profession as a group of men and women "pursuing a learned art as a common calling in the spirit of public service." And many of us remember at least hearing about a professional golden age when the respected general practitioner or local judge would serve on a school board, sponsor a Scout Troop, or give a Fourth of July speech.

Yet as we spoke, we were both aware of modern pressures that make it difficult for any of us, whether judge or lawyer, to live up to that past ideal. For the judge those pressures may take the form of workload, keeping us at our desks, or internally generated concerns about conflicts of interest that may lead us to believe the safest way to avoid public criticism is through total isolation. But ethics rules, which must be followed, do not mandate total isolation. Indeed, just after the judicial conference, Justice O'Connor and I went on to visit several Indian reservations, where we saw tribal courts in action. On the Spokane Reservation we saw a drug court draw upon a host of community resources in order to prevent a teenager's recidivism. In the Navajo Nation we witnessed highly successful mediation techniques. We also began to understand the great benefits that a few additional resources might bring. During these visits, we shared views and experiences—which, we hope, will prove beneficial in the continuing effort to improve the quality of justice (and therefore the quality of life) on Indian reservations.

Lawyers face different, more immediate, more serious pressures. Many of my practitioner friends talk about the "treadmill." How can a lawyer undertake pro bono work, engage in law reform efforts, even attend bar association meetings, if that lawyer must produce 2,100 or more billable hours each year, say sixty-five or seventy hours in the office each week? That kind of number reflects a pace, which, according to one lawyer, is like "drinking water from a fire hose." The treadmill's pressure is partly financial, aggravated for younger lawyers by law school loans that may amount to $100,000 or more, which must be paid back from their earnings in practice. The pressure also reflects the increased complexity and specialization of law itself. . . .

All of us want to resist these isolating pressures. Perhaps it will help if in the next few minutes I try to explain why, from my own perspective, it is so important that we do so. I shall describe three different "public service" roles that the lawyer traditionally has played and which still, taken together, make up that "spirit of public service" that must continue to characterize the American Bar.

I shall touch upon the first—pro bono legal work—only briefly, simply because it is so well known to you. The Supreme Court is itself a direct beneficiary of that work, for public interest organizations and law firms representing pro bono clients often file briefs. And they represent clients ranging from death row prisoners in habeas corpus cases to property owners in "Takings Clause" cases. The briefs are almost always helpful, whatever political or ideological view they represent.

But more broadly, pro bono work means that those who cannot afford legal representation to protect their legal rights will have it. The need is there. A 1994 ABA Report says that between 70% and 80% of those with low incomes who needed a lawyer in a civil case failed to find one. . . .

And the critical importance of satisfying the resulting need was explained to me in a sentence two summers ago by a foreign judge. He told me that most villagers in his country had never seen a lawyer or a judge. He had persuaded a local bar group to lend him a small private plane; and he spent weekends flying to distant villages, mediating disputes, most of which he resolved rather quickly. Why? Because, he explained, by helping make the legal system work for everyone, he would help to build public confidence necessary to sustain the legal system itself.

32

The author's primary purpose in speaking is to

A) explain why judges often isolate themselves from the community.
B) convince his listeners of the importance of public service on the part of lawyers.
C) explain why lawyers often find it difficult to engage in public service.
D) hold himself up as an example of how judges can engage in public service.

33

The author most likely included the quote from Roscoe Pound in lines 11-12 in order to

A) provide expert testimony to prove that public service is mandatory for lawyers.
B) explain why he believes that public service is vital to the legal profession.
C) better illustrate the ideals of the golden age of the legal profession.
D) define the legal profession.

34

As it is used in line 33, "host" most nearly means

A) moderator.
B) crowd.
C) presenter.
D) array.

35

It can be inferred from the passage that

A) the tribal courts operate differently from other courts.
B) Justices Breyer and O'Connor visited the tribal courts to tell tribal judges what they were doing wrong.
C) tribal courts lack access to helpful community resources.
D) tribal courts do not follow judicial rules of ethics.

36

Which of the following provides the best evidence for the answer of the previous question?

A) Lines 26-28 ("But ethics...isolation")
B) Lines 29-31 ("Justice...action")
C) Lines 31-34 ("On the...recidivism")
D) Lines 38-43 ("During...reservations")

37

Based on information in the passage, what does the author mean by the term "treadmill" (line 45)?

A) Lawyers are under constant pressure to perform pro bono work.
B) Lawyers enjoy working constantly in the same way that many other people enjoy exercise.
C) Lawyers must work constantly in order to pay student loans and get ahead, leaving little time for other pursuits.
D) The increased complexity of the legal profession requires that lawyers work constantly to stay ahead of changes.

38

The author likely included the question in lines 46-52 in order to

A) show that the speaker doesn't fully understand the issue himself.
B) present a problem that the speaker intends to solve.
C) pose a question that will be answered later in the speech.
D) illustrate the pressures that prevent many lawyers from doing pro bono work.

39

As it is used in line 55, "aggravated" most nearly means

A) worsened.
B) irritated.
C) enhanced.
D) teased.

40

Based on the passage, which of the following best describes the "isolating pressures" that prevent judges and lawyers from engaging in public service?

A) Judges are forbidden from public service by ethics rules while lawyers lack the "spirit of public service."
B) Judges are too busy sitting on school boards while lawyers are overwhelmed by the complexity of the profession.
C) Judges fear ethics violations while lawyers simply lack the time.
D) Judges are overworked while lawyers fear ethics violations.

41

According to the passage, why is pro bono work vital to the legal profession?

A) Because by providing access to legal service for those who can't afford it, pro bono work builds public confidence in the legal system.
B) Because without pro bono work, 70% of Americans would not have access to vital legal services.
C) Because pro bono work makes up the vast majority of the cases presented before the Supreme Court, and those cases shape the nation's policies.
D) Because most people have never seen a lawyer or a judge.

42

Which of the following provides the best evidence for the answer to the previous question?

A) Lines 72-75 ("The Supreme...briefs")
B) Lines 84-87 ("A 1994...one")
C) Lines 92-96 ("He told...quickly")
D) Lines 97-100 ("Because...itself")

Questions 43-52 are based on the following passage.

The following is adapted from an article titled "Why North Europeans Are the Happiest People on Earth."

According to the 2015 World Happiness Report, a report published by a group of influential economists, the world's happiest countries are Switzerland, Iceland, Denmark, and Norway. What exactly are these nations doing right that the rest of the world is doing wrong?

Jeffrey Sachs of Columbia University, Richard Layard of the London School of Economics, and John Helliwell of the University of British Columbia have been publishing the World Happiness Report since 2012. Their goal is to remind governments that success is about more than economic growth and other such statistics. Certainly people tend to be happier when they're wealthier and healthier, as they tend to be in more developed countries, but there are many other factors that influence well-being. That's what the report measures: People in various countries are asked how they perceive various aspects of their lives.

After years of conducting these surveys, the authors have identified six variables that account for three-quarters of the differences in happiness levels among countries: Gross domestic product per capita, social support, healthy life expectancy, freedom to make life choices, generosity, and freedom from corruption. Two of these—social support and generosity—are relatively independent of economic development or politics, which explains why some fairly poor, institutionally weak countries have happier populations than the strongest Western democracies. For example, Mexicans are happier than Americans, and Brazilians report being happier than the residents of Luxembourg.

The happiest countries are rich, healthy, free, and populated with generous people who support one another when there's trouble. One has to wonder if Northern Europe's so-called Law of Jante might not be responsible for the fact that Iceland, Denmark, Norway, Finland, and Sweden are among the world's ten happiest nations. Though Scandinavians may scoff at the cultural creed that considers individual success to be unworthy, it does make for unusually strong social support networks. It is this cultural phenomenon that the study's authors point to as an explanation for Iceland's surprising resilience during an economic collapse, as well as the country's second place in the rankings. Iceland has the highest percentage in the world of people who say they have someone to count on in times of crisis.

The report includes a chapter that emphasizes the role of "relational goods," such as reciprocity and simultaneity (which describes people taking part in meaningful activities together), in building happy nations. People are happier when they're socially fulfilled, particularly as members of a group. The happiest countries are participatory. That is true for Switzerland, with its direct democracy and close-knit local communities, as well as for the Scandinavian countries, which have perhaps the highest social capital in the world. Participation and democracy help to build mutual trust, an important part of social capital, a term that describes the networks of relationships among people in a society. People are more willing to pay taxes, less likely to become corrupt, and more likely to embrace expansive social safety nets.

Though it might seem that such a social fabric ought to be strong, it is, in fact, quite delicate. The happiest countries in the world have small populations (the biggest country in the top ten is Canada, at 35 million residents). Bringing smaller countries together into a bigger bloc, such as the European Union, doesn't help to increase social capital. In fact, when some countries in such a union are outperformed by others, their social fabric rips, trust erodes, and the decline in happiness is greater than economic losses can explain. The ideal example of this is Greece, the biggest happiness loser compared with data for 2005-2007.

One of the policy implications of the findings of Sachs, Layard, and Helliwell is that countries need to nurture their natural social fabric rather than seek to impose contrived rules that might have worked elsewhere. If laws are passed that run counter to the social and moral rules prevailing in a society, then those laws will fail to produce the desired results because they will not be followed because not all infringers of such rules can be punished. Worse, such laws are likely to threaten the stability of the social order by trying to impose unnatural change on a culture.

In other words, a country like the U.S. cannot improve happiness simply by passing laws or establishing government programs that imitate those of countries like Sweden. No matter how much we may like big, ambitious programs, aiming for happiness may mean thinking small and being careful with the fragile web of relationships that make human society function.

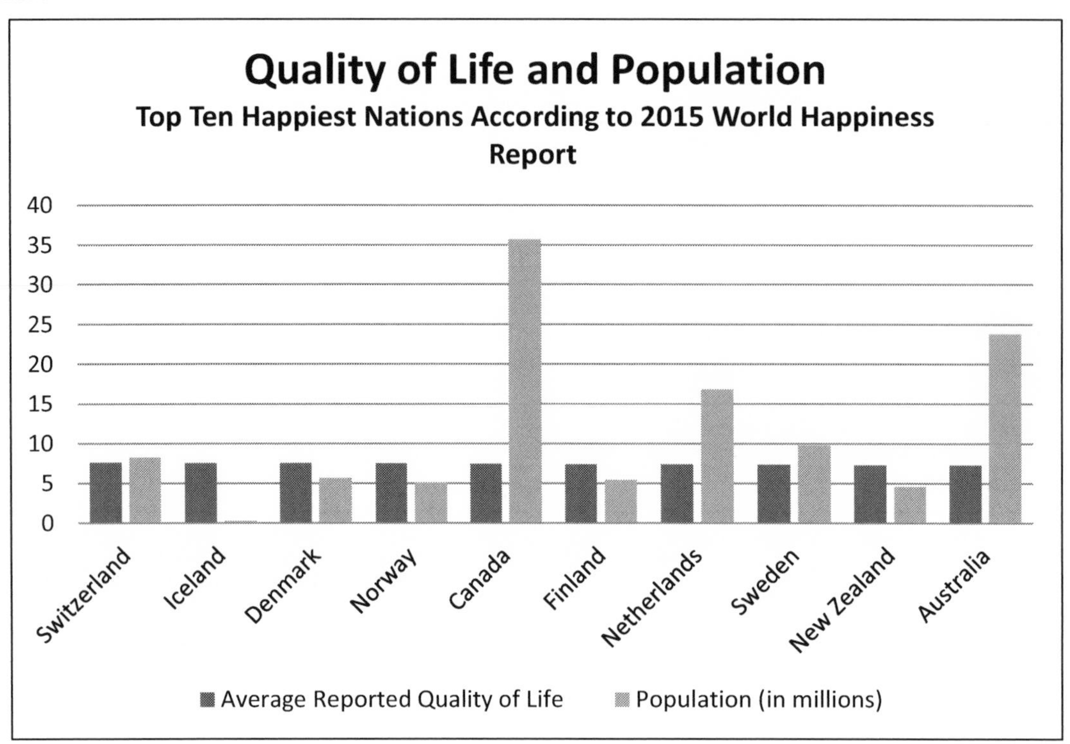

43

Which of the following best establishes the main idea of the passage?

A) Lines 5-7 ("What...wrong")
B) Lines 8-13 ("Jeffrey...2012")
C) Lines 20-21 ("People...lives")
D) Lines 32-34 ("institutionally...democracies")

44

Which of the following can be inferred from the second paragraph (lines 8-21)?

A) The only factor that should be considered in evaluating a government's success is the happiness of its people.
B) A government's success can best be measured by a country's economic health.
C) Governments use the World Happiness Report when measuring their success or failure.
D) Governments often forget to consider things like happiness when considering their success or failure.

45

As it is used in line 22, "conducting" most nearly means

A) accompanying.
B) administering.
C) transporting.
D) acquitting.

46

How would the author most likely explain why Mexicans are happier than Americans?

A) The Mexican economy is stronger than the American economy.
B) The Mexican government is less corrupt than the American government.
C) The Mexican government is stronger than the American government.
D) Mexicans report enjoying greater social support and generosity than Americans.

47

Which of the following provides the best evidence in support of the answer to the previous question?

A) Lines 19-21 ("That's...lives")
B) Lines 22-29 ("After...corruption")
C) Lines 29-34 ("Two of these...democracies.")
D) Lines 38-40 ("The...trouble")

48

It can be inferred that the author believes which of the following about the Law of Jante (line 42)?

A) By minimizing the importance of individual success, it encourages group cooperation.
B) It causes a decline in happiness by degrading individual achievement.
C) It is a written law that is strongly enforced in Northern European countries.
D) It was enacted during one of Iceland's economic collapses.

49

Which of the following is most strongly implied by the passage?

A) Smaller countries are more likely to be happier countries.
B) Greece is a part of the European Union.
C) Mexico and Brazil tend to favor reciprocity and simultaneity above all else.
D) Because the United States is a union of many parts, it has a weak social fabric.

50

Which of the following provides the best evidence in support of the answer to the previous question?

A) Lines 34-37 ("For... Luxembourg.")
B) Lines 45-48 ("Though... networks.")
C) Lines 75-79 ("Though... residents.)")
D) Lines 82-89 ("In fact... 2007.")

51

As it is used in line 95, "counter" most nearly means

A) opposite.
B) retaliate.
C) backwards.
D) offset.

52

Based on the graphic, which of the following countries could be considered an outlier based on the information found in the sixth paragraph (lines 75-89)?

A) Switzerland
B) Iceland
C) Sweden
D) Australia

52

STOP

If you finish before time is called, you may check your work on this section only.
Do not turn to any other section.

Writing and Language Test

35 MINUTES, 44 QUESTIONS

Mark your responses on this test. Use the "How to Calculate Your Scores in the back of this book to determine your scores.

DIRECTIONS

Each passage below is accompanied by a number of questions. For some questions, you will consider how the passage might be revised to improve the expression of ideas. For other questions, you will consider how the passage might be edited to correct errors in sentence structure, usage, or punctuation. A passage or a question may be accompanied by one or more graphics (such as a table or graph) that you will consider as you make revising and editing decisions.

Some questions will direct you to an underlined portion of a passage. Other questions will direct you to a location in a passage or ask you to think about the passage as a whole.

After reading each passage, choose the answer to each question that most effectively improves the quality of writing in the passage or that makes the passage conform to the conventions of standard written English. Many questions include a "NO CHANGE" option. Choose that option if you think the best choice is to leave the relevant portion of the passage as it is.

Questions 1-11 are based on the following passage.

Though American parents spend more time with their children than any other parents in the world, many feel guilty because they don't believe it's enough. There's a widespread cultural assumption that the time parents, particularly mothers, spend with children is key to ensuring a bright future. **1** A new study confirms the importance of parent time in child development.

1

Which of the following provides the best thesis for the passage as a whole?

A) NO CHANGE
B) New research suggests that even the large amounts of time that Americans spend with their children isn't enough.
C) It turns out that parent time is completely unimportant to child development.
D) Groundbreaking new research upends that conventional wisdom.

In fact, it appears that the amount of time parents spend with their children between the ages of 3 and 11 has virtually no impact on how children turn out. This is the primary finding of the first large-scale longitudinal study of parent time, published in April 2015 in the Journal of Marriage and Family, which examined parental time and **2** it's impact on such factors as children's academic achievement, behavior, and emotional well-being.

3 That's not to say that parent time isn't important. Plenty of studies have shown links between quality parent time—such as reading to a **4** child; sharing meals; talking with them, or otherwise engaging with them one-on-one—and positive outcomes for kids. The same is true for parents' warmth and sensitivity toward their children. It's just that the quantity of time doesn't appear to matter.

2

A) NO CHANGE
B) its
C) it
D) its'

3

Which of the following creates the best transition between the second and third paragraphs?

A) NO CHANGE
B) These findings are confusing since other studies show the exact opposite.
C) Other researchers question these findings.
D) Clearly, these findings show that parent time is unimportant.

4

A) NO CHANGE
B) child; sharing meals; talking with them; or otherwise
C) child, sharing meals, talking with them, or otherwise
D) child, sharing meals (talking with them), or otherwise

The one instance the study identified in which the quantity of time parents spend does indeed matter is during adolescence: the more time a teen spends engaged with **5** their mother, the fewer instances of delinquent behavior. And the more time a teen spends with both parents together in family time, **6** the less likely he or she is to engage in drug and alcohol use and to engage in other risky, dangerous, or illegal behavior. Students who spend plenty of time with family also achieve higher math scores. Interestingly, the study found positive **7** conclusions for teens who spent an average of just six hours a week engaged in family time with **8** parents, so the time required to see beneficial results is minimal.

5

A) NO CHANGE
B) him or her
C) his or her
D) they're

6

A) NO CHANGE
B) the lower the likelihood of the teen engaging in drug and alcohol abuse or engaging in illegal and risky behavior.
C) the less likely they are to do drugs, drink, or do illegal things.
D) the less likely he or she is to abuse drugs and alcohol or engage in other risky behavior.

7

A) NO CHANGE
B) outcomes
C) events
D) consequences

8

A) NO CHANGE
B) parents;
C) parents, for
D) parents, but

These findings could have significant impacts on modern parenting. The study's findings shook some parents, many of whom had built their lives around the idea that the more time with children, the better. **9** Working mothers today spend as much time with their children as at-home mothers did in the early 1970s. This is despite the fact that modern mothers often work full time outside of the home. **10** They quit or cut back on work, have downsized their houses, or will have struggled to cram it all in. **11** Turns out, all those sacrifices were totally pointless.

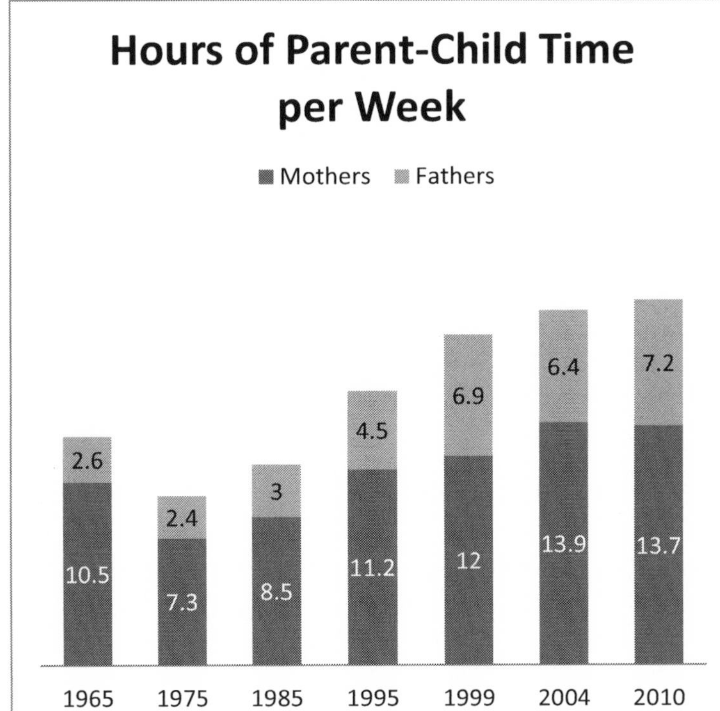

9

Which of the following best suits the paragraph based on the information in the graph?

A) NO CHANGE
B) Mothers today spend significantly more time with their children than mothers in past decades.
C) Modern fathers still fail to spend more time with their children than they did several decades ago.
D) Mothers spent little time with their children in the 1970s and 1980s.

10

A) NO CHANGE
B) They quit or cut back on work, have downsized their houses, or struggled to cram it all in.
C) They quit or cut back on work, downsized their houses, or struggled to cram it all in.
D) They quit or cut back on work or downsized their houses or struggled to cram it all in.

11

Which of the following provides the best conclusion to the passage as a whole?

A) NO CHANGE
B) Instead, it is building relationships in order to seize quality moments of connection that is most important for both parent and child well-being.
C) And when mothers failed to meet the standards they set for themselves by not being able to balance everything, they realized that it just didn't matter.
D) Who knew that spending time with kids was pointless?

Questions 12-22 are based on the following passage.

Food is energy for the body. The digestive process breaks complex food structures down into simpler structures, such as sugars, that travel to our cells. The energy stored in the chemical bonds of these simpler molecules powers our **12** bodies. We measure this energy in calories.

In the 19th century, chemist Wilbur Olin Atwater developed the calorie system that we still use today. Every calorie count on every food label you have ever seen is based on Atwater's measurements. What if these measurements are wrong? **13** Even modern research shows that Atwater was very careful in his calculations. To truly calculate the total calories that someone gets out of a given food, you would have to take into account a dizzying array of factors.

12

Which of the following best combines the sentences at the underlined portion?

A) bodies, yet we
B) bodies, and we
C) bodies since we
D) bodies; and we

13

Which of the following best establishes the main idea of the passage as a whole?

A) NO CHANGE
B) There have been many advances in nutritional knowledge since the 19th century.
C) In fact, new research suggests that these calculations are significantly inaccurate.
D) The caloric count for a hamburger could turn out to be different if you looked at different aspects of the meal itself.

One of the first factors that scientists must consider is the **14** variable digestibility of foods. For instance, nuts are far less easily digested than spinach; as a result, nuts require more energy to digest. But even within the same category of food, digestibility can vary. A new study by Janet A. Novotny at the Department of Agriculture suggests that peanuts, pistachios, and almonds are less completely digested than other foods with similar levels of proteins, carbohydrates, and **15** fats meaning that they relinquish fewer calories than one would expect. **16**

14

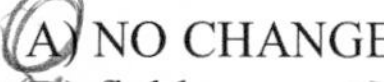

A) NO CHANGE
B) fickle
C) irregular
D) wavering

15

A) NO CHANGE
B) fats; meaning
C) fats—meaning
D) fats, meaning

16

The author is considering adding the following sentence at this point:

Almonds, for instance, yield just 129 calories per serving, far less than the 170 calories reported on the label.

Should the author make this addition?

A) Yes, because the sentence provides an example to clarify the idea presented in the previous sentence.
B) Yes, because the sentence meaningfully develops the main idea of the passage.
C) No, because the sentence fails to meaningfully develop the ideas of the paragraph.
D) No, because the sentence is unrelated to the main idea of the paragraph.

17 Cooking affects the calorie counts of foods, too. One Harvard study showed that cooking made calories in foods more readily accessible. In the study, adult mice were fed either sweet potatoes or lean beef. Some mice received cooked foods while others received raw foods. **18** The mice that ate cooked foods retained or gained significantly more weight when compared to the mice that ate raw foods. This is to be expected: heating hastens the unraveling of proteins, **19** makes them more easily digestible.

[1] Yet even if people eat the exact same food cooked in the exact same way, **20** they will not get the same number of calories out of it. [2] For example, studies from the early 1900s found that some populations have longer colons than others, and since the final stages of nutrient absorption occur in the large intestine, a larger colon means that more calories can be absorbed from the same food. [3] People differ in nearly all traits, and many of those traits impact digestion. [4] People also differ immensely in the community of bacteria that populates the intestines. [5] These bacteria have been shown to not only impact our digestive abilities, but can even cause us to crave specific foods. **21**

17

Which sentence provides the best transition between this paragraph and the previous paragraph?

A) NO CHANGE
B) Yet another complicating factor is the change that the food undergoes when cooked.
C) Beyond the variability of foods themselves, we must also consider the impact that cooking has on our foods.
D) However, the foods we eat have to be cooked.

18

A) NO CHANGE
B) Mice that are fed raw foods often gain less weight than the weight that is gained by mice that eat cooked foods.
C) When food is cooked for the mice, the mice often gain more weight from cooked foods than their weight gain from raw foods.
D) The mice that ate cooked foods retained or gained significantly more weight than those that ate raw foods.

19

A) NO CHANGE
B) making
C) made
D) having made

20

A) NO CHANGE
B) one
C) he
D) he or she

21

To improve the logical flow of the previous paragraph, sentence 3 should be placed

A) where it is now.
B) after sentence 1.
C) after sentence 4.
D) after sentence 5.

Because of the myriad of minute factors that can alter the number of calories we absorb from any given food item, it would be nearly impossible to develop totally accurate food labels. But one thing is **22** <u>certain, a</u> calorie isn't necessarily a calorie.

22

A) NO CHANGE
B) certain, that a
C) certain because a
D) certain: a

Questions 23-33 are based on the following passage.

[1] We often think of African politics and governments as being dominated by a single ethnic group. [2] The exclusion of certain groups then **23** translated into ethnic tensions as groups attempt to wrestle power from one another. [3] It makes a certain amount of sense. [4] We rely on this narrative to explain the root cause of the civil wars, revolutions, and coups we've seen in the last half-century. **24**

But a new paper published by economists Patrick Francois, Franceso Trebbi, and Illia Rainer **25** argue that we may have the story backwards. **26** It is not ethnic dominance that causes coups, but coups that cause ethnic dominance. Moreover, they are inclusive because leaders hope to reduce the probability of revolutions and coups against them. The authors **27** administered their analysis based on data that they carefully compiled on the ethnic composition of cabinet ministers in 15 African countries from 1960 to 2004.

23

A) NO CHANGE
B) translates
C) will have translated
D) has translated

24

Which sentence should be eliminated in order to improve the cohesion of the paragraph?

A) Sentence 1
B) Sentence 2
C) Sentence 3
D) Sentence 4

25

A) NO CHANGE
B) argues
C) will argue
D) have argued

26

Which of the following best establishes the main idea of the passage as a whole?

A) NO CHANGE
B) Coups are hostile takeovers of official governments, which happen often in Africa.
C) Ruling coalitions in Africa are, in fact, ethnically inclusive.
D) Ethnic tensions in Africa have been a considerably reliable trend throughout Africa's modern history.

27

A) NO CHANGE
B) conducted
C) regulated
D) transported

On average, ruling coalitions in Africa are broad, representing roughly 80% of a country's population. Moreover, the study's authors found that an ethnic group's share in the total population matched **28** its share in the cabinet. In other words, an ethnic group making up 20% of the total population held roughly 20% of the cabinet seats. This pattern of ethnic representation also held for the top cabinet posts of Finance, Defense, Justice, Home Affairs, Foreign Affairs, and so on.

These findings also undermine the popular belief that African heads of state disproportionately favor **29** their own ethnic groups in the allocation of cabinet posts. The study's authors found that this ethnic advantage is actual very small. They estimate that heads of state only allocate an additional 2 cabinet posts out of an average 25-member cabinet to their own ethnic group over and above their group's share in the population.

28

A) NO CHANGE
B) it's
C) its'
D) their

29

A) NO CHANGE
B) one's
C) his or her
D) his

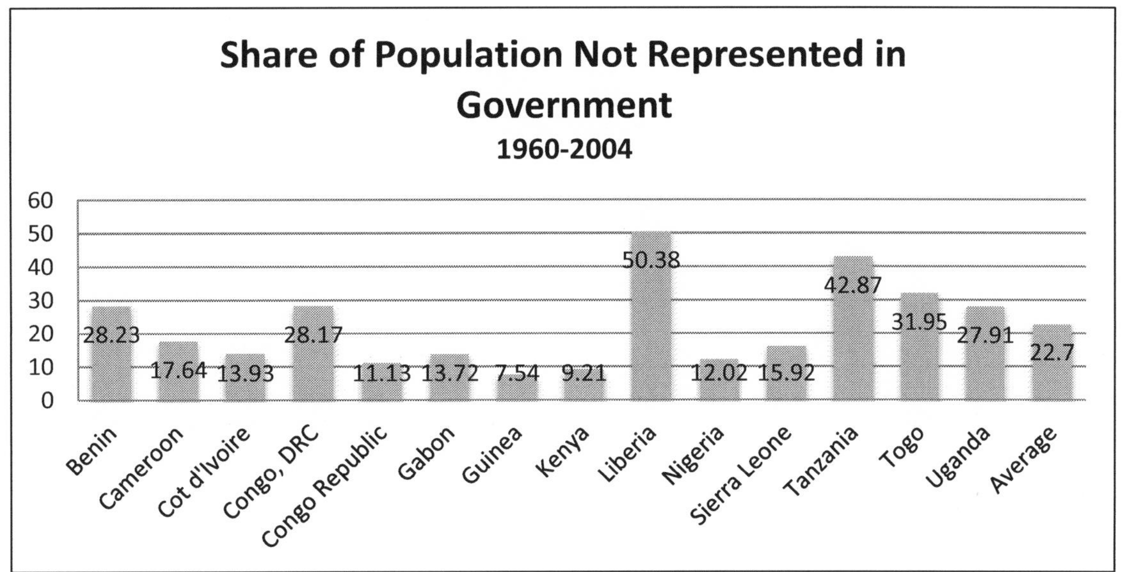

[1] Liberia seems to be the biggest **30** eccentricity in the study. **31** [2] Currently, only about 50% of the country's population is represented in government. [3] Once American help waned, the rule of the Americo-Liberians collapsed. [4] Interestingly, the authors found that most of this ethnic exclusiveness was limited to the period before 1980 when Liberia was ruled by Americo-Liberians, a very small minority of freed American slaves. [5] Americo-Liberians made up just 4% of the **32** population, they were able to set aside about 50% of cabinet posts for themselves. [6] Their minority rule was largely reinforced by outside help from the U.S. **33**

Western views of African politics are, at best, inaccurate and, at worst, prejudicial. We tend to generate over-simplified narratives in an attempt to explain a complex political situation. If western nations are to play a role in the development of African nations, then westerners must take the time to better understand African politics.

30

A) NO CHANGE
B) outlier
C) quirk
D) aberration

31

Which of the following provides accurate information based on the graph?

A) NO CHANGE
B) The population of Liberia is better represented in its government than other countries such as Nigeria or Sierra Leone.
C) In comparison to other African countries, Liberia has a much higher rate of citizens getting involved in their governments.
D) Only about 50% of the population found representation in government during the time period studied.

32

A) NO CHANGE
B) population, yet they
C) population; they
D) population, so they

33

In order to improve the logical flow of the previous paragraph, sentence 3 should be placed

A) where it is now.
B) before sentence 1.
C) after sentence 4.
D) after sentence 5.

Questions 34-44 are based on the following passage.

34 Although a molecule of DNA holds the complex blueprints for life, it measures just 2.5 billionths of a meter in diameter. DNA isn't simply responsible for a person's eye color or stature; many scientists believe that DNA may also hold the key to understanding and treating many diseases. To accomplish that goal, researchers have turned to nanotechnology. 35

34

The author is considering eliminating this sentence. Should this change be made?

A) Yes, because the sentence provides no meaningful information to the reader.
B) Yes, because the sentence misleads the reader into believing that DNA is the focus of the passage.
C) No, because the sentence provides context regarding the scale of work in the field of nanotechnology.
D) No, because the sentence provides vital information regarding the role of DNA.

35

The author is considering adding the following clause to the end of this sentence:

, the science of manipulating matter on a miniscule scale.

Should the author make this addition?

A) Yes, because it defines a term that is vital to the reader's understanding of the passage.
B) Yes, because it meaningfully develops the concept of DNA research.
C) No, because it unnecessarily defines a term that is in common use.
D) No, because it introduces a redundancy to the passage.

Through painstaking work over the last decade, scientists have learned to **36** manipulate and building molecules similar in size to a molecule of DNA. **37** This knowledge has revealed all of the medical applications of nanotechnology.

Regarding cancer alone, nanotechnology may provide multiple means of treatment. One potential treatment involves nanobots **38** molecule-sized robots that target cancer cells. Researchers at Harvard have developed a nanorobot that is designed to transport a collection of molecules. These molecules contain instructions that make cells behave in a particular way. In their study, the researchers successfully demonstrated the delivery of molecules that trigger cell suicide in leukemia and lymphoma cells.

Researchers at Northwestern University have taken a different approach. Scientists used gold to make "nanostars," simple star-shaped nanoparticles that can deliver drugs straight to the nuclei of cancer cells. These drug-loaded nanostars behave like tiny hitchhikers; after being attracted to an over-expressed protein found on the surface of human cervical and ovarian cancer cells, these little hitchhikers deposit their payload **39** promptly into the nuclei of those cells.

Scientists have long known that these kinds of protein-based drugs hold great promise. Unlike conventional cancer treatments, which kill not only the cancerous cells but also the surrounding healthy cells, protein-based drugs can be programmed to deliver specific signals to certain cells, **40** targeting treatment more effectively. The problem with current methods of delivery of such drugs is that the body breaks most of them down before the drugs are able to reach **41** their destination.

36

A) NO CHANGE
B) manipulate and build
C) manipulating and building
D) manipulate, build

37

Which of the following best establishes the main idea of the passage as a whole?

A) NO CHANGE
B) DNA studies have expanded in leaps and bounds thanks to the introduction of nanotechnology.
C) This knowledge is leading to new medicines and diagnostic methods, revealing some of the many possible medical applications of nanotechnology.
D) Nanotechnology allows scientists to work on a previously unimaginably small scale.

38

A) NO CHANGE
B) —molecule-sized robots—
C) molecule-sized robots,
D) (molecule-sized robots)

39

A) NO CHANGE
B) directly
C) openly
D) unswervingly

40

A) NO CHANGE
B) targets
C) will target
D) targeted

41

Which of the following best clarifies the pronoun reference?

A) the methods'
B) the drugs'
C) the body's
D) the delivery's

42 Therefore, researchers at the Massachusetts Institute of Technology (MIT) have begun exploring the possibility of creating self-assembling "nanofactories" that manufacture the necessary protein compounds on demand at target sites. The MIT team came up with this idea while trying to find a way to attack metastatic tumors, those that grow from cancer cells that have 43 journeyed from the original site to other parts of the body. Over 90% of cancer deaths are due to metastatic 44 cancer, so that successful treatments would be groundbreaking. Work has begun on the development of the nanofactories that may one day synthesize cancer drugs exactly where they are needed most—where the cancer grows.

42

Which of the following provides the best transition from the previous paragraph?

A) NO CHANGE
B) To discover this problem
C) To solve this problem
D) However,

43

A) NO CHANGE
B) emigrated
C) wandered
D) migrated

44

A) NO CHANGE
B) cancer, and successful
C) cancer, so successful
D) cancer, successful

STOP

If you finish before time is called, you may check your work on this section only.
Do not turn to any other section.

Math Test – No Calculator

25 MINUTES, 20 QUESTIONS

Mark your responses on this test. Use the "How to Calculate Your Scores in the back of this book to determine your scores.

DIRECTIONS

For questions 1-15, solve each problem, choose the best answer from the choices provided, and fill in the corresponding circle on your answer sheet. **For questions 16-20**, solve the problem and enter your answer in the grid on the answer sheet. Please refer to the directions before question 16 on how to enter your answers in the grid. You may use any available space in your test booklet for scratch work.

NOTES

1. The use of a calculator **is not permitted**.
2. All variables and expressions used represent real numbers unless otherwise indicated.
3. Figures provided in the test are drawn to scale unless otherwise indicated.
4. All figures lie in a plane unless otherwise indicated.
5. Unless otherwise indicated, the domain of a given function f is the set of all real numbers x for which $f(x)$ is a real number.

REFERENCE

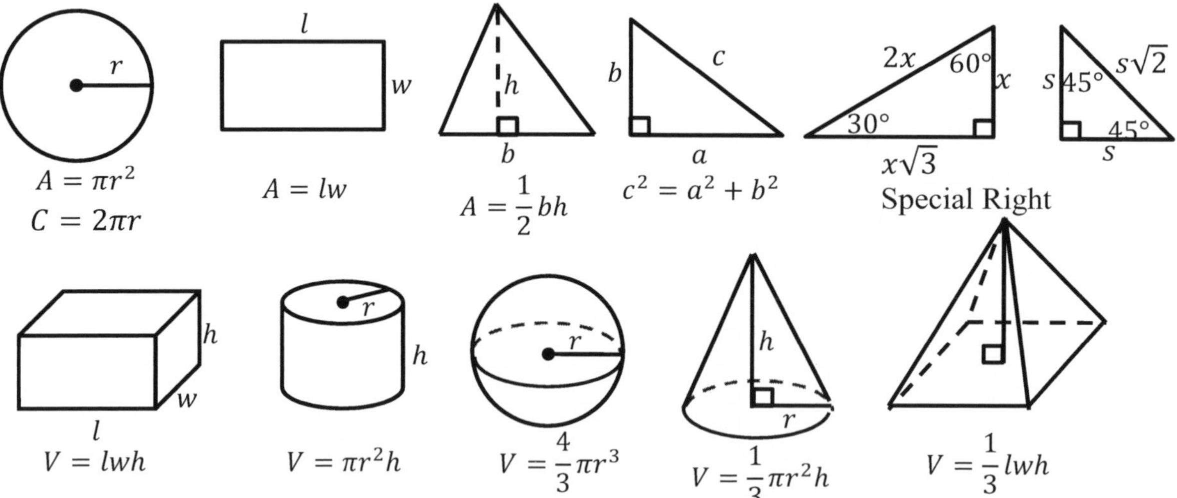

The number of degrees of arc in a circle is 360.

The number of radians of arc in a circle is 2π.

The sum of the measures in degrees of the angles of a triangle is 180.

1

The function $f(x) = x^2 - 2$ is graphed in the xy-plane. If $f(x)$ is translated up 3 units and then flipped over the x-axis, its new vertex is what?

A) $(0, -5)$
B) $(0, -1)$
C) $(0, 1)$
D) $(0, 5)$

2

The amount of money, in dollars, Kenji makes each month from his online blog series, y, can be estimated using the equation
$y = 2.25(x - 100) + 193.69$, where x represents the number of subscribers to his blog and $x \geq 100$. Which of the following statements is the best interpretation of the number 2.25 in the context of this problem?

A) The estimated amount of money Kenji makes per subscriber
B) The estimated amount of money Kenji makes for each subscriber after the 100th
C) The estimated amount of money Kenji makes when he has no subscribers
D) The estimated amount of money Kenji makes when he has 100 subscribers

3

If $|x - 3| < \frac{1}{2}$, what is a possible value of $3x$?

A) -9
B) $\frac{21}{2}$
C) $\frac{17}{2}$
D) $\frac{15}{2}$

4

If $xy - 3 = 2z$, $x \neq 0$, $y \neq 0$, and $z \neq 0$, what is y in terms of x and z?

A) $y = \frac{2z-3}{x}$
B) $y = \frac{2z+3}{x}$
C) $y = \frac{x}{2z+3}$
D) $y = \frac{x}{2z-3}$

5

If $A = x^2 + 6x + 9$, $B = x + 3$, and $x \neq -3$, what is $\frac{A}{2B}$ in terms of x?

A) $\frac{x^2+5x+6}{2}$
B) $\frac{x^2+9}{2}$
C) $\frac{x^2+6x+3}{2}$
D) $\frac{x+3}{2}$

6

The graph of $y = (x + 3)(3x + 15)$ is a parabola in the xy-plane. In which of the following equivalent equations do the x- and y-coordinates of the vertex of the parabola appear as constants or coefficients?

A) $3x^2 + 24x + 45$
B) $3x(x + 8) + 45$
C) $3(x + 4)^2 - 3$
D) $(3x + 9)(x + 5)$

7

$$5x + 7y = 13$$
$$5y - 2x = -17$$

Based on the system of equations above, what is the value of $7x + 2y$?

A) -4
B) $-\frac{15}{13}$
C) 30
D) $\frac{1406}{39}$

8

Which of the following is equal to $\cos\left(-\frac{\pi}{6}\right)$?

A) $\sin\left(-\frac{\pi}{3}\right)$
B) $\sin\left(-\frac{\pi}{6}\right)$
C) $\sin\left(\frac{\pi}{6}\right)$
D) $\sin\left(\frac{\pi}{3}\right)$

9

$$\frac{1}{t} + \frac{3}{t} = \frac{1}{7}$$

Corey and Trevor need to build a new greenhouse for their father. Corey works three times as quickly as Trevor does, and together they can build the greenhouse in seven hours. The equation above represents the situation described. Which of the following describes what the expression $\frac{3}{t}$ represents in this equation?

A) The portion of the greenhouse that Corey would complete in one hour
B) The portion of the greenhouse that Trevor would complete in one hour
C) The time, in hours, that it takes for Corey to finish the greenhouse alone
D) The time, in hours, that it takes for Trevor to finish the greenhouse alone

10

Which of the following is equal to $\frac{2-i}{2+i}$?

A) $\frac{3-4i}{5}$
B) $\frac{5-4i}{5}$
C) $\frac{3-4i}{3}$
D) $\frac{5-4i}{3}$

11

$$\frac{1-2(x-3)}{4}=\frac{3(2-x)-5}{7}$$

In the equation above, what is the value of x?

A) $\frac{-39}{2}$
B) $-\frac{21}{13}$
C) 4
D) $\frac{45}{2}$

12

$$(x-3)^2+(y+2)^2=16$$

Which of the following is the center of the equation of the circle above graphed in the xy-plane?

A) $(-3,-2)$
B) $(-3,2)$
C) $(3,-2)$
D) $(3,2)$

13

In the xy-plane, if the parabola with equation $y=x^2-x$ passes through the point (a,a), where a is a constant, what are all of the possible values of a?

A) -1
B) -1 and 0
C) 2
D) 0 and 2

14

Jason needs to buy at least 20 pounds of meat for the cookout he's holding. Hamburger costs \$7.50 per pound and chicken costs \$5.75 per pound, and Jason can only spend a maximum of \$150 on meat. If Jason buys x pounds of hamburger and y pounds of chicken, which of the following lists a solution, (x,y) that meet both of Jason's constraints?

A) $(10,10)$, $(13,6)$
B) $(2,19)$, $(19,3)$
C) $(12,8)$, $(15,7)$
D) $(8,15)$, $(12,10)$

15

Which of the following is equivalent to $s^2(\frac{1}{s}-\frac{1}{s^2})$?

A) $s-1$
B) $1-s$
C) $s-\frac{1}{s^2}$
D) $\frac{1}{s}-1$

DIRECTIONS

For questions 16-20, solve the problem and enter your answer in the grid, as described below, on the answer sheet.

1. Although not required, it is suggested that you write your answer in the boxes at the top of the columns to help you fill in the circles accurately. You will receive credit only if the circles are filled in correctly.
2. Mark no more than one circle in any column.
3. No question has a negative answer.
4. Some problems may have more than one correct answer. In such cases, grid only one answer.
5. **Mixed numbers** such as $3\frac{1}{2}$ must be gridded as 3.5 or 7/2.

   (If 3 1 / 2 is entered into the grid, it will be interpreted as $\frac{31}{2}$, not $3\frac{1}{2}$.)
6. **Decimal answers:** If you obtain a decimal answer with more digits than the grid can accommodate, it may be either rounded or truncated, but it must fill the entire grid.

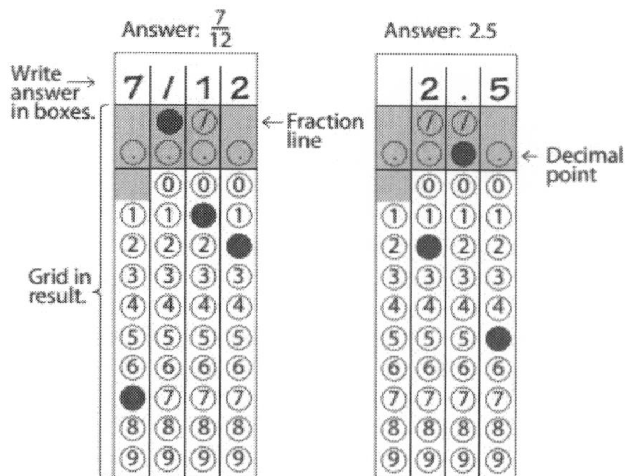

Acceptable ways to grid $\frac{2}{3}$ are:

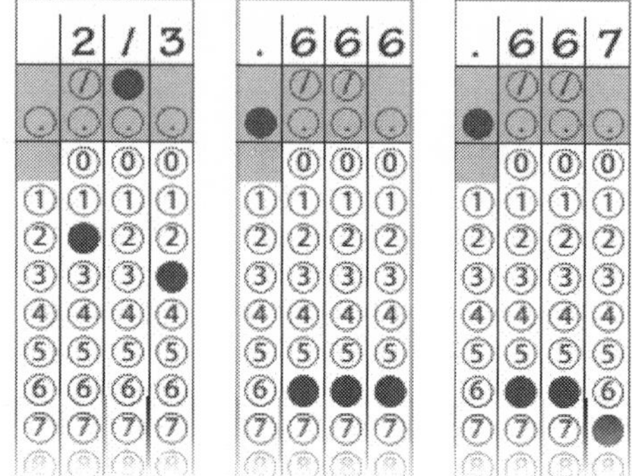

Answer: 201 – either position is correct

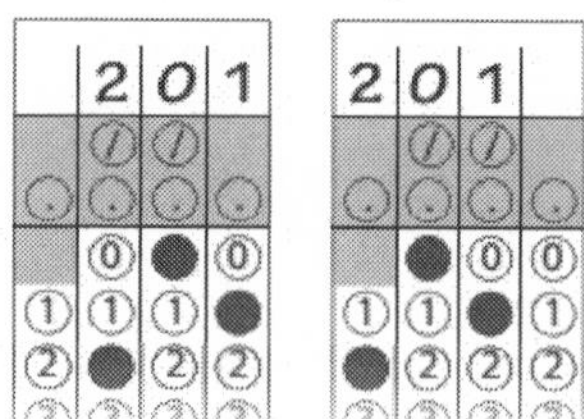

NOTE: You may start your answers in any column, space permitting. Columns you don't need to use should be left blank.

16

If $\frac{3}{5}a + \frac{2}{3}b = 7$, what is the value of $9a + 10b$?

17

What is the perimeter of the triangle with vertex coordinates in the xy-plane at $(-3, 2)$, $(-3, 5)$, and $(-7, 2)$?

18

If $(x + 3) + 3(x - 4) = x$ and $x > 0$, what is the value of x?

19

$$3x - \frac{1}{2}y = 12$$
$$py - 6x = -24$$

In the system of linear equations above, p is a constant. If the system has an infinite number of solutions, what is the value of p?

20

What is a possible solution to the equation $\frac{30}{x+4} = \frac{45}{4(x+1)}$?

STOP

If you finish before time is called, you may check your work on this section only. Do not turn to any other section.

Math Test –Calculator

55 MINUTES, 38 QUESTIONS

Mark your responses on this test. Use the "How to Calculate Your Scores in the back of this book to determine your scores.

DIRECTIONS

For questions **1-30**, solve each problem, choose the best answer from the choices provided, and fill in the corresponding circle on your answer sheet. **For questions 31-38**, solve the problem and enter your answer in the grid on the answer sheet. Please refer to the directions before question 31 on how to enter your answers in the grid. You may use any available space in your test booklet for scratch work.

NOTES

1. The use of a calculator **is permitted**.
2. All variables and expressions used represent real numbers unless otherwise indicated.
3. Figures provided in the test are drawn to scale unless otherwise indicated.
4. All figures lie in a plane unless otherwise indicated.
5. Unless otherwise indicated, the domain of a given function f is the set of all real numbers x for which $f(x)$ is a real number.

REFERENCE

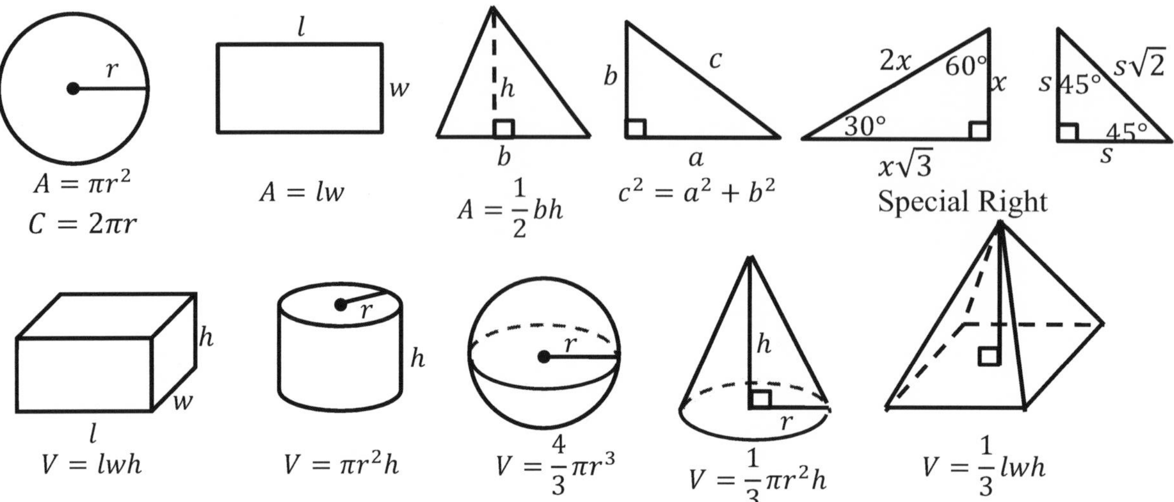

The number of degrees of arc in a circle is 360.

The number of radians of arc in a circle is 2π.

The sum of the measures in degrees of the angles of a triangle is 180.

1

A charity video game livestream needs to earn \$10,000. Silver viewers pay \$3.50 to watch the stream, while gold viewers pay \$5.25 to watch the stream. Which of the following inequalities represents the number of silver viewers s and gold viewers g the charity needs to meet or exceed its goal?

A) $\frac{3.50}{s} + \frac{5.25}{g} > 10{,}000$
B) $\frac{3.50}{s} + \frac{5.25}{g} \geq 10{,}000$
C) $3.50s + 5.25g > 10{,}000$
D) $3.50s + 5.25g \geq 10{,}000$

2

Sierra is shopping at an organic grocery store. She didn't bring her own grocery bags with her, so the grocery store charges her an untaxed fee of \$2.50 for grocery bags. A tax of x percent is applied to the cost of her groceries, \$78.53. Which of the following represents Sierra's total charge, in dollars?

A) $\frac{x}{100}(78.53) + 2.50$
B) $\frac{x}{100}(78.53 + 2.50)$
C) $\frac{x+100}{100}(78.53) + 2.50$
D) $\frac{x+100}{100}(78.53 + 2.50)$

3

Group	Mean (min)	Margin of Error (min)
A	125	9.21
B	121	4.32
C	131	2.59
D	152	5.36

A university official randomly selected four different groups of sophomore chemical engineering students and asked each student "How many minutes per day do you typically spend studying?" The results are shown in the table above. Which group most likely had the largest number of students surveyed?

A) Group A
B) Group B
C) Group C
D) Group D

Questions 4-6 refer to the following information.

The scatterplot below shows the relationship between the mass, in pounds, of a lobster and age, in years, of 12 lobsters.

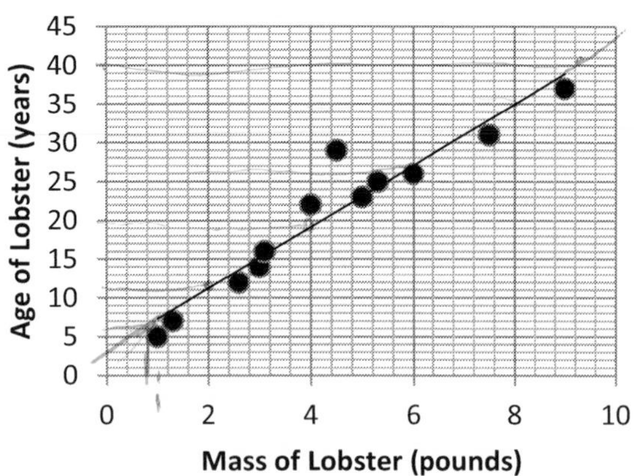

4

Based on the line of best fit, a 10-pound lobster would be expected to be approximately how many years old?

A) 1.6
B) 39.0
C) 43.0
D) 47.0

5

Which of the following is the best interpretation of the slope of the line of best fit in the context of this problem?

A) The predicted mass of a one-year-old lobster.
B) The predicted age of a one pound lobster.
C) The predicted mass increase in pounds for every year increase in age.
D) The predicted age increase in years for one pound increase in mass.

6

Based on the line of best fit, a 6-year-old lobster would have what mass, in pounds?

A) 0.6
B) 1.2
C) 1.8
D) 2.7

7

$$x^2 + y^2 = 16$$
$$x = -\frac{1}{2}y - 1$$

A system of equations is shown above. How many solutions does the system have?

A) Zero
B) One
C) Two
D) Four

8

Elise is starting a lemonade stand to make money for her trip to Nicaragua. She estimates that her startup costs will be $35, and that it will cost approximately 75 cents to produce a cup of lemonade. If she plans to sell each cup of lemonade for $1.50, what is the minimum number of cups that she must sell to raise at least $200?

A) 134
B) 157
C) 314
D) 470

9

Employee	Salary
Johnson	$60,000
Parvathi	$100,000
Lee	$30,000
Angelo	$60,000
Takas	$45,000
Tsumura	$35,000

What is the positive difference in the mean and median salaries, in dollars, of the employees listed above?

A) $2,500
B) $5,000
C) $7,500
D) $10,000

10

A biologist researched the population of a local group of elephants and recorded the data below:

Year	Population
1995	7
2000	14
2005	28

The population adheres to the same model over time. If P represents the population n years after 1995, then which of the following equations represents the biologist's model of the population over time?

A) $P = 7 + 2n$
B) $P = 7 + 7n$
C) $P = 7(2)^{5n}$
D) $P = 7(2)^{\frac{n}{5}}$

11

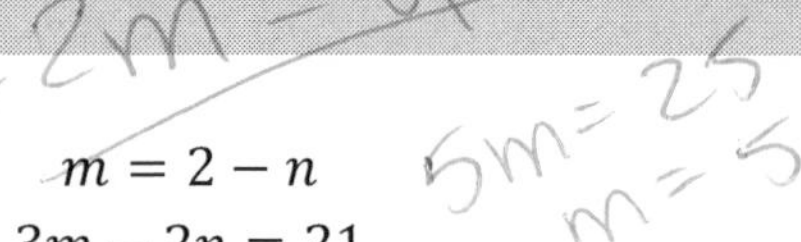

$$m = 2 - n$$
$$3m - 2n = 21$$

Based on the system of equations above, what is the value of n^2?

A) –9
B) –3
C) 3
D) 9

12

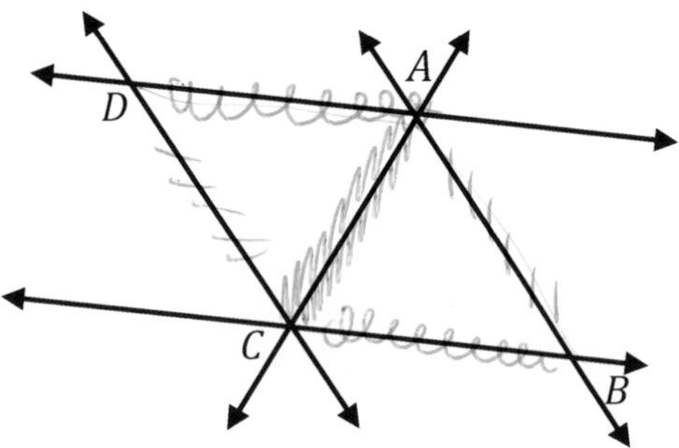

Note: Figure not drawn to scale.

In the figure above, $\Delta ABC \sim \Delta CDA$. Which of the following is NOT necessarily true?

A) $\angle DAB \cong \angle DCB$
B) $\angle ADC \cong \angle ACB$
C) $DA \parallel CB$
D) $DC \parallel AB$

13

A shipping truck at a local distributor has a gas mileage of 15 miles per gallon when the truck travels at an average speed of 60 miles per hour. The truck's gas tank starts with 24 gallons of gas at the beginning of the trip. If the truck travels at an average speed of 60 miles per hour, which of the following functions f models the number of gallons of gas remaining in the tank m minutes after the trip begins?

A) $24 - 4m$
B) $24 - \frac{m}{15}$
C) $\frac{24-m}{15}$
D) $\frac{24-4m}{15}$

14

Jenny needs to buy at least 1,500 hot dog buns for her school's end of the year picnic. Hot dog buns come in two sizes: packs of wheat buns and packs of white buns. Each 12-pack of wheat hot dog buns costs \$1.69, while each 18-pack of white hot dog buns costs \$1.89. If Jenny has a maximum of \$200.00 to spend on the hot dog buns, and the number of wheat and white buns she buys is inconsequential, solving which of the following systems of inequalities yields the number of packs of wheat buns, a, and white buns, b, she could buy?

A) $a + b \geq 1{,}500$
$1.69a + 1.89b \leq 200$
B) $12a + 18b \geq 1{,}500$
$1.69a + 1.89b \leq 200$
C) $12a + 18b \leq 1{,}500$
$1.69a + 1.89b \geq 200$
D) $a + b \leq 1{,}500$
$12(1.69a) + 18(1.89b) \geq 200$

15

When mining a particular region of the United States, the average mass of gold found per cubic meter of dirt unearthed increases linearly with the depth at which the dirt is mined. At a depth of 300 meters, an average of 3.7 g of gold is found per cubic meter of dirt unearthed. At a depth of 500 meters, an average of 4.8 g of gold is found per cubic meter of dirt unearthed. How much gold would be expected to be unearthed, on average, in 10 cubic meters of dirt at a depth of 100 meters?

A) 2.6 g
B) 5.9 g
C) 26.0 g
D) 59.0 g

look @ pairs diagrams

16

If $2k^2 + 7k = 15$ and $k > 0$, what is the value of k^2?

A) -5
B) $\frac{3}{2}$
C) $\frac{9}{4}$
D) 25

look @ Q.

reread Q. by bubbling

17

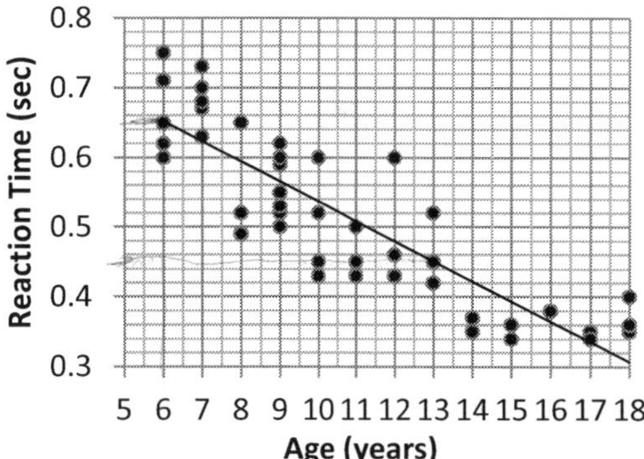

The scatterplot above shows the reaction time, in seconds, of several people based on their age, in years. Based on the line of best fit to the data shown, which of the following values is closest to the average yearly decrease in reaction time, in seconds?

A) 0.01
B) 0.03
C) 0.05
D) 0.07

18

Which of the following equations can be used to find the area of a circle, A, in terms of its circumference, C?

A) $A = \frac{C^2}{4\pi}$
B) $A = \frac{\pi C^2}{4}$
C) $A = \frac{4}{\pi C^2}$
D) $A = \frac{4\pi}{C^2}$

19

If $\frac{-2(x-2)+5}{3} = \frac{3-(2x-5)}{2}$, then $x =$

A) -6
B) -4
C) 3
D) $\frac{9}{2}$

20

A research assistant wants to know if there is an association between time spent watching television and physical fitness for the population of middle school students in the United States. She obtained responses from a random sample of 5,000 middle school students and found convincing evidence of an indirect correlation between time spent watching television and physical fitness. Which of the following conclusions is well supported by the data?

A) Using time spent watching television and physical fitness as defined by the study, an increase in time spent watching television is caused by a decrease in physical fitness for middle school students in the United States.
B) Using time spent watching television and physical fitness as defined by the study, a decrease in time spent watching television is caused by an increase in physical fitness for middle school students in the United States.
C) There is a negative association between time spent watching television and physical fitness for students in the United States.
D) There is a negative association between time spent watching television and physical fitness for middle school students in the United States.

21

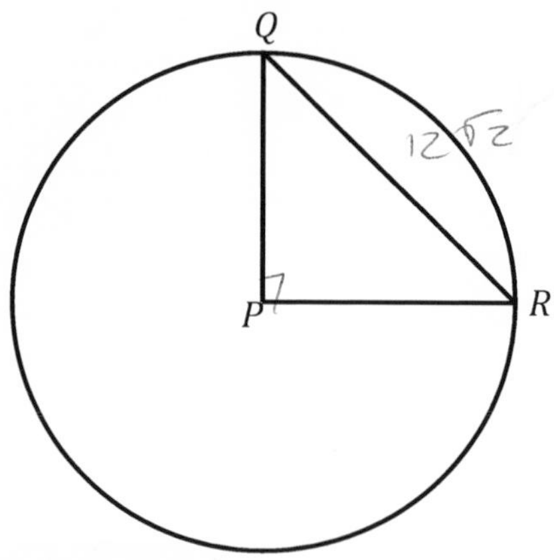

Circle P above contains right triangle QPR. If QR has a length of $12\sqrt{2}$, what is the area of circle P?

A) 24π
B) 72π
C) 144π
D) 288π

22

$$x + y = 3x$$
$$4x - \frac{1}{2}y = 12$$

Which of the following is a solution to the system of equations above?

A) (8, 4)
B) (7, 14)
C) (6, 6)
D) (4, 8)

23

A botanist plants two different varieties of grass on two different lawns in order to measure their rates of growth. After the initial planting of the grass ($t = 0$ days), the botanist measures and records the area covered by the grass every 12 hours. The data for each grass were fit by a smooth curve, as shown above, where each curve represents the area of a lawn covered by grass as a function of time, in days. Which of the following is a correct statement about the data above?

A) Grass B initially covers more of the lawn than Grass A does.
B) After 4 days, both grass varieties covered the same amount of the lawn.
C) After 6 days, both grass varieties covered the same amount of the lawn.
D) For the first 2 days, Grass A spreads more slowly than does Grass B.

Questions 24-26 refer to the following information.

A survey was conducted among a randomly chosen sample of registered voters from four different states about participation in the November 2008 presidential election. The table below displays a summary of the survey results.

Reported Voting by State				
	Voted	Did Not Vote	Did Not Respond	Total
Alabama	951	1,237	36	2,224
Georgia	1,639	2,364	73	4,076
Florida	3,134	4,752	108	7,994
Tennessee	1,030	1,781	43	2,854
Total	6,754	10,134	260	17,148

24

Which of the following is closest to the percent of those surveyed who reported voting?

A) 1.5%
B) 19.7%
C) 39.4%
D) 59.1%

25

Which state had the highest proportion of registered voters who did NOT vote?

A) Alabama
B) Georgia
C) Florida
D) Tennessee

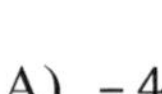

26

Based on the data, how many times more likely is it for a registered voter in Alabama to not vote than to vote? (Round the answer to the nearest hundredth)

A) 0.67 times as likely
B) 0.77 times as likely
C) 1.30 times as likely
D) 1.50 times as likely

27

A metal sphere of density 11.34 g/cm^3 and mass 1.282 kg is dropped into a cylindrical container with radius 4 cm and height 20 cm. If the container is originally half-filled with water, by approximately how many cm does the height of water in the beaker rise?

A) 0.23 cm
B) 1.13 cm
C) 2.25 cm
D) 6.00 cm

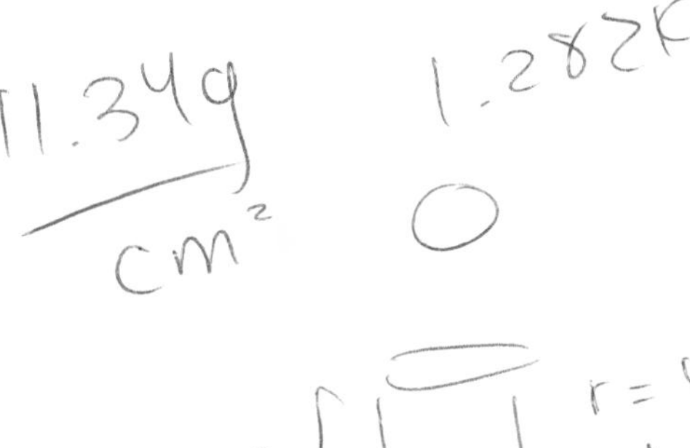

28

$$3(2-x)+2x=6(5+x)-7x$$

Which of the following is a solution to the equation above?

A) -4
B) 4
C) 12
D) No solution exists.

29

$$(x-3)^{-0.5}=2$$

Which value of x satisfies the equation above?

A) $3-\sqrt{2}$
B) $\frac{11}{4}$
C) $\frac{13}{4}$
D) $3+\sqrt{2}$

30

If the expression $\frac{x^3}{x-3}$ is written in the equivalent form $\frac{27}{x-3}+K$, what is K in terms of x?

A) x^2+3x+9
B) x^2-3x+9
C) x^2+3x-9
D) x^2-3x-9

DIRECTIONS

For questions 31-38, solve the problem and enter your answer in the grid, as described below, on the answer sheet.

1. Although not required, it is suggested that you write your answer in the boxes at the top of the columns to help you fill in the circles accurately. You will receive credit only if the circles are filled in correctly.
2. Mark no more than one circle in any column.
3. No question has a negative answer.
4. Some problems may have more than one correct answer. In such cases, grid only one answer.
5. **Mixed numbers** such as $3\frac{1}{2}$ must be gridded as 3.5 or 7/2.

   (If [3|1|/|2] is entered into the grid, it will be interpreted as $\frac{31}{2}$, not $3\frac{1}{2}$.)
6. **Decimal answers:** If you obtain a decimal answer with more digits than the grid can accommodate, it may be either rounded or truncated, but it must fill the entire grid.

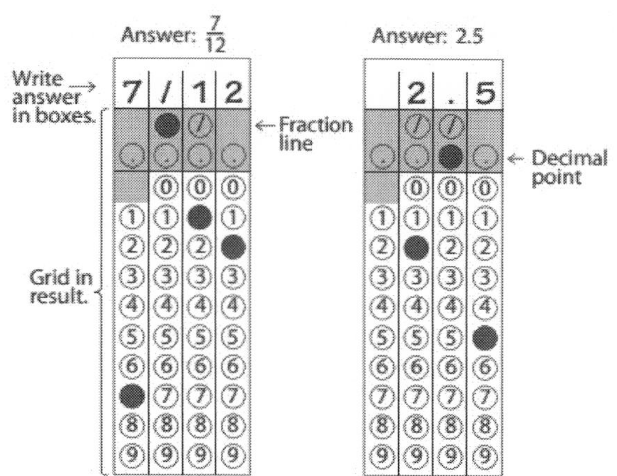

Acceptable ways to grid $\frac{2}{3}$ are:

2 / 3 . 6 6 6 . 6 6 7

Answer: 201 – either position is correct

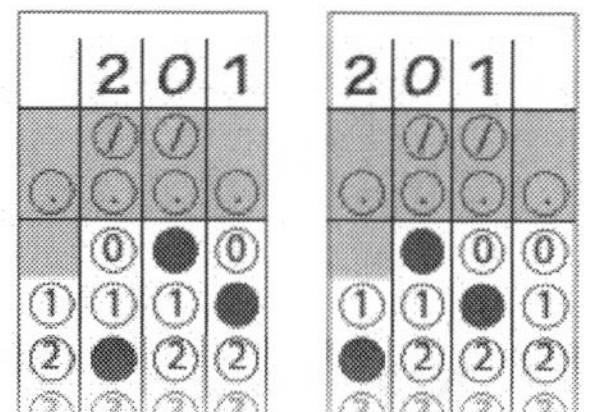

NOTE: You may start your answers in any column, space permitting. Columns you don't need to use should be left blank.

31

If $-\frac{7}{3} > -\frac{1}{2}k \;\; - 2 > -\frac{13}{4}$, what is one possible value of $2k + 8$?

32

The table below classifies 66 people based on two different physical characteristics.

	Widow's Peak	No Widow's Peak	Total
Attached Earlobes	10	32	42
Detached Earlobes	6	18	24
Total	16	50	66

What fraction of all people in the table with detached earlobes have a widow's peak as well?

33

An airline has 341 passengers for an overseas flight from Miami to London. If the number of passengers who want non-vegetarian meals is 20% more than the number of passengers who want vegetarian meals, how many fewer passengers on the flight requested vegetarian meals than requested non-vegetarian meals?

34

$$\frac{x^2 - 3x - 2}{x - 2} = 1$$

What is a possible value of x that satisfies the equation above?

35

$$y + x^2 = 3$$
$$2x + y = 0$$

If (x, y) is a solution to the system of equations above, and $y > x$, what is the value of $y - x$?

36

In the xy-coordinate plane, line FG is perpendicular to line segment DE and intersects DE at its midpoint. DE has endpoints at $(1, 5)$ and $(-3, -1)$. If FG intersects the y-axis at $(0, b)$, what is the value of b?

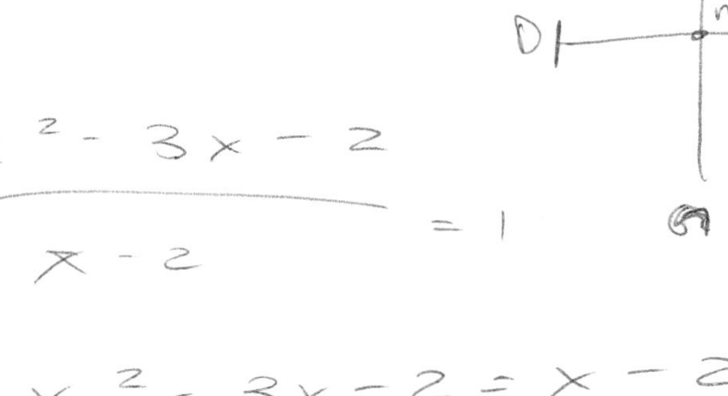

Questions 37 and 38 refer to the following information.

A popular cellphone provider offers the following plans for data usage:

Low Usage: $15.00 per month for 200 MB of data. For each 1 MB of data used over 200 MB, a charge of 7.5 cents is added to the user's bill.

High Usage: $25.00 per month for 1 GB of data. For each 1 MB of data used over 1 GB, a charge of 1.5 cents is added to the user's bill.

(Note: 1 GB = 1024 MB)

37

Gregory uses exactly 500 MB of data each month. How much money, to the nearest dollar, would he save per year by switching from the Low Usage plan to the High Usage plan?

38

Hannah currently uses 6 GB of data per month under the High Usage plan. She is considering switching to a competitor's plan. This plan charges $120.00 per month. However, since she is switching from a competitor, the new company is offering her a 20% discount on her data bill. How much money, to the nearest hundredth of a dollar, will Hannah save the first month when she makes her switch?

STOP

If you finish before time is called, you may check your work on this section only.

Do not turn to any other section.

ANSWER KEY

Section 1: Reading Test		Section 2: Writing and Language Test		Section 3: Math Test – No Calculator	Section 4: Math Test – Calculator Allowed
1. C	27. D	1. C	23. B	1. B	1. D
2. A	28. C	2. B	24. C	2. B	2. C
3. D	29. A	3. A	25. B	3. C	3. C
4. C	30. D	4. C	26. A	4. B	4. C
5. D	31. B	5. C	27. B	5. D	5. D
6. D	32. B	6. D	28. A	6. C	6. A
7. B	33. B	7. D	29. A	7. C	7. C
8. B	34. D	8. A	30. B	8. D	8. C
9. C	35. A	9. B	31. D	9. A	9. A
10. A	36. C	10. C	32. B	10. A	10. D
11. C	37. C	11. B	33. D	11. D	11. D
12. A	38. D	12. B	34. C	12. C	12. B
13. B	39. A	13. C	35. A	13. D	13. B
14. B	40. C	14. A	36. B	14. D	14. B
15. C	41. A	15. D	37. C	15. A	15. C
16. B	42. D	16. A	38. B	16. 105	16. C
17. A	43. A	17. B	39. B	17. 12	17. B
18. C	44. D	18. D	40. A	18. 3	18. A
19. A	45. B	19. B	41. B	19. 1	19. C
20. D	46. D	20. A	42. C	20. 0.8 or $\frac{4}{5}$	20. D
21. A	47. C	21. B	43. D		21. C
22. D	48. A	22. D	44. C		22. D
23. B	49. A				23. B
24. D	50. C				24. C
25. A	51. A				25. D
26. C	52. D				26. C
					27. C
					28. D
					29. C
					30. A
					31. $\frac{28}{3} < x < 13$
					32. $\frac{1}{4}$ or 0.25
					33. 31
					34. 0 or 4
					35. 3
					36. $\frac{4}{3}$ or 1.33
					37. 150
					38. 5.8

Reading Test

65 MINUTES, 52 QUESTIONS

Mark your responses on this test. Use the "How to Calculate Your Scores in the back of this book to determine your scores.

DIRECTIONS

Each passage or pair of passages below is followed by a number of questions. After reading each passage or pair, choose the best answer to each question based on what is stated or implied in the passage or passages and in any accompanying graphics (such as a table or graph).

Questions 1-11 are based on the following passage.

Adapted from "Oil for the Taking?", this passage discusses a 2011 fossil fuel discovery in Argentina.

A Spanish company called Repsol has discovered a huge amount of shale oil in Argentina, a find that could boost Argentina's potential to cash in on energy. However, some people are concerned about the cost—both financial and environmental—of extracting the oil.

The oil was discovered in the "VacaMuerta," or "Dead Cow," formation of the arid Neuquén Basin in northern Patagonia, a region of rocky, treeless plains dotted with dry brush, with only two lakes in close proximity. According to Repsol, the discovery comprises 927 million barrels of recoverable oil and natural gas, of which 741 million barrels are shale oil, and there may be even more than that—other areas of Argentina have yet to be explored and may also hold oil.

Oil is a widely used energy source and can be extremely valuable, so the find is big news—Argentina's economy stands to benefit from the export of oil.

Still, many people are not prepared to celebrate the discovery just yet. Experts say that the find is very promising, but they warn that the amount of time and financial resources needed to capitalize on the oil is still ambiguous.

"It must be proven, first of all, that [Repsol has found] commercially exploitable reserves," said Daniel Bosque, editor of the Argentina-based Web site Enernews. Bosque says a fundamental question is economic feasibility: whether there's a profit to be made from the shale oil. Unlike regular crude oil, which comes out of rock formations in liquid form, shale oil is drilled from rocks and is generally in solid form, making it more expensive to extract than normal crude oil.

Jason Schenker, an energy analyst, also had mixed emotions about the news because such oil discoveries "will be critical to meet rising global oil demand. Now the questions will be: How quickly can this oil be brought into production...and at what price?"

These are questions that Repsol wasn't immediately ready to answer with specific details. However, Repsol spokesperson Kristian Rix said that because 15 vertical wells have already been drilled and are producing 5,000 barrels of shale oil a day, developing the area "is uncomplicated from our point of view."

"It's [already an oil-producing] region, [and] all the infrastructure is there already, so putting new wells on line is very fast," Rix said. Typically, there is a lag time of five to seven years between oil exploration and oil production. "This is clearly not the case here, because we're already producing from wells."

Rix said it's still too early to comment on how long it would take or how much it would cost to get all of the oil from the area.

Some have also expressed apprehension about the environmental impact of getting the oil. The oil would be extracted by hydraulic fracturing, or "fracking," a technique that entails injecting water, sand, and chemicals into the rock, using high pressure to expel the fuel. It's not yet clear which water sources would be used for that process. In a recent report, the environmental group Greenpeace admonished that fracking puts considerable pressure on water supplies, particularly in arid regions.

Greenpeace also warned that chemicals used in the fracking process can taint underground aquifers and that little is known about other potential effects. The organization noted that up to 600 chemicals are used in fracking fluid, including known carcinogens and toxins such as lead, uranium, mercury, and formaldehyde. These chemicals have been found to leach into the groundwater, water that is stored underground in the soil, which can contaminate water used by local flora and fauna, as well as drinking water for any nearby towns.

Greenpeace opposes oil developments like the one in Argentina unless "it's shown that there's no [environmental] impact," said Ernesto Boerio, an energy and climate campaign coordinator for the organization in Argentina, adding, "More needs to be known about this project."

Speaking for Repsol, Rix said, "We operate to the highest standards of safety and environmental protection."

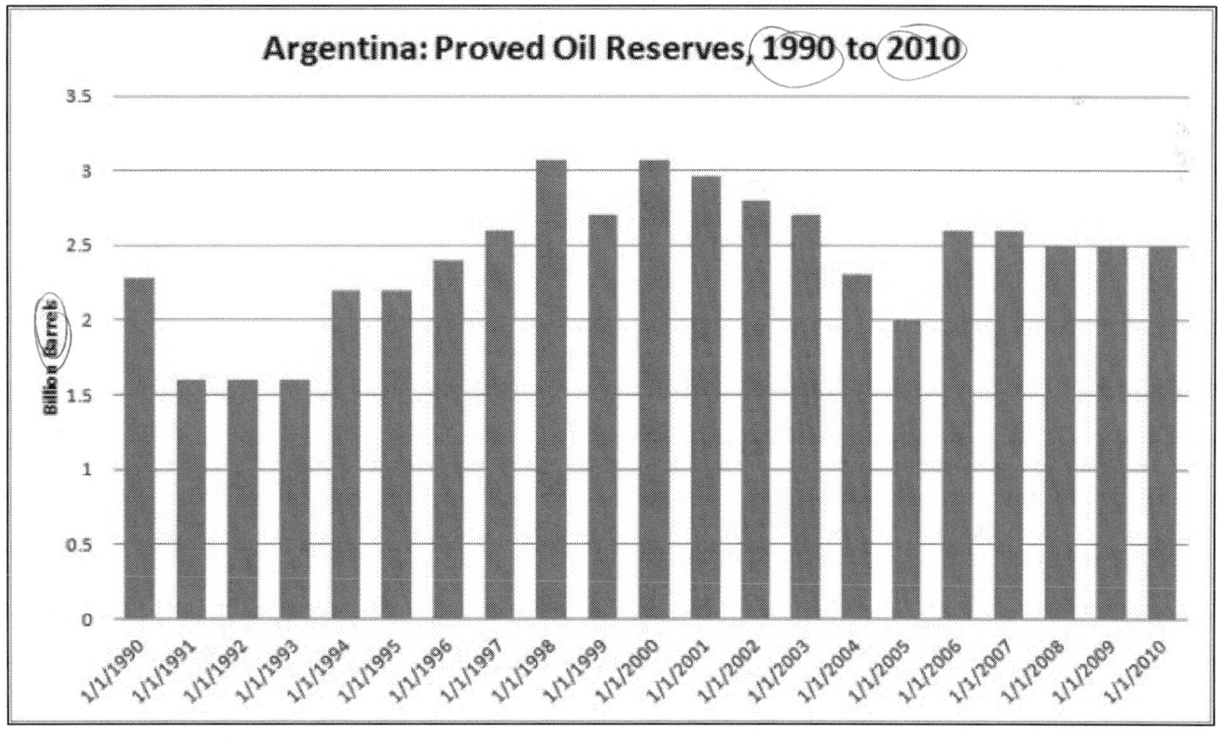

1

Which of the following best describes the purpose of the first paragraph?

A) To celebrate the new oil discovery in Argentina
B) To show that the author feels that the oil discovery will be very harmful
C) To introduce the potential benefits and harms of the new oil discovery
D) To demonstrate the relative insignificance of the new oil discovery

2

The author most likely included the information that the Vaca Muerta region has "only two lakes in close proximity" (lines 12) in order to

A) demonstrate the fact that the region has limited water reserves.
B) provide imagery to allow the reader to visualize the region.
C) show that the region has ample water to use in extracting the oil.
D) suggest that there are few plants and animals that could be impacted by the extraction of the oil.

3

Based on information from the passage and the graph, the new oil discovery will likely

A) not be a significant increase over Argentina's existing oil reserves.
B) bring Argentina's oil reserves to higher levels than were seen in any other year shown in the graph.
C) reduce Argentina's oil reserves to levels similar to those seen in 1991-1993.
D) allow Argentina to maintain the same oil reserve levels seen in 2010.

4

According to the passage, the biggest benefit likely to come from the oil discovery is that it will

A) improve the drinking water for nearby towns.
B) provide much needed fuel to South Americans.
C) improve Spain's economy.
D) improve Argentina's economy.

5

Which of the following provides the best evidence to support the answer to the previous question?

A) Lines 1-3 ("A Spanish...Argentina")
B) Lines 8-12 ("The oil...proximity")
C) Lines 13-15 ("According...gas")
D) Lines 21-22 ("Argentina's...oil")

6

As it is used in line 30, "reserves" most nearly means

A) supplies.
B) cautions.
C) preserves.
D) secures.

7

According to the passage, crude oil is preferable to shale oil because

A) crude oil can be extracted using water.
B) there is more crude oil than there is shale oil.
C) shale oil is easier to access.
D) crude oil is cheaper to extract.

8

Repsol believes that concerns regarding the production of oil in the Vaca Muerta region are unfounded because

A) there is almost always a lag time of five to seven years before production begins.
B) it is far too early to tell whether there would be difficulties in production.
C) wells in the region are already producing significant amounts of oil.
D) the technology to extract shale oil is already available.

9

Which of the following provides the best evidence in support of the answer to the previous question?

A) Lines 35-39 ("Unlike...oil")
B) Lines 48-52 ("However...view")
C) Lines 56-58 ("Typically...production")
D) Lines 60-62 ("Rix...area")

10

As it is used in line 63, "expressed" most nearly means

A) voiced.
B) discharged.
C) hastened.
D) protested.

11

According to the passage, which of the following is not a concern about fracking?

A) It pollutes water used by nearby plants, animals, and people.
B) It produces fossil fuels that result in air pollution.
C) It uses dangerous chemicals that may have unknown environmental effects.
D) It uses up a lot of water, putting pressure on local water sources.

Questions 12-22 are based on the following passage.

The following passages describe two rebellions in early U.S. history. The first discusses Shays' Rebellion, while the second discusses Bacon's Rebellion.

Passage 1

The last cannonade of the War of Independence did not occur on the fields of Yorktown but instead was fired "waistband" high, as an eyewitness later recorded, into a crowd of irate Massachusetts farmers as they rebelled against unfair taxes and foreclosures. The farmers were led by thirty-nine-year-old Revolutionary War veteran, Daniel Shays.

The year was 1787. The United States was only a loose alliance between thirteen former colonies. Ironically, three young farmers lying dead on a road had as much to do with uniting the states' disparate interests as Washington, Jefferson, and Hamilton combined. The danger of anarchy posed by this revolt inspired patriots to write a strong constitution, restrain states' rights, and establish a federal government that would secure the future of the United States.

Prior to the adoption of the Constitution, the young country was paralyzed by an enormous war debt. Many colonists who had just resisted the tyranny of a king preferred to resist the creation of a strong federal authority. The weak Articles of Confederation had created a government that could not levy taxes, control trade, or defend against foreign countries. There were neither federal judges nor a chief executive. When the Confederation Congress tried to impose an import duty to pay government bills, the vote of one state kept it from being approved.

Wealthy eastern merchants in the big cities dominated state legislatures and favored higher taxes on land to pay the war debt. This placed a heavier burden on smaller farmers who owned land but little cash. In order to stop the courts from foreclosing on their lands, mobs of farmers in Western Massachusetts organized themselves behind Shays. They kept regional courts from opening and on January 25, 1787 they marched on the federal arsenal at Springfield, intent on seizing its weapons.

Shays and his men never thought their fellow citizens would try to stop them, but they were wrong. After a warning, the militia fired a volley of grapeshot at Shays's men, scattering them, and killing three. As a result of this rebellion, the Confederation Congress endorsed a constitution that created a strong central government that could tax its own citizens to support and sustain itself.

Passage 2

A century before the American Revolution, the charismatic Nathaniel Bacon led a full-scale insurrection against the king's appointed governor for the Virginia Colony, William Berkeley. Bacon's Rebellion began in opposition to Governor Berkeley's Indian policy.

In 1676, former indentured servants wanted to establish small farms, but Native Americans lived on the treaty-guaranteed land. Governor Berkeley and his allies opposed the poorer whites' expansion into Indian lands for two reasons. First, they wanted these men to be wage laborers on their plantations. Second, this landed gentry wanted to trade with the Native Americans for furs.

The rebellion erupted when Native Americans stole corn from the poorer colonists. The colonists retaliated by attacking the Susquehannocks, and the Susquehannocks retaliated by killing settlers along the frontier. In the meantime, King Phillip's War was pitting Natives against colonists in New England, and the news of it heightened the Virginia colonists' fear of an all-out Indian war. Additionally, economic pressures from falling tobacco prices increased the colonists' desire for Indian land. The frustrated settlers asked Nathaniel Bacon to lead an army against the Natives.

Bacon was a member of the governor's council and owned a frontier estate. When he answered the call of his terrified neighbors, Governor Berkeley ordered him to desist, but Bacon refused. The governor expelled Bacon from his council and declared him a "rebel."

Bacon marched on the capital, Jamestown, but he was promptly arrested. Under pressure, the governor pardoned him. However, the governor failed to deliver on a promise to let Bacon return to fighting Indians. Bacon again raised 600 men and took over Jamestown, personally challenging Berkeley to a duel. The "rebel" issued a "Declaration of the People," which condemned unjust taxes. Sadly, the rebellion fell apart after Bacon died of an illness.

This clash of personalities led to more control of the colony by the English king. The most important long-term effect was an increase in slave labor. Fearing future rebellions by former indentured servants,

Virginia plantation owners imported more and more slaves from Africa. This expansion of slavery would culminate in a tragic civil war two centuries later.

12

The author of the first passage most likely chose to include the sentence in lines 11-14 (“Ironically...combined”) in order to

A) show that Washington, Jefferson, and Hamilton were not as influential as historians believe.
B) introduce humor to the passage through the use of irony.
C) foreshadow the effect of the rebellion on the nation's development.
D) establish the fact that the nation was not yet established at the time of the rebellion.

13

It can be inferred from the first passage that the reason the Articles of Confederation limited central control was that

A) the nation faced too great a war debt to properly organize a central government.
B) the colonists did not expect to need to control trade or defend against foreign countries.
C) the states couldn't agree on a form of central government.
D) the colonists feared that a strong federal authority would lead to tyranny.

14

Which of the following provides the strongest support for the answer to the previous question?

A) Lines 19-21 (“Prior...debt”)
B) Lines 21-23 (“Many...authority”)
C) Lines 24-26 (“The weak...countries”)
D) Lines 28-31 (“When...approved”)

15

The first passage suggests which of the following about the government under the Articles of Confederation?

A) Land-owners dominated the legislature.
B) The primary duty of the federal government was to pay war debt.
C) There was an executive branch and a judicial branch, but no legislative branch.
D) All states were required to agree before measures could be passed.

16

The author of the first passage most likely included the information found in lines 32-39 (“Wealthy...Shays”) in order to

A) explain the root causes of Shays' Rebellion.
B) justify the actions of the “wealthy eastern merchants.”
C) demonstrate how taxation worked under the Articles of Confederation.
D) illustrate Shays' leadership abilities.

17

As it is used in line 51, “support” most nearly means

A) bolster.
B) endorse.
C) strengthen.
D) tolerate.

18

According to the second passage, former indentured servants were forbidden from settling in Native American lands because

A) a treaty promised that whites would not settle in those lands, and colonial leaders feared violating the treaty.

B) wealthy leaders wanted these men to labor on their plantations and wanted to continue to trade with the Native Americans.

C) Native American tribes commonly stole supplies from settlers who settled near those lands.

D) falling tobacco prices prevented these men from being able to afford to settle in the Native American land.

19

Which of the following provides the best evidence in support of the answer to the previous question?

A) Lines 59-61 ("In 1676...land")

B) Lines 62-67 ("Governor...furs")

C) Lines 68-69 ("The rebellion...colonists")

D) Lines 76-78 ("Additionally...land")

20

As it is used in line 77, "pressures" most nearly means

A) urgency.

B) compels.

C) heaviness.

D) burdens.

21

It can be inferred from the second passage that Bacon's Rebellion

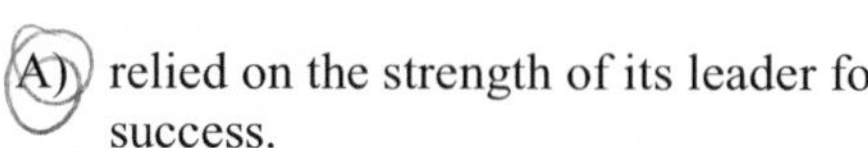
A) relied on the strength of its leader for success.

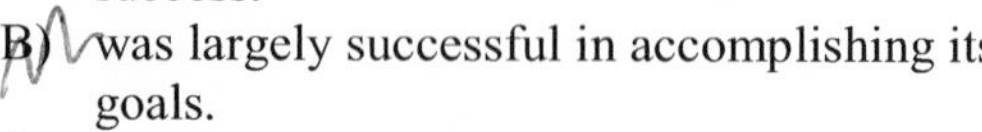
B) was largely successful in accomplishing its goals.

C) proved the necessity of continuing the practice of indentured servitude.

D) resulted in all-out war against the Native Americans.

22

The rebellions discussed in each passage are similar in that both

A) began in opposition to taxes and land seizures.

B) were in response to limitations on where people could settle.

C) involved New England farmers.

D) resulted in changes that had long term effects on the nation as a whole.

Questions 23-32 are based on the following passage.

The following is excerpted from Mark Twain's The Prince and the Pauper, *a tale about a prince and a poor boy who switch places. This excerpt discusses the life of Tom, the poor boy in the story.*

London was fifteen hundred years old, and was a great town. It had a hundred thousand inhabitants. The streets were very narrow, and crooked, and dirty, especially in the part where Tom Canty lived.

The house which Tom's father lived in was up a foul little pocket called Offal Court. It was small, decayed, and rickety, but it was packed full of wretchedly poor families. Canty's tribe occupied a room on the third floor. The mother and father had a sort of bedstead in the corner; but Tom, his grandmother, and his two sisters, Bet and Nan, were not restricted—they had all the floor to themselves, and might sleep where they chose. There were the remains of a blanket or two, and some bundles of ancient and dirty straw, but these could not rightly be called beds.

Bet and Nan were fifteen years old—twins. They were good-hearted girls, unclean, clothed in rags, and profoundly ignorant. Their mother was like them. But the father and the grandmother were a couple of fiends. They fought each other or anybody else who came in the way; they cursed and swore always; John Canty was a thief, and his mother a beggar. They made beggars of the children, but failed to make thieves of them. Among, but not of, the dreadful rabble that inhabited the house, was a good old priest, and Father Andrew taught Tom how to read and write; and would have done the same with the girls, but they were afraid of the jeers of their friends, who could not have endured such a queer accomplishment in them.

All Offal Court was just such another hive as Canty's house. Drunkenness, riot and brawling were the order, there, every night and nearly all night long. Broken heads were as common as hunger in that place. Yet little Tom was not unhappy. He had a hard time of it, but did not know it. It was the sort of time that all the Offal Court boys had, therefore he supposed it was the correct and comfortable thing. When he came home empty-handed at night, he knew his father would curse him and thrash him first, and that when he was done the awful grandmother would do it all over again and improve on it; and that away in the night his starving mother would slip to him stealthily with any miserable scrap or crust she had been able to save for him by going hungry herself, notwithstanding she was often caught in that sort of treason and soundly beaten for it by her husband.

No, Tom's life went along well enough. He only begged just enough to save himself, for the laws against mendicancy were stringent, and the penalties heavy; so he put in a good deal of his time listening to good Father Andrew's charming old tales and legends about giants and fairies, dwarfs, and enchanted castles, and gorgeous kings and princes. His head grew to be full of these wonderful things, and many a night as he lay on his scant and offensive straw, tired, hungry, and smarting from a thrashing, he unleashed his imagination and soon forgot is aches and pains in delicious picturings to himself of the charmed life of a prince in a regal palace. One desire came to haunt him day and night: it was to see a real prince, with his own eyes. He spoke of it once to some of his Offal Court comrades; but they jeered him so unmercifully that he was glad to keep his dream to himself after that.

By-and-by Tom's reading and dreaming about princely life wrought such a strong effect upon him that he began to *act* the prince, unconsciously. His speech and manners became curiously ceremonious and courtly, to the vast admiration of his intimates. But Tom's influence among these young people began to grow now, day by day; and in time he came to be looked up to with a sort of wondering awe, as a superior being. He seemed to know so much! and he could do and say such marvelous things! and withal, he was so deep and wise! Tom's remarks were reported by the boys to their elders; and these, also, presently began to discuss Tom Canty and to regard him as a most gifted and extraordinary creature. Full-grown people brought their perplexities to Tom for solution, and were often astonished at the wit and wisdom of his decisions.

23

Within the context of the passage, what is the effect of the author's use of the phrase "great town" in line 2?

A) It creates vivid imagery of London's richness.
B) It emphasizes the size and spaciousness of London.
C) It underscores the magnificence of London, which is further explained later in the passage.
D) It introduces irony since the description of London makes it seem shabby rather than great.

24

As it is used in line 6, "pocket" most nearly means

A) small.
B) sack.
C) corner.
D) concealment.

25

The author most likely included the information in the third paragraph (lines 18-33) in order to

A) illustrate the poverty in which Tom was raised.
B) show that Tom had a loving family in spite of their poverty.
C) explain why Tom became a beggar instead of a thief.
D) provide a thorough description of the people who have the greatest impact on Tom.

26

It can be inferred from the passage that

A) it was uncommon for girls to learn to read.
B) Bet and Nan were well-educated thanks to Father Andrew.
C) Tom's family was unique among the other residents of Offal Court.
D) Tom had a strong relationship with his father.

27

Which of the following provides the best evidence in support of the answer to the previous question?

A) Lines 27-30 ("Among...write")
B) Lines 30-33 ("and would...them")
C) Lines 34-35 ("All...house")
D) Lines 42-44 ("When...first")

28

Which of the following is a reason given in the passage for Tom's satisfaction with his life?

A) Tom's mother ensured that he wanted for nothing.
B) Tom did not know better since he had never seen a different life.
C) Tom's sisters were kind and loving toward him.
D) Tom enjoyed begging during the days.

29

Which of the following provides the best evidence to support the answer to the previous question?

A) Lines 18-20 ("Bet...ignorant")
B) Lines 39-42 ("He...thing")
C) Lines 47-50 ("his...herself")
D) Lines 54-57 ("He...heavy")

30

As it is used in line 36, "order" most nearly means

A) application.
B) authorization.
C) lawfulness.
D) status.

31

Which of the following best describes Tom's begging?

A) He refused to beg because he preferred to listen to Father Andrew's tales.

B) He greatly preferred to steal than to beg, much to his father's approval.

C) He begged because he was punished if he didn't, but limited his begging to avoid being caught by the authorities.

D) He eagerly learned the art of begging from his father and grandmother.

32

How did Tom earn the respect of the other people in Offal Court?

A) By winning fights against the other boys

B) By adopting an impressive demeanor to seem more intelligent

C) By earning enough money to leave Offal Court

D) By seeing a real prince and sharing the experience with his friends

Questions 33-42 are based on the following passage.

The following is adapted from an April 2015 article titled "Why 'Natural' Doesn't Mean Anything Anymore."

In the past few years, several lawsuits have challenged the definition of an English word that is ubiquitous in common parlance: "natural." During the past several years, some 200 class-action suits have been filed against food manufacturers, charging them with misuse of the term "natural" in their advertising. Examples include such oxymoronic products as "natural" Cheetos, "all-natural" Sun Chips, "all-natural" Naked Juice, and "100 percent all-natural" Tyson chicken nuggets. The plaintiffs argue that these products contain ingredients that few consumers would consider to be natural—high-fructose corn syrup, artificial flavors and colorings, chemical preservatives, and genetically modified organisms, just to name a few.

The judges hearing these cases have sought some standard definition of the word "natural" that could be used to adjudicate such claims, only to discover that no such thing exists. The very word is impressively slippery, its use steeped in dubious assumptions that are easy to overlook. Perhaps the most difficult to grasp definition is the notion that nature consists of everything in the world except for us and all that we have created.

For example, many in the anti-vaccine crowd use the argument that vaccines are unnatural. By their logic, we would be better off relying on "natural immunity" acquired through exposure to the live virus; injecting dead or deactivated viruses into ourselves is, by their reasoning, completely unnatural and thus undesirable. The concept of "natural immunity" implies the absence of human intervention, allowing for a process to unfold as it would if we did nothing—in other words, "letting nature take its course." Yet even the most ardent anti-vaxxer likely interrupts nature's course from time to time. After all, most of medicine sets itself *against* nature's course, which is precisely what we like about it—at least when it's saving us from dying, an eventuality that is perhaps more natural than is desirable.

At this end of the spectrum of possible meanings, we stand outside nature. By this definition, what is left of the natural that we haven't altered in some way? We've inserted ourselves into everything by now, from the chemical composition of the atmosphere to the genome of every plant or animal in the grocery store to the human body itself, which has long since evolved in response to cultural practices we created, like agriculture and cooking.

At the other extreme end of the spectrum, there isn't anything but nature. Our species is a result of the same process—natural selection—that created every other species, meaning that we and our actions are natural, too. By this definition, those processed chicken nuggets most certainly are natural: They're made of matter, after all.

Like the maddening whiteness of Ahab's whale, nature is an obligingly blank screen on which we can project what we want to see. But this doesn't mean that when it comes to determining what is and isn't natural, anything goes. I think that we can harvest some philosophical wisdom from, of all places, the Food and Drug Administration. When federal judges couldn't find a definition of "natural" to apply to the class-action suits before them, three of them wrote to the F.D.A., ordering the agency to define the word. The F.D.A. had already considered the question several times before without reaching a consensus; they refused another attempt at a definition. The only advice the F.D.A. was willing to offer on the issue is that a food labeled "natural" should have "nothing artificial or synthetic" in it "that would not normally be expected in the food." The F.D.A. states on its website that "it is difficult to define a food produce as 'natural' because the food has probably been processed and is no longer the product of the earth." The food industry may not want to push the issue too hard because the F.D.A.'s current stance suggests that if forced to define "natural," it may well decide that nothing the food industry produces is natural.

The F.D.A.'s philosopher-bureaucrats are probably right: It's difficult, if not impossible, to establish a workable definition of "natural." But we can rely on common sense. "Natural" has a fairly concrete antonym: artificial or synthetic. On a scale of relative values, it's not very difficult to say which of two things is more natural than the other: cane sugar or high-fructose corn syrup, chicken or chicken nuggets, genetically modified organisms or heirloom seeds? In fact, the most natural foods in the store rarely bother labeling themselves as natural; food products that feel compelled to tell you that they are natural probably are not.

33

Which of the following best summarizes the main idea of the passage?

A) Food manufacturers should be allowed to label their products in any way they chose in order to improve sales.
B) Food manufacturers frequently lie about the ingredients in their products.
C) On food labels, the word "natural" likely doesn't mean that the food item is not synthetic.
D) Judges should establish a common definition of the word "natural" in order to help consumers.

34

As it is used in line 5, "charging" most nearly means

A) assaulting.
B) requesting.
C) demanding.
D) accusing.

35

The author likely used the phrase "oxymoronic products" to describe the items listed in lines 8-10 in order to

A) show that the use of the word "natural" in describing those items is very inaccurate.
B) introduce literary terminology to add color and flair to the article.
C) create a humorous tone in the passage.
D) help provide a clear definition of the word "natural."

36

Which of the following is NOT a definition of "natural" discussed in the passage?

A) Natural things are those things that humans have not impacted.
B) Everything comes from nature, including humans and our inventions.
C) Natural is a philosophical concept established by the F.D.A.
D) Natural things include nothing that is artificial or synthetic.

37

According to the passage, why should food manufacturers not press the F.D.A. to define "natural"?

A) The F.D.A. has suggested that any processed food likely isn't natural, so the F.D.A. may decide that no manufactured food items are natural.
B) In the absence of a definition, food manufacturers can label anything natural without fear of condemnation.
C) Food manufacturers will likely find a more favorable definition by relying on the courts rather than on the F.D.A.
D) All foods are natural, regardless of whether they have been processed, so an F.D.A. definition is unnecessary.

38

Which of the following provides the best support for the answer to the previous question?

A) Lines 17-19 ("The judges...claims")
B) Lines 60-62 ("those...all")
C) Lines 74-77 ("The F.D.A....definition")
D) Lines 82-85 ("The F.D.A...earth")

39

As it is used in line 95, "concrete" most nearly means

A) tangible.
B) objective.
C) compact.
D) hardened.

40

Within the context of the passage as a whole, what is the purpose of the third paragraph (lines 27-44)?

A) To show that the definition of natural is equally murky in the field of medicine
B) To provide an example to better explain the ideas presented in the previous paragraph
C) To provide an example to better explain the ideas presented in the fifth paragraph (lines 55-62)
D) To show the author's expertise in fields other than the food industry

41

The author would most likely agree with which of the following?

A) The judges deciding the lawsuits should rule in favor of the plaintiffs.
B) The F.D.A. should establish a clear definition of the term "natural."
C) Nearly all foods are natural in one way or another.
D) Consumers should rely on common sense rather than food labels to determine whether a food is natural.

42

Which of the following best supports the answer to the previous question?

A) Lines 3-6 ("During...advertising")
B) Lines 59-62 ("By this...all")
C) Lines 85-90 ("The food...natural")
D) Lines 94-101 ("But we...seeds")

Questions 43-52 are based on the following passage.

The following is excerpted from a radio speech delivered by Franklin Delano Roosevelt while he was running for his first term as president in 1932.

Although I understand that I am talking under the auspices of the Democratic National Committee, I do not want to limit myself to politics. I do not want to feel that I am addressing an audience of Democrats or that I speak merely as a Democrat myself. The present condition of our national affairs is too serious to be viewed through partisan eyes for partisan purposes.

It is the habit of the unthinking to turn in times like this to the illusions of economic magic. People suggest that a huge expenditure of public funds by the Federal Government and by State and local governments will completely solve the unemployment problem. A real economic cure must go to the killing of the bacteria in the system rather than to the treatment of external symptoms.

How much do the shallow thinkers realize, for example, that approximately one half of our whole population, fifty or sixty million people, earn their living by farming or in small towns whose existence immediately depends on farms. They have today lost their purchasing power. Why? They are receiving for farm products less than the cost to them of growing these farm products. The result of this loss of purchasing power is that many other millions of people engaged in industry in the cities cannot sell industrial products to the farming half of the Nation.

I cannot escape the conclusion that one of the essential parts of a national program of restoration must be to restore purchasing power to the farming half of the country. Without this the wheels of railroads and of factories will not turn.

Closely associated with this first objective is the problem of keeping the home-owner and the farm-owner where he is, without being dispossessed through the foreclosure of his mortgage. His relationship to the great banks of Chicago and New York is pretty remote.

His is a relationship to his little local bank or local loan company. It is a sad fact that even though the local lender in many cases does not want to evict the farmer or home-owner by foreclosure proceedings, he is forced to do so in order to keep his bank or company solvent. Here should be an objective of Government itself, to provide at least as much assistance to the little fellow as it is now giving to the large banks and corporations.

One other objective closely related to the problem of selling American products is to provide a tariff policy based upon economic common sense rather than upon politics, hot-air, and pull.

Every man and woman who gives any thought to the subject knows that if our factories run even 80 percent of capacity, they will turn out more products than we as a Nation can possibly use ourselves. And we know by sad experience that they cannot do that.

What we must do is this: revise our tariff on the basis of a reciprocal exchange of goods, allowing other Nations to buy and to pay for our goods by sending us such of their goods as will not seriously throw any of our industries out of balance, and incidentally making impossible in this country the continuance of pure monopolies which cause us to pay excessive prices for many of the necessities of life.

Such objectives as these three, restoring farmers' buying power, relief to the small banks and home-owners and a reconstructed tariff policy, are only a part of ten or a dozen vital factors. But they seem to be beyond the concern of a national administration which can think in terms only of the top of the social and economic structure. It has sought temporary relief from the top down rather than permanent relief from the bottom up. It has totally failed to plan ahead in a comprehensive way. It has waited until something has cracked and then at the last moment has sought to prevent total collapse.

It is high time to get back to fundamentals. It is high time to admit with courage that we are in the midst of an emergency at least equal to that of war. Let us mobilize to meet it.

43

Which of the following best describes the author's attitude towards partisanship?

A) Partisanship must come second to solving the nation's serious economic problems.
B) Ideally, partisan politics shouldn't have a role in government, but they do anyway.
C) Democrats are overly partisan, often at the expense of the American people.
D) Parties other than the Democrats are overly partisan, often at the expense of the American people.

44

In the metaphor presented in lines 14-17, "bacteria" is most analogous to

A) politically-based tariff policies.
B) partisan politics.
C) economic reliance on farming.
D) fundamental economic problems.

45

As it is used in line 28, "engaged" most nearly means

A) committed.
B) absorbed.
C) employed.
D) matched.

46

Which of the following best summarizes the author's reasoning in the fourth paragraph (lines 31-36)?

A) The entire nation is part of an agrarian economy.
B) If half the population lacks purchasing power, then no part of the economy can succeed.
C) The government must give money to farmers and those engaged in industry.
D) Agriculture is more important than any other part of the U.S. economy.

47

Which of the following is NOT a goal set forth in this speech?

A) To provide support to small banks
B) To eliminate partisanship from politics
C) To restore purchasing power to farmers
D) To establish new tariff policies

48

Which of the following provides the best support for the answer to the previous question?

A) Lines 2-5 ("I do...myself")
B) Lines 31-34 ("I cannot...country")
C) Lines 53-57 ("One other...pull")
D) Lines 74-77 ("Such...policy")

49

As it is used in line 60, "capacity" most nearly means

A) space.
B) maximum.
C) competence.
D) scope.

50

You can infer which of the following about the national administration at the time the speech was given?

A) It has refused to allow the export of American goods.
B) It has forced factories to manufacture more products than the nation could possibly purchase.
C) It has responded to the economic crisis by helping the nation's wealthiest rather than the poorest.
D) It has solved the economic problem through huge government expenditures.

51

Which of the following provides the best support for the answer to the previous question?

A) Lines 11-14 ("People...problem")
B) Lines 60-63 ("they...do that")
C) Lines 64-69 ("What...balance")
D) Lines 78-83 ("But they...up")

52

The author most likely included the reference to "war" in line 91 in order to

A) encourage his audience to rise to a challenge.
B) demonstrate how violent the economic crisis has been.
C) show his belief that the nation will soon enter a war.
D) subtly call his audience cowardly.

STOP

If you finish before time is called, you may check your work on this section only.

Do not turn to any other section.

Writing and Language Test

35 MINUTES, 44 QUESTIONS

Mark your responses on this test. Use the "How to Calculate Your Scores in the back of this book to determine your scores.

DIRECTIONS

Each passage below is accompanied by a number of questions. For some questions, you will consider how the passage might be revised to improve the expression of ideas. For other questions, you will consider how the passage might be edited to correct errors in sentence structure, usage, or punctuation. A passage or a question may be accompanied by one or more graphics (such as a table or graph) that you will consider as you make revising and editing decisions.

Some questions will direct you to an underlined portion of a passage. Other questions will direct you to a location in a passage or ask you to think about the passage as a whole.

After reading each passage, choose the answer to each question that most effectively improves the quality of writing in the passage or that makes the passage conform to the conventions of standard written English. Many questions include a "NO CHANGE" option. Choose that option if you think the best choice is to leave the relevant portion of the passage as it is.

Questions 1-11 are based on the following passage.

1 Beans. Many of us rarely think about these tiny legumes, but for tens of millions of people across the globe they are vital food, staples of an everyday diet. Scientists are well **2** aware of this fact, and of the fact that beans are one of the most versatile types of agriculture. **3** This versatility may serve us well in the years to come, if scientists in Colombia have anything to say about it.

1

A) NO CHANGE
B) Beans: many
C) Beans; many
D) Beans? Many

2

A) NO CHANGE
B) aware of this fact, and that beans
C) aware of this fact, and also the fact that beans
D) aware of this and that beans

Question 3 is on the next page.

[1] In Valle de Cauca, Colombia, the International Center for Tropical Agriculture (CIAT) **4** will be researching beans and other staple foods. [2] Under the auspices of the United Nations, the CIAT works to safeguard important crops, such as beans, rice, and cassava, in an effort to make sure that the rising food needs of the human race are met. [3] With issues like unpredictable weather and crop diseases, they have their hands full. [4] Yet they have risen to the task before: CIAT came about during the Green Revolution, a **5** time in which agricultural innovation staved off starvation in third-world countries by introducing new and stronger strains of beans, rice, and wheat. [5] One scientist who worked with the CIAT, Norman Borlaug, won the Nobel Peace Prize for helping fight world hunger. **6**

The largest problem that CIAT and their beans face today is that ever-present bogeyman, climate change. In 2013, the Intergovernmental Panel on Climate Change released a report that suggested that global temperatures may **7** raise up 2 to 5 degrees Celsius over the next hundred years. Computer simulations run by CIAT revealed a horrifying fact: by 2050, the areas suitable for growing beans may shrink by as much as 50%. This could have disastrous consequences for many areas in tropical regions, such as the Caribbean and central Africa.

3

Which of the following best establishes the main idea of the passage as a whole?

A) NO CHANGE
B) The versatility of the bean leads to an endless variety of foods to be made.
C) Colombia is a place where many bean varieties are kept.
D) The question remains: how will beans fare as global temperatures rise?

4

A) NO CHANGE
B) was researching
C) is researching
D) has been researching

5

A) NO CHANGE
B) time where
C) time during which
D) time while

6

Which of the following sentences should be removed in order to improve the focus of this paragraph?

A) NO CHANGE
B) Sentence 1
C) Sentence 3
D) Sentence 5

7

A) NO CHANGE
B) raise by
C) rise to
D) rise by

CIAT's center in Valle de Cauca has over 36,000 varieties of beans – what some of them call "the largest bean stash in the world." It certainly is the **8** largest and most extensive collection of beans in the world. Researchers began combing through the bean **9** varieties, they were trying to find a strain that could withstand the heightened temperatures predicted by the IPCC.

One bean stood out: the tepary bean, cultivated by Native Americans since pre-Columbian times in particularly **10** toasty areas— the American southwest and northern Mexico. Crossing the tepary bean with more common varieties of beans, the scientists then planted the new variety in various areas of Colombia and in their own greenhouses. Some of the crossed beans showed promising signs: some could withstand a 3 degree rise, while others withstood 4 degrees or more.

11 If this new variety of bean proves hardy enough, it could preclude difficulties in growing staple foods caused by rising temperatures.

8

A) NO CHANGE
B) most extensively large
C) most extensive
D) most impressively and largely extensive

9

A) NO CHANGE
B) varieties, trying
C) varieties, while trying
D) varieties—they were trying

10

A) NO CHANGE
B) heated
C) scorching
D) sweltering

11

Which of the following sentences would best conclude this passage?

A) NO CHANGE
B) Growing a new bean shows that the difficulties presented by climate change are surmountable.
C) Another Green Revolution might be just around the corner.
D) Experiments with genetics can have incredibly positive effects.

Questions 12-22 are based on the following passage.

[1] In May of 2015, a federal circuit court ruled that a program under the auspices of the NSA **12** <u>is and always was</u> illegal. [2] The program in question? [3] A broad federal 'wire-tap' that enabled the NSA to log any and every call that took place **13** <u>on</u> the continental U.S. [4] Using this program, **14** <u>they have compelled</u> phone service providers such as T-Mobile and Sprint to provide records of phone calls of regular Americans, all in the name of homeland security. [5] This program was held under the broad umbrella of the Patriot Act, a sweeping security bill that was passed in the wake of the 9/11 attacks. **15**

The program first came to light when a contractor at the NSA, Edward Snowden, **16** <u>released</u> the program in June 2013 by bringing it to the attention of the Washington Post. Since this action, Snowden has had to seek asylum in various other countries, as he would be jailed and prosecuted for releasing state secrets had he stayed in the U.S. **17**

12

A) NO CHANGE
B) is, will be, and was
C) was and will be
D) might be

13

A) NO CHANGE
B) throughout
C) within
D) into

14

A) NO CHANGE
B) they have been compelling
C) it has compelled
D) the NSA has compelled

15

Which of the following should be eliminated to improve the focus of this paragraph?

A) NO CHANGE
B) Sentence 2.
C) Sentence 4.
D) Sentence 5.

16

A) NO CHANGE
B) exposed
C) publicized
D) uncovered

17

Which of the following, if added after this sentence, would best support the claim made in the previous sentence?

A) Snowden has become a cause for celebration among hackers and internet activists.
B) U.S. law prohibits the release of information that could endanger U.S. citizens or assets.
C) His sentence could last anywhere from 10 to 40 years.
D) Recently, Snowden has found asylum in Russia.

18 While Snowden did violate the non-disclosure agreement he had to sign to work for the NSA, his release of this information allowed average Americans to discover what their government had been doing. The three-judge panel that examined this case found that agencies of the government **19** had gone far above and beyond what the original homeland security bills had requested. One judge noted, "[These] statutes…. Have never been interpreted to authorize anything approaching the breadth of sweeping surveillance at issue here. The sheer volume of information sought is staggering."

20 What's more, this program was carried on under the utmost secrecy: as one of the judges put it, it was a program "…which many members of Congress – and all members of the public were not aware…only a limited subset of members of Congress had a comprehensive understanding of the program." In fact, the program was classified as a state **21** secret, thus keeping any litigation regarding these leaks out of Article III courts. The judicial branch, therefore, could not review whether the information gathered by the NSA was done in a legitimate manner. This goes against one of the oldest tenets of the American government: judicial review, that the courts can decide whether a particular law or action of the government is constitutional.

While Edward Snowden leaked a great deal of information – not all of it beneficial to the nation's safety—in this case, he may have done his country a service. The overreach of the government in monitoring its citizens' every phone call has been **22** exposed; citizens and representatives of the United States must now decide what to do about this information.

18

Which of the following, if inserted here, would best connect the previous paragraph with this paragraph?

A) Though his release of information has helped Americans, Snowden should still be jailed.
B) Snowden's critics have disputed this most recent ruling.
C) However, with the May 2015 ruling, he has been somewhat vindicated.
D) The release of information has elicited a strong response from the American people.

19

A) NO CHANGE
B) had gone beyond
C) have gone above
D) have gone above and beyond

20

Which of the following provides the best transition from the previous paragraph while maintaining the style and tone of the passage?

A) NO CHANGE
B) Not just that,
C) Furthermore,
D) Even so,

21

A) NO CHANGE
B) secret, and thus
C) secret; thus
D) secret. Thus

22

A) NO CHANGE
B) exposed, yet citizens
C) exposed, for citizens
D) exposed, citizens

Questions 23-33 are based on the following passage.

The recipe for economic growth, though elusive to many **23** nations, is really quite simple. Add rising labor productivity measured by the total output per worker to an increase in the number of people working. Shake vigorously. The end. **24**

Japan is home to the world's third largest economy; unfortunately, it is also home to a rapidly declining population. This population decline is due to Japan's rapidly aging populace, low birth rates, and traditional ambivalence about immigration. It is Japan's weak population **25** growth is one of the reasons that Japan has been locked in a decades-long battle to reenergize an economy that remains deeply damaged by the real estate and banking **26** bust it had suffered more than two decades ago.

[1] In fact, Prime Minister Shinzo Abe was elected largely because of his economic platform, which has popularly become known as "Abenomics." [2] Abe's three-part program calls for aggressive monetary policy, aggressive government spending, and labor market reform. [3] Japan's heavy investment in technology has ensured that it is a leader in the technology sector; imagine the many brands that have gained prominence internationally that have come from Japan. [4] There are some signs that the program is working; one of the most promising indicators of economic change in Japan is that women are entering the workforce. **27**

23

A) NO CHANGE
B) nations, are
C) nations, it is
D) nations, simply is

24

Which of the following choices would best express the main idea of the following paragraph?

A) Most of the most prominent countries in the world have a positive economic outlook.
B) Yet economic growth remains a struggle for countries where populations are stagnant or shrinking.
C) The economic growth of a country allows the country to provide better lives for its people.
D) Many sub-Saharan African nations have quickly growing populations, but weak economic growth.

25

A) NO CHANGE
B) growth one
C) growth, is one
D) growth that is one

26

A) NO CHANGE
B) bust it has suffered
C) bust it is suffering
D) bust it suffered

27

Which of the following sentences should be removed in order to improve the focus of the paragraph?

A) Sentence 1
B) Sentence 2
C) Sentence 3
D) Sentence 4

To residents of a country like the U.S., where women have long made up roughly half of the workforce, this hardly seems revolutionary, but Japanese women have traditionally worked **28** far less than other wealthy nations' females working. **29** When Japan's population peaked in the early 2000s, one of the few ways of increasing the number of workers is to pull women into the labor force. Realizing this, Abe has famously claimed that Japan's women are the nation's **30** "most-underutilized-resource."

Adam Posen, president of the Petersen Institution for International Economics, argues that the addition of Japanese women to the labor force is actually a double whammy. Not only does it boost the size of the labor force, **31** but it does also increase labor force productivity thanks to the high levels of education of Japanese women. Although Japanese women have not participated in the work force, there has long been parity in education between Japanese men and women.

28

A) NO CHANGE
B) far less than many other wealthy nations
C) far fewer in number than those in many other wealthy nations
D) far less than females in many other wealthy nations

29

Which of the following best reflects the information in the passage and the graph?

A) NO CHANGE
B) As Japan's population growth has decreased to zero,
C) Since the overall population is in decline,
D) With the population of Japan at its highest level since the 1970s,

30

A) NO CHANGE
B) "most underutilized-resource."
C) "most-underutilized resource."
D) "mostly under-utilized-resource."

31

A) NO CHANGE
B) but it also increases
C) but also increasing
D) but also it increases

Unfortunately, bringing women in the work force presents a bit of a catch-22. Although there are clear economic benefits to growing Japan's labor force, an increase in working women might result in a sharper decline in Japan's already **32** dire fertility rates. This is because Japanese work culture is notoriously difficult to balance with family life. **33**

The government is not unaware of this problem. Abe's administration recently announced a plan to open 400,000 new childcare spaces by 2018, and last year Japan made parental leave policies more generous.

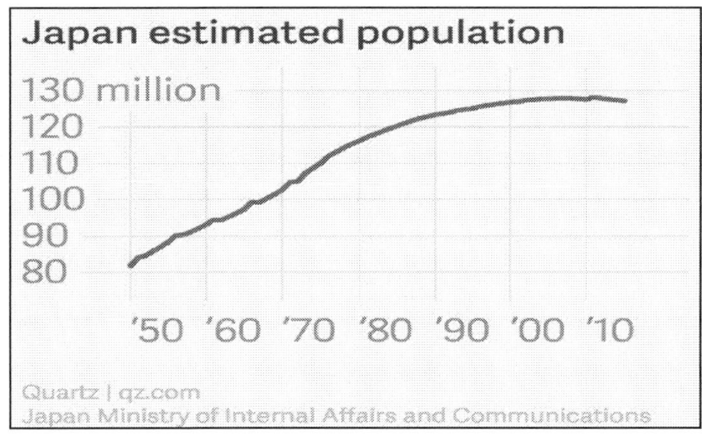

32

A) NO CHANGE
B) weak
C) treacherous
D) degraded

33

Which of the following would provide the best support for the previous sentence?

A) Many Japanese businessmen never see their families.
B) Japanese corporations don't entirely discourage spending time with family, but they don't emphasize it either.
C) Japanese work culture is highly stringent, expecting a great deal of work from employees.
D) An employee who hopes to rise in a corporation is expected to work between 10 and 15 hours a day, leaving little time for family life.

Questions 34-44 are based on the following passage.

Fracking is the latest process of extracting gas and oil from previously inaccessible sources. The process involves injecting liquid at high pressure into rocks or shale in order to open up **34** fissures which gas or oil can be extracted. While fracking has greatly increased the amount of gas and oil produced in the U.S., it is not without its dangers. **35**

The study focused on Pennsylvania's Marcellus Shale region and found that fracking wells are disproportionately located in poor rural communities, which then bear the brunt of the associated pollution. The study **36** shows concerns that poor people are more likely to deal with hydraulic fracturing in their community **37** and raises concerns that such vulnerable populations will suffer the potential health impacts of air and water pollution associated with fracking.

Researchers from Clark University mapped hydraulic fracturing wells and then examined local demographics. **38** They found that poverty levels were strongly associated with active fracking wells. The researchers then used a series of tests to estimate exposure to potential pollution. "No matter how you estimate proximity, it always came up that exposure was significantly, much higher" in poor Pennsylvania communities, said the study's lead author, Yelena Ogneva-Himmelberger. She said the study raises environmental justice concerns as people under the poverty line often "have less mobility and access to information" about the potential ills of fracking, especially since the communities she looked at were rural areas without the amenities of larger cities and towns. **39**

34

A) NO CHANGE
B) fissures through which
C) fissures, in which
D) fissures through that

35

Which of the following, if placed here, best establishes the main idea of the passage as a whole?

A) The question arises, however, whether fracking is fair to all classes of Americans.
B) And, according to a new study, fracking unfairly burdens some of our poorest populations.
C) Many activist and environmental groups have protested the excessive use of fracking.
D) Scientists have debated the pros and cons of fracking in recent years.

36

A) NO CHANGE
B) augments
C) alleviates
D) bolsters

37

A) NO CHANGE
B) and rises
C) and raised
D) and raise

38

Which of the following would best support the main idea of this paragraph?

A) NO CHANGE
B) It was found that poverty had very little to do with fracking.
C) Their findings suggested that regions with fracking wells were often in very rural areas.
D) They found that residents were often very grateful for the aid of the coal and oil industry.

Recent headlines have only provoked alarm in fracking communities. The Proceedings of the National Academies of Sciences recently released a study that found traces of a common fracking chemical in water from three different homes in Bradford County, Pennsylvania. A separate study found that **40** radon; the world's second leading cause of lung cancer; is much more prevalent in Pennsylvania buildings near natural gas development than in other parts of the state. Yet another study recently found that sulfur dioxide emissions, which harm the respiratory system and exacerbate conditions like asthma, **41** soaring 57 percent from 2012 to 2013 at Pennsylvania natural gas sites.

Industry groups, **42** in fact, say that hydraulic fracturing is in rural farming regions of Pennsylvania out of necessity and is providing some much needed economic stimulus. According to industry representatives, oil and natural gas leases allow poor farmers to supplement **43** their incomes, and fracking provides local tax revenue and jobs.

39

Which of the following would best support the idea mentioned in the previous sentence?

A) NO CHANGE
B) especially since these communities lacked infrastructure and had very little access to the internet.
C) especially because the communities in question had poor education opportunities.
D) especially since many communities have few healthcare opportunities to deal with the potential dangers of the chemicals fracking releases.

40

A) NO CHANGE
B) radon: the world's second leading cause of lung cancer is
C) radon, the world's second leading cause of lung cancer, is
D) radon – the world's second leading cause of lung cancer, is

41

A) NO CHANGE
B) soared
C) has soared
D) had soared

42

A) NO CHANGE
B) meanwhile,
C) concurrently,
D) however,

43

A) NO CHANGE
B) his or her income
C) their income
D) his or her incomes

Still, many believe that the short term economic benefits of **44** fracking is heavily outweighed by the environmental and health concerns associated with the process.

44

A) NO CHANGE
B) fracking are heavily
C) fracking heavily
D) fracking, heavily

STOP

If you finish before time is called, you may check your work on this section only. Do not turn to any other section.

Math Test – No Calculator

25 MINUTES, 20 QUESTIONS

Mark your responses on this test. Use the "How to Calculate Your Scores in the back of this book to determine your scores.

DIRECTIONS

For questions 1-15, solve each problem, choose the best answer from the choices provided, and fill in the corresponding circle on your answer sheet. **For questions 16-20**, solve the problem and enter your answer in the grid on the answer sheet. Please refer to the directions before question 16 on how to enter your answers in the grid. You may use any available space in your test booklet for scratch work.

NOTES

1. The use of a calculator **is not permitted**.
2. All variables and expressions used represent real numbers unless otherwise indicated.
3. Figures provided in the test are drawn to scale unless otherwise indicated.
4. All figures lie in a plane unless otherwise indicated.
5. Unless otherwise indicated, the domain of a given function f is the set of all real numbers x for which $f(x)$ is a real number.

REFERENCE

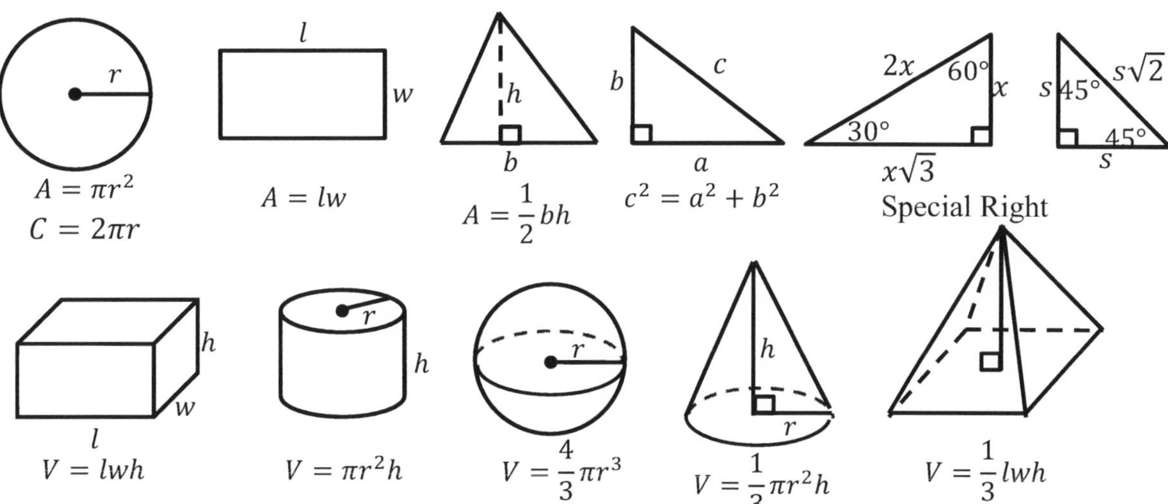

The number of degrees of arc in a circle is 360.

The number of radians of arc in a circle is 2π.

The sum of the measures in degrees of the angles of a triangle is 180.

1

An entry-level game developer earns \$150 per day for debugging the code of 5 different video games and an additional \$500 bonus if any of her ideas get used by the company. If the game developer comes up with an idea that is used by the company, what expression could be used to determine how much the game developer earned?

A) $150x + 500$, where x is the number of days worked
B) $500x + 150$, where x is the number of days worked
C) $x(150 + 5) + 500$, where x is the number of video games worked on
D) $(150 + 5) + 500x$, where x is the number of video games worked on

2

$$2y + x = 2(x + 2y)$$

If (x, y) is a solution to the equation above and $x \neq 0$, what is the ratio $\frac{y}{x}$?

A) -2
B) $-\frac{1}{2}$
C) $\frac{1}{2}$
D) 2

3

$$\frac{1}{3}x - \frac{1}{6}y = 18$$

$$\frac{1}{12}x + \frac{1}{12}y = \frac{9}{2}$$

Which ordered pair (x, y) satisfies the system of equations above?

A) $(-54, 0)$
B) $(0, -54)$
C) $(0, 54)$
D) $(54, 0)$

4

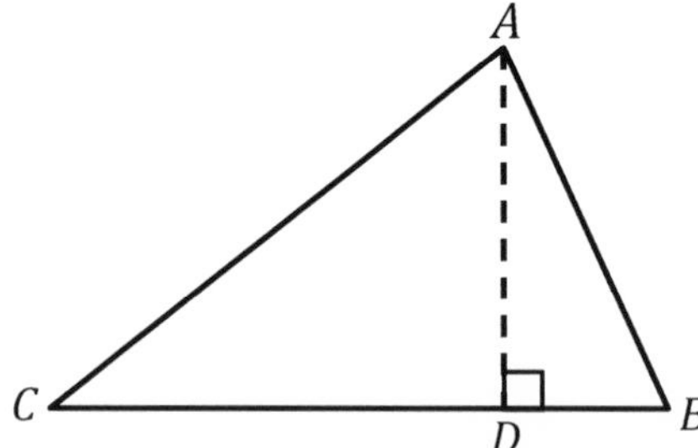

Note: Figure not drawn to scale.

Triangle ABC pictured above has an area of 900. If the length of CB is twice the length of AD, what is the length of CB?

A) 30
B) 60
C) 300
D) 600

5

A certain national forest is allowing the hunting of deer because of overpopulation. To regulate the number of deer killed, the forest rangers assign point values to male and female deer. Each female deer killed is worth 3 points, while each male deer killed is worth 5 points. If a total of 100 deer, worth 420 points, were killed, how many male deer were killed?

A) 20
B) 40
C) 60
D) 80

6

What is the slope of the line that passes through the points $(-3,5)$ and $(-8,-1)$ in the xy-plane?

A) $-\frac{6}{5}$
B) $-\frac{5}{6}$
C) $\frac{5}{6}$
D) $\frac{6}{5}$

7

$$x^2 + 4b = 0$$

If 12 and -12 are solutions to the equation above and b is a constant, what is the value of b?

A) -36
B) $-4\sqrt{3}$
C) $4\sqrt{3}$
D) 36

8

If $y^{-\frac{1}{3}} - 6 = z$, what is the value of y in terms of z?

A) $-(z+6)^3$
B) $\frac{-1}{(z+6)^3}$
C) $\frac{1}{(z+6)^3}$
D) $(z+6)^3$

9

If $f(2x) = 6x + 4x^2$ for all values of x, what is the value of $f(-4)$?

A) 4
B) 28
C) 208
D) 304

10

Which of the following is equivalent to $(xy - x^2)(x + y)$?

A) $2x^2y - xy^2 - x^3$
B) $xy^2 - x^3$
C) $x^3 - xy^2 + 2x^2y$
D) $6xy - 2x^2$

11

i^{17} is equivalent to which of the following? (Note: $i = \sqrt{-1}$)

A) i^{13}
B) i^{14}
C) i^{15}
D) i^{16}

12

The temperature inside of an industrial freezer must be kept between $-1.5°C$ and $-2.9°C$, inclusive. Which of the following inequalities contains the entire range of Celsius temperatures, x, at which the freezer can be kept?

A) $|2.2 - x| \geq 0.7$
B) $|2.2 - x| \leq 0.7$
C) $|x + 2.2| \geq 0.7$
D) $|x + 2.2| \leq 0.7$

13

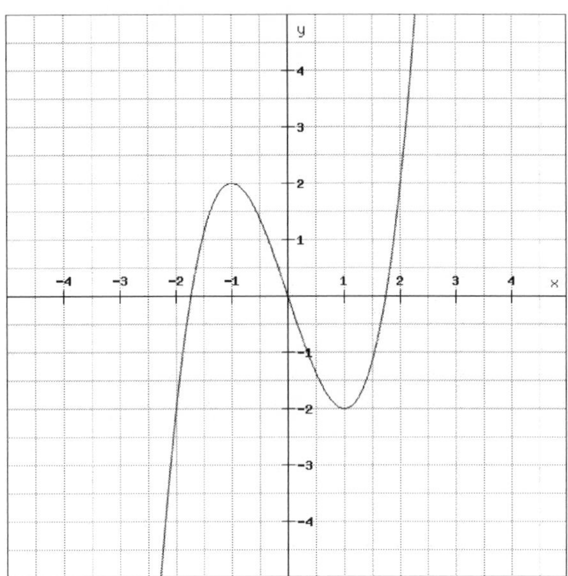

What is the maximum value of the function graphed on the xy-plane above, for $-2 \leq x \leq 2$?

A) -1
B) 1
C) 2
D) ∞

14

The population of a species of goat doubles every year. If the initial population of the goat species is 10 animals, after how many years will the population exceed 100 animals?

A) 2
B) 3
C) 4
D) 9

15

$$x^2 + y^2 - 2x + 8y = 64$$

The equation of a circle in the xy-plane is shown above. What is the diameter of the circle?

A) 8
B) 9
C) 16
D) 18

DIRECTIONS

For questions 16-20, solve the problem and enter your answer in the grid, as described below, on the answer sheet.

1. Although not required, it is suggested that you write your answer in the boxes at the top of the columns to help you fill in the circles accurately. You will receive credit only if the circles are filled in correctly.
2. Mark no more than one circle in any column.
3. No question has a negative answer.
4. Some problems may have more than one correct answer. In such cases, grid only one answer.
5. **Mixed numbers** such as $3\frac{1}{2}$ must be gridded as 3.5 or 7/2.

   (If 3 1 / 2 is entered into the grid, it will be interpreted as $\frac{31}{2}$, not $3\frac{1}{2}$.)
6. **Decimal answers:** If you obtain a decimal answer with more digits than the grid can accommodate, it may be either rounded or truncated, but it must fill the entire grid.

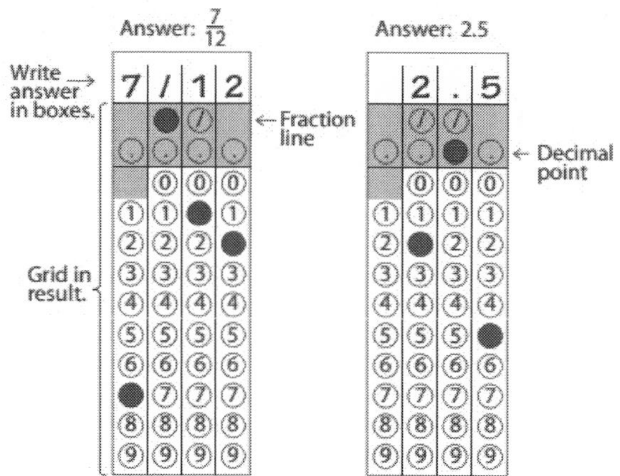

Acceptable ways to grid $\frac{2}{3}$ are:

2 / 3   . 6 6 6   . 6 6 7

Answer: 201 – either position is correct

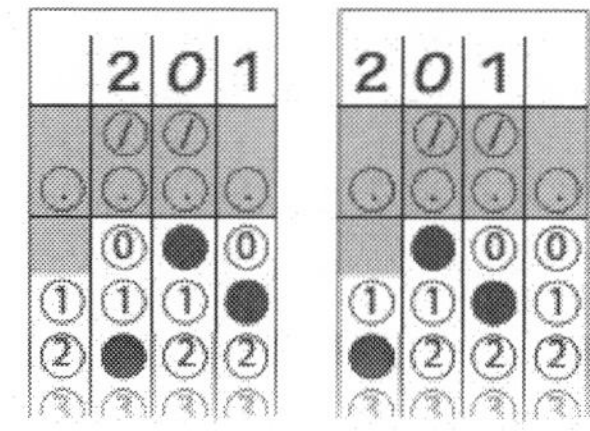

NOTE: You may start your answers in any column, space permitting. Columns you don't need to use should be left blank.

16

For what value of a does $\frac{1}{2}a - \frac{3}{5} = \frac{1}{3}a + \frac{3}{10}$?

17

If x is not equal to zero, what is the value of $\frac{3(-x)^3}{(-2x)^3}$?

18

If $x - p$ is a factor of $x^2 - 19x + 48$, where p is a constant, what is a possible value of p?

19

A group of 5 girls, working at the same rate, can paint a building in a total of 20 hours. How much longer, in hours, would it take for a group of 4 girls who work at the same rate to do the same job?

20

If $s > 0$, for what value of s does $\sqrt{s^2 - 11} = 5$

STOP

If you finish before time is called, you may check your work on this section only. Do not turn to any other section.

Math Test – Calculator

55 MINUTES, 38 QUESTIONS

Mark your responses on this test. Use the "How to Calculate Your Scores in the back of this book to determine your scores.

DIRECTIONS

For questions 1-30, solve each problem, choose the best answer from the choices provided, and fill in the corresponding circle on your answer sheet. **For questions 31-38**, solve the problem and enter your answer in the grid on the answer sheet. Please refer to the directions before question 31 on how to enter your answers in the grid. You may use any available space in your test booklet for scratch work.

NOTES

1. The use of a calculator **is permitted**.
2. All variables and expressions used represent real numbers unless otherwise indicated.
3. Figures provided in the test are drawn to scale unless otherwise indicated.
4. All figures lie in a plane unless otherwise indicated.
5. Unless otherwise indicated, the domain of a given function f is the set of all real numbers x for which $f(x)$ is a real number.

REFERENCE

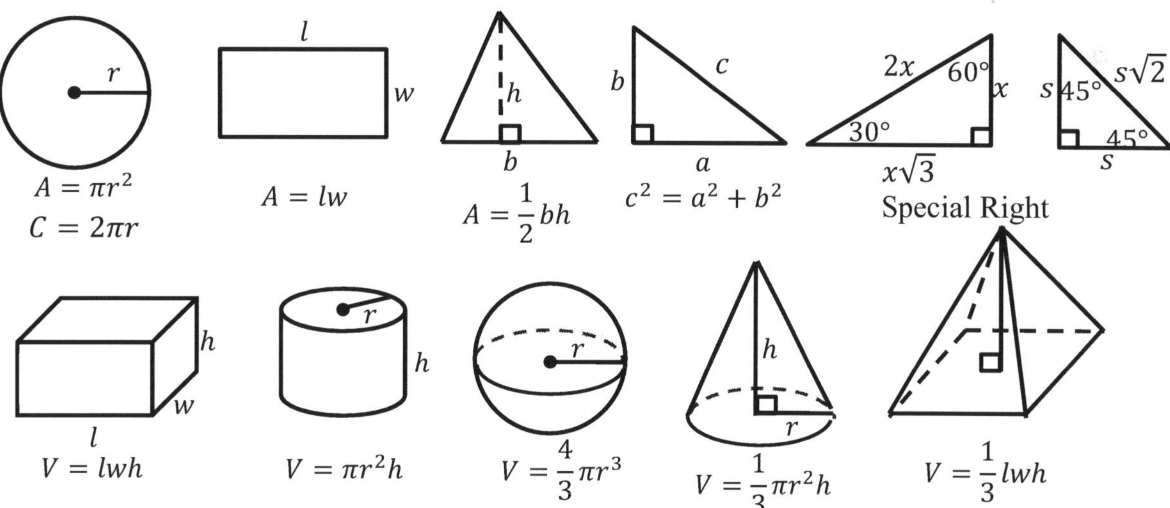

The number of degrees of arc in a circle is 360.

The number of radians of arc in a circle is 2π.

The sum of the measures in degrees of the angles of a triangle is 180.

1

The recommended maximum amount of added sugars an adult woman should eat per day is 25,000 milligrams (mg). An 8-ounce cup of orange juice contains 24 grams (g) of sugar, while an 8-ounce cup of soy milk contains 8 grams of sugar. Which of the following inequalities represents the possible number of ounces of soy milk, m, and ounces of orange juice, j, an adult woman could drink in a day and not meet or exceed the maximum recommended daily sugar intake from those drinks alone?

A) $\frac{24j}{8} + \frac{8m}{8} < 25{,}000$

B) $\frac{8j}{24} + \frac{8m}{8} < 25{,}000$

C) $\frac{24j}{8} + \frac{8m}{8} < 25$

D) $\frac{8j}{24} + \frac{8m}{8} < 25$

2

A national survey was given to 1000 randomly selected high-school freshmen. Among survey participants, the mean GPA was 2.8, and the margin of error for the estimate was 0.025. Another survey was given to 500 randomly selected high-school students and a mean GPA of 2.75 was obtained. The margin of error of the second survey is most likely

A) Four times as small as that of the first survey
B) Twice as small as that of the first survey
C) Equal to that of the first survey
D) Larger than that of the first survey

3

$$2x + 5 = 3y$$
$$3x - 6y = -\frac{21}{2}$$

If (x, y) is a solution to the system of equations above, what is the value of $2x$?

A) -1
B) $-\frac{1}{2}$
C) $\frac{1}{2}$
D) 1

4

Marion is going to a spa resort that charges \$156.95 per night. Marion has a coupon for 15% off the total price of her stay, and a tax of 6% is applied to her final cost. Which of the following represents Marion's total charge, in dollars, for staying n nights?

A) $0.91(156.95n)$
B) $1.06(0.85(156.95n))$
C) $1.06(1.15(156.95n))$
D) $1.21(156.95n)$

5

$$\frac{\sqrt{18x^5}}{-3x^2}$$

If $x \neq 0$, which of the following is equivalent to the expression above?

A) $-3x$
B) $-\sqrt{2x}$
C) $\sqrt{2x}$
D) $3x$

6

A hardware store sells decorative shelf brackets individually and in packs of 8 brackets. On a certain day, x brackets were sold, of which 15 were sold as individual brackets. Which equation shows the number of packs of brackets, p, sold that day?

A) $p = \frac{x-15}{8}$
B) $p = \frac{x+15}{8}$
C) $p = \frac{x}{8} - 15$
D) $p = \frac{x}{8} + 15$

7

The cost to tour Cave of the Winds is $20 for adults and $12 for children. During a one-week period, at least 325 people toured Cave of the Winds, and the total collected in entry fees was no more than $5,500. Solving which of the following systems of equations yields the number of adults, a, and children, c, who entered the cave during the week?

A) $a + c \geq 325$
$20a + 12c \geq 5{,}500$
B) $a + c \geq 325$
$20a + 12c \leq 5{,}500$
C) $a + c \leq 325$
$20a + 12c \geq 5{,}500$
D) $a + c \leq 325$
$20a + 12c \leq 5{,}500$

Questions 8-10 refer to the following information.

A survey of 314 adults in the United States was conducted to gather data on their television watching habits. The data are shown in the table below.

	< 1 hour per day	1 – 2 hours per day	> 2 hours per day	Total
Male	62	52	28	142
Female	76	46	50	172
Total	138	98	78	314

8

Which of the following is closest to the percent of those surveyed who watched more than 1 hour of television per day?

A) 24%
B) 31%
C) 43%
D) 56%

9

In 2014, the total population of adult females in the United States was approximately 121 million. If the survey results are used to estimate information about television watching habits across the country, which of the following is the best estimate of the total number of adult females in the United States who watch less than 1 hour of television per day?

A) 52,200,000
B) 52,800,000
C) 53,500,000
D) 65,000,000

10

Based on the data, how many times more likely is it for a male to watch more than 2 hours of television per day than a female to watch more than 2 hours of television per day?

A) 0.61 times as likely
B) 0.73 times as likely
C) 1.37 times as likely
D) 1.47 times as likely

11

Which scatterplot shows an association that is neither positive nor negative? (Note: A negative association between two variables is one in which higher values of one variable correspond to lower values of the other variable, and vice versa. A positive association between two variables is one in which lower values of one variable correspond to lower values of the other variable, and vice versa.)

A)

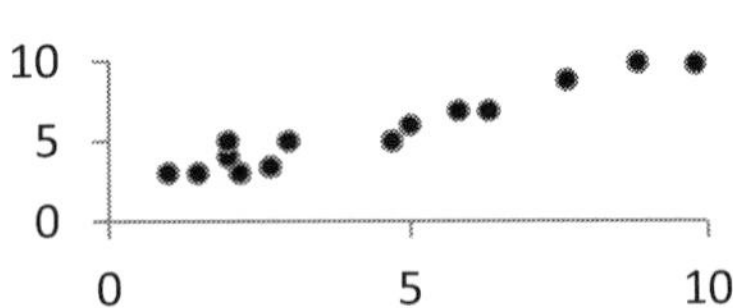

B)

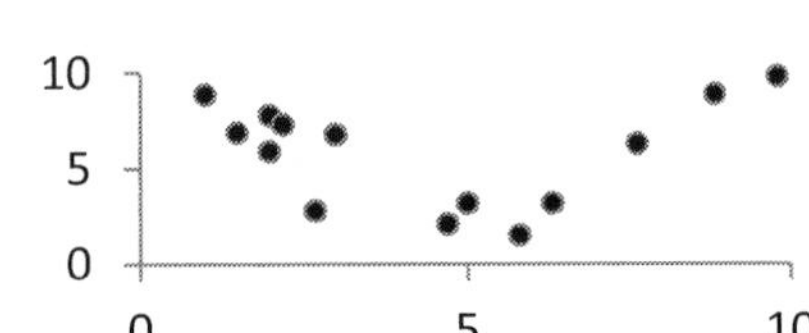

C)

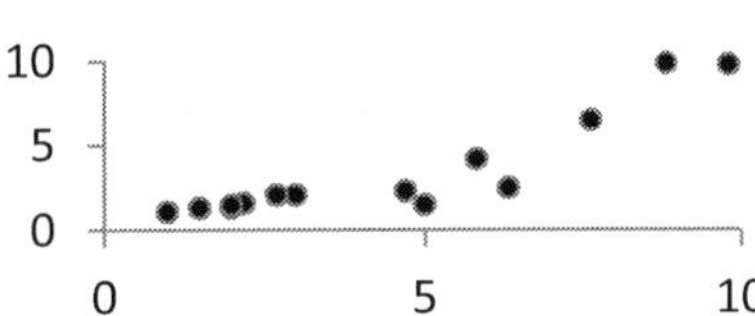

D)

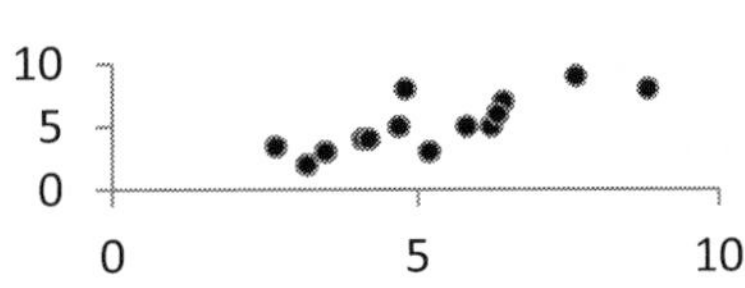

12

A square has area, A, perimeter, P, and side length, s. Which of the following represents A in terms of P?

A) $\frac{P}{4}$
B) $\frac{P}{16}$
C) $\frac{P^2}{4}$
D) $\frac{P^2}{16}$

13

A car is driving down the highway at a speed of 65 miles per hour. To the nearest second, how long will it take the car to drive 100 yards?
(1 mile = 5280 feet, 1 yard = 3 feet)

A) 1
B) 3
C) 4
D) 9

14

An aquarium has 3 types of fish: guppies, cichlids, and angelfish. The mean length of the guppies is 3 cm, the mean length of the cichlids is 6 cm, and the mean length of the angelfish is 4 cm. Which of the following must be true about the mean length l of the combined group of fish in the aquarium?

A) $l = 4\frac{1}{3}$ cm
B) $l < 4\frac{1}{3}$ cm
C) $l > 4\frac{1}{3}$ cm
D) $3 \text{ cm} < l < 6 \text{ cm}$

15

Every year, the number of members of an honor society grows by 3 people every 5 years. The number of members of the group numbered 168 in 2010. If M represents the number of members of the honor society n years after 2010, then which of the following equations represents the best model of the honor society's membership over time?

A) $M = 3 + \frac{168n}{5}$
B) $M = 168 + \frac{3n}{5}$
C) $M = 168(3)^{\frac{n}{5}}$
D) $M = 3(168)^{\frac{n}{5}}$

16

Peter is going on a 10-mile hike and plans to bring 32 ounces of water with him. Peter plans to take a 15-minute break after every 2 hours of hiking, and he plans to drink 2 ounces of water at the end of every 15-minute interval, whether he is hiking or resting. If Peter wants to drink the last of his water at the very end of his hike, at what rate, in miles per hour, should he hike?

A) $5\frac{1}{3}$
B) 5
C) $2\frac{2}{3}$
D) $2\frac{1}{2}$

17

$$y = x^2 - 3x + 2$$
$$y = -2x + 1$$

How many points of intersection does the system of equations above contain?

A) Zero
B) One
C) Two
D) Three

18

If $ax^{-\frac{1}{2}} = a^2$, $a \neq 0$, and $x > 0$, which of the following gives x in terms of a?

A) $x = \frac{1}{(a^2-a)^2}$
B) $x = \frac{1}{a^2-a}$
C) $x = \frac{1}{a^2}$
D) $x = \frac{1}{a}$

19

A biologist periodically measures the number of mold cells present on a piece of bread. At the start of the experiment, there are approximately 1,000 mold cells. Each time a periodic observation is made, the number of mold cells triples. This type of growth is best described as

A) linear.
B) cubic.
C) exponential.
D) none of the above.

20

If m is a positive constant greater than 1, which of the following equations of a line is perpendicular to the graph of $y + x = m(y - x)$ in the xy-plane?

A) $x - y = m(y + x)$
B) $x + y = m(x + y)$
C) $y - x = m(y - x)$
D) $x + y = -\frac{1}{m}(y - x)$

21

The function f is defined by $f(x) = 3x^3 + 2x^2 - bx + 6$, where b is a constant. In the xy-plane, the graph of f intersects the x-axis at the three points $(-3, 0)$, $\left(\frac{1}{3}, 0\right)$, and $(r, 0)$. What is the value of r?

A) -19
B) -2
C) 2
D) 19

22

If the expression $\frac{2x^2+6x-8}{x-3}$ is written in the equivalent form $2x + 12 + \frac{R}{x-3}$, what is the value of R?

A) -8
B) 8
C) 28
D) 44

23

Jason makes two different types folk art which he sells locally: baskets, for which he makes a profit of \$3.50, and painted rocks, for which he makes a profit of \$2.75. Last year, Jason sold 150 baskets and 200 rocks. This year, Jason managed to sell 20% more baskets and 10% more rocks. To the nearest percent, by what percentage did Jason's profits increase by?

A) 14%
B) 15%
C) 22%
D) 30%

24

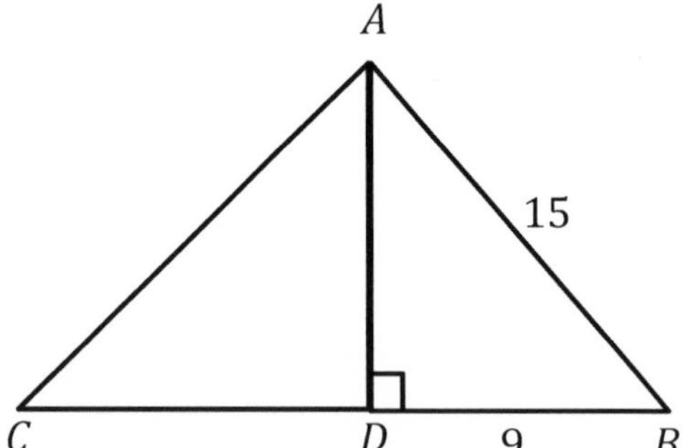

Note: Figure not drawn to scale.

Triangle ACD is isosceles, the length of DB is 9 and the length of AB is 15. What is the perimeter of triangle ACD?

A) 24
B) 36
C) $24 + 12\sqrt{2}$
D) $24 + 12\sqrt{3}$

Questions 25-27 refer to the following information.

The data in the graph below shows the volume, in cubic meters, of a tree relative to its height, in meters.

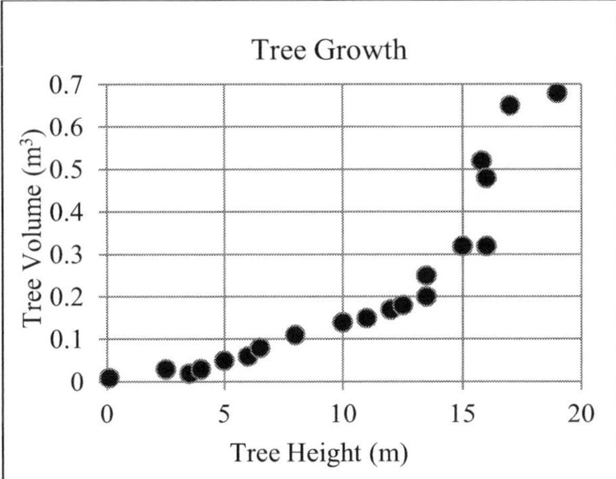

The data can be modeled by the equation $v = 0.015(1.24)^h$, where h is the tree height, in meters, and v is the tree volume, in cubic meters. Assume that the relationship is valid for both shorter and taller trees than are shown in the graph.

25

According to the equation used to model the data, a tree with a volume of 0.3 cubic meters would be *expected* to be approximately how many centimeters tall?

A) 0.014
B) 0.016
C) 1400
D) 1600

26

What is the approximate range of volumes of the trees with heights between 10 and 15 meters, inclusive, listed in the data shown?

A) 0.09 m^3
B) 0.18 m^3
C) 0.27 m^3
D) 5 m^3

27

Based on the model, what is the volume, in cubic meters, of a tree that is 25 meters tall?

A) 2.00 m^3
B) 3.25 m^3
C) 4.50 m^3
D) It is unable to be determined from the information given.

28

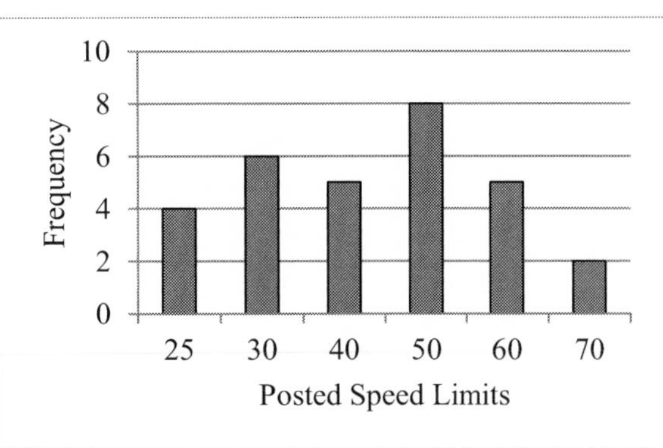

The graph above shows the frequency distribution of the speed limits of all of the roads in a certain county. What is the median of the list of numbers?

A) 40
B) 44
C) 45
D) 50

29

What is the minimum value of the function $f(x) = 2x^2 - 8x - 4$?

A) –12
B) –4
C) –2
D) 4

30

A 15-meter tall oak tree casts a 18-meter shadow. *What* is the angle of elevation, to the nearest tenth of a degree, from the end of the shadow to the top of the tree with respect to the ground?

A) 33.6°
B) 39.8°
C) 50.2°
D) 56.4°

DIRECTIONS

For questions 31-38, solve the problem and enter your answer in the grid, as described below, on the answer sheet.

1. Although not required, it is suggested that you write your answer in the boxes at the top of the columns to help you fill in the circles accurately. You will receive credit only if the circles are filled in correctly.
2. Mark no more than one circle in any column.
3. No question has a negative answer.
4. Some problems may have more than one correct answer. In such cases, grid only one answer.
5. **Mixed numbers** such as $3\frac{1}{2}$ must be gridded as 3.5 or 7/2.

   (If 3 1 / 2 is entered into the grid, it will be interpreted as $\frac{31}{2}$, not $3\frac{1}{2}$.)
6. **Decimal answers:** If you obtain a decimal answer with more digits than the grid can accommodate, it may be either rounded or truncated, but it must fill the entire grid.

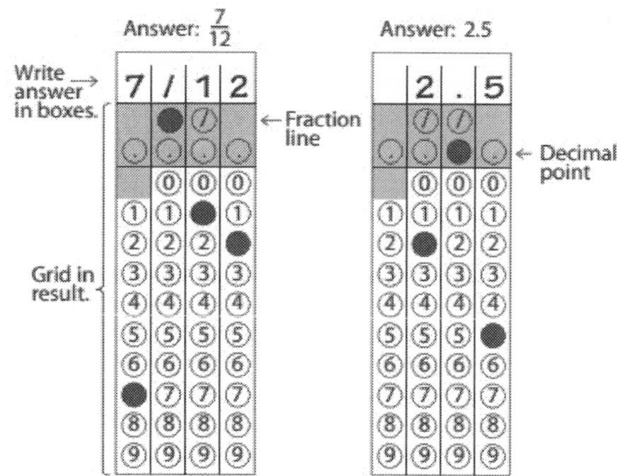

Acceptable ways to grid $\frac{2}{3}$ are:

2 / 3 | . 6 6 6 | . 6 6 7

Answer: 201 – either position is correct

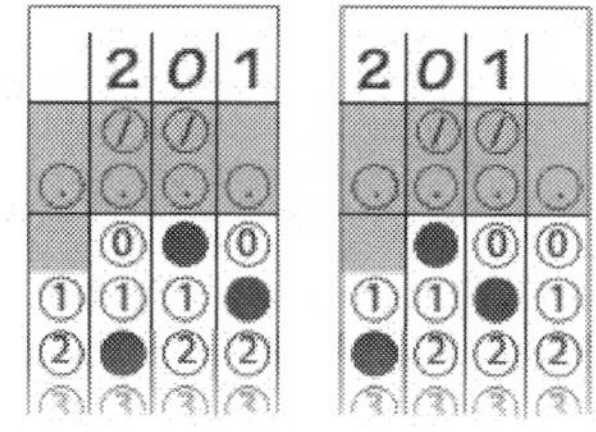

NOTE: You may start your answers in any column, space permitting. Columns you don't need to use should be left blank.

31

If $f(x) = -\frac{3}{x} - 2x$, *what* is the value of $f(-2)$?

32

If $\sqrt{x^2 - 2} = \frac{1}{2}$, *what* is the value of $4x$?

33

If $-\frac{3}{4} < 1 - 2x < -\frac{1}{3}$, *what* is one possible value of $4x - 2$?

34

Bob can write a 10,000-word English paper in 5 hours while working at a constant rate. If Bob has a 15,000-word English paper due in 6 hours, by what percentage must he increase his rate of work to complete the paper on time?

35

What is the value of $(3 - 2i)(3 + 2i)$? (Note: $i = \sqrt{-1}$)

36

A parking garage has at most 500 square meters of space to park cars for an event and charges \$1.50 for a parking spot. If each car is allotted 13.5 square meters of space to park, what is the most money, in dollars, the parking garage can hope to make for the event?

Questions 37 and 38 refer to the following information.

$$f(x) = \frac{3 - \frac{1}{2}(3x - 2)}{2}$$

$$g(x) = \frac{2 - 2(1 - 2x)}{3}$$

37

For what value of x, rounded to the nearest hundredth, is $f(x) = g(x)$?

38

For what $value$ of x, rounded to the nearest hundredth, is $f(x)$ twice the value of $g(x)$?

STOP

If you finish before time is called, you may check your work on this section only. Do not turn to any other section.

ANSWER KEY

Section 1: Reading Test		Section 2: Writing and Language Test		Section 3: Math Test – No Calculator	Section 4: Math Test – Calculator Allowed
1. C	27. B	1. B	23. A	1. A	1. C
2. A	28. B	2. B	24. B	2. B	2. D
3. B	29. B	3. A	25. D	3. D	3. D
4. D	30. D	4. D	26. D	4. B	4. B
5. D	31. C	5. C	27. C	5. C	5. B
6. A	32. B	6. D	28. D	6. D	6. A
7. D	33. C	7. D	29. C	7. A	7. B
8. C	34. D	8. C	30. C	8. C	8. D
9. B	35. A	9. B	31. B	9. A	9. C
10. A	36. C	10. C	32. A	10. B	10. A
11. B	37. A	11. A	33. D	11. A	11. B
12. C	38. D	12. A	34. B	12. D	12. D
13. D	39. B	13. C	35. B	13. C	13. B
14. B	40. B	14. D	36. D	14. C	14. D
15. D	41. D	15. D	37. A	15. D	15. B
16. A	42. D	16. B	38. A	16. 5.4 or $\frac{27}{5}$	16. C
17. C	43. A	17. B	39. A	17. $3/8$ or 0.37 or 0.38	17. A
18. B	44. D	18. C	40. C	18. 3 or 16	18. C
19. B	45. C	19. B	41. B	19. 5	19. C
20. D	46. B	20. C	42. D	20. 6	20. A
21. A	47. B	21. A	43. A		21. C
22. D	48. D	22. A	44. B		22. C
23. D	49. B				23. B
24. C	50. C				24. C
25. D	51. D				25. C
26. A	52. A				26. B
					27. B
					28. C
					29. A
					30. B
					31. 5.5 or $\frac{11}{2}$
					32. 6
					33. $\frac{2}{3} < x < \frac{3}{2}$
					34. 25
					35. 13
					36. 55.5
					37. 0.96
					38. 0.59

Reading Test

65 MINUTES, 52 QUESTIONS

Mark your responses on this test. Use the "How to Calculate Your Scores in the back of this book to determine your scores.

DIRECTIONS

Each passage or pair of passages below is followed by a number of questions. After reading each passage or pair, choose the best answer to each question based on what is stated or implied in the passage or passages and in any accompanying graphics (such as a table or graph).

Questions 1-10 are based on the following passage.

Adapted from "Baltimore's Mortgage Crisis Destroyed Dreams," a 2015 article written by Martha S. Jones, an Associate Professor at the University of Michigan. The article was written shortly after a series of riots shook the city of Baltimore in the wake of the death of Freddie Gray.

On the steps of the city courthouse, a monument to equality and the rule of law, Baltimore residents have learned how dreams can be brutally deferred. There, the property of the city's poor and working families has been, by order of the court, auctioned to the highest bidder.

When tensions erupted in Baltimore following the death of Freddie Gray in 2015, most of the media coverage ignored the role of these lost homes in creating a sense of outrage and injustice. But in truth, Baltimore's foreclosure crisis was one of many factors that contributed to the racial and social tensions that boiled over that April.

Foreclosures in the wake of the subprime mortgage scandal of 2008 have been the end game in predatory lending schemes that took the single asset held by many black Baltimore residents: their homes. The University of Baltimore's Baltimore Neighborhood Indicators Alliance has found that, between 2008 and 2009, foreclosure filings in Baltimore increased by over 38%. More than 14,000 foreclosure proceedings were brought against the city's homeowners between 2009 and 2012.

Too much of what happens daily on the courthouse steps is not new. The court's 19th century records show how justice has been denied those seeking the dream of homeownership for over 150 years.

Two hundred years ago, Maryland was a slave state, yet by the 1850s no more than 1,000 enslaved people lived in Baltimore. In fact, the city was home to the largest community of free African Americans in the nation. Despite this seemingly unusual level of freedom, courthouse records show that the lives of free African Americans in Baltimore were framed by grim facts. The period's court dockets show that Baltimore judges routinely sentenced free black men and women to enslavement, selling them to bidders gathered on the courthouse steps.

In the decades before the Civil War, homeownership was rare among Baltimore's black residents. Wages were too low and work too unsteady to allow most families to purchase any dwelling, no matter how modest. Yet a man named Jonathan Trusty defied the odds. At 55, Trusty, a dockworker, amassed just enough to buy a two-story home on Bethel Street. The tiny property became home to Trusty, his wife, their eight children, and two grandchildren.

In 1854, Trusty fell on hard times. His petition for debt relief shows that he had slowly incurred a series of small debts to several dozen creditors. He tried to use a state bankruptcy law to settle his debts. Under the law, the court would inventory his property and satisfy creditors to the extent possible. Trusty's sole asset was his home. Trusty's creditors banded together to ensure that the house was sold. They pressured Trusty to file for insolvency and pressured the court to take control of Trusty's house and land. Just six weeks after his initial filing, Trusty's home was auctioned for $460, more than enough money to settle Trusty's debts.

But the loss of his family home certainly felt less than just. Trusty's story reminds us that today's Baltimore is shaped, in part, by nearly two centuries of policy that have kept too many black residents on the city's economic margins.

Just as in Trusty's day, the organized actions of modern creditors still influence the Baltimore city courthouse as many African-American families lose their primary assets through predatory lending practices that end in foreclosures.

This modern drama still begins with notices published in local newspapers and online, a source of personal embarrassment to people who already face incredible personal loss. At the announced day and time, an auctioneer positions himself at the top of courthouse steps, flanked by crates filled with files. Sometimes a small crowd gathers, but other times, only a few interested parties appear. The staccato song of the auctioneer always ends with the same refrain: "Sold!"

Baltimore was not the only city whose minority residents were targeted for subprime loans and who ultimately paid the price by losing their homes. Too many people watched as their homes went to the highest bidder and their dreams were deferred indefinitely. And when the pain of the foreclosure crisis is compounded by centuries of policies that actively worked to keep minority residents on the fringes of the city's society, it is only a matter of time before the injustice of it all explodes.

1

Which of the following best describes the author's tone in the passage?

A) Callously apathetic
B) Passionately indignant
C) Derisively accusatory
D) Lyrically wistful

2

According to the author, which of the following describes the relationship between foreclosures and the riots in Baltimore in 2015?

A) The foreclosure crisis was one cause of the 2015 riots.
B) The 2015 riots were one cause of the foreclosure crisis.
C) The 2015 riots were a direct response to the foreclosure crisis.
D) The 2015 riots and the foreclosure crisis happened simultaneously.

3

Which of the following provides the best support for the answer to the previous question?

A) Lines 1-4 (“On the...deferred”)
B) Lines 12-15 (“Baltimore's...April”)
C) Lines 16-20 (“Foreclosures...homes”)
D) Lines 22-26 (“between...2012”)

4

How does the author support her assertion that the foreclosure crisis had a widespread impact in Baltimore?

A) By sharing her personal experiences with foreclosures
B) By offering witness testimony establishing that foreclosure auctions occur daily
C) By sharing the personal story of Jonathan Trusty
D) By providing a series of statistics regarding the number of Baltimore foreclosures

5

As it is used in line 39, “framed” most nearly means

A) mounted.
B) bound.
C) faked.
D) trussed.

6

As it is used in line 48, “modest” most nearly means

A) prudent.
B) discreet.
C) humble.
D) shy.

7

Within the context of the passage as a whole, which of the following best describes the purpose of Jonathan Trusty's story (lines 48-68)?

A) To illustrate the fact that problems like the modern foreclosure crisis have been going on for centuries
B) To put a face to the recent foreclosure crisis in order to personify the problems facing Baltimore
C) To show that bad lending practices resulted in foreclosure crises in the past as well as today
D) To show that unfair home foreclosures have led to protests and riots in the past

8

Which of the following provides the best support for the answer to the previous question?

A) Lines 12-15 (“Baltimore's...April”)
B) Lines 16-20 (“Foreclosures...homes”)
C) Lines 48-54 (“Yet a...grandchildren”)
D) Lines 70-73 (“Trusty's...margins”)

9

Which of the following identifies a similarity between the challenges faced by African American families in Baltimore in the 19th century and today?

A) Subprime loans result in foreclosures.
B) The courts refuse to apply bankruptcy laws.
C) Creditors heavily influence the courts.
D) Auctioneers sing on the court steps.

10

What is the effect of the author's choice of words in the sentence in lines 89-90?

A) The sentence adds an artistic flair to the writing that contrasts the dry and unemotional tone of the rest of the passage.
B) The sentence creates imagery to help elicit an emotional response from the reader.
C) The sentence adds humor to an otherwise serious passage.
D) The sentence creates a more persuasive argument by suggesting that the author has experienced this scene in person.

Questions 11-21 are based on the following passage.

The following pair of articles were written by Peace Corps volunteers in different parts of the world. The first is titled "From a Ghetto Brownstone to a Jungle Brown Hut," and the second is titled "From Hawaii to Benin."

Passage 1

It was April of 1975 when I began my Peace Corps service in the Central American nation of Belize. Fresh out of junior college, I longed for an opportunity to travel, to meet new people, to experience new cultures, and to apply my skills as an apiculturist (beekeeper).

I was stationed in the southernmost portion of Belize, living in the rural village of San Antonio among Mayan Indians. The ancient Mayans were empire builders in Mesoamerica and were the first beekeepers in the New World. Ironically, 1,200 years later, this young African-American from Brooklyn, New York would be teaching the Mayans how to raise the European honeybee.

Belize has many ethnic groups, represented by people of African, Hispanic, Asian, and Indian descent. To the Mayans, I later discovered, I looked to be Creole (mixed race), but I confused them with my distinctive "Brooklyn" accent. For weeks, many of San Antonio's villagers did not believe that I was a Peace Corps Volunteer. The only Peace Corps Volunteers the Mayans ever knew or saw had been Caucasian Americans.

The Mayans and I accomplished more than expected. We increased the number of beehives in the country five-fold, built a honey processing plant and exported tons of honey to England. Never lost was the fact that the Mayans now had a new, dependable cash crop to purchase seed, soap, and kerosene.

Still, some of my fondest memories are of the Mayan children who would come to my village extension office in droves and inquire about every conceivable item on my desk. I can still hear the short staccato sounds of their Mopan language, "*Qua a bail ada* Mista Hendree?"

"That's a label maker," I would say before spend an hour or so making everyone labels of their names.

They weren't the only ones who learned, however. My time in the village in the Mayan mountains helped me to realize that in order to truly appreciate life, one must experience a different way of living.

Passage 2

Growing up in Hawaii, I was always surrounded by varying cultures and languages: Japanese, Chinese, Filipino, Samoan, native Hawaiian, and so on. Even most white people I knew claimed a European heritage like Portuguese. As an African American woman, I was different from everyone around me. I grew up experiencing and appreciating ethnic diversity, cultural exchange, and religious differences. This multi-cultural, multi-lingual setting was the foundation for my pursuing the Peace Corps.

The Peace Corps was the ultimate cross-cultural experience, and so I will be sad to say farewell to it. Learning new cultures was always my main goal. I didn't go in with arrogant ideas of saving native villagers from themselves by teaching them the American way of doing things. I wanted to learn and experience what they could teach me. When I was posted in a small bush village in Benin, I was thrilled, thinking that I had gotten exactly what I wanted—a remote place with optimal opportunity for cultural immersion. Little did I know how much the Beninese would learn about Americans through me.

As an environmental volunteer, I have helped women's groups find money and supplies to start tree nurseries as both reforestation and money-earning ventures. I taught schoolchildren the importance of tree planting and wood conservation. In Benin, the Sahara desert slowly encroaches from the north because of severe deforestation. Trees hold the topsoil from washing away, so conservation becomes vital in keeping the desert at bay.

I vividly remember the way that women and girls would sit for hours and watch me write letters home or read a novel. My reading and writing fascinated them. Perhaps because of this, during my second year, the number of girls in elementary school in my neighborhood has risen significantly.

From my time in Peace Corps, I have learned much from the Beninese, such as unending generosity. Numerous times, villagers offered me chicken, fish, and eggs, all of which they needed far more than I did. No matter who you are, what you look like, or where you are from, in Benin, you will always have food to eat, shelter out of a rainstorm, and a place to rest your head for the night.

What I will recall most about my Peace Corps experience is learning to appreciate small details about myself and others. In the end, it's the little things that make a lasting difference.

11

Which of the following is NOT a similarity between the two Peace Corps volunteers?

A) Both managed to help the villagers succeed economically.
B) Both learned valuable lessons from their experiences.
C) Both wanted to experience new cultures.
D) Both had to convince the villagers that they were Peace Corps volunteers.

12

In both passages, the first paragraph serves to

A) explain the author's reasons for becoming a Peace Corps volunteer.
B) describe the people the author helped.
C) provide a description of the author's upbringing.
D) convince the reader to consider joining the Peace Corps.

13

During his assignment in Belize, the author of Passage 1 primarily intended to

A) teach children about American culture.
B) help Mayans learn to keep honeybees.
C) earn extra money by selling honey.
D) purchase seed, soap, and kerosene.

14

Which of the following best supports the answer to the previous question?

A) Lines 12-15 (“this young...honeybee”)
B) Lines 27-30 (“We...England”)
C) Lines 30-32 (“Never...kerosene”)
D) Lines 33-36 (“Still...desk”)

15

The author of Passage 1 most likely included the story about the children and the label maker (lines 33-42) in order to

A) explain why he enjoyed the children's company more than the adults'.
B) show how the children taught him valuable lessons.
C) illustrate his warm interactions with the villagers.
D) show how remote the village in Belize was.

16

As it is used in line 46, “appreciate” most nearly means

A) acknowledge.
B) enjoy.
C) gain.
D) praise.

17

It can be inferred from Passage 2 that the author

A) taught the girls of the village to read.
B) studied environmental science in college.
C) was disappointed by her experience in the Peace Corps.
D) will be leaving the Peace Corps.

18

Which of the following provides the best support for the answer to the previous question?

A) Lines 60-62 (“The...to it”)
B) Lines 67-71 (“When I...immersion”)
C) Lines 74-77 (“As...ventures”)
D) Lines 87-90 (“Perhaps...significantly”)

19

As it is used in line 70, "remote" most nearly means

A) unlikely.
B) aloof.
C) irrelevant.
D) distant.

20

According to Passage 2, how does reforestation keep the desert away?

A) Trees can't grow in the desert, so if there are trees, there is no desert.
B) Trees keep the topsoil in place, and without topsoil, the desert takes over.
C) Tree nurseries provide income that allows the villagers to purchase topsoil to replace what washes away.
D) Trees help to create moisture, which keeps the desert away.

21

The author of Passage 2 suggests that

A) she tutored the women and girls in reading and writing.
B) girls were not allowed to attend school before she visited Benin.
C) her example of reading encouraged girls in Benin to attend school.
D) she acted as a schoolteacher while in Benin.

Questions 22-31 are based on the following passage.

Excerpted from "The Legend of Perseus" as written by E.M. Berens in The Myths and Legends of Ancient Greece and Rome.

Perseus, one of the most renowned of the legendary heroes of antiquity, was the son of Zeus and Danaë, daughter of Acrisius, king of Argos.

An oracle having foretold to Acrisius that a son of Danaë would be the cause of his death, he imprisoned her in a tower of brass in order to keep her secluded from the world. Zeus, however, descended through the roof of the tower in the form of a shower of gold, and the lovely Danaë became his bride.

For four years Acrisius remained in ignorance of this union, but one evening as he chanced to pass by the brazen chamber, he heard the cry of a young child proceeding from within, which led to the discovery of his daughter's marriage with Zeus. Enraged, Acrisius commanded the mother and child to be placed in a chest and thrown into the sea.

But it was not the will of Zeus that they should perish. He directed Poseidon to calm the troubled waters, and caused the chest to float safely to the island of Seriphus, [where Polydectes, king of the island, treated them] with the greatest kindness.

Polydectes eventually became united to Danaë, and bestowed upon Perseus an education befitting a hero. When he saw his stepson develop into a noble and manly youth he endeavored to instill into his mind a desire to signalize himself by the achievement of some great and heroic deed, and it was decided that the slaying of the Gorgon, Medusa, would bring him the greatest renown.

For the successful accomplishment of his object it was necessary for him to be provided with a pair of winged sandals, a magic wallet, and the helmet of Aïdes, which rendered the wearer invisible. He attached to his feet the winged sandals, and flew to the abode of the Gorgons, whom he found fast asleep. Now as Perseus had been warned by his celestial guides that whoever looked upon these weird sisters would be transformed into stone, he stood with averted face before the sleepers, and caught on his bright metal shield their triple image. Then he cut off the head of the Medusa, which he placed in his wallet. He now hastened to elude the pursuit of the two surviving sisters, who, aroused from their slumbers, eagerly rushed to avenge the death of their sister.

His invisible helmet and winged sandals here stood him in good stead; for the former concealed him from the view of the Gorgons, whilst the latter bore him swiftly over land and sea, far beyond the reach of pursuit.

His winged sandals bore him over deserts and mountains, until he arrived at Æthiopia, the kingdom of King Cepheus. Here he found the country inundated with disastrous floods. On a projecting cliff close to the shore he beheld a lovely maiden chained to a rock. This was Andromeda, the king's daughter. Her mother Cassiopea, having boasted that her beauty surpassed that of the Nereides, [angered the sea nymphs, who appealed to Poseidon, the sea god, to avenge them. He] devastated the country with a terrible inundation, which brought with it a huge monster who devoured all that came in his way. Only by the sacrifice of the king's daughter to the monster could the country and people be saved.

On being informed of the meaning of this tragic scene, Perseus proposed to slay the dragon, on condition that the lovely victim should become his bride. Perseus, assuming once more the helmet of Aïdes, mounted into the air, and awaited the approach of the monster.

Presently the sea opened, and the shark's head of the gigantic beast of the deep raised itself above the waves. Lashing his tail furiously from side to side, he leaped forward to seize his victim; but the gallant hero suddenly darted down, and [held the head of Medusa] before the eyes of the dragon, whose hideous body became gradually transformed into a huge black rock.

Perseus now took leave of the Ethiopian king, and, accompanied by his beautiful bride, returned to Seriphus. He then sent a messenger to his grandfather, informing him that he intended returning to Argos; but Acrisius, fearing the fulfilment of the oracular prediction, fled for protection to his friend Teutemias. Anxious to induce the aged monarch to return to Argos, Perseus followed him thither. Whilst taking part in some funereal games, celebrated in honour of the king's father, Perseus, by an unfortunate throw of the discus, accidentally struck his grandfather, and thereby was the innocent cause of his death.

22

Which of the following best describes the order of events in the story?

A) Chronological order
B) Reverse chronological order
C) Problem-solution
D) Order of importance

23

It can be inferred from the passage that Acrisius threw his daughter and grandchild into the sea in order to

A) test Zeus's devotion to his daughter.
B) seek revenge on Zeus for betraying his wishes.
C) avoid the fate that was foretold by the oracle.
D) make a sacrifice to the gods.

24

As it is used in line 29, "develop" most nearly means

A) expand.
B) grow.
C) establish.
D) realize.

25

Perseus decided to slay Medusa in order to

A) establish himself as a hero.
B) make his parents proud.
C) save the islanders from Medusa.
D) get the winged sandals, magic wallet, and helmet of Aïdes.

26

Which of the following provides the best evidence to support the answer to the previous question?

A) Lines 26-28 ("Polydectes...hero")
B) Lines 28-34 ("When...renown")
C) Lines 35-39 ("For...invisible")
D) Lines 41-44 ("Now...stone")

27

Of what use was Medusa's head to Perseus?

A) He used it as a weapon against another monster.
B) He showed it to his stepfather to prove that he had accomplished his goal.
C) He showed it to his grandfather in an attempt to win praise.
D) He gave it to King Cepheus in exchange for his daughter's hand in marriage.

28

As it is used in line 36, "object" most nearly means

A) item.
B) complaint.
C) recipient.
D) purpose.

29

It can be inferred from the passage that Perseus wore the helmet of Aïdes while fighting the monster in Æthiopia because

A) it protected him from turning to stone when he pulled out Medusa's head.
B) he knew it would impress King Cepheus and Andromeda.
C) it allowed him to attack the dragon without being seen.
D) it allowed him to fly above the sea without danger of drowning.

30

Which of the following provides the best evidence in support of the answer to the previous question?

A) Lines 35-39 ("For...invisible")
B) Lines 41-44 ("Now...stone")
C) Lines 59-60 ("Here...floods")
D) Lines 74-76 ("Perseus...bride")

31

The author most likely included the final paragraph (lines 89-102) because

A) it explains how Perseus became king of Argos.
B) it concludes the story by referencing the beginning of the tale.
C) it further illustrates why Perseus is known as a legendary hero.
D) it creates suspense to leave the reader wanting more.

Questions 32-42 are based on the following passage.

Excerpted from Barack Obama's remarks at the 2014 United Nations Climate Change Summit, given at UN Headquarters in New York.

There's one issue that will define the contours of this century more dramatically than any other, and that is the urgent and growing threat of a changing climate.

Five years have passed since many of us met in Copenhagen. And since then, our understanding of climate change has advanced—both in the deepening science that says this once-distant threat has moved "firmly into the present," and into the sting of more frequent extreme weather events that show us exactly what these changes may mean for future generations.

No nation is immune. In America, the past decade has been our hottest on record. Along our eastern coast, the city of Miami now floods at high tide. In our west, wildfire season now stretches most of the year. In our heartland, farms have been parched by the worst drought in generations, and drenched by the wettest spring in our history. A hurricane left parts of this great city dark and underwater. And some nations already live with far worse. Worldwide, this summer was the hottest ever recorded—with global carbon emissions still on the rise.

So the climate is changing faster than our efforts to address it. We know what we have to do to avoid irreparable harm. We have to cut carbon pollution in our own countries to prevent the worst effects of climate change. We have to adapt to the impacts that, unfortunately, we can no longer avoid. And we have to work together as a global community to tackle this global threat before it is too late.

We cannot condemn our children, and their children, to a future that is beyond their capacity to repair. Not when we have the means—the technological innovation and the scientific imagination—to begin the work of repairing it right now. So today, I'm here personally, as the leader of the world's largest economy and its second largest emitter, to say that we have begun to do something about it.

The United States has made ambitious investments in clean energy, and ambitious reductions in our carbon emissions. We now harness three times as much electricity from the wind and 10 times as much from the sun as we did when I came into office. Within a decade, our cars will go twice as far on a gallon of gas, and already, every major automaker offers electric vehicles. We've made unprecedented investments to cut energy waste in our homes and our buildings and our appliances, all of which will save consumers billions of dollars. And we are committed to helping communities build climate-resilient infrastructure.

So, all told, these advances have helped create jobs, grow our economy, and drive our carbon pollution to its lowest levels in nearly two decades—proving that there does not have to be a conflict between a sound environment and strong economic growth.

Over the past eight years, the United States has reduced our total carbon pollution by more than any other nation on Earth. But we have to do more. Last year, I issued America's first Climate Action Plan to double down on our efforts. Under that plan, my administration is working with states and utilities to set first-ever standards to cut the amount of carbon pollution our power plants can dump into the air. And when completed, this will mark the single most important and significant step the United States has ever taken to reduce our carbon emissions.

Last week alone, we announced an array of new actions in renewable energy and energy efficiency that will save consumers more than $10 billion on their energy bills and cut carbon pollution by nearly 300 million metric tons through 2030. That's the equivalent of taking more than 60 million cars off the road for one year.

And today, I call on all countries to join us—not next year, or the year after, but right now, because no nation can meet this global threat alone.

Yes, this is hard. But there should be no question that the United States of America is stepping up to the plate. We recognize our role in creating this problem; we embrace our responsibility to combat it. We will do our part, and we will help developing nations do theirs. But we can only succeed in combating climate change if we are joined in this effort by every nation—developed and developing alike. Nobody gets a pass.

32

It can be inferred from the passage that

A) UN members have already discovered a means of solving climate change.
B) most UN members feel that climate change is an unimportant issue.
C) all UN members have made great strides to address climate change.
D) UN members met to discuss climate change several years earlier.

33

Which of the following best describes the rhetorical effect of the sentence ("No…immune") in line 14?

A) It warns of a coming disease epidemic.
B) It suggests that the speaker is threatening his listeners.
C) It creates a sense of urgency among the speaker's listeners.
D) It utilizes repetition to underscore the speaker's argument.

34

What proof does the speaker offer to support the contention that climate change is worsening?

A) Examples of extreme weather in the U.S. and elsewhere
B) Statistics establishing record-breaking weather
C) The results of scientific studies showing increasing temperatures
D) Expert testimony regarding changes to the climate in the U.S.

35

Which of the following provides the best support for the answer to the previous question?

A) Lines 5-10 ("Five...present")
B) Lines 14-25 ("In...rise")
C) Lines 35-43 ("We...it")
D) Lines 44-58 ("The...infrastructure")

36

As it is used in line 27, "address" most nearly means

A) undertake.
B) discuss.
C) direct.
D) solve.

37

The speaker most likely referenced "children" in lines 35 and 36 in order to

A) establish the speaker's authority on the subject.
B) create an emotional appeal to motivate his listeners.
C) show how long the speaker expects climate change to last.
D) show how cynical those who oppose taking action are.

38

It can be inferred from the passage that

A) the U.S. is the only nation to have taken steps to address climate change.
B) the U.S. government has required that automakers offer electric vehicles.
C) wind and solar energy produce little pollution.
D) the U.S. plans to require that consumers reduce energy usage.

39

Which of the following provides the best support for the answer to the previous question?

A) Lines 44-49 ("The United...office")
B) Lines 49-52 ("Within...vehicles")
C) Lines 52-56 ("We've...dollars")
D) Lines 65-67 ("Over...Earth")

40

Which of the following is a counterclaim addressed in the passage?

A) Countries other than the U.S. cannot afford to address climate change.
B) Climate change has gone too far for any actions to make a difference.
C) Reducing carbon emissions is economically disadvantageous.
D) It is not the U.N.'s place to take action on climate change.

41

As it is used in line 77, “array” most nearly means

A) display.
B) multitude.
C) attire.
D) design.

42

What is the author's primary purpose in speaking?

A) To boast of the U.S.'s actions to combat climate change
B) To encourage all world leaders to join him in fighting climate change
C) To explain that climate change is a legitimate issue
D) To address a series of arguments against combating climate change

Questions 43-52 are based on the following passage.

Adapted from a 2015 article titled "The Case for Drinking Whole Milk," written by Deena Shanker.

At one time, Americans primarily drank whole milk—no-fat and lower-fat milks were relatively rare. When the anti-fat movement of the 1980s took hold, these low-fat alternatives saw their popularity rise. Today, most people consider creamy whole milk, like the milkmen who once delivered it, to be a relic of the past.

Though it would seem logical that consuming less fat would lead to being less fat, that's not what the science says, especially when it comes to dairy fat. In 2006, a study published in the *American Journal of Clinical Nutrition* looked at the role of dairy consumption in weight regulation for 19,352 Swedish women. It found that the women who consumed one or more servings per day of whole dairy products was "inversely associated with weight gain." More recently, the *European Journal of Nutrition* published a meta-analysis of 16 studies on the relationship between dairy fat, obesity, and cardiometabolic disease. It found that "high-fat dairy consumption within typical dietary patterns is inversely associated with obesity risk."

This paradox begs the question: Why does eating high-fat foods seem to lower the risk of obesity?

One possible explanation, according to Walter Willett of the Harvard School of Public Health, is that full-fat dairy better satiates the appetite. "It is also possible that some of the fatty acids in milk products have an additional effect on weight regulation," he says. In addition, many low-fat and fat-free dairy products compensate for lost flavor by adding sugar, which certainly induces weight gain.

But what about the other health risks associated with consumption of saturated fat? Saturated fat has long been associated with heart disease, but science is challenging this conventional wisdom as well. A 2010 meta-analysis published in the *American Journal of Clinical Nutrition* found "no significant evidence for concluding that dietary saturated fat is associated with an increased risk of coronary heart disease or cardiovascular disease." Further meta-analyses also concluded that the evidence simply does not support a recommendation of low consumption of saturated fats.

And while whole milk seems far less harmful than it has been made out to be, it certainly has health benefits. Milk is a good source of vitamins A, D, and B, calcium, protein, potassium, riboflavin, niacin, and phosphorous. Milk certainly isn't the only—or even the best—source of these nutrients, but whole milk provides far better nutrition than skim milk. This is because many nutrients, including vitamins A and D, are fat soluble—the body can't absorb them without fat.

Health advocates like to promote eating "whole foods" that haven't been overly processed. Lower fat milks go through more processing than their whole counterpart. Taking the fat out of milk is a high-tech endeavor. First, fat is removed in a centrifuge; next, synthetic vitamins are added to the milk to replace those that have been lost; for 1% or 2% milk, fat is then added back in through additional processing. Whole milk undergoes processing as well since almost all milk is pasteurized, but because it remains closer to its original state, it is a more natural—and more nutritious—food than reduced-fat milk.

All of this leads to the same conclusion that most nutritionists agree on: Everything in moderation. Eat too much of anything, and it will likely hurt you. But in moderation, whole fat dairy is not only safe, but beneficial.

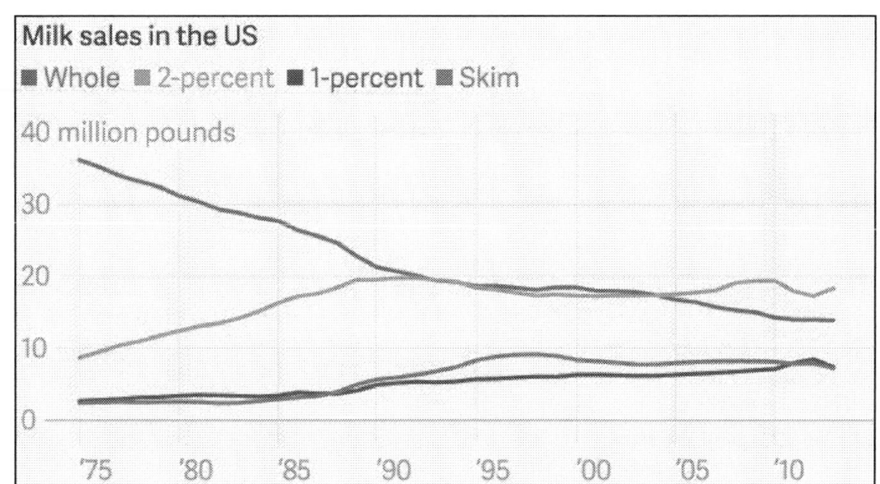

Figure 1: Shows the change in milk sales in the U.S. from 1975 to 2010.

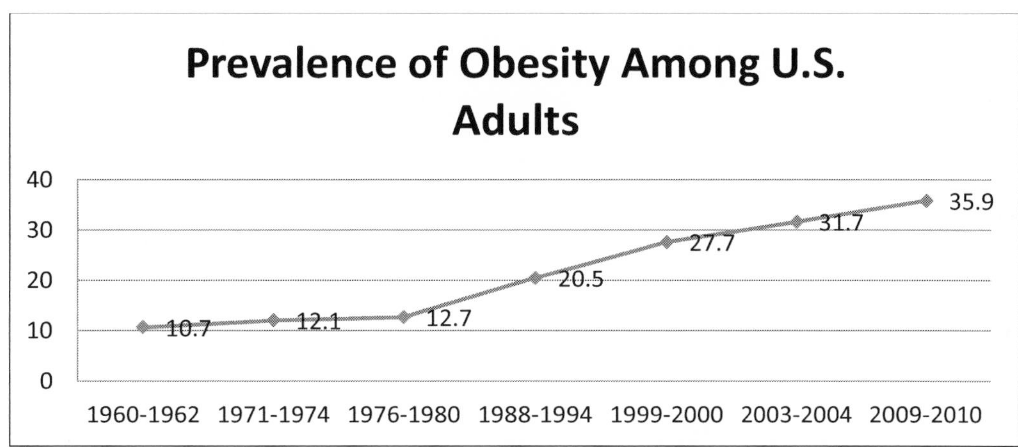

Figure 2: Shows the percentage of U.S. adults who were obese from 1960 to 2010.

43

The author likely included the phrase "like the milkmen who once delivered it" (lines 6-7) in order to

A) show that the switch from whole milk to low-fat milk also destroyed jobs.
B) provide an image to emphasize how old-fashioned whole milk seems.
C) show that whole milk has been eliminated from modern stores.
D) explain that whole milk can only be purchased from milkmen.

44

How does the author support the contention that consuming whole milk does not lead to obesity?

A) By citing several modern studies that show that people who consume whole milk are less likely to be obese
B) By citing expert testimony that claims that whole milk has no detrimental health effects
C) By citing the results of a survey that asked people how much milk they drank and how much they weighed
D) By citing an example of a person who regularly drinks whole milk but is not overweight

45

Which of the following is not given as a possible reason for why whole milk consumption seems to lower the risk of obesity?

A) Whole milk better satiates the appetite.
B) Fatty acids in whole milk help to regulate weight.
C) Whole milk is lower in sugar than reduced fat products are.
D) Whole milk has more vitamins A and D than reduced fat milk does.

46

As it is used in line 35, "compensate" most nearly means

A) refund.
B) atone.
C) offset.
D) improve.

47

According to the passage, whole milk's high levels of saturated fat

A) do not cause heart disease.
B) prevent the absorption of valuable nutrients.
C) prevent the absorption of sugar.
D) made milk popular during the 1980s.

48

Which of the following best supports the answer to the previous question?

A) Lines 3-5 ("When...rise")
B) Lines 33-36 ("In...gain")
C) Lines 41-47 ("A 2010...disease")
D) Lines 59-61 ("This...fat")

49

As it is used in line 61, "absorb" most nearly means

A) assimilate.
B) process.
C) consume.
D) involve.

50

Which of the following is one reason given in the passage for why whole milk is more nutritious than reduced-fat milk?

A) Whole milk does not cause heart disease.
B) Whole milk contains fatty acids.
C) Whole milk is less processed.
D) Whole milk is more processed.

51

Which of the following provides the best evidence in support of the answer to the previous question?

A) Lines 31-33 ("It...says")
B) Lines 39-41 ("Saturated...well")
C) Lines 67-71 ("First...processing")
D) Lines 71-75 ("Whole...milk")

52

It can be most strongly inferred from the passage and the graphs that

A) the obesity rate began to increase substantially around the same time that whole milk sales began to fall significantly.
B) the primary cause of the rise in obesity from 1975 to today has been the reduction in whole milk consumption.
C) because milk sales have held relatively steady since the 1990s even as the obesity rate has continued to rise, milk consumption can have no impact on obesity.
D) people who stopped drinking whole milk began to consume large amounts of saturated fat from other sources.

STOP

If you finish before time is called, you may check your work on this section only.
Do not turn to any other section.

Writing and Language Test

35 MINUTES, 44 QUESTIONS

Mark your responses on this test. Use the "How to Calculate Your Scores in the back of this book to determine your scores.

DIRECTIONS

Each passage below is accompanied by a number of questions. For some questions, you will consider how the passage might be revised to improve the expression of ideas. For other questions, you will consider how the passage might be edited to correct errors in sentence structure, usage, or punctuation. A passage or a question may be accompanied by one or more graphics (such as a table or graph) that you will consider as you make revising and editing decisions.

Some questions will direct you to an underlined portion of a passage. Other questions will direct you to a location in a passage or ask you to think about the passage as a whole.

After reading each passage, choose the answer to each question that most effectively improves the quality of writing in the passage or that makes the passage conform to the conventions of standard written English. Many questions include a "NO CHANGE" option. Choose that option if you think the best choice is to leave the relevant portion of the passage as it is.

Questions 1-11 are based on the following passage.

Though many people believe in the benefits of marrying young, recent research **1** will show that age may be the biggest predictor of marriage success. There are several factors related to age that strongly shape the health of a marriage, including income, education level, and whether couples live together.

1

A) NO CHANGE
B) will be showing
C) has shown
D) showed

Based solely on common statistics, **2** this may seem counterintuitive. Over the last half-century, Americans have married later and later. According to the U.S. census, today's young adults marry **3** at least eight years later than **4** there counterparts did in the 1950s. Yet as marriage ages have risen, marriage has also become less common and less stable. In 1960, less than 9 percent of people over the age of 25 had never married. Today, that proportion is 20%, meaning that 42 million Americans have never tied the knot. Moreover, divorce rates have increased by more than 100% since the mid-20th century and, by some evidence, approximately one in two marriages now end in divorce.

[1] On the surface, these statistics suggest that as marriage age went up, so did divorce rates; thus, it would seem that there is, at the very least, a **5** corollary between higher marriage age and divorce. [2] This is misleading, however. [3] Divorce rates skyrocketed for decades, **6** so they peaked in the mid-1990s. [4] Since then, divorce rates have been declining, and many sociologists believe that this is because marriage age has been increasing. [5] Other sociologists are not yet ready to make an opinion based on the data. **7**

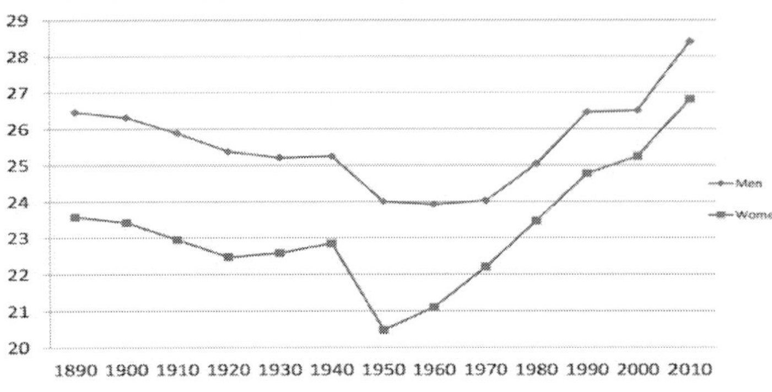

2

Which choice results in the most effective transition to the information that follows in the following paragraph?

A) NO CHANGE
B) this is the most logical result.
C) it is clear which of these factors is most important.
D) income and education seem to be the most important factors in marital success.

3

Which choice offers an accurate interpretation of the data in the chart?

A) NO CHANGE
B) no more than five years later
C) between five and six years later
D) between six and eight years later

4

A) NO CHANGE
B) their
C) they're
D) our

5

A) NO CHANGE
B) causation
C) causality
D) correlation

6

A) NO CHANGE
B) but
C) however
D) although

7

Which of the following sentences should be removed in order to improve the focus of this paragraph?

A) Sentence 1
B) Sentence 3
C) Sentence 4
D) Sentence 5

In fact, the relationship between age and marriage stability seems to **8** go above and beyond the actual marriage itself. For years, researchers wondered why couples who cohabit before getting married are more likely to get divorced. Recent research suggests that it is not, in fact, cohabitation that impacts divorce rates, but rather the age of the couple when they began living together that most strongly predicted an eventual divorce.

The secret to a stable marriage might be waiting to marry, but not because wisdom comes with age (or, at least, not only because wisdom comes with age). People who marry older generally have **9** great education, high incomes, and strong support systems than those who marry young. All of these factors greatly contribute to the stability of a marriage. In other words, while marrying older does correlate with likelihood for marital success, it's still unclear whether age-related factors or age itself which **10** determine marital stability. **11**

8

A) NO CHANGE
B) go above and beyond the actual marriage
C) extend the actual length of the marriage itself
D) extend beyond the actual marriage

9

A) NO CHANGE
B) greater education, higher incomes, and strong support systems
C) greater education, higher incomes, and stronger support systems
D) great education, incomes, and support systems

10

A) NO CHANGE
B) determines
C) is determining
D) are determining

11

Which of the following sentences would best conclude this passage?

A) In the end, modern people are not mature enough to marry early in their lives.
B) The data are even more skewed when the ages of the couple differ by more than ten years.
C) Ultimately, people should wait as long as possible for marriage.
D) Either way, the data do seem to suggest that it's best to wait on marriage.

Questions 12-22 are based on the following passage.

When we think of the moon, **12** one thinks of a dead, cratered planetoid without an atmosphere. Yet other moons in our solar system can be very **13** different. The innermost of Jupiter's moons, Io, is a volcanic powerhouse with constant eruptions and seismic shifts that constantly reshape the moon's surface. In recent months, however, scientists have gotten a clear and close look at Io's volcanic activity, especially in one spot.

The Large Binocular telescope Interferometer, an extremely powerful telescope, has given scientists a hi-definition look at Io. The image is not crystal clear, but what makes it impressive is the distance **14** at which these photographs have been taken: 600 million kilometers away. Each pixel in the pictures this telescope takes is the rough equivalent of 100 square kilometers.

One particular spot on Io is heavily **15** volcanic, and has been spotted by scientists in decades past. They named this volcanic spot "Loki" after the Norse trickster god. Over 200km – or 120 miles – in diameter, the "Loki" spot is what is known as a patera. **16** As the lake fills with lava, this crust **17** periodically sinks into the lava below, and then as the lake cools, the crust becomes solid again. These cycles are what the scientists are able to spot from Earth. Before the use of the Large Binocular telescope Interferometer, all they could see was a single spot. Now, astronomers can tell that almost all of the 200km area is subject to a great deal of seismic activity. Not only that, they also spotted two other areas of heavy volcanic activity—Io was, perhaps, more active than anyone could have guessed.

12

A) NO CHANGE
B) we think
C) you think
D) they think

13

Which choice most effectively combines the sentences at the underlined portion?

A) different and the
B) different, like the
C) different: the
D) different, for example, the

14

A) NO CHANGE
B) where
C) that
D) and how

15

A) NO CHANGE
B) volcanic and has
C) volcanic. Io has
D) volcanic which has

16

The writer is considering adding the following sentence here. Should the writer make this insertion?

A patera is an entire lake of lava, covered by a solidified lava crust.

A) No, because the reader should already know what a patera is.
B) No, because it detracts from the overall focus of the passage.
C) Yes, because knowing the definition of patera is important to understanding the passage.
D) Yes, because the paragraph is currently lacking in factual information.

17

A) NO CHANGE
B) occasionally
C) sporadically
D) irregularly

[1] **18** What benefit does the study of a moon of Jupiter allow? Scientists argue that by studying volcanism on worlds other than Earth, they can get a better grasp of how it works here. [2] "It's becoming **19** clear" said one researcher, "that volcanism on the Earth is part and parcel of what makes it a habitable planet, and so understanding how these processes work off-world helps us address a number of issues in exoplanetary science." [3] Understanding how Io's seismic properties work could also aid our understanding of what makes a planet livable. [4] The **20** excepted idea of habitable planets posits that they must be in a "Goldilocks zone" – not too hot, not too cold – but Io's volcanoes offer another solution: **21** they must be seismically active. **22**

18

Which choice most effectively sets up the paragraph?

A) NO CHANGE
B) Why would anyone care about studying volcanoes?
C) The study of Io may not have too many ramifications on Earth, however.
D) Many of the volcanoes on Io are much more seismically powerful than those on Earth.

19

A) NO CHANGE
B) clear said
C) clear", said
D) clear," said

20

A) NO CHANGE
B) exceptable
C) acceptable
D) accepted

21

A) NO CHANGE
B) it
C) habitable planets
D) volcanoes

22

To make this paragraph most logical, sentence 3 should be placed

A) where it is now.
B) before sentence 1.
C) before sentence 2.
D) after sentence 4.

Questions 23-33 are based on the following passage.

It was on a flat, cactus-studded coastal plain of South Texas that the American Civil War ended in its final battle, 150 years ago. When news of General Robert E. Lee's surrender at Appomattox reached the westernmost Confederate state, chaos **23** controlled as the remnants of the Confederate Army turned upon Texas itself. And it was here that the Confederate Army made **24** their final and most futile stand.

Within days of Lee's surrender, much of the Confederate Army in Texas deserted. In several Texas cities, the remaining troops rioted for their back pay. The soldiers attacked and looted government warehouses and even commandeered a train. **25** Before long, civilians joined in the pillaging. Some 20 children were injured after playing with looted ammunition, and in Austin, $17,000 worth of gold was stolen from the state treasury.

Near the coast, Union Major General Lew Wallace, fearing that Confederate troops would slip across the border into Mexico **26** and using it as a staging ground to continue the war using guerrilla tactics, negotiated terms of surrender. These terms were vetoed in Austin, and several thousand Union troops, mostly African-American, landed at nearby Brazos Santiago.

Even as the Confederate army unraveled, Colonel Rip Ford, the Confederate commander in far South Texas, **27** was holding his men together with glorious speeches. On May 11, a Union force of 250 Colored Infantry troops and 50 members of the Texas Second United States Cavalry headed for the town of Brownsville and presented a target to one of the last intact units of Confederates. More than a month after Lee's surrender, the Texas Cavalry Battalion under George H. Giddings ambushed the Union **28** detachment; and bullets flew across the coastal plain.

23

A) NO CHANGE
B) governed
C) reigned
D) ruled

24

A) NO CHANGE
B) there
C) it's
D) its

25

At this point, the author is considering starting a new paragraph. Should the writer make this change?

A) Yes, because the topic of the paragraph shifts from discussing government entities to civilians.
B) Yes, because the tone of the passage becomes much more negative.
C) No, because the author is still discussing the aftermath of Lee's surrender.
D) No because it does not change the structure of the passage.

26

A) NO CHANGE
B) and use it
C) by using it
D) and, using it

27

A) NO CHANGE
B) held his men together because of the glorious speeches he was giving
C) held his men together
D) used glorious speeches to hold his men together

28

A) NO CHANGE
B) detachment and bullets
C) detachment as bullets
D) detachment, so bullets

The federal troops fell back to a farm to rest for the night, but at 3 a.m., the rebels attacked again. By 5 a.m., 200 troops from the 34th Indiana Infantry had arrived to reinforce the Union troops, bringing their total strength to about 500, versus fewer than 200 rebels. **29**

[1] That afternoon, the numbers were evened out by the addition of 300 Confederates. [2] Ford brought artillery and cavalry, **30** who were leading the rebels in an all-out attack. [3] Relying on African-American troops to provide a screen, the Union line finally **31** broke and they bolted for the coast. [4] The Confederates chased them for seven miles. [5] When all was said and done, there were a few dozen wounded among the Confederates; over 100 Union officers and men were captured and some 30 lay dead or wounded. [6] The Confederates seemed to have the upper hand for now. **32**

Ford's victory was short-lived. Even as the battle raged in Texas, the governors of the southern states were busy authorizing the Confederate commanders to disband their armies and conclude the war. **33**

29

If inserted at this point, which sentence provides the best transition to the next paragraph?

A) The Union needed a miracle to weather the attack.
B) Undermanned, the Confederates appeared to be in dire straits.
C) Both sides new the winner of this next battle would win the war.
D) Weary-eyed, the Indiana Infantry would not be much help in the upcoming battle.

30

A) NO CHANGE
B) they were leading
C) lead
D) leading

31

A) NO CHANGE
B) was broken, its soldiers
C) was broken; so its soldiers
D) was broken, and its soldiers

32

Which sentence should be removed to improve the focus of the paragraph?

A) Sentence 1
B) Sentence 3
C) Sentence 5
D) Sentence 6

33

Which choice provides a supporting example that reinforces the main point?

A) Ford soon retired from military service, content with the role he had played.
B) Over 600,000 men had perished in America's deadliest war, but it was finally over.
C) Racial harmony was soon to follow, thanks to the soldiers who fought that day.
D) The battle marked one of the last instances of cavalry use in modern warfare.

Questions 34-44 are based on the following passage.

A geologist has discovered a palm-like plant in Liberia that seems to only grow on top of columns of volcanic rock **34** that extends deep into Earth, left by ancient eruptions that exhumed diamonds from the Earth's mantle. Stephen Haggerty, a researcher at Florida International University in Miami and the chief exploration officer of Youssef Diamond Mining Company, which owns mining operations in Liberia, suspects that the plant grows only on top of kimberlite columns because the soils are rich in magnesium, potassium, and phosphorous. **35**

[1] Diamonds are formed hundreds of kilometers below the Earth's surface, **36** in which carbon is placed under **37** passionate temperatures and pressures. [2] Kimberlite pipes carry the gems to the surface in eruptions that sometimes rise faster than the speed of sound. [3] Haggerty says that the pipes are rare, and that pipes containing diamonds are even rarer: of the more than 6,000 known kimberlite pipes in the world, about 600 contain diamonds, and only about 60 are rich enough in quality diamonds to be worth mining. **38**

34

A) NO CHANGE
B) that extend
C) that are extending
D) that is extending

35

Which of the following best establishes the main idea of the passage as a whole?

A) If the plant is as picky as it seems, diamond hunters in West Africa will have a simple means of locating diamond deposits.
B) The versatility of the plant, however, makes it far more useful than simply finding diamonds.
C) The plant, which is only found in Liberia, may help researchers find these mineral-rich soils.
D) The question remains: which mining company will be able to use this information most effectively to increase its profits?

36

A) NO CHANGE
B) because
C) while
D) where

37

A) NO CHANGE
B) extreme
C) punishing
D) arduous

38

Which of the following sentences should be removed in order to improve the focus of this paragraph?

A) NO CHANGE
B) Sentence 1
C) Sentence 2
D) Sentence 3

Haggerty has focused his prospecting efforts in the northwest part of Liberia. By examining soil samples, he was able to identify a new kimberlite pipe that has proven rich in diamonds. **39** Out of the blue, Haggerty noticed a plant that seemed to grow only in the soil above the pipe. Working with botanists from the Royal Botanic Garden, Kew, in the United Kingdom, and the Missouri Botanical Garden in St. Louis, **40** the plant has been identified as *P. candelabrum*, a poorly-understood species that seems to grow only above kimberlite pipes.

This new discovery **41** will be particularly helpful to prospectors attempting to locate diamonds in the thick jungle areas of Africa. The bush is often nearly impenetrable, so few kimberlite pipes have been identified. But, if **42** they can be found, they could help to guide prospectors. Haggerty hopes to evaluate whether the plant can be recognized from aerial imagery, which could help West African nations find and develop valuable diamond deposits. Kimberlite mines tend to have much smaller **43** routes than other mines, and the resulting waste is simply kimberlite soil, which is about as toxic as garden fertilizer. **44**

39

A) NO CHANGE
B) Doing a double take
C) More importantly,
D) Raising eyebrows,

40

A) NO CHANGE
B) he believes the plant has been identified
C) Haggerty has identified the plant
D) identified by Haggerty, the plant is now known

41

A) NO CHANGE
B) has been
C) had been
D) would have been

42

A) NO CHANGE
B) the plants
C) the prospectors
D) the diamonds

43

A) NO CHANGE
B) paths
C) footprints
D) leftovers

44

Which of the following sentences would best conclude this passage?

A) Developing countries must start researching kimberlite minding or else they will fall behind their global competitors.
B) Every country must start finding its diamond mines using *P. candelabrum*, or the environment might never recover.
C) Since most countries do not regulate garden fertilizer, why would they regulate kimberlite mining?
D) For many countries, kimberlite mining could offer vital revenue without great damage to the environment.

STOP

If you finish before time is called, you may check your work on this section only. Do not turn to any other section.

Math Test – No Calculator

25 MINUTES, 20 QUESTIONS

Mark your responses on this test. Use the "How to Calculate Your back of this book to determine your scores.

DIRECTIONS

For questions 1-15, solve each problem, choose the best answer from the choices provided, and fill in the corresponding circle on your answer sheet. **For questions 16-20**, solve the problem and enter your answer in the grid on the answer sheet. Please refer to the directions before question 16 on how to enter your answers in the grid. You may use any available space in your test booklet for scratch work.

NOTES

1. The use of a calculator **is not permitted**.
2. All variables and expressions used represent real numbers unless otherwise indicated.
3. Figures provided in the test are drawn to scale unless otherwise indicated.
4. All figures lie in a plane unless otherwise indicated.
5. Unless otherwise indicated, the domain of a given function f is the set of all real numbers x for which $f(x)$ is a real number.

REFERENCE

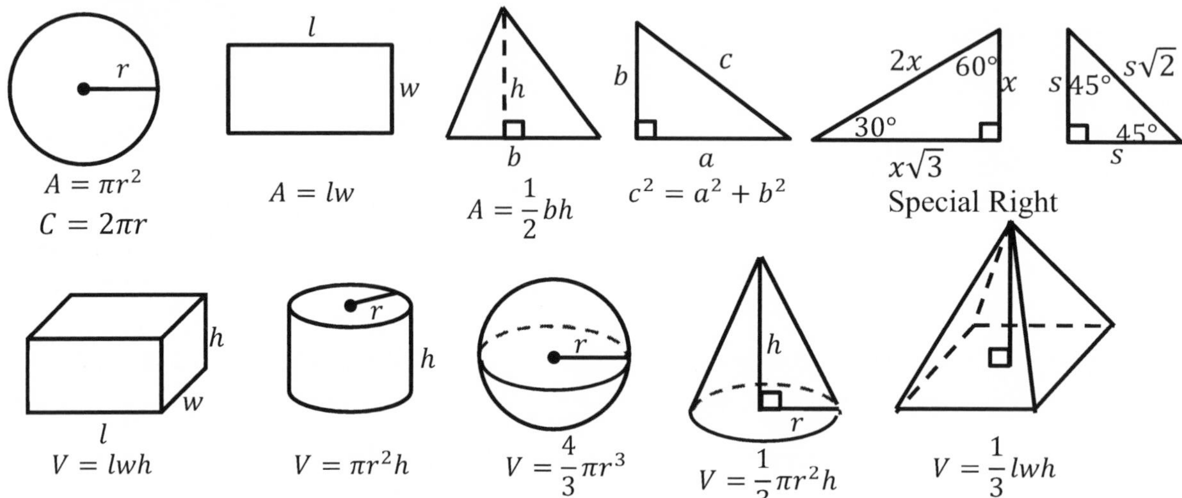

The number of degrees of arc in a circle is 360.

The number of radians of arc in a circle is 2π.

The sum of the measures in degrees of the angles of a triangle is 180.

1

Victoria needs to have at least \$30 dollars to be able to go on her class field trip to an amusement park. Currently, she has \$5.00. For every dog she washes, she earns \$3.50. Which of the following inequalities can be solved to find x, the minimum number of dogs she must wash to be able to go on her field trip?

A) $5.00 + 3.50x \leq 30.00$
B) $3.50 + 5.00x \leq 30.00$
C) $5.00 + 3.50x \geq 30.00$
D) $3.50 + 5.00x \geq 30.00$

2

What is the y-intercept of the line that passes through the points $(1, 3)$ and $(-2, -5)$?

A) $-\frac{1}{8}$
B) $\frac{1}{3}$
C) $\frac{8}{3}$
D) 8

3

$$\frac{x^2}{16} = \frac{y^2}{4}$$

If (x, y) is a solution to the equation above and $y \neq 0$, what is a possible value of the ratio $\frac{x}{y}$?

A) –8
B) –4
C) –2
D) 8

4

$$3y - 2x = 12$$
$$8x + 48 = 12y$$

Which ordered pair (x, y) satisfies the system of equations shown above?

A) $(3, 6)$
B) $(-3, 2)$
C) $(-6, 0)$
D) All of the above ordered pairs satisfy the system of equations given.

5

$$4x^2 - 16 = 9$$

If a and b are two solutions of the equation above and $a > b$, which of the following is the value of ab?

A) $-\frac{25}{4}$
B) $-\frac{5}{2}$
C) $\frac{5}{2}$
D) $\frac{25}{4}$

6

A hockey team won exactly one-third of its games last season and tied exactly one-tenth of its games last season. Which of the following could be the total number of games the team played last season?

A) 66
B) 80
C) 100
D) 120

7

$$62x + y = 720$$

A video game store is running a promotion in which a number of 20%-off coupons are given away each day. The equation above can be used to model the number of coupons, y, that remain to be given away x hours after the promotion began. What does it mean that $(10, 100)$ is a solution to this equation?

A) During the promotion, 100 coupons are given away for the first 10 hours.
B) It takes 10 hours for 720 coupons to be given away.
C) After 10 hours, 100 coupons still remain to be given away.
D) After 62 hours, 100 coupons still remain to be given away.

8

$$(x - 1)^2 + (y + 2)^2 = 9$$

The equation of a circle in the xy-plane is shown above. What is the area of the circle?

A) 1π
B) 4π
C) 9π
D) 81π

9

A biology professor gives 5 points for each correct answer and –2 points for each incorrect or blank answer. Each test has 20 questions, and Marissa scored 65 points on the exam. How many questions did she get incorrect or leave blank?

A) 5
B) 7
C) 13
D) 15

10

If $f(x) = x^2 - 6$ and $g(x) = \frac{3}{x} - x$ for all non zero values of x, what is the value of $f(g(2))$?

A) $-\frac{23}{4}$
B) $-\frac{11}{2}$
C) $-\frac{7}{2}$
D) $\frac{1}{2}$

11

The population of a species of turtle decreases by half every 3 years. The population at the beginning of 2012 was estimated to be 1,000 turtles. If P represents the population n years after 2012, then which of the following represents the class's model of the population over time?

A) $P = 1000 - \frac{1}{2}(3)^n$
B) $P = 1000 - 3\left(\frac{1}{2}\right)^n$
C) $P = 1000\left(\frac{1}{2}\right)^{3n}$
D) $P = 1000\left(\frac{1}{2}\right)^{\frac{n}{3}}$

12

If $x^{-\frac{2}{3}} = \frac{1}{4}$, then $x =$

A) 2
B) 4
C) 8
D) 16

13

Patricia is responsible for catering the meal of a large wedding; she knows that there will need to be enough meals to feed at least 200 people. The food budget for the wedding is \$1,500; each vegetarian meal costs \$8.50, while each non-vegetarian meal costs \$9.75. Solving which of the following systems of inequalities yields the number of vegetarian meals, v, and non-vegetarian meals, n, that Patricia could prepare while meeting her budget requirements?

A) $8.50v + 9.75n \geq 1{,}500$
$n + v \geq 200$

B) $8.50v + 9.75n \leq 1{,}500$
$n + v \geq 200$

C) $8.50v + 9.75n \geq 1{,}500$
$n + v \leq 200$

D) $8.50v + 9.75n \leq 1{,}500$
$n + v \leq 200$

14

$$x^2 + y^2 = 9$$
$$x = \sqrt{3}y$$

What is a possible solution,(x, y), to the system of equations above?

A) $\left(-\frac{\sqrt{3}}{2}, \frac{3}{2}\right)$

B) $\left(\frac{3\sqrt{3}}{2}, \frac{3}{2}\right)$

C) $\left(-\sqrt{3}, 1\right)$

D) $\left(\sqrt{3}, 1\right)$

15

It is given that $\sin x = u$, where x is the radian measure of an angle and $0 < x < \frac{\pi}{2}$. If $\sin y = -u$, which of the following could be the value of y?

A) $x - 2\pi$

B) $x + \frac{\pi}{2}$

C) $x + \pi$

D) $x + 2\pi$

DIRECTIONS

For questions 16-20, solve the problem and enter your answer in the grid, as described below, on the answer sheet.

1. Although not required, it is suggested that you write your answer in the boxes at the top of the columns to help you fill in the circles accurately. You will receive credit only if the circles are filled in correctly.
2. Mark no more than one circle in any column.
3. No question has a negative answer.
4. Some problems may have more than one correct answer. In such cases, grid only one answer.
5. **Mixed numbers** such as $3\frac{1}{2}$ must be gridded as 3.5 or 7/2.

   (If 3 1 / 2 is entered into the grid, it will be interpreted as $\frac{31}{2}$, not $3\frac{1}{2}$.)
6. **Decimal answers:** If you obtain a decimal answer with more digits than the grid can accommodate, it may be either rounded or truncated, but it must fill the entire grid.

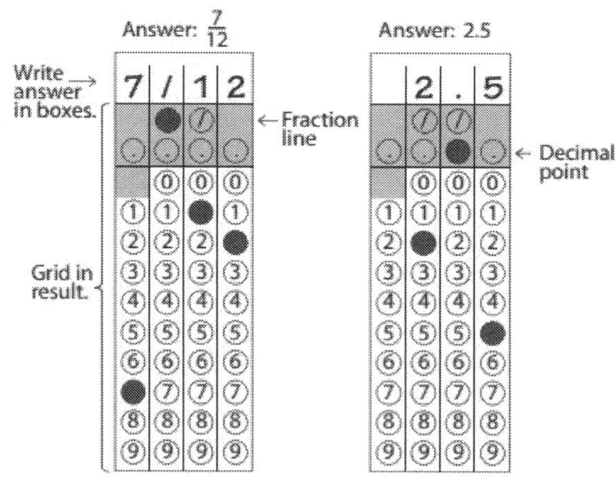

Acceptable ways to grid $\frac{2}{3}$ are:

2 / 3   . 6 6 6   . 6 6 7

Answer: 201 – either position is correct

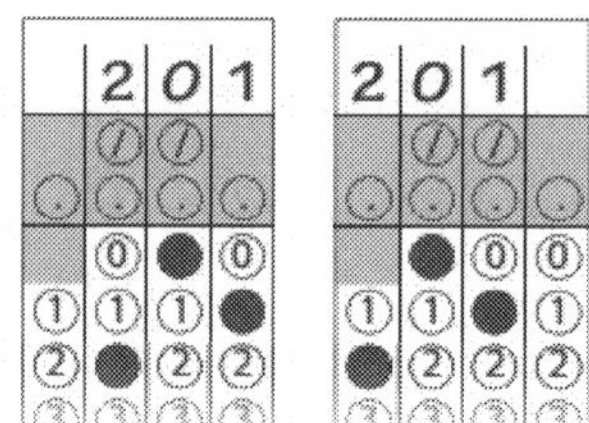

NOTE: You may start your answers in any column, space permitting. Columns you don't need to use should be left blank.

16

If x is not equal to zero, what is the value of $\frac{-3(4x)^3}{(-2x)^3}$?

17

If $\frac{1}{3}x - \frac{2}{5}y = 12$, what is the value of $5x - 6y$?

18

If $x - 5$ is a factor of $x^2 - 2ax + 5a$, where a is a constant, what is the value of a?

19

The length of a rectangular-shaped garden is twice its width. If the area of the garden is 128 square feet, what is the perimeter of the garden, in feet?

20

What is the solution to the equation $\frac{1}{x^2-7x+10} - \frac{6}{x-2} = -\frac{1}{x-2}$?

STOP

If you finish before time is called, you may check your work on this section only.
Do not turn to any other section.

Math Test – Calculator

55 MINUTES, 38 QUESTIONS

Mark your responses on this test. Use the "How to Calculate Your Scores in the back of this book to determine your scores.

DIRECTIONS

For questions 1-30, solve each problem, choose the best answer from the choices provided, and fill in the corresponding circle on your answer sheet. **For questions 31-38**, solve the problem and enter your answer in the grid on the answer sheet. Please refer to the directions before question 31 on how to enter your answers in the grid. You may use any available space in your test booklet for scratch work.

NOTES

1. The use of a calculator **is permitted**.
2. All variables and expressions used represent real numbers unless otherwise indicated.
3. Figures provided in the test are drawn to scale unless otherwise indicated.
4. All figures lie in a plane unless otherwise indicated.
5. Unless otherwise indicated, the domain of a given function f is the set of all real numbers x for which $f(x)$ is a real number.

REFERENCE

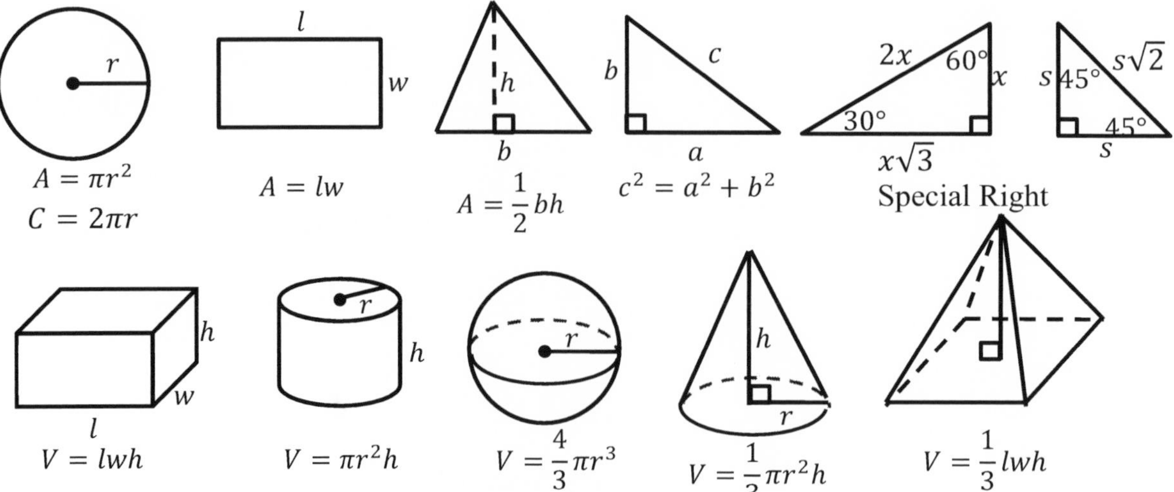

The number of degrees of arc in a circle is 360.

The number of radians of arc in a circle is 2π.

The sum of the measures in degrees of the angles of a triangle is 180.

1

The line graph above shows the yearly sales constant, from 2000 to 2006 of a commissioned employee. According to the graph, what was the greatest change (in absolute value) in the yearly sales constant value between two consecutive years?

A) 6
B) 7
C) 8
D) 9

2

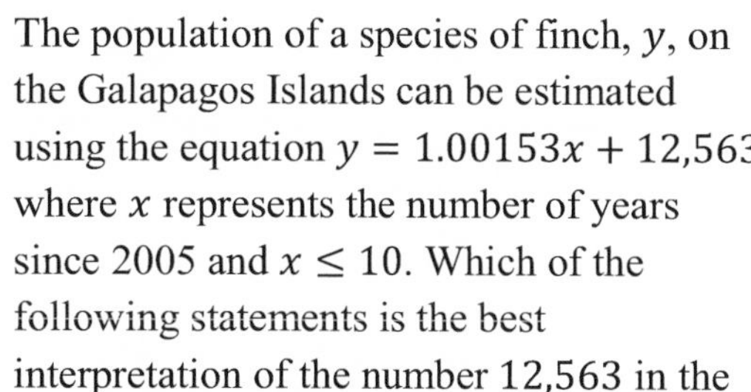

The population of a species of finch, y, on the Galapagos Islands can be estimated using the equation $y = 1.00153x + 12{,}563$, where x represents the number of years since 2005 and $x \leq 10$. Which of the following statements is the best interpretation of the number 12,563 in the context of the problem?

A) The estimated population of the finch species on the Galapagos Islands in 2005.
B) The estimated population of the finch species on the Galapagos Islands in 2015.
C) The estimated yearly increase in the population of the finch species on the Galapagos Islands.
D) The estimated yearly decrease in the population of the finch species on the Galapagos Islands.

3

What is the slope of the line that passes through the points $(-\frac{2}{3}, 4)$ and $(\frac{4}{3}, 0)$?

A) -2
B) $-\frac{1}{2}$
C) $\frac{1}{2}$
D) 2

4

A printer uses paper at a rate of 20 sheets per minute. How many hours would it take the printer to print a 5000-page document?

A) $\frac{6}{25}$
B) $4\frac{1}{6}$
C) 25
D) $41\frac{2}{3}$

5

If $\frac{1}{x-2} = \frac{a}{3}$, where $x \neq 2$ and $a \neq 0$, what is x in terms of a?

A) $\frac{a+6}{3}$
B) $\frac{5}{a}$
C) $\frac{2a-3}{a}$
D) $\frac{2a+3}{a}$

6

The number of bacteria in a petri dish has increased by 11% each hour. If there were 1,692 bacteria in the petri dish at 6:00 PM, approximately how many bacteria were present at 12:00 noon earlier that day?

A) 815
B) 905
C) 1,004
D) 3,165

7

$$x^2 + 16 = 0$$

Which of the following is a solution to the above equation? (Note: $i = \sqrt{-1}$)

A) -4
B) 2
C) $2i$
D) $-4i$

8

A popular videogame streamer receives one-tenth of a cent per advertisement viewed during her streams. She shows an advertisement at the end of every 30-minute increment of streaming, including previous advertisements, and 40% of her 3,500 viewers do not watch her advertisements because of advertisement-blocking software. If the streamer streams for 4 hours, how many dollars does she make during her stream?

A) \$11.20
B) \$16.80
C) \$112.00
D) \$168.00

9

Gerrard is building a circular pen of diameter d for his sheep. Each sheep needs at least 75 square meters of room within the pen. Which of the following inequalities models the diameter of the pen, in meters, that Gerrard must build to keep s sheep?

A) $d \geq \sqrt{\frac{300s}{\pi}}$
B) $d \geq \sqrt{\frac{75s}{\pi}}$
C) $d \geq \frac{75s}{\pi}$
D) $d \geq \frac{300s}{\pi}$

10

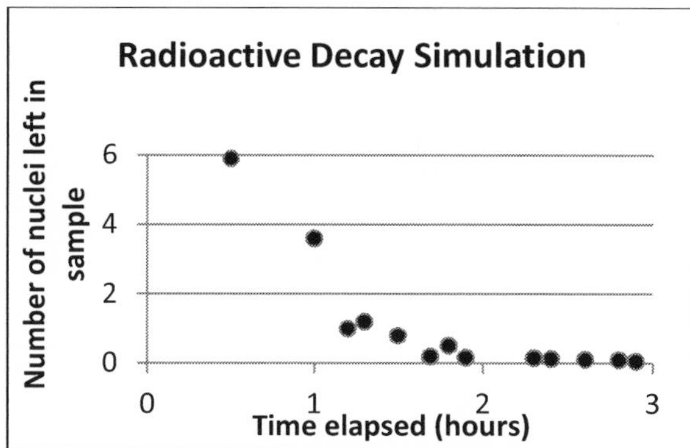

The scatterplot above shows the number of nuclei left in several samples of a radioactive isotope based on the amount of time that has elapsed, in hours. Based on the data above, the relationship that exists between time elapsed and the number of nuclei left in a sample of the radioactive isotope can best be described as what?

A) Positive and linear
B) Positive and exponential
C) Negative and linear
D) Negative and exponential

11

A car traveled at an average speed of 55 miles per hour and consumed fuel at a rate of 26 miles per gallon. If the driver starts with a full 15-gallon fuel tank and wants to drive until his fuel tank is one-eighth full, approximately how long can he drive until he needs to stop to refuel?

A) 53 minutes
B) 3 hours and 28 minutes
C) 6 hours and 12 minutes
D) 7 hours and 6 minutes

12

3, 3, 3, 6, 7, 10, 11, 12, 12, 17, 19, 20, 20, 25

What is the positive difference between the mean and median of the dataset above?

A) 0.0
B) 0.5
C) 1.0
D) 1.5

13

If $2(x - y) = \frac{1}{3}x$ and $y \neq 0$, then the ratio $\frac{x}{y} =$

A) $-\frac{6}{5}$
B) $-\frac{5}{6}$
C) $\frac{5}{6}$
D) $\frac{6}{5}$

14

The cost of a taxi in Jersey City is \$2.50 for the first one-eighth of a mile, 25 cents for each additional one-eighth of a mile, and 35 cents per minute the taxi has to wait for the rider. If Gwendolyn takes a 2-mile taxi ride to the airport, has the rider wait 15 minutes, and wants to give the driver a 20% tip, how much will her fare be, to the nearest cent?

A) \$9.20
B) \$9.86
C) \$13.80
D) \$14.10

Questions 15 and 16 refer to the following information.

A new country, which uses the U.S. dollar as currency, decides to tax the income of its citizens in the following way:

- The first \$20,000 of income is taxed at 16.6%
- The next \$20,000 of income is taxed at 21.1%
- All income over \$40,000 is taxed at 32.4%

15

How much would a citizen with an income of \$80,000 be taxed by the country?

A) \$20,500
B) \$24,720
C) \$25,920
D) \$33,460

16

If the income of a citizen of the new country increases from \$40,000 the first year to \$60,000 the next year, how much more will he be taxed the second year than the first year?

A) \$3,320
B) \$6,480
C) \$11,000
D) \$11,900

Questions 17-19 refer to the following information.

A survey of 268 children in the United States was conducted to gather data on their approval of a new game currently in beta testing. The data are shown in the table below.

	Rate favorably	Rate unfavorably	Total
5- to 8-year-olds	27	53	80
9- to 12-year-olds	48	27	75
13- to 15-year-olds	42	23	65
16- to 18-year-olds	16	32	48
Total	133	135	268

17

According to the table, for which age group did the greatest percentage of people rate the game favorably?

A) 5- to 8-year-olds
B) 9- to 12-year-olds
C) 13- to 15-year-olds
D) 16- to 18-year-olds

18

What fraction of the children who rated the game unfavorably were 9- to 12-year-olds?

A) $\frac{1}{5}$
B) $\frac{75}{268}$
C) $\frac{9}{25}$
D) $\frac{5}{9}$

19

After the initial survey, the game designers decided to survey 1,000 children, spread out equally among the two youngest age groups. Within each age group, the ratio of favorable to unfavorable ratings remained the same. Approximately what percentage of the 1,000 children rated the game favorably?

A) 46.9%
B) 48.9%
C) 51.1%
D) 53.1%

20

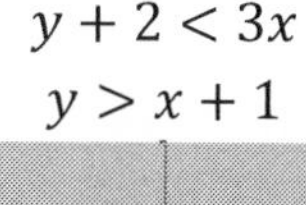

$$y + 2 < 3x$$
$$y > x + 1$$

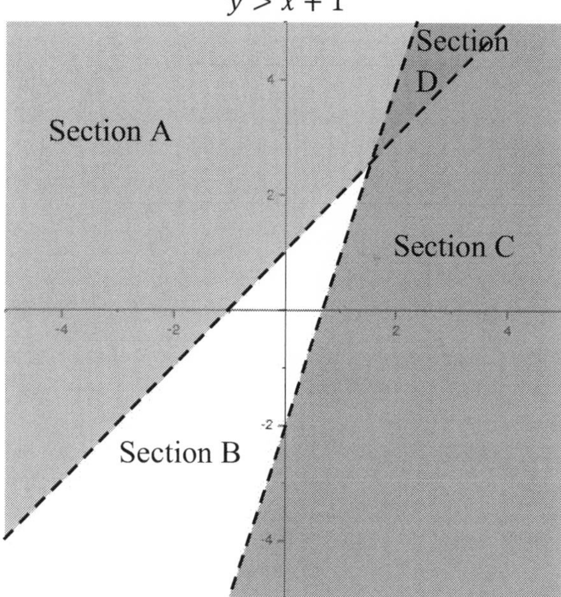

A system of inequalities and a graph are shown above. Which section of the graph could represent all of the solutions to the system?

A) Section A
B) Section B
C) Section C
D) Section D

21

Maurice wants to decrease the concentration of a beaker of hydrogen peroxide and water by adding more water. Currently, the beaker contains 200 mL of liquid and is 2% hydrogen peroxide. How much water should he add to the beaker to reduce the contents of the beaker to 1.25% hydrogen peroxide?

A) 47 mL
B) 120 mL
C) 152 mL
D) 200 mL

22

$\sin 135°$ is equivalent to which of the following?

A) $\cos\frac{\pi}{4}$
B) $\cos\frac{3\pi}{4}$
C) $\cos\frac{5\pi}{4}$
D) $\cos\frac{11\pi}{4}$

23

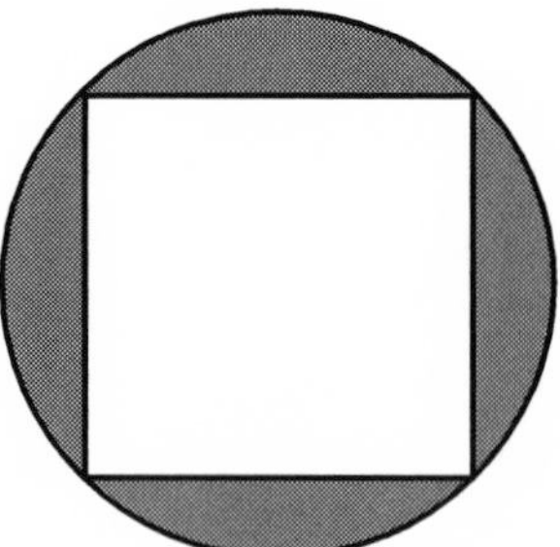

A square with side length 6 is inscribed inside of a circle, as shown above. What is the area of the shaded portion of the image?

A) $18\pi - 18$
B) $18\pi - 36$
C) $36\pi - 18$
D) $36\pi - 36$

24

A typical image taken of the ocean floor by camera is 10.6 gigabits in size. A submarine near the surface can receive data from the camera at a data rate of 2.4 megabits per second for 18 hours each day. If 1 gigabit equals 1,024 megabits, what is the maximum number of typical images that the submarine could receive from the camera each day?

A) 2
B) 14
C) 15
D) 19

25

$$h = v_0 t - \frac{1}{2}gt^2$$

Based on the equation above, which of the following represents g in terms of h, v_0, and t for all values of $t \neq 0$?

A) $g = \frac{2v_0t-h}{t^2}$
B) $g = \frac{2v_0t-2h}{t^2}$
C) $g = \frac{2h-v_0t}{t^2}$
D) $g = \frac{2h-2v_0t}{t^2}$

26

The line $y = -\frac{3}{4}x + 5$ intersects the line $y = mx + b$ on the x-axis. If the two lines are perpendicular to each other, what is the value of b?

A) $-\frac{80}{9}$
B) $-\frac{4}{3}$
C) $\frac{4}{3}$
D) $\frac{80}{9}$

27

$$x - 7 = \sqrt{x-1}$$

Which of the following lists all values of x that satisfy the equation above?

A) 5
B) 10
C) –5 and 5
D) 5 and 10

28

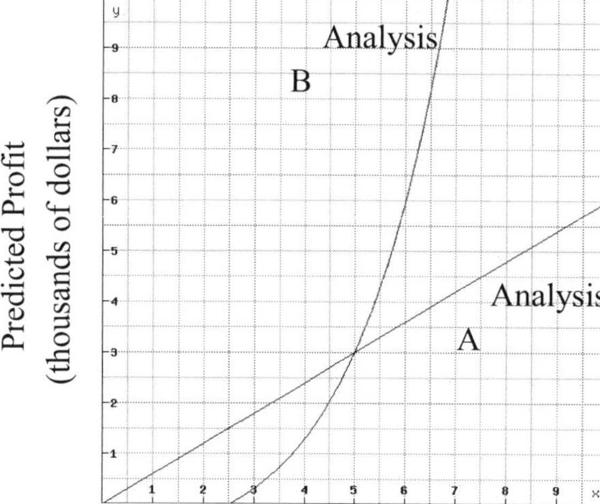

Two financial analysts created two different models of a company's predicted profits, as shown above. Which of the following is a correct statement about the data above?

A) Analysis B predicts the company to not make any profit until 3 years later.
B) At 5 years, both analysts predict the same amount of profit for the company.
C) Analysis A offers a more reasonable prediction of the company's projected future profits.
D) Analysis B offers a more reasonable prediction of the company's projected future profits.

29

The function f is defined by $f(x) = x^3 - ax^2 - 4x + 8$, where a is a constant. In the xy-plane, the graph of f interests the x-axis at two points $(-2, 0)$ and $(b, 0)$. What is the value of $a + b$?

A) –4
B) –2
C) 2
D) 4

30

$$(x - 4)^2 \leq 16$$
$$x > 4$$

Which value of x does NOT satisfy both equations listed above?

A) 5
B) 6
C) 8
D) 9

IRECTIONS

For questions 31-38, solve the problem and enter your answer in the grid, as described below, on the answer sheet.

1. Although not required, it is suggested that you write your answer in the boxes at the top of the columns to help you fill in the circles accurately. You will receive credit only if the circles are filled in correctly.
2. Mark no more than one circle in any column.
3. No question has a negative answer.
4. Some problems may have more than one correct answer. In such cases, grid only one answer.
5. **Mixed numbers** such as $3\frac{1}{2}$ must be gridded as 3.5 or 7/2.

   (If 3 1 / 2 is entered into the grid, it will be interpreted as $\frac{31}{2}$, not $3\frac{1}{2}$.)
6. **Decimal answers:** If you obtain a decimal answer with more digits than the grid can accommodate, it may be either rounded or truncated, but it must fill the entire grid.

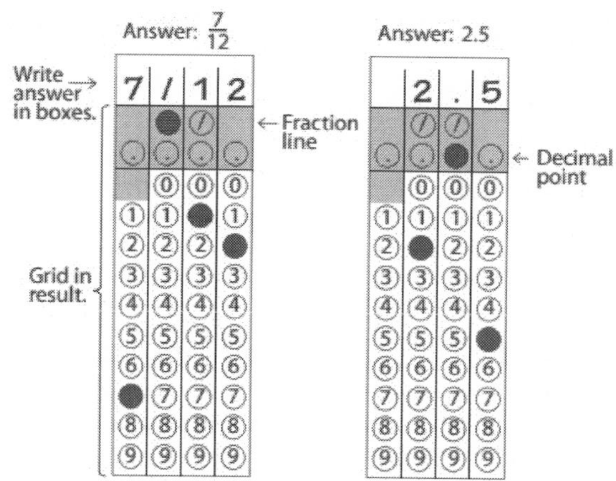

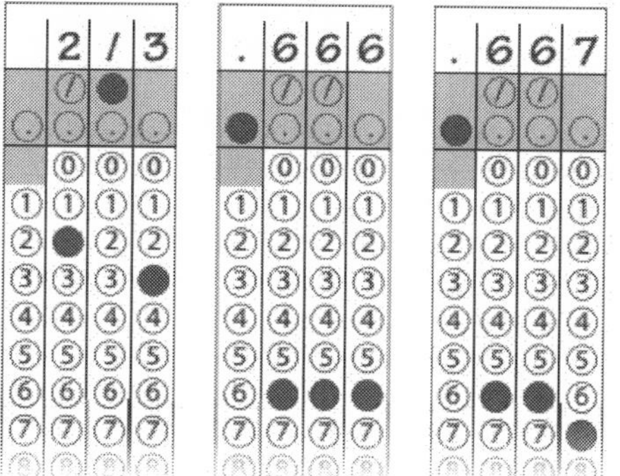

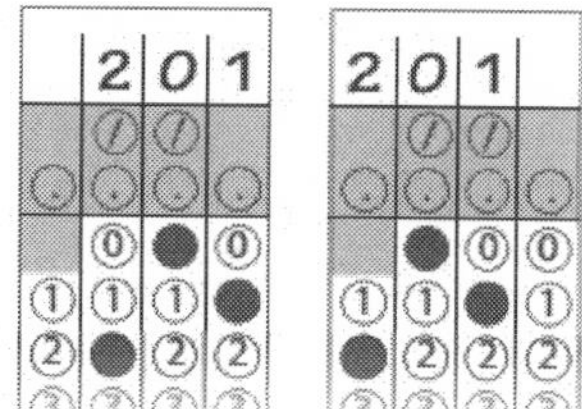

NOTE: You may start your answers in any column, space permitting. Columns you don't need to use should be left blank.

31

$$\frac{f-3}{-3} = 2 - 3f$$

What value of f satisfies the equation above?

32

A survey company is grouping the 50 U.S. states into groups of 3 states and groups of 4 states to conduct a survey. If the company ends up with a total of 13 groups, how many more 4-state groups than 3-state groups did the company form?

33

$$y = -x^2 + 6x - 9$$
$$y - 3 = 0$$

How many solutions exist to the system of equations shown above?

34

$$\frac{3}{x} + \frac{1}{x} = \frac{2}{5}$$

Jackson needs to paint a bedroom and enlists his brother Percy for help. Percy can paint 3 bedrooms in x hours, while Jackson can paint 1 bedroom in x hours. Working together, the two brothers can paint two bedrooms in 5 hours. The equation above represents the situation described. What is the value of x, in hours?

35

The table below classifies the 36 species of animals at a local wildlife preserve as reptile, amphibian, or mammal. The wildlife preserve is partitioned into 3 distinct sections.

	Reptile	Amphibian	Mammal	Total
Section A	2	4	3	9
Section B	5	1	8	14
Section C	0	3	10	13
Total	7	8	21	36

What fraction of all of the reptiles and amphibians at the wildlife preserve are in Section B?

36

$$\frac{3}{x-2}+\frac{2}{x-1}=\frac{1}{x-1}$$

What is the solution to the equation above?

Questions 37 and 38 refer to the following information.

A bank charges a 5% fee to exchange one country's currency to another country's currency. This exchange cost is already included in the transaction, so the cost of the transaction has already been taken out when the customer receives his or her money.

37

Marcellus goes to the bank above and exchanges \$50 for 51,917.50 Korean Won. Ignoring exchange fees, \$1 is worth how many Korean Won?

38

Kima goes to the bank to exchange U.S. dollars for Euros. She exchanges \$100 to Euros at a rate of \$1 = 0.89 Euro. However, her plans to travel to France get cancelled, so she exchanges her Euros back to dollars. What percentage of her initial money did she lose in making these exchanges due to transaction fees?

STOP

If you finish before time is called, you may check your work on this section only. Do not turn to any other section.

ANSWER KEY

Section 1: Reading Test		Section 2: Writing and Language Test		Section 3: Math Test – No Calculator	Section 4: Math Test – Calculator Allowed
1. B	27. A	1. C	23. C	1. C	1. C
2. A	28. D	2. A	24. D	2. B	2. A
3. B	29. C	3. C	25. C	3. C	3. A
4. D	30. A	4. B	26. B	4. D	4. B
5. B	31. B	5. D	27. C	5. A	5. D
6. C	32. D	6. B	28. C	6. D	6. B
7. A	33. C	7. D	29. B	7. C	7. D
8. D	34. A	8. D	30. D	8. C	8. B
9. C	35. B	9. C	31. D	9. A	9. A
10. B	36. D	10. B	32. D	10. A	10. D
11. D	37. B	11. D	33. B	11. D	11. C
12. A	38. C	12. B	34. B	12. C	12. B
13. B	39. A	13. C	35. A	13. B	13. D
14. A	40. C	14. A	36. D	14. B	14. C
15. C	41. B	15. B	37. B	15. C	15. A
16. B	42. B	16. C	38. C	16. 24	16. B
17. D	43. B	17. A	39. C	17. 180	17. C
18. A	44. A	18. A	40. C	18. 5	18. A
19. D	45. D	19. D	41. A	19. 48	19. B
20. B	46. C	20. D	42. B	20. $\frac{26}{5}$ or 5.2	20. D
21. C	47. A	21. C	43. C		21. B
22. A	48. C	22. A	44. D		22. A
23. C	49. B				23. B
24. B	50. C				24. B
25. A	51. D				25. B
26. B	52. A				26. A
					27. D
					28. B
					29. D
					30. D
					31. $\frac{3}{8}$ or $.375$
					32. 9
					33. 0
					34. 10
					35. 0.4 or $\frac{2}{5}$
					36. 1.25 or $\frac{5}{4}$
					37. 1093
					38. 9.75

How to Calculate Your Scores

Once you have completed an assessment, use the following steps to calculate your scores. The score(s) you calculate will be *general estimates* of your official scores for a number of reasons:

- Because standardized test score calculations are based on normative scaling and statistical analysis, your scores will differ depending your official test date – the final score calculations are impacted by the number of students, per-question performance by all students on each test date, and other numerical factors.
- College Board determines the final curve for official tests. Therefore, the scores you calculate for yourself on Test Prep Genius tests are within a general range of scores.

Calculate Your Raw Scores

Evidence-based Reading and Writing Section Raw Score

1) Count the number of correct answers you got on Section 1 (Reading Test). There is no penalty for wrong answers. The number of correct answers is your raw score.
2) Go to the Raw Score Conversion Table on the next page. Look in the "Raw Score" column for your raw score and match it to the number in the "Reading Test Score" column.
3) Do the same with Section 2 (Writing Test) to determine your Writing and Language Test Score. Make sure to use the "Writing Test Score" column.
4) Add your Reading Test Score and your Writing and Language Test Score.
5) Multiply that number by 10. This is your final Evidence-based Reading and Writing Section Score.

Math Section Score

1) Count the number of correct answers you got on Section 3 (Math Test – No Calculator) and Section 4 (Math Test – Calculator). There is no penalty for wrong answers.
2) Add the two numbers together.
3) Use the Raw Score Conversion Table on the next page to your final Math Section Score.

Use the following Raw Score Conversion Table to determine your test scores

Raw Score Conversion Table							
Raw Score (# of correct answers)	Math Section Score	Reading Test Score	Writing Test Score	**Raw Score (# of correct answers)**	Math Section Score	Reading Test Score	Writing Test Score
0	200	10	10	**30**	540	28	29
1	200	10	10	**31**	550	28	30
2	210	10	10	**32**	550	29	30
3	230	11	11	**33**	560	29	31
4	240	12	11	**34**	560	30	32
5	260	13	12	**35**	570	30	32
6	280	14	13	**36**	580	31	33
7	290	15	14	**37**	590	31	34
8	310	15	15	**38**	600	32	34
9	320	16	16	**39**	600	32	35
10	330	17	16	**40**	610	33	36
11	340	17	17	**41**	620	33	37
12	360	18	18	**42**	630	34	38
13	370	19	19	**43**	640	35	39
14	380	19	19	**44**	650	35	40
15	390	20	20	**45**	660	36	
16	410	20	21	**46**	670	37	
17	420	21	21	**47**	670	37	
18	430	21	22	**48**	680	38	
19	440	22	23	**49**	690	38	
20	450	22	23	**50**	700	39	
21	460	23	24	**51**	710	40	
22	470	23	25	**52**	730	40	
23	490	24	25	**53**	740		
24	500	24	26	**54**	750		
25	510	25	26	**55**	760		
26	510	25	27	**56**	770		
27	520	26	28	**57**	790		
28	520	26	28	**58**	800		
29	530	27	29				

For Evidenced-based Reading and Writing and Language Test Scores, add them together and multiply by 10 for your final Section Score for Reading and Writing and Language.

Add your two Section Scores together to get your final Score on a 400-1600 scale

Calculating Subscores

The Redesigned, New SAT will offer more detailed information in specific areas within math, reading, and writing. These subscores are reported on a scale of 1-15.

Math: Heart of Algebra

The Heart of Algebra subscore is calculated based on questions from the two Math Tests that focus on linear equations and inequalities.

1) Each practice test's Heart of Algebra questions are specified below. Add up your total correct answers from the specified set of questions for each test to get your raw scores for each test.
   Practice Test 1:
      Math Test – No Calculator: Questions 2-4; 7; 9; 11; 15-16; 18; 20
      Math Test – Calculator: Questions 2; 8; 11; 13-15; 19; 22; 28-29; 31
   Practice Test 2:
      Math Test – No Calculator: Questions 1-3; 5; 8; 12; 16; 20
      Math Test – Calculator: Questions 3; 7; 12; 14; 31-34; 36-38
   Practice Test 3:
      Math Test – No Calculator: Questions 1; 4; 7; 12-13; 17; 20
      Math Test – Calculator: Questions 4-5; 8; 13; 25; 27; 30-34; 36
2) Use the Subscore Conversion Table on Page 532 to calculate your Heart of Algebra Subscore.

Math: Problem Solving and Data Analysis

The Problem Solving and Data Analysis subscore is calculated based on questions from the two Math Tests that focus on quantitative reasoning, interpretation and synthesis of data, and solving problems with rich and varied contexts.

1) Each practice test's Problem Solving and Data Analysis questions are specified below. Add up your total correct answers from the specified set of questions for each test to get your raw scores for each test.
   Practice Test 1:
      Math Test – No Calculator: No Questions
      Math Test – Calculator: Questions 1-6; 9-10; 17; 20; 23-27; 32-33
   Practice Test 2:
      Math Test – No Calculator: No Questions
      Math Test – Calculator: Questions 1-2; 4; 6-10; 14-16; 19; 23; 25-28
   Practice Test 3:
      Math Test – No Calculator: No Questions
      Math Test – Calculator: Questions 1-2; 8; 10-11; 14-19; 21; 23-24; 35; 37-38
2) Use the Subscore Conversion Table on Page 532 to calculate your Problem Solving and Data Analysis Subscore.

Math: Passport to Advanced Math

The Passport to Advanced Math subscore is calculated based on questions from the two Math Tests that focus on topics critical to the ability of students to handle more advanced math topics, such as expressions, complex equations, and analysis of functions.

1) Each practice test's Passport to Advanced Math questions are specified below. Add up your total correct answers from the specified set of questions for each test to get your raw scores for each test.

   Practice Test 1:

   Math Test – No Calculator: Questions 1; 5-6; 8; 10; 12-13; 19
   Math Test – Calculator: Questions 7; 16; 18; 30; 34-35; 37-38

   Practice Test 2:

   Math Test – No Calculator: Questions 7; 9-11; 13; 15; 17-18
   Math Test – Calculator: Questions 5; 11; 17-18; 21-22; 29-30

   Practice Test 3:

   Math Test – No Calculator: Questions 3; 5; 8; 10-11; 14-16; 18
   Math Test – Calculator: Questions 7; 9; 10; 20; 22; 28-29;

2) Use the Subscore Conversion Table on Page 532 to calculate your Passport to Advanced Math Subscore.

Writing and Language: Expression of Ideas

The Expression of Ideas subscore is calculated based on questions from the Writing and Language Test that focus on topic development, organization, and rhetorical, effective use of language.

1) Each practice test's Expression of Ideas questions are specified below. Your total number of correct answers in the specified set below is your raw score.

   Practice Test 1: Questions 1; 3; 6-7; 9; 11; 13-14; 16-18; 21; 24; 26-27; 30-31; 33-35; 37; 39; 42-43
   Practice Test 2: Questions 3; 5-6; 7; 10-11; 13; 15-18; 20; 24; 27-30; 32-33; 34-36; 38-39; 42
   Practice Test 3: Questions 2-3; 5; 7; 11; 13; 16-18; 20; 22-23; 25; 27; 29; 32-33; 35; 37-39; 43-44

2) Use the Subscore Conversion Table on Page 532 to calculate your Expression of Ideas Subscore

Writing and Language: Standard English Conventions

The Standard English Conventions subscore is calculated based on questions from the Writing and Language Test that focus on sentence structure, usage, and punctuation (basic grammar).

1) Each practice test's Standard English Conventions questions are specified below. Your total number of correct answers in the specified set below is your raw score.

   Practice Test 1: Questions 2; 4; 5; 8; 10; 12; 15; 19-20; 22-23; 25; 28-29; 32; 36; 38; 40-41; 44
   Practice Test 2: Questions 1-2; 4; 8-9; 12; 14; 19; 21-22; 23; 25-26; 31; 37; 40-41; 43-44
   Practice Test 3: Questions 1; 4; 6; 8-10; 12; 14-15; 19; 21; 24; 26; 28; 30-31; 34; 36; 40-42

2) Use the Subscore Conversion Table on Page 532 to calculate your Standard English Conventions Subscore

Writing and Language + Reading: Words in Context

The Words in Context subscore is based on questions from both Reading and Writing Tests that focus on the meaning of words in context and rhetorical word choice.

1) Each practice test's Words in Context questions are specified below. Your total number of correct answers in the specified set below is your raw score.
   Practice Test 1:
      Reading Test: Questions 1; 7; 14-15; 24; 28; 34; 39; 45; 51
      Writing Test: Questions 7; 14; 27; 30; 34-35; 39; 43
   Practice Test 2:
      Reading Test: Questions 6; 10; 17; 20; 24; 30; 34; 39; 45; 49
      Writing Test: Questions 7; 10; 13; 16; 30; 32; 36; 42
   Practice Test 3:
      Reading Test: Questions 5-6; 16; 19; 24; 28; 36; 41; 46; 49
      Writing Test: Questions 5; 8; 17; 20; 23; 27; 37; 43
2) Use the Subscore Conversion Table on Page 532 to calculate your Words in Context Subscore

Writing and Language + Reading: Command of Evidence

The Command of Evidence subscore is based on questions from both the Reading and Writing Tests that focus on the student's ability to interpret and use evidence found in passages and informational graphics such as tables, graphs, and charts.

1) Each practice test's Command of Evidence questions are specified below. Your total number of correct answers in the specified set below is your raw score.
   Practice Test 1:
      Reading Test: Questions 6; 9; 17; 20; 22; 27; 36; 42; 47; 50
      Writing Test: Questions 1; 9; 11; 13; 16; 26; 31; 37
   Practice Test 2:
      Reading Test: Questions 5; 9; 14; 19; 27; 29; 38; 42; 48; 51
      Writing Test: Questions 3; 11; 15; 17; 29; 33; 38; 39
   Practice Test 3:
      Reading Test: Questions 3; 8; 14; 18; 26; 30; 35; 39; 48; 51
      Writing Test: Questions 3; 11; 18; 22; 29; 33; 35; 44
2) Use the Subscore Conversion Table on Page 532 to calculate your Command of Evidence Subscore

Use the following Subscore Conversion Table to calculate your Subscores

Subscore Conversion Table							
Raw Score (# of correct answers)	Expression of Ideas	Standard English Conventions	Heart of Algebra	Problem Solving and Data Analysis	Passport to Advanced Math	Words in Context	Command of Evidence
0	1	1	1	1	1	1	1
1	1	1	1	1	2	1	1
2	1	1	2	2	3	2	2
3	2	2	3	3	5	3	3
4	3	2	4	4	6	4	4
5	4	3	5	5	7	5	5
6	5	4	6	6	8	6	6
7	6	5	6	7	9	6	7
8	6	6	7	8	10	7	8
9	7	6	8	8	11	8	8
10	7	7	8	9	12	8	9
11	8	7	9	10	12	9	10
12	8	8	9	10	13	9	10
13	9	8	9	111	13	10	11
14	9	9	10	12	14	11	12
15	10	10	10	13	14	12	13
16	10	10	11	14	15	13	14
17	11	11	12	15		14	15
18	11	12	13			15	15
19	12	13	15				
20	12	15					
21	13						
22	14						
23	14						
24	15						

Calculating Cross-Test Scores

The Redesigned, New SAT also offers detailed information in the form of two Cross-Test scores. These scores are based on questions in the Reading, Writing and Language, and Math Tests that focus on analytical thinking about texts and questions in specific subject areas. Cross-Test Scores are reported on a scale from 1-40.

Analysis in History/Social Studies

1) Each practice test's History/Social Studies questions are specified below. Your total number of correct answers in the specified set below is your raw score.
   Practice Test 1:
   - Reading Test: Questions 32-42; 43-52
   - Writing Test: Questions 1; 9; 11; 26; 31; 33
   - Math Test – No Calculator: No Questions
   - Math Test – Calculator: Questions 3; 9; 17; 20; 24-26; 32

   Practice Test 2:
   - Reading Test: Questions 12-22; 43-52
   - Writing Test: Questions 15; 17; 20; 24; 27; 29
   - Math Test – No Calculator: No Questions
   - Math Test – Calculator: Questions 2; 8-10; 15-16; 23; 28

   Practice Test 3:
   - Reading Test: Questions 1-10; 11-21
   - Writing Test: Questions 3; 7; 11; 25; 29; 33
   - Math Test – No Calculator: No Questions
   - Math Test – Calculator: Questions 15-16; 17-19; 28; 37-38
2) Use the Cross-Test Conversion Table on the next page to calculate your Cross-Test Score for Analysis in History/Social Studies.

Analysis in Science

1) Each practice test's Science questions are specified below. Your total number of correct answers in the specified set below is your raw score.
   Practice Test 1:
   - Reading Test: Questions 1-10; 21-31
   - Writing Test: Questions 13; 16; 17; 34-35; 37
   - Math Test – No Calculator: No Questions
   - Math Test – Calculator: Questions 4-6; 10; 23; 27; 37-38

   Practice Test 2:
   - Reading Test: Questions 1-11; 33-42
   - Writing Test: Questions 3; 6; 11; 35; 38; 39
   - Math Test – No Calculator: Questions 5; 14
   - Math Test – Calculator: Questions 14; 19; 25-27; 30

   Practice Test 3:
   - Reading Test: Questions 32-42; 43-52
   - Writing Test: Questions 16; 18; 22; 35; 38; 44
   - Math Test – No Calculator: Question 11
   - Math Test – Calculator: Questions 2; 6; 10; 21; 24-25; 35
2) Use the Cross-Test Conversion Table on the next page to calculate your Cross-Test Score for Analysis in Science.

Use the following Cross-Test Conversion Table to calculate your Cross-Test Scores

Cross-Test Score Conversion Table					
Raw Score (# of correct answers)	Analysis in History/Social Studies Cross-Test Score	Analysis in Science Cross-Test Score	**Raw Score (# of correct answers)**	Analysis in History/Social Studies Cross-Test Score	Analysis in Science Cross-Test Score
0	10	10	**18**	28	26
1	10	11	**19**	29	27
2	11	12	**20**	30	27
3	12	13	**21**	30	28
4	14	14	**22**	31	29
5	15	15	**23**	32	30
6	16	16	**24**	32	30
7	17	17	**25**	33	31
8	18	18	**26**	34	32
9	29	19	**27**	35	33
10	21	20	**28**	35	33
11	22	20	**29**	36	34
12	23	21	**30**	37	35
13	24	22	**31**	38	36
14	25	23	**32**	38	37
15	26	24	**33**	39	38
16	27	24	**34**	40	39
17	28	25	**35**	40	40

Made in the USA
Middletown, DE
07 January 2022